MATHEMATICS INSTRUCTION
in the Elementary Grades

SILVER BURDETT PROFESSIONAL PUBLICATIONS

MATHEMATICS INSTRUCTION
in the Elementary Grades

William D. McKillip
University of Georgia

Thomas J. Cooney
University of Georgia

Edward J. Davis
University of Georgia

James W. Wilson
University of Georgia

SILVER BURDETT COMPANY
Morristown, New Jersey
Glenview, Illinois • *Palo Alto* • *Dallas* • *Atlanta*

Illustrations by Victoria Christian

© 1978 SILVER BURDETT COMPANY.
All Rights Reserved.
Printed in the United States of America.
Published simultaneously in Canada.

This publication, or parts thereof,
may not be reproduced in any form
by photographic, electrostatic,
mechanical or any other method, for any use,
including information storage and retrieval,
without written permission from the publisher.

Library of Congress Card Number: 77–15283

ISBN 0–382–01363–8

ISBN 0–382–01528–2

Preface

How This Book Came to Be

In attempting to improve student learning, many school systems are seeking to specify what teachers should be doing in the classroom. The question, *What are the observable characteristics of effective teaching?* is an old one and one to which no fully satisfactory answer has been given. The Atlanta City School System asked mathematics educators from the University of Georgia to observe their teachers and students, state in specific terms what the teachers should be doing, and write materials to help the teachers learn how to do those things.

This team, including the authors of this book, observed and analyzed the mathematics teaching in Atlanta, added their own observations from a variety of other locations, and developed specific techniques and materials to help teachers improve mathematics teaching. These materials have been extensively revised and tested over a five-year period. Hundreds of teachers, inservice and preservice, have used the materials and reported on the effects of the techniques on their students. We hope you will agree that the results are practical—that these techniques *work* in the classroom.

We take this opportunity to thank Dr. Ruel Morrison and Mr. Heywood Thomas, of the Atlanta City Schools, for their valuable cooperation and assistance in the original project. We are particularly indebted to the many fine elementary school teachers from whom we have all learned so much.

Contents

PART TWO · CONTENT 217

2. Make the problem simpler (suggestion 4 on page 93). Think about some specific amounts for Pam to start with. If Pam had a dime then Sam would have to have 24 cents. Could Pam start with no money?

3. Similar to D on page 89. Each connecting line segment could be a handshake (also see discussion on page 93–94). Four people could have 6 handshakes, five people could have 10.

4. If 2 rolls and 3 pennies in some sense equals 13 pennies, then 2 rolls by themselves would weigh the same as ten pennies. The mathematics sentence could be $2 \cdot \square + 3 = 13$.

If 2 rolls + 5 "equals" 1 roll + 17 then 2 rolls would "equal" 1 roll + 12. Now remove one roll from each situation.

5. Make a table:

Number	Product	2X Product
10	$1 \times 0 = 0$	0
11	$1 \times 1 = 1$	2

6. Draw a picture of the action of the ball and record it as a series: $(16 + 8) + (8 + 4) + (4 + 2) + (2 + 1) = 45$. To answer the second question, continue the series: $(1 + 1/2) + (1/2 + 1/4) + (1/4 + 1/8) + (1/8 + 1/16) + \ldots$ Note that this is an infinite geometric series, with a ratio of 1/2. The sum of such a series is a finite number and can be found by using the formula $\dfrac{a}{1 - r}$, where a is the first term and r is the ratio. Substituting in the formula, we find $S = 3$. Thus, the ball will travel $(45 + 3)$ feet if it bounces forever.

7. Filling the 3 twice and pouring it into the 5 each time would leave 1 quart in the 3. Now empty the 5. You take it from here.

10. Let x = number of children in B; $x + 6$ = number in A. Then $x + 5 = 2(x + 1)$. Solve for x.

11. If the thousands digit and the hundreds digit add to one, the thousands digit must be 1 and the hundreds digit 0. Our number then looks like this 10 __ __. (Answer: 1070)

12. List the primes from 10 to 99. Can an even number in the range be prime? Can the multiples of 3, 4 or 5 be prime? (Answer: 13, 31; 37, 73; 79, 97)

13. Similar to problem 4. Double the first condition, giving 2 dozen and 2 loaves costing $5.60. Now "remove" (subtract) the second condition. (Answer, $1.00).

14. Total Sales − Total Cost = Profit (Answer: $20.00).

15. A table could help. What must be the sum of the numbers in the boxes?

Pretty	$\square$	$\Big\}$ ...30
Pretty and Smart	$\square \Big\}$	...35
Smart	$\square$	
Neither	10	
Total	50	

Another approach would be to draw a 50-dot array; encircle dots to match the various combinations.

17. Sue's square was 18 inches on each side. Peg had one half of a 36 × 36 inch square. Compare 18 × 18 with (36 × 36) ÷ 2. (Peggy has more).

18. Add 3's and 4's to total 31: fewer than ten 3's; fewer than seven 4's. Three combinations of chairs and stools are possible: 7, 1; 4, 5; 1, 9.

19. Sum the series: $1 + 2 + 3 + \ldots$ Remember the formula for the sum of a finite series? $\left(S_n = \dfrac{n}{2} + a_n\right)$

20. Make a table.

	Event	Mathematical Statement
	Begin	x = people on streetcar
1	+ Wilson, + 1	x + 2
2	+ 3	x + 5
3	+ 2, − 1	x + 6
4	− 3	x + 3
5	− 6, + 2	x − 1
6	− 1/2(x − 1)	(x − 1) − 1/2(x − 1) = 1

Solution: $2(x - 1) - (x - 1) = 2$
$$x - 1 = 2$$
$$x = 3$$

21. Try a series of simpler problems. If you had 4 pennies you couldn't make change for a nickel. If you had 4 pennies and a nickel you couldn't make change for a nickel or a dime. If you had 4 pennies, a nickel, and a dime you couldn't make change for a nickel, dime, or quarter. (4 pennies, 1 nickel, 1 dime, 1 quarter, 1 half dollar = $.94)

If you take away the nickel you could replace it with ___ dimes and still not make change for a quarter, half dollar, or dollar? (New total: $1.19)

22. In the second method of payment you would get $(1 + 2^1 + 2^2 + 2^3 + 2^4 + \text{---} 2^{29})$ cents. That turns out to be $10,737,418.23!!

23. Make a table, using numbers to show relative ages.

Pilot	5	4	3	2	1
		4	3	2	1
Possible		3	2	1	
copilots		2	1		
		1			

24. Use trial and error and rely on your knowledge of basic facts. There is more than one possible solution.

2	7	6
9	5	1
4	3	8

25. Nine times.

26. The number of blocks with 3 red faces is always eight. The number of cubes with no red side is 0^3, 1^3, and 2^3. Those with 2 red faces is 12×1 and 12×2. Do you think the patterns continue?

Red on	2" cube	3" cube	4" cube
none of the sides	0	1	8
one face only	0	6	24
two faces only	0	12	24
three faces only	8	8	8
more than three faces	0	0	0

27. Draw a sketch. Six cuts and welds are necessary. The cost is $6 \times 35¢$ or $2.10.

28. The problem can be solved by using algebra and adding and subtracting equations. The answer is R = 160, S = 115, Q = 130, P = 120, T = 155.

29. a. yes; **b.** 6; **c.** 4

30. a. 3 dimes, 3 nickels, 3 pennies
   b. 6 (1 quarter, 2 dimes, 3 pennies)
   c. 7 (1 quarter, 1 dime, 2 nickels, 3 pennies)

31. On the ninth day. Draw a sketch to determine the snail's progress after each day.

32. 14. There are nine 1×1 squares, four 2×2 squares, and one 3×3 squares. $14 = 9 + 4 + 1$.

33. 18. There are 14 squares as determined in problem 32 plus 4 more.

34. 6. Observe that there are three different sized squares, 4 of one type and one each on the other two types. $6 = 4 + 1 + 1$.

35. 20. There are four different sized triangles. Count the number of each type. There are 8 of one type and 4 each of the remaining types. $20 = 8 + 4 + 4 + 4$.

36. Determine the different sized triangles and then count the number of each.
   a. 5. (4 small triangles and one large triangle)
   b. 13. (9 small triangles, 3 of a second size, and one large triangle)
   c. 27. ($16 + 7 + 3 + 1 = 27$. There are four different sized triangles)

37. 204 squares. Make a table and observe the pattern.

Size of squares	Number of squares
1×1	64 (8^2)
2×2	49 (7^2)
3×3	36 (6^2)
4×4	25 (5^2)
5×5	16 (4^2)
6×6	9 (3^2)
7×7	4 (2^2)
8×8	1 (1^2)
	Sum = 204

38. There is more than one possible sollution.

① ② ④
③ ⑤ ⑥

39. Draw a sketch; count the posts. 15; 16; 70'

40. The problem becomes one of finding numbers which satisfy the equation $2(l + w) = l \times w$ where l is the length and w is the width. The following dimensions satisfy the equation: 3 by 6, 4 by 4, 8 by 2 2/3. Others exist also.

41. The largest area will occur when the rectangle is a square. Each side of the square would be 25 inches ($100 \div 4$). Hence the largest possible area would be 25×25 or 625 square inches.

ONE · METHODS

1 · An Overview

In this chapter we discuss some general issues in teaching and in learning to teach mathematics to children. We describe the relationship between this textbook and the things you do, or will do, when you are teaching mathematics. In this book we have attempted to collect, organize, and describe as clearly as we can effective techniques for teaching elementary mathematics. We do not merely *present* these techniques; we frankly *advocate* that you use them and we will explain why you should use them. We believe that their use will lead to desirable student achievement and attitudes. For almost all teachers, these techniques and instructional procedures are absolutely essential to effective teaching. It is true that some teachers develop personalized teaching styles, seeming to break all the rules, and yet their teaching results in good student achievement. A few teachers have able students for whom meeting "normal" achievement standards is virtually assured, no matter how they teach. For the vast majority of elementary school teachers, however, the techniques described in this textbook are essential for achieving desired results. As you study these techniques and apply them in your teaching situation, be open-minded and observant. Ask, "What changes can I see in students' achievement as a result of using this technique?" If you observe desirable outcomes from particular techniques, continue to use and develop those techniques in your teaching.

1. THE SECRET OF SUCCESSFUL TEACHING

Some people just entering the profession ask questions such as, "How do you really teach mathematics?" or "What can you do with a student who just can't learn multiplication?" Those who ask such questions are often looking for a technique that, if it could only be revealed, would enable them to solve their students' learning problems. They assume there must be a best method that will solve all the problems.

And there is, of course, a secret for teaching mathematics: If you will study your materials carefully, plan your objectives, activities, and lessons, evaluate the outcomes frequently, and consider these outcomes when making future plans, you will do an excellent job of teaching. The secret is hard work!

When so-called experts, mathematics supervisors, or college professors (!) teach elementary school mathematics for two weeks, a month, or a year, they have exactly the same problems you have: children with vastly different backgrounds, different learning problems, behavior disorders (those are discipline problems!), lack of motivation—you name it. Do they "solve" all of these problems and quickly produce a group of uniform, highly motivated, well-behaved, model students? Of course not! They struggle with learning problems, try to detect and remedy students' misconceptions, try to get socially acceptable behavior and a reasonable learning atmosphere, set learning goals and attain some of them, and experience both failure and success as teachers. Sounds familiar? It should, because that's teaching. Now that you know the secret of teaching success, we will discuss some things that are important for *making* the secret work. There are a few general ideas of primary importance in teaching *all* aspects of mathematics.

What is Really Important in Teaching Mathematics?

It is really important to study each topic you are going to teach. When you undertake to teach a topic, you should know what the students already know about the topic, what is expected of the students in subsequent lessons, and what is expected of them during the year and in years to come. In this way you can put your lesson activities in proper perspective, anticipate and diagnose probable learning difficulties, and properly prepare the students for coming topics. You can learn much of what you need to know by examining the textbook series or other program you are using, considering *at least* the year before and the year after the grade you are teaching.

Careful study of the textbook you are using is particularly important. Frequently, a sequence of lessons is planned to lead up to the introduction of an algorithm; in the sequence all subskills and prerequisites are covered. Teachers must be aware of this organization so that they can use the lessons to maximum advantage. Further, a teacher who is planning to present the skill in a manner different from the textbook will also need to plan a different sequence of les-

sons on the prerequisites. Whether or not you follow the textbook on a topic, you need to be fully aware of the development being used!

It is really important for you to plan the material you are going to cover and keep track of each student's progress. At the beginning of the year you should set target points to be sure your students are making progress. If you group children for mathematics, and you should, you will express different goals for each group. These goals will be tentative, and, as you find out what progress your students make, you may revise the goals. Progress toward goals is an indication of learning; lack of progress is a signal that learning problems are developing. If you find that you are "stalled" with a group, look for the causes. As you look for causes, you may consider the background of the children and study the chapter on diagnosis and remediation of mathematics learning problems. When planning for your groups you may get help from the chapter on individualizing instruction.

It is really important to get to know your students, so you can work with them as individuals. Each child brings a unique background into every learning situation, unique not only in terms of prerequisite knowledge of mathematics, but unique in personality and learning style. Some children seem to do everything first-rate. They possess good work habits, remember facts and procedures, profit from their mistakes, relish challenging problems, enjoy encountering new ideas, and are successful in integrating new knowledge with previous learning.

Other children are not so fortunate — they have trouble paying attention and getting started at work. They seem to have short attention spans and do not appear to remember facts and procedures. Some are unenthusiastic about learning new things and seem unable to profit from errors or to think clearly in problem contexts. The reason behind these difficulties is the different social, intellectual, and emotional blend of each child. You should try to understand children in making decisions concerning the way you work with them. With some children you will be extra patient, with some you will pace the presentation of new material very slowly. With others you will try to be firm and require them to adhere to a schedule. Some will need extra practice and additional explanations; others will need an abundance of reassurance and praise. Some will need to be challenged to work on advanced or enrichment topics. Only by getting to know your students as individuals can you intelligently decide which of these strategies to employ.

It is really important to spend a substantial block of time on mathematics each day. One of the most important factors in determining how much mathematics, or any subject, children will learn is the "opportunity to learn." This means (among other things) the time spent each day on the subject. There are several things that influence the "opportunity to learn" mathematics, including schedule and the organization of the teacher. The schedule should provide ample time for mathematics. It is widely recognized that mathematics is one of the most important subjects taught in the elementary school. Mathematics is usually scheduled for a substantial block of time, often in the morning when the children are rested and ready for work. This is as it should be! In early grades at least 40 minutes and in later grades 60 minutes of

real working time should be scheduled for mathematics every day, without fail. It is likely that simply adhering to this schedule would improve children's mathematics achievement substantially. Of course, teachers must follow the schedule. Sometimes a teacher who does not like mathematics or who fears it will find reasons to reduce or eliminate mathematics class time.

Observations of teachers reveal great differences in the way in which they manage the classroom and utilize their time and their students' time. Good management procedures and a "businesslike" approach to school are associated with higher student achievement. When a teacher wastes five minutes of class time, the actual loss, five minutes times the number of children, may be hours of students' time. Have your materials ready to start on time. Be clearly aware of what each group or your whole class is going to do. Aim to have every student working every minute!

It is really important to be highly motivated, to put in the hard work and energy needed to help children learn. Many people succeed in teaching and do really outstanding work because they are highly motivated to help children learn. It is important to like children and to desire to see them grow up as happy adults, but this is not enough. You must also see their intellectual growth as an important, essential feature of their relationship with you. Few teachers are equipped to help children resolve deep-seated problems; we teachers probably function best as helpful, sympathetic *adult* friends. But teaching is our profession and our reason for being employed, as we are, in contact with children. We must and should see teaching as our primary purpose!

The Danger in Comfort and Security

This paragraph is addressed mainly to interns, student teachers, and other "preservice" teachers. Teaching is a demanding enterprise. Even with very young children there are problems of class control and behavior management. The difficulty of getting young children, kindergarteners and first and second graders, to attend to a lesson is as great as the problem of defiance or noncooperation in some older children. Most people approach their first teaching experience with nervousness or even fear. Will the children do what I tell them? Will my lessons work? Nothing we know of will prevent these feelings; even experienced teachers have them to some degree when they start a new class. The fact is that almost always teachers quickly get over these feelings of insecurity and nervousness and develop feelings of comfort and security. The problem is that when you get comfortable, you may think you have discovered how to teach! Some may say, "Now I know how to do it. I have this job whipped—there wasn't much to it, after all." These people never really begin to learn how to teach because they do not go on to try new teaching techniques. They simply stay with whatever techniques they first found comfortable. *It is important for you to be willing to go beyond "comfort and security," to venture, to try new and different teaching techniques, even though you may again feel uncomfortable and insecure for a time.* Without trying new methods and new activities you stifle your professional growth. You may end up in the proverbial "rut." Do not be afraid or reluctant to try out new ideas in your classroom. Variety is a spice in life and lessons. Make use of it.

A Framework for Teaching

We believe a very useful part of this overview is to provide you a model, or a framework, for thinking about the goals of your mathematics instruction. Lots of people have done this sort of thing in planning, teaching, and evaluating mathematics instruction. The one presented here is similar to other attempts.

A table of specifications can be constructed by describing two dimensions — a *content* dimension and a *behavior* (or objectives) dimension. Our table may not be suited exactly to your particular teaching situation. That is all right. We hope you will learn enough about the strategies of specifying a model to identify goals of instruction in mathematics for your own program. That is, we hope you will be able to modify our model to fit your particular curriculum or classroom situation.

Mathematics achievement has many facets. It is not a unitary trait; therefore, a strategy that ensures consideration of many *different* goals, lessons, and measures of mathematics achievement is necessary. Our strategy is to stratify the outcomes of mathematics instruction in two ways: first, by types of mathematics content, and second, by levels of behavior.

The categories of mathematics content should reflect the curriculum. Since this is a general model we use the content categories reflecting the mathematics content of the whole elementary school. (A modified set of content categories might be used if you were elaborating the table of specifications just for third grade or fourth grade, for example.) The content categories used here are those discussed in the chapters in Part Two of this book.

Table of Specifications for Elementary School Mathematics.

	Computational Skills	Understanding	Problem Solving	Feelings
Whole Numbers and Numeration				
Fractions and Numeration				
Decimals, Percent, and Numeration				
Measurement and Geometry				
Probability, Statistics, and Graphing				
Functions and Relations				

The levels of behavior include *computational skills, understanding, problem solving,* and *feelings*. These levels are somewhat ordered and hierarchical. They tend to run from the least complex to the most complex, and the more complex tend to require the less complex as a part. For example, problem solving is more complex than computation or understanding, and it subsumes both.

Computational skills include recall and recognition of basic facts and terminology as well as the routine and practiced manipulation of problem elements the students are presumed to have learned. Emphasis is on knowing and performing operations, and not on deciding which operations are appropriate.

Understanding emphasizes concepts, principles and generalizations, and their relationships. Translation from one form to another (e.g., words to figures) is one type of understanding behavior, as is transfer from one context to another.

Problem-solving behaviors demand the use of concepts, computational skills, and relevant knowledge to accomplish some end or goal. The transfer of problem-solving skills from one context to another is also a part of this level of behavior.

Feelings include various types of emotional or affective goals, such as attitudes, appreciation, self-concept, anxiety, and motivation. While the cognitive outcomes of mathematics are extremely important and take up a lot of attention, we believe the affective outcomes deserve emphasis and we attempt to give them due consideration in this book.

Throughout the book we will be stressing objectives of instruction. We will discuss teaching for computational skills, teaching for understanding, teaching for problem solving, and how learning mathematics can be a positive experience. This model, or your own adaptations of it, will prove helpful.

2. PART ONE: METHODS

How This Textbook Helps You Teach Mathematics

A teacher of elementary school mathematics has a variety of decisions to make and a still wider variety of things to do to implement those decisions. First, the teacher begins with a group of children and some general ideas about the sequence of mathematics learnings in elementary school. The teacher evaluates the status of the children in the mathematics sequence and decides what topic would be appropriate to study. In planning this topic the teacher will almost certainly include some things the children should *understand,* some *problems* they should solve, and some *computational skills* they should acquire. Thus, the teacher has selected a topic and objectives based on knowledge of the children in the class and their knowledge of mathematics.

In the course of teaching the topic the teacher will utilize teaching techniques appropriate for developing *understanding, problem-solving ability,* and *computational skill.* The teacher will use the resources contained in *textbooks* and stimulate students to learn by reading books and other material. The teacher will make use of *concrete materials* where they will contribute to under-standing and will use *laboratory activities* to provide applications of the mathematics being learned.

In the course of teaching a topic the teacher will undoubtedly encounter students' learning difficulties caused by inadequate past learning. He or she will attempt to *diagnose* the causes of these problems and provide *remedial instruction* so that the students can progress. Some students will progress more rapidly than others and the teacher will *individualize* instruction. Throughout, and at the conclusion of the topic, the teacher will *evaluate,* assessing his or her efforts and the status of the children relative to the sequence of learnings in the mathematics curriculum. The teacher will then select another topic and begin the cycle again.

While this is an oversimplified view of teaching, you can see in it elements of judgment that are highly complex. It is far more complicated to evaluate children's present achievement and select a topic than to cover page after page in a textbook. It is more complex to state objectives and choose methods and materials than to run off three or four ditto sheets a day.

We trust you will see your job as a teacher as one of judgment and decision making about both content and learning activities. In the chapters that follow we have attempted to help you learn how to teach for a wide variety of objectives, selecting appropriate content and learning activities for your students.

Planning Your Mathematics Program

You will read in this text many specific suggestions for teaching—often in direct language: Do this! You may have

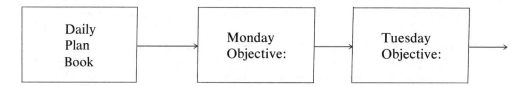

the opportunity to try these suggested techniques with children. How do you "put it all together" and create a classroom situation that results in effective mathematics learning? No one can keep all the details in mind at once. It is humanly impossible.

In the next few pages we suggest a way to organize your arithmetic program mentally in broad categories of activities. This conceptualization, or mental picture, of your program will help you include all the important activities. Use this book as a source of help in the details—as a desk reference of ideas for developing computational skill and problem-solving ability, planning specific lessons, and so forth. But keep the broad, overall plan clear in your mind!

It is very helpful to have a way of organizing the jobs you are to do and some ways of organizing are more effective than others. Mathematics is a subject that has a great many long-range objectives. These long-range objectives are changes taking place in students over months or years and are not, cannot be, the result of a lesson or two. Contrast these two instructional objectives:

1. Given a number between two and two hundred, the student will test it by division and identify it as a prime or a composite number.

2. Given an unfamiliar problem, the student will attempt to solve it by using the mathematics he knows, employing various problem-solving strategies in a flexible and persistent manner.

These are both legitimate and important objectives of mathematics instruction. The first can be achieved, assuming a fairly normal student group, in a day or two of good, sound teaching. After that, occasional review will keep the concept and procedure fresh in the mind of the student. The second objective is not a "can" or "cannot" sort of proposition. It is observable only as a gradual growth in problem-solving power, perseverance, and flexibility. The difference between these two objectives has implications for our planning and teaching.

A short-range objective can be accomplished through planning the work of a day, a week, or a unit or chapter. The lessons can be planned a day or two at a time, building one on another until the objective is accomplished. This kind of planning and teaching is very effective for short-range objectives, but in thinking only of a day or two at a time there is a tendency to neglect long-range objectives.

Long-range objectives must be given consideration in planning and in teaching. Here is a way of organizing and planning so that long-range objectives receive the consideration they deserve. Think of the time, 45 minutes or an hour, you spend on mathematics each day—but also think of the days forming a connected stream.

Planning now becomes more like filling stripes on a roll of paper towel than like filling the pages of a book. What things should you plan in these stripes on the

	Mon.	Tues.	Wed.	Thur.	Fri.	
60						
50						And
40						so
30						on
20						till
10						June!
0						

(Minutes)

roll of towel? The chapters on particular techniques describe several activities that should be included in every daily lesson. (See the table below.)

Think of it as an unwinding scroll on which practice, problem solving, and other activities flow from day to day.

WRITTEN PRACTICE
VERBAL DRILL
TEACHING
MENTAL ARITHMETIC
PROBLEM SOLVING

With this concept of planning you can see growth in problem-solving skill as a gradual process — you will start with the children at some point and move them to some more advanced point. You will do this by seeing problem solving as a band running through the entire year. The same may be said of mental arithmetic, written computational skills, and other long-range objectives. We hope that you will permanently retain the mental image of the scroll on which the bands of related activities develop. This will provide an organized structure into which you can fit the details of various teaching techniques.

Organization of the Chapters

In each of the chapters on methodology the organizing features are essentially the same. You will find a list of competencies to be attained, an introduction describing the contents of the chapter, sections describing specific teaching techniques, suggested activities, and a

	Mon.	Tues.	Wed.	Thur.	Fri.	June
60	WRITTEN PRACTICE on Computational Skills Should Take No More					→
50	Than One Third of Your Time and Preferably Less					→
40	VERBAL DRILL: A few minutes every day					→
30	TEACHING! Explaining, Demonstrating, Using Concrete Materials,				
20	Boardwork, Laboratory Activities, Applications, Discussion, Group work, and so on.					→
10	MENTAL ARITHMETIC PRACTICE.					→
0	A STORY PROBLEM EACH DAY: Less Than Ten Minutes					→

(Minutes)

summary set of "maxims" to guide teaching practice.

Competencies. The objectives of each chapter are expressed as "competencies." Some definitions of competency tend to emphasize the overt behavior of a teacher in a classroom setting; others focus on the knowledge needed by a teacher. The definition we present here attempts to synthesize these two aspects. Any observable teaching performance is, or should be, the result of the teacher's knowledge of content, knowledge of methods, and attitudes, as well as consideration of the particular students whose learning is the object of the teaching performance.

A competency is a teaching performance observed in a selection of appropriate situations, together with the supporting knowledge that enables the teacher to describe how, when, with whom, and for what outcomes to use it. This use of the word *competency* is nearly synonymous with our usual use of the phrase "specific teaching technique," with reference to techniques that have specific kinds of learning outcomes. To have attained a competency, one must have the knowledge of content and method that enables the teacher to decide when, how, and with whom to use the "observable teaching performance."

Discussion questions. At the ends of sections in each chapter are discussion questions related to the ideas being developed in the chapter. The questions frequently identify controversial issues in the teaching of mathematics, issues on which the "experts" will not all agree. These questions may be used as a springboard for class discussion and debate. Whether they are used in class or not, you should read them as they occur and think out what your answers to the questions would be.

Assignments and projects. At the end of each chapter are assignments planned to help you master the teaching techniques discussed in the chapter. Some assignments require planning, study of other material, written work, or simulated teaching. These assignments can all be done in the traditional college class setting. A further set of assignments are for your guidance in teaching children. These assignments can be used if you are already a full-time teacher or if you are an intern or a student teacher.

Maxims. Each chapter of Part One concludes with a section of maxims that summarize and highlight the important ideas for action in the classroom setting. Trying out a new technique in a classroom situation is facilitated by simple statements of *what to do* in the classroom. The statements have been called, as we call them here, "maxims for teaching." These maxims are supported by the experience of successful teachers, by research, or by expert opinion—sometimes by all three. The maxims are valid in the sense that most teachers who apply them in the classroom find they get desired results or improvements.

3. PART TWO: CONTENT

In Part Two we review the development of the important topics in the elementary mathematics curriculum. This review concentrates on an examination of the meanings of ideas of elementary mathematics and on explanations of those ideas. As each mathematical topic is considered, you will note that concrete and semiconcrete models are used to establish meanings, that operations are related to these meanings and to previous operations, that many illustrations are used, and that the emphasis is on the way teachers may present and explain mathematics to their students.

What does one do with meanings and models? Why should a teacher use models extensively in teaching?

A. Models are used to give meaning to numbers and operations and to obtain answers before any computational procedures are known. Thus, if a child can use counting objects to find answers to addition problems, he knows a lot about addition even though he does not know a paper and pencil algorithm.

1. The child should be able to start with a problem, construct or draw a model of it, and use the model to solve the problem.

2. The child should be able to start with a model, state the problem that the model illustrates, and use the model to solve the problem.

3. The child should understand the relationships between the problem and the model and how the problem and the solution can be seen in the model.

B. Meanings and models are used as a basis for explaining some algorithms, making the steps meaningful and justifying the procedures.

1. The child should be able to relate the algorithm and the steps within the algorithm to a variety of models.

2. The child should be able to relate each step in the algorithm to a manipulation of the model.

3. The child should be able to explain how the answer obtained through the algorithm is represented in the model.

C. Problem solving is closely related to meaning. When a situation arises in a problem, how does a student know that multiplication of fractions, say, is the required operation? The student knows this because the situation "fits" one of the meanings he or she has attached to multiplication of fractions. Thus, the more different meanings or models are associated with an operation, the greater will be its applicability in problem solving.

Organizing Concepts

In the next few paragraphs we describe four organizing concepts helpful in grasping the relationships within the curriculum: strands, scope and sequence, and spiral curriculum organization.

Strands. In elementary mathematics almost all topics are developed through several grade levels. Various items of content are placed at different grade levels and the mode of presentation is adapted to the age of the students. For example, you may think of geometry: It begins in kindergarten with simple concepts, such as *inside* and *outside,* and increases in formality and complexity to analytic geometry in high school. Such topics are called "strands," the image of a strand being that of a common thread running through the curriculum. Further, one presumes the strand has been carefully planned so that over the years the student gains a complete and well-organized view of the topic.

Scope and sequence. It is usual for the elementary curriculum to be conceptualized in terms of "scope" and "sequence." The scope of a curriculum is the

The SEQUENCE, division of the topic into parts for each grade ↓ ↓	The SCOPE, a list of the topics in the curriculum	
	Operations and properties	Numbers and numeration
Beginners (K)		
Grade 1		
Grade 2		
and so forth		

sum total of all the topics developed in the curriculum, that is, all the strands. The sequence for each strand is the assignment of parts of that strand to appropriate grade levels. A very efficient way to describe a curriculum is to make a scope-and-sequence chart like the one started above.

This scope-and-sequence chart is incomplete; it does not list all topics or all grade levels. In the spaces under a topic the specific content to be taught in each grade would be listed. Sometimes the content is expressed in terms of behavioral objectives.

The spiral curriculum. All elementary mathematics curricula are organized in what is called spiral form. That means that students encounter a topic more than once; they spiral back to the topic and meet it again at a higher level. The topic spirals upward. We would not want the students to "circle back" and meet the topic at the same level. The spiral shown here illustrates the spiral curriculum. As students move up through the grades, they study addition at each grade level. Other major topics also spiral upward.

The chapters in Part Two are related to the scope and sequence of the elemen-

tary mathematics curriculum. Each chapter represents a strand in the curriculum: a major topic which is developed over a period of years. These chapters cover whole numbers, fractional numbers, decimals, geometry and measurement, probability and statistics, and functions and relations. Each of these chapters contains some mathematical explanation of the topic. The major emphasis, however, is on how the children are to learn each topic and how the ideas can be explained and made meaningful to children.

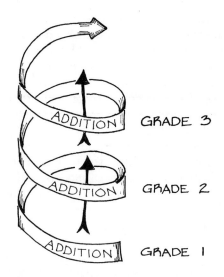

GRADE 3

GRADE 2

GRADE 1

2 · Teaching for Understanding

INTRODUCTION

In elementary mathematics we frequently assert that our purpose is to teach students not just to compute but to understand the mathematics they study. This is a goal most teachers are striving to achieve. Our purpose in this chapter is to provide specific suggestions about how to enable students to understand the mathematics they learn.

Understanding, more than any other issue, is at the heart of teaching. It is the base on which all other mathematical objectives should rest. Computational skill should be preceded by and be based on understanding of: (1) the operation to be performed and (2) in most cases, the algorithm by which it is performed. Problem-solving activities are facilitated by understanding the mathematics involved, even though understanding may increase during the process of solving a problem. The *use of mathematical ideas in situations other than the situation in which they were learned — transfer — is not only based on understanding but is itself part of the definition of understanding.*

This chapter does not emphasize any one method, any one approach, or any one device for teaching. Teachers develop styles and preferences for different approaches; some achieve better results with one approach, some with another. The best teachers can use a variety of different ways to present and explain material. Consequently, we describe many effective ways to present and explain mathematics. A varied approach can improve learning in three ways. First, students often need another approach to a topic after failing to learn satisfactorily the first time. The more varied ways teachers have to present topics, the more effective they will be. Second, any one way of conducting lessons will become boring after a time. Third, varying the instructional techniques helps meet individual differences.

Understanding is synonymous with comprehension, knowing, and, possibly, a great many other words. When teachers say, "That child really knows the subject," they are referring to a child who understands. Understanding, like knowledge and comprehension, is inside the head. Since we cannot get a direct look at this quality, we will spend a considerable part of this chapter on ways of finding out whether a student does, in fact, understand what has been taught and, if the student does understand, at what level.

1. OBJECTIVES AND EVALUATION

In this section we will look at the problems involved in selecting objectives and evaluating students' understanding of a mathematical topic. Our first goal is to enable you to state objectives at several levels of understanding and to write test questions to determine whether students have achieved those levels of understanding. Some teachers limit themselves to recognition and recall in testing for understanding; it is our hope that, knowing about higher levels of understanding, you will teach for and test for these levels as well. Our second goal is to enable you to plan and carry out an evaluation of your students' understanding of material you have taught and, as an outgrowth of this, to evaluate your own teaching.

Not everyone will agree on the proper assessment of understanding. Consequently, whether a student does indeed "understand" a topic is a matter of interpretation of the evidence. To illustrate this problem, let us examine several examples.

Let us suppose we have just completed a unit on area in Grade 5 and we wish to determine whether a student "understands" area and the formula for the area of a rectangle. We might use some or all of the following test items.
Recognition and recall:
Which formula could you always use to find the area of a rectangle?

(a) $A = \pi r^2$ (b) $A = s^2$
(c) $A = lw$ (d) $A = \frac{1}{2}bh$

What is the formula for finding the area of a rectangle?
Application:
Sam's back yard is a rectangle, 180 feet long by 52 feet wide. What is the area of Sam's yard?
Relationship:
How would the area of a rectangle change if the width were doubled? How would the area change if both length and

width were doubled?

Transformation:

John says he knows that the area of this rectangle is 15, even without using the formula. How could he figure it out?

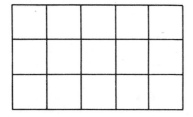

Transfer:

Get a tin can and find the area of the metal used to make it. Include the top and the bottom in your calculation.

Which of these items would you accept, if the student succeeded on the item, as evidence of understanding? These items are arranged in order from an indication of least understanding to an indication of most understanding. Success on each item must be judged as some evidence of understanding, great or small.

It is fairly easy to decide whether the evidence shows that a student possesses a computational skill. It is not nearly so easy to decide whether a student understands a topic. Imagine this exchange between teachers.

Teacher A:

I want my students to understand prime numbers.

Teacher B:

How can you tell whether they do or not?

Teacher A:

Well, I have them write the definition of a prime number. If they can do that, I think they understand prime numbers.

Teacher B:

But some students have just memorized the definition; they don't really understand at all.

So it goes. What behaviors by students indicate this thing we call understanding? While there is no final or indisputable answer to this question, we now list some behaviors which are frequently thought to imply understanding.

Types of "Understanding" Objectives

Let us look at these behaviors in order from the least difficult to the most difficult. As we move from easier to more difficult items, or from lower to higher cognitive processes, we would find greater agreement on our right to infer understanding from success on the task. A student who succeeds on a recognition item may understand the material but many will debate this. When a student succeeds on a transfer task, almost everybody will agree that he understands the material involved.

Recognition and recall. Recognition and recall are grouped together because they both represent "low-level" cognitive abilities. Can the student *recognize* the object in the form in which it was studied? Whether this ability implies understanding or not is sometimes questioned. If a student is unable to recognize the object he has been studying, he would seem to lack understanding. Here are some sample items in which the ability to recognize the correct answer is being tested.

A. Mark X on the triangle.

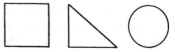

B. Mark each improper fraction with an X.

$\frac{2}{3}$ $\frac{5}{4}$ $\frac{1}{2}$ $\frac{4}{7}$ $\frac{7}{4}$ $\frac{5}{2}$

C. Which symbol means "greater than"?

a. =   b. <   c. >   d. □   e. ⊥

D. Circle the prime numbers.

2, 3, 5, 10, 12, 13

While recognition requires only that students "know it when they see it," objectives requiring *recall* demand that students produce appropriate responses from memory. This is a more difficult task than recognition, and so more agreement could be expected for the notion that recall implies understanding. We know, however, that people are capable of memorizing and recalling perfectly meaningless items. We see this in the memorization of nonsense syllables, in learning phone numbers and license plate numbers, and in many other instances. Students *can* learn a definition and repeat it on a test without being able to give any other evidence of understanding. Rote recall, unaccompanied by other capabilities, is not convincing evidence of understanding. Here are some examples of items that require recall.

A. Write the definition of a prime number. _____

_____

_____

B. If the numerator of a fraction is larger than the denominator, then the fraction is _____ than 1.

C. A whole number which has more than two factors is called a _____ number.

Application. The use of a mathematical idea in the solution of a word problem is frequently taken as evidence of understanding. Application items are the standard or commonplace word problems, which students work frequently. This kind of item is treated in detail in the chapter, "Teaching for Problem-Solving Skill."

A. Amanda had $\frac{5}{3}$ yards of ribbon. How much more does she need in order to have two yards?

B. Kathy can save $1.50 per week from her allowance. How long will it take her to save $16.50?

Relationships. We may ask students to identify relationships between the idea they are presently learning and other ideas. If they can correctly state these relationships, we are likely to conclude they understand not only the idea being learned but the other idea also. Here are some items which illustrate ways a student may demonstrate understanding by stating relationships.

A. Show how the problem $238 \div 51$ could be done by subtraction.

B. Tell how a parallelogram helps you to find the area of this triangle. Draw the parallelogram and explain.

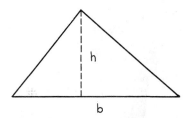

C. N is a prime number between 40 and 50. Is N divisible by 2? How can you be sure? Do you need to know what N is to be sure? Why not?

D. How can you change $\frac{3.1}{8}$ to a decimal fraction? Will the result be less than 1 or greater than 1?

Transformation. Given a problem, a statement, or an idea in one form, we are often called on to transform or translate it to another form. For example, we may have to write an equation from a word problem, make a graph of numerical data, restate or explain something in our own words, or draw a diagram illustrating a number concept or a problem. The ability to do this seems to be a proof of understanding.

One of the most important and significant ways in which students transform ideas is to restate ideas in other words. A student who can thus express the essential nature of the idea he or she has learned, without parroting the language used to teach it, gives compelling evidence of understanding. Here are some examples of transformation items.

A. How can you recognize whether a number is a prime number? (This item attempts to stimulate students to tell about prime numbers in their own words. The next item does also. The instruction "Write the definition of prime number" would probably elicit the words used in the text.)

B. What is the difference between a prime number and a composite number?

C. Write an equation for this problem: John earned $4.30 on Monday and 20% more than that on Tuesday. How much did he earn altogether?

D. Draw a picture illustrating the fraction $\frac{5}{3}$.

E. Draw arrows on the number line to illustrate the problem

$$6 - 2 = \square$$

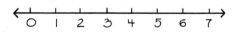

Transfer. If students can see the use of an item of information in a context different from the context in which they learned it, and can use the item successfully in the new context, they are said to have transferred the item from the former context to the new context. This is, in most people's thinking, powerful evidence of understanding. In many educational research studies the ability of students to transfer what they have learned in one situation to another situation is used as the definition of understanding.

Transfer from one context to another is our ultimate goal in education. What students learn in school must function in their future education or in out-of-school contexts or it is of little use to them.

Not all examples of transfer are alike. In some cases a student will use an item of information in a context just slightly different from the context in which it was learned. We then wonder if this is really transfer or, perhaps, if the two situations are exactly alike in the student's mind. In other cases a student will use an item of information in a context so radically different from the context in which we taught it that we feel certain transfer has taken place.

Because transfer depends on the context in which the item is used being different from the context in which it was learned, it is not possible simply to examine an item and tell whether it requires transfer. We must also know about the learner's experiences during the time the information was learned. Suppose a student has learned the formula $A = lw$ for the area of a rectangle. If the student can find the area of a figure labelled as shown on the next page, he or she has transferred the knowledge of the area of a rectangle to a slightly different situation.

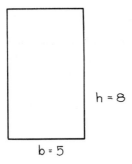

In the paragraphs above we attempted to explain what "understanding" means in terms of a student's behavior. We will use these kinds of objectives — recognition and recall, application, relationships, transformation, and transfer — repeatedly in evaluating understanding. Now we will describe a step-by-step procedure for evaluating students' growth in understanding of a topic during the time you are teaching the topic.

Evaluating Growth in Understanding

Evaluation of student's understanding is an important part of teaching. This evaluation will tell us how much the students have learned and will tell us about the depth of their knowledge; it will provide us with guidance in deciding what topics to review and what new topics to take up. If we carefully evaluate students' understanding, we can, in the process, analyze and evaluate our own teaching.

The evaluation of understanding is frequently limited to low-level items, involving only recognition and recall. When children discover the correct response requires *recalling* exactly the teacher's words, they study for memorization rather than for deeper understanding of the material. The use of a

variety of kinds of items — recognition, recall, application, stating relationships, transformation, and transfer — encourages students to study for understanding and not merely for memorization. Another reason for using a variety of items is to assess the depth or degree to which your teaching produces understanding and to get an idea, from the items your students get right and wrong, what the results of your teaching have been.

1. *Select the topic you are going to cover.* In most cases, if you are following a textbook or syllabus, you will proceed to the next topic. You may decide, however, to go back and review some material which was not thoroughly learned during the previous unit. You may decide to review some of a previous year's work in preparation for further progress. Many teachers now feel free to alter the order of textbook material and to add or delete material, based on their evaluation of the needs of the children. This is a good thing as long as teachers are careful children possess the background necessary for the topic selected.

2. *State the objectives for the unit.* A good procedure for stating objectives is to list the items of content you want the students to understand at the conclusion of the unit. Often this will be a much shorter list than you might imagine. When you have listed these items, then write one or more objectives for each of the levels of understanding, *and* at the same time write one or two test questions for each objective. The number of test items is potentially infinite; you will never have a "complete" list of all the items you want students to do. Get as wide a variety of items as you can.

Suppose, in the second grade, we wish to teach a unit on subtraction; certainly one of our objectives will be that the students "understand" the operation of subtraction. Here are some selected objectives and test items for these objectives.

Recognition and recall
Given set and number-line pictures of operations, the students will mark those which show subtraction situations.

A. Which shows subtraction?

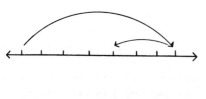

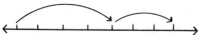

B. Which shows subtraction?

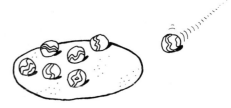

Given subtraction sentences and number-line illustrations, the students will recognize the illustration corresponding to each sentence.

C. Draw a line from each sentence to the number line that matches it.

5 - 3 = ☐

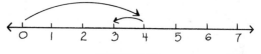

4 - 1 = ☐

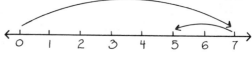

7 - 2 = ☐

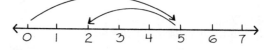

6 - 2 = ☐

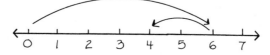

Application
Given a word problem involving subtraction of whole numbers, the student can solve it.

A. Solve this problem:

John went to the store with 8 cents. He spent 3 cents. How much did he have then?

Relationship

Given an addition sentence, the student will write two related subtraction sentences.

A. Write two subtraction sentences using the numbers in this addition sentence: $4 + 2 = 6$.

Transformation

Given a set or number-line picture, the students can write the subtraction sentence and vice versa.

A. Draw a number line and show this problem on it.

$$7 - 4 = \square$$

B. Write the subtraction sentence that goes with this set picture.

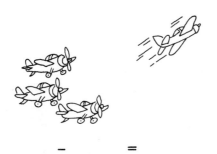

$$\underline{\hspace{1.2cm}} - \underline{\hspace{1.2cm}} = \underline{\hspace{1.2cm}}$$

Transfer

Given a problem describing an unfamiliar situation, the students will recognize whether subtraction is the appropriate operation and, if so, use it to solve the problem.

A. Alice had 18 seeds. Of these, 11 were bean seeds. How many were not bean seeds?

B. Kathy has 59 cents. A toy costs 87 cents. How much more does Kathy need?

3. *Pretest.* Select from the items you have written enough questions to give you an idea of what the students may already know and in what depth they know it. Since you have already decided in your diagnosis that this is a topic the students need to study, you may expect the students will not know much about it. There are, however, always a few surprises. Some students may know enough about the topic to skip on to something else. Some students may not know enough to start study of the topic, and this is something else you can find out through pretesting. When you pretest, you will also get some solid information to use in comparing what students know at pretesting to what they know at posttesting, and thus help evaluate the effectiveness of the unit and your teaching.

4. *Plan and teach lessons appropriate to the content and objectives of the unit.* This is the topic of Section 3, below, Teaching for Understanding, so we will not go into detail on planning or teaching at this time.

5. *Posttest.* Use the items you wrote at the beginning of the unit but not those used on the pretest. To get an accurate idea of students' *real* progress, do not use any item which you taught directly or repeatedly, except for memory items. If you teach a "transfer" item directly, then for those students it is memory, not transfer.

6. *Evaluate your students' growth in understanding; evaluate your teaching effectiveness.* Look at the changes that have taken place in your students' understanding. Which students who formerly had no understanding of the topic now have some understanding? To what degree have students made progress in achieving deeper levels of understanding? In which areas has your teaching been most effective? least effective? Is there one type of item on which students are not doing well? If so, perhaps you can find out why or work on finding improved teaching procedures for that type of objective.

Summary

Objectives of understanding are complex to state and to evaluate. There are various levels of understanding that may be described as recognition and recall, applications, stating relations, transformation, and transfer. A teacher who emphasizes low-level test items, such as recall, will stimulate the students merely to memorize. A teacher who plans for and tests for the full range of objectives will achieve better results and will also be able to evaluate his or her own teaching in a more meaningful way.

Discussion Questions

1. Which of the five levels of understanding do *you* accept as implying that a student "really understands"?

2. What objectives and test items would you use to determine whether a student understands place value? Choose a grade level and relate your answer to that grade.

3. What do you see as the difference(s) between the application and transfer levels of understanding? Could a problem be at the transfer level for one student and at the application level for another? Explain.

4. Here are some "opening lines" of questions for students. See if you can predict the level of understanding that the entire question is testing. It is possible that you

may wish to assign more than one level to a given item below.

a. Which of these is a picture of . . . ?
b. Make three examples of . . . .
c. What is the difference between . . . ?
d. Use the rule . . . to find . . . .
e. Why is a . . . also a . . . ?
f. Write a number sentence that says . . . .
g. Create a story to go with this number sentence. . . .
h. Create a story that describes this picture. . . .
i. Show . . . on the number line.
j. Why is a . . . not a . . . ?
k. This is a well known puzzle. See if you can solve it. . . .
l. In your own words tell why . . . .
m. In your own words tell what a . . . is.
n. Solve the following story problems. . . .
o. Which of these is not a . . . ?
p. Tell three things you know that are true about . . . .

5. Review Step 2, under Evaluating Growth in Understanding. Why do you think it was recommended that a teacher write sample test questions for each objective? Why wasn't just writing down the objectives seen as sufficient?

2. THE DEVELOPMENT OF UNDERSTANDING

Mathematicians, educators, and psychologists have many views on how understanding develops. While their views are not all the same, they are not as opposed as they are complementary. The different views seem to be the result of people with different backgrounds and interests looking at pretty much the same idea but analyzing it in terms of their backgrounds. Of course, some contradictions emerge, and in the course of debate these theoreticians have tended to emphasize the points of disagreement. Because all of these views have applications in teaching elementary mathematics and are of great utility in one context or another, we will not debate the issues nor will we draw conclusions as to a "correct" position. Instead, we will examine several of these views of understanding and how understanding develops or is developed. Where a particular individual is closely associated with a position, it will, for simplicity, be ascribed to him and generally illustrated through his work.

We will now look at the development of understanding in four ways: through concrete and semiconcrete representations; through the structure of the subject; through meaningful verbal learning; and through the reasoning which explains mathematics and convinces one that it is correct. The teaching suggestions in the next section flow from the positions taken here and in Section 1.

Concrete and Semiconcrete Representation

There seems to be little disagreement that children should learn mathematics through a progression from the use of concrete materials to semiconcrete materials and finally to abstract statements. Again, there is little disagreement that the use of concrete material, and to some extent semiconcrete material also, will be more frequent in lower grades and less frequent in upper grades.

These ideas are not new. In 1918, the authors of *Practical Methods and Devices for Teachers* spoke of first graders as follows: "Examples in the concrete are better for the child at this stage of his development, as he can more readily

comprehend these."[1] The rationale for using concrete materials has been developed further since that time, and guidelines have been provided that will assist us in deciding when, where, and how to use them. For guidance we turn mainly to the works of Bruner and Dienes. First, consider these statements by Jerome Bruner.

Any idea or problem or body of knowledge can be presented in a form simple enough so that any particular learner can understand it in a recognizable form. . . .

Any domain of knowledge (or any problem within that domain of knowledge) can be represented in three ways: by a set of actions appropriate for achieving a certain result (enactive representation); by a set of summary images or graphics that stand for a concept without defining it fully (iconic representation); and by a set of symbolic or logical propositions drawn from a symbolic system that is governed by rules or laws for forming and transforming propositions (symbolic representation). . . .

If it is true that the usual course of intellectual development moves from enactive through iconic to symbolic representation of the world, it is likely that an optimum sequence will progress in the same direction. Obviously, this is a conservative doctrine. For when the learner has a well-developed symbolic system, it may be possible to by-pass the first two stages. But one does so with the risk that the learner may not possess the imagery to fall back on when his symbolic transformations fail to achieve a goal in problem solving.[2]

[1]Beecher and Faxon (Eds.), *Practical Methods and Devices for Teachers*, Volume 1. (Dansville, N. Y.: F. W. Owen Publishing Company, 1918). p. 47

[2]Jerome S. Bruner, *Toward a Theory of Instruction.* (Cambridge, Mass.: The Belknap Press of Harvard University Press, 1966.) © Copyright 1966 by the President and Fellows of Harvard College. pp. 44–45, 49. Reprinted by permission.

These quotations from Bruner are rich in implications for teaching elementary school mathematics. The first quotation is an optimistic appraisal of the capabilities of children to learn and teachers to teach. "Any idea . . . can be presented . . . so that any . . . learner can understand it. . . ." The burden is on the teacher because the idea ". . . can be presented . . ." It is not, however, always easy to find the mode of presentation that will succeed!

Bruner advances three ways to represent, or in the case of the teacher to present, a "domain of knowledge." We see that there is an active ("enactive") representation. The action implies the use of concrete materials, that is, concrete representations, or "embodiments," of the content to be taught. We next see the "iconic" form of representation, including pictures, charts, diagrams, drawings, or any images or graphics which may represent the content. These are the semiconcrete presentations which are used extensively in textbooks and on the chalkboard. The third form is the "symbolic" presentation, through sentences or equations, relating statements to each other, relying on reasoning more than on objects or drawings. All of these modes of presentation are used in elementary mathematics. The second quoted paragraph describes the sequence in which they are used.

Take, as a simple example, the early development of the addition of whole numbers. We can see clearly the development described by Bruner:

Enactive: The child is asked to combine sets of real objects and find the number of objects in the resulting set.

Iconic: The child interprets as addition a variety of pictured situations and uses the pictures to find the sums.

Symbolic: The child is presented with the addition fact expressed in an abstract form and obtains the answer.

In the last case there is, of course, no guarantee that the child has solved the problem abstractly just because it was presented abstractly. The child may have solved the problem in a concrete or semiconcrete mode. This is important to remember, for we are going to use that fact in a discussion below. Here are some things a child may do to find the answer to $4 + 2 = \square$:

a. Knows the answer from memory and writes $4 + 2 = 6$.

b. Knows $4 + 1 = 5$ and can think two is one more than one; $4 + 1 = 5$, so $4 + 2 = 6$. The child may not produce each step mentally but in many cases *can* if asked.

c. Thinks of a picture or draws a picture and counts.

d. Counts fingers.

For purposes of finding the answer, any of these is effective. While we expect a child to make progress (from *d* toward *a* in our list), we recognize that if the child forgets or is unable to process the problem abstractly, as in *a* or *b*, the most sensible thing the child can do is to use some concrete or semiconcrete model to solve the problem.

Thus, for young children it is appropriate to develop instruction in concrete, semiconcrete, and abstract modes, and in that order. Does this apply only to young children? No! For older learners it may be possible to bypass the first two stages. The result, however, may be that the learner may not have models to fall back on when trying to solve a problem. It seems desirable to begin most topics at the concrete and semiconcrete level. This may be just as desirable for older learners as for young ones.

A further analysis of the use of concrete material is provided in the ideas of Zoltan Dienes. The work of Z. P. Dienes is replete with ideas or principles which can be applied in teaching.[1] Dienes' Multiple Embodiment Principle is one that teachers can use to get a variety of interesting lessons on the same topic. The multiple embodiment principle asserts it is best to use a wide variety of different, and different looking, materials in teaching a mathematical idea. The argument for the principle is this: In learning an abstraction one needs to see many different examples in order to separate what is relevant or crucial from what is related to only one example. When a young child learns the meaning of the word *dog,* it is learned by example. "This is a dog," "That is a dog," and so forth. Imagine a child whose only contact with dogs has been with tiny, clipped poodles. Would the child say that a Saint Bernard is a dog? Probably not; to that child a dog is small and has a fancy hair cut! Unless we have many different examples of the things we are trying to learn about, we get incorrect concepts because we mistake the characteristics of the example for the characteristics of the concept.

Another reason for using many different concrete representations (embodiments) of a mathematical idea is that many ideas apply to a variety of different situations. A child who learns only one of these situations may have difficulty extending the idea to the other situations. Let us make this clearer by an example in multiplication of whole numbers. Suppose a child learns about multiplication of whole numbers only through

[1]Z. P. Dienes, "A Theory of Mathematics Learning." Chapter 2 in *Building Up Mathematics,* 3rd Edition. (London: Hutchinson Publishing Group, Ltd., 1967)

the "set of sets" approach. In this approach 3×5 is "embodied" as 3 sets of 5.

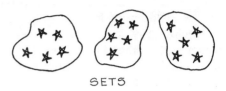

SETS

There are, however, at least four other common meanings of 3×5: jumps on the number line, rectangular array, Cartesian product, and repeated addition. They are illustrated on page 25.

If children learn about multiplication through only one approach, they will have to find for themselves the relation between multiplication and the other situations. Thus, to give multiplication its full range of meanings, we would use all of the embodiments which relate to it, that is, multiple embodiments of the same concept.

Let us examine, in the light of the multiple embodiment principle, a common error made by children and see how the use of this principle can help to prevent this error. Look at the rectangle below. Is one half of the rectangle shaded?

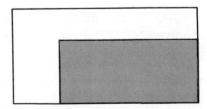

Most elementary school students will answer the question incorrectly because their experience with fraction concepts has been limited to situations in which a geometric figure is divided into congruent parts. When the parts are not

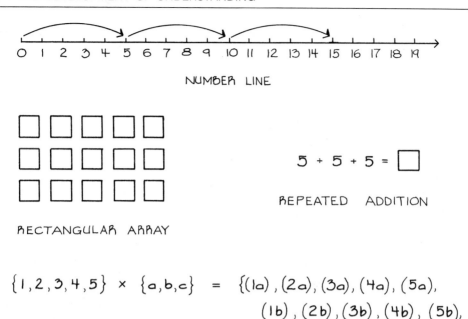

NUMBER LINE

$5 + 5 + 5 = \boxed{}$

REPEATED ADDITION

RECTANGULAR ARRAY

$$\{1,2,3,4,5\} \times \{a,b,c\} = \{(1a),(2a),(3a),(4a),(5a),$$
$$(1b),(2b),(3b),(4b),(5b),$$
$$(1c),(2c),(3c),(4c),(5c)\}$$

CARTESIAN PRODUCT

congruent, they will say, "No, the rectangle is not divided in half." The multiple embodiment principle would imply that examples should be given in which children work with halves that are the same size but are *not* always congruent.

Let us look further at fraction concepts and apply the multiple embodiment principle. Each embodiment could give rise to a lesson at almost any grade level. Fractions may also be visualized, represented, *embodied,* as sets of objects divided into equally numerous subsets. For example, four of the eight circles, or half of the circles, are shaded.

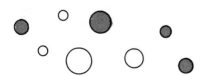

The main point is that fractions can be related to sets, area, volume, distance, and a number of other topics. A child should see and use all of these embodiments to get the full meaning of the fraction concept. When we teach an idea, such as the concept of a fraction, which is rich in various meanings and uses, we should bring into our teaching as many different kinds of things as we can find to illustrate that concept. We attempt to have the range of our examples and illustrations match the range of uses of the idea.

Structure Within the Subject

The trend toward meaningful instruction in arithmetic, which was started by William A. Brownell in the thirties, has been so completely accepted that it is difficult to imagine advocating that arithmetic be taught any other way. We have seen the "drill only" theory and the "incidental learning" theory virtually vanish. The meaning theory emphasizes understanding the structure of the subject. In the words of Brownell,

> The "meaning" theory conceives of arithmetic as a closely knit system of understandable ideas, principles, and processes. According to this theory, the test of learning is not mere mechanical facility in "figuring." The true test is an intelligent grasp upon number relations and the ability to deal with arithmetical situations with proper comprehension of their mathematical as well as their practical significance.[1]

While Brownell objected to the meaning theory being called "eclectic," he did allow that there were appropriate uses of both drill and incidental learning in teaching mathematics. His writings suggest that not only the structure of the subject, ". . . a closely knit system of understandable ideas, principles, and processes. . . ," but also the use of concrete materials and practical applications have a place in meaning theory. At present this view has prevailed. The teaching of mathematics is an interweaving of concrete representations, structure and relations within the subject, appropriate drill and practice, and relevant applications. Having discussed the use of concrete representations, we will now look at the use of the structure of elementary mathematics as a device for teaching for understanding.

Emphasis on structures (properties) and relations within mathematics often make learning more efficient. In some cases this is absolutely necessary because there are too many individual cases to learn separately. The use of the commutative property assists learning the basic facts of addition and multiplication. When a child has learned $2 \times 9 = 18$, learning $9 \times 2 = 18$ can be materially assisted by emphasizing the commutative property. Consider also search techniques used in trying to remember forgotten facts. If I forget $9 \times 6 = \square$, I may try $6 \times 9 = \square$ as a first step in trying to remember. In learning division facts the relationship between multiplication and division will also help to make learning more efficient. The problem $54 \div 6 = \square$ is surely easier to learn and remember, and to reconstruct if forgotten, if it is closely tied to $6 \times 9 = 54$.

When an addition problem involves numbers such as $28 + 5 = \square$, we may call on a relation within our place value system of numeration. This relation is illustrated here.

$$8 + 5 = 13$$
$$18 + 5 = 23$$
$$28 + 5 = 33$$
$$38 + 5 = 43$$
$$48 + 5 = 53$$
$$58 + 5 = 63$$
$$68 + 5 = 73$$

We notice that when we add 5 to a number ending in 8, the sum has two properties: Its final digit is 3 and the number of tens is one larger than before. It is easier to see this relation than to state it, and we use it constantly in addition. We sometimes do such a problem in the more formal way, thinking of regrouping, but more often we do not, as this problem shows.

[1]William A. Brownell, "Psychological Considerations in the Learning and the Teaching of Arithmetic." In *The Teaching of Arithmetic*, Tenth Yearbook of The National Council of Teachers of Mathematics, 1935. Copyright, 1935, by The National Council of Teachers of Mathematics. p. 19. Reprinted by permission.

```
2 1 5     What we think
  3 7      7 + 5 = 12
4 2 9        + 9 = 21
2 6 5        + 5 = 26
  3 2        + 2 = 28
4 3 5        + 5 = 33
+   2 6      + 6 =
```

In the display, which shows what we think as we work the problem, we use the adding by endings procedure without any formal regrouping and we do this many times in each problem. Note that $28 + 5 = 33$ occurs in step 5.

Emphasis on structures and relationships also helps justify statements, explaining in a logical way why they are true. To illustrate this, we may take a statement which is frequently memorized and more frequently not understood at all. The statement: Division by zero does not produce an answer and so we never consider such problems. The short way to say this is, "Division by zero is undefined." Let us try a division by zero.

$$5 \div 0 = \square$$

I don't know what the answer is, but I do know an important and useful structural property or relation. This is the relation between multiplication and division.

If $a \div b = c$, then $b \times c = a$
So if $5 \div 0 = \square$, then $0 \times \square = 5$

Now I may ask whether I know a number, $\square$, for which $0 \times \square = 5$. Again, another property states that zero times any number equals zero. Whatever number I put in the box, I will get 0, not 5, for the answer. Thus, there is no answer for the multiplication problem, so there is no answer for division by zero.

Meanings may be derived from two sources: directly from experience in manipulating concrete materials or through elaboration of previously understood ideas. To illustrate this, glance back at the different meanings which multiplication may, and in fact should, have. Four of these—sets, the number line, rectangular arrays, and the Cartesian product—involve concrete or at least semiconcrete material. The idea of multiplication arises and, in fact, products can be found by direct experience with objects. The fifth, repeated addition, does not have to involve concrete objects. The child is led to an understanding of multiplication through an understanding of addition. As we progress through the grades in the mathematics curriculum, more and more topics are based on previously learned abstractions; that is as it should be. However, whenever it is also possible to root an idea or operation in a concrete model, this should be done; many children need far more support from concrete models than they typically receive.

Meaning and significance. A very useful distinction pointed out by Brownell and others is the one between the "meaning" and the "significance" of a subject. In this context the word *significance* means social significance and might encompass anything from counting change to advanced scientific and technical applications. There has been, and in all likelihood will continue to be, a shifting balance of emphasis between meaning and significance. The drill-only theory of teaching arithmetic gave little emphasis to meaning. Once the mathematics was learned through drill, however, practice in applications was provided. In this way the drill-only theory gave far more emphasis to significance than to meaning. The curriculum reforms which occurred during the 1950's and 1960's emphasized structural properties of mathematics and mathematical relations. Meaning then outpaced significance, and relevant interesting applications were in short supply in the curriculum. It is now generally agreed that more work on interesting applications is needed at the elementary level, and actually at all levels. One cannot expect to see any final resolution of this problem. Certainly both meaning and significant applications are essential in the curriculum, but the relative emphasis may be expected to continue to change in response to the forces that influence curriculum.

Meaningful Verbal Learning

Even though we have lately experienced an emphasis on discovery learning and we are now experiencing an increase in the popularity of mathematics laboratories, we still find there is a vast amount of teaching by telling and learning by listening in classrooms. There is some at every grade level and the proportion of instruction that is intended for verbal reception increases, quite properly, at higher grade levels. David P. Ausubel has discussed meaningful verbal learning. He presents some characteristics distinguishing *effective, meaningful* verbal learning from *ineffective, rote* verbal learning. We emphasize here that verbal learning, when properly organized, can be very effective and, in fact, is a proper way to present many topics. We undertake here to present and exemplify Ausubel's most important principles for obtaining effective, that is, meaningful, verbal learning.[1]

Ausubel points out there are three conditions necessary for verbally learned material to be meaningful:

1. *The subject or topic or concept must be inherently meaningful or meaningful learning will be impossible.* If the learning task is itself meaningless, you cannot make it meaningful. I can figure out what 8×7 is, if I forget, because it has a variety of meanings for me. If I forget my telephone number, I can't "figure it out" because it has no meaning. Arbitrary material *must* be learned by rote reception learning.

2. *The student must intend to learn meaningfully.* In making this assertion, Ausubel means the student must not intend solely to memorize the words of the textbook or teacher. In fact, a student's capacity to retain memorized statements is limited and any significant, permanent educational attainment on that basis is impossible. Some students try to learn this way; you may have memorized a lot of material the night before a test, knowing that in 48 hours it would be forgotten. What good was it? Ausubel speculates about one reason for this kind of learning strategy:

> One reason why pupils commonly develop a rote-learning set in relation to potentially meaningful subject matter is that they learn from sad experience that substantively correct answers lacking in verbatim correspondence to what they have been taught receive no credit whatsoever from certain teachers.[2]

This is surely true, and it is true for a variety of reasons. Some teachers simply lack the depth of understanding to recog-

[1]David P. Ausubel, "Facilitating Meaningful Verbal Learning in the Classroom," *The Arithmetic Teacher*, Vol. 15, No. 2, (Feb. 1968), pp. 126–132.

[2]David P. Ausubel, "Facilitating Meaningful Verbal Learning in the Classroom," *The Arithmetic Teacher*, Vol. 15, No. 2, (Feb. 1968). Copyright © 1968, The National Council of Teachers of Mathematics, Inc. p. 128. Reprinted by permission.

nize an essentially correct statement in words other than the exact words of the text. Some think it is their proper task to get children to memorize exactly the words of the text. Some do not recognize the importance of the alternate statement "in the student's own words" as evidence of understanding. Put simply, if learned material is meaningful to the students, they will be able to restate the ideas in language other than the verbatum language in which it was taught. The students must also recognize the idea when presented in other words. If the statement has meaning for the students, then they will be able to recognize and use many different ways to express it. This is the same point expressed in Section 1 on the importance of transformation of material from one form to another in evaluating understanding.

Let us take, for example, the definition of prime number, given in one fifth-grade text as, "A prime number is any whole number greater than 1 that has only two factors, itself and 1." Choose from the statements below those which are correct, nearly correct, or wrong.

a. A prime number is a whole number which has exactly two factors.

b. A prime number is a whole number which can be divided evenly only by 1 and by itself.

c. A prime number is any whole number greater than 1 that has 1 and itself as factors.

d. A prime number is a number you can't get by multiplying two other numbers together, except using 1 and the number.

What were your choices? *a* is correct, *b* and *d* are nearly correct, and *c*, which looks the closest in wording to the given definition, is wrong. The point, of course, is this: If students are to go be-yond memorization and understand meanings, we must be willing and able to accept statements which are essentially correct but different in wording from the statements in the textbook.

A very important point made by Ausubel is that students must actively attempt to make the new material meaningful.

> The main danger relative to meaningful reception learning is not so much that the learner will frankly adopt a rote-learning set but that he will be insufficiently energetic in reformulating presented propositions so that they have real meaning for him in terms of his own structure of knowledge, . . .[1]

Notice the emphasis by Ausubel on the activity of the learner in a form of learning generally thought to be passive. There is no such thing as passive learning of any substantial organized body of information. Learning by whatever avenue depends on the activity of the learner. As teachers, we may arrange circumstances so that learning is possible, probable, or even joyous, but it is ultimately the student who must learn.

3. *The student must have a background of previous learning to which to relate the new learning.* The new item, to be learned meaningfully, must be "fitted in" or "hooked on" to the learner's existing ideas. For this to happen, prior learning must be available and must be clear and stable. If these conditions are met, then there is a good chance that the new learning will be related meaningfully to the student's existing cognitive structure.

---

[1]David P. Ausubel, "Facilitating Meaningful Verbal Learning in the Classroom," *The Arithmetic Teacher,* Vol. 15, No. 2, (Feb. 1968). Copyright © 1968, The National Council of Teachers of Mathematics, Inc. p. 129. Reprinted by permission.

Let us look at an example which illustrates how the position of an item of information in cognitive structure affects the degree to which it will be meaningful and the degree to which it will be retained. In learning multiplication in the third and fourth grades, the operation of multiplication is related to addition. Students learn, through verbal reception, that multiplication is a short way of repeated addition of the same number. Those students for whom the groundwork has been properly prepared will find this verbal reception is quite meaningful, and they can solve multiplication problems by repeated addition. They will do this until they learn more efficient procedures which, in this case,

$$6 \times 4 = 4 + 4 + 4 + 4 + 4 + 4 = 24$$

means memorizing either the fact in question or some closely related fact. Children for whom addition is not a "clear and stable anchoring idea" will use more primitive strategies, such as making six sets of four marks each and counting to solve the problem.

The point, again, is this: For an item to be meaningful, relevant explanatory anchoring ideas must be available in the cognitive structure of the students. These ideas must be clear and stable. We have also seen that the students must actively seek to establish the meanings relative to their own cognitive structure. In the next section we will apply these ideas and other ideas to the task of developing effective lessons.

Explaining Mathematics

A basic characteristic of mathematics, and one which should be communicated to students through all mathematics teaching, is this: There is evidence that the things we say are true, and there are reasons why things are done as they are. In most of our teaching it is just as important for the students to learn *why* a statement is true and to be able to justify it as it is to memorize the fact involved. In many cases the reasoning leads to the conclusion itself. Even in computation, where the performance of the algorithm and the production of answers are important goals, it is desirable in most cases that the students should be able to explain why the algorithm is performed as it is. One way to evaluate students' comprehension is to ask them to explain in their own words why a statement is true or why an algorithm is done as it is. As you proceed through the next section, observe that several ways of presenting evidence are used in the development of lessons.

Experience. One reason for believing a statement to be true is that the statement corresponds to (accurately describes) something you have actually experienced. The thing which is experienced is believed because direct sensory evidence supports it. In providing evidence for a mathematical statement, try to arrange lessons where students experience directly the truth of the statement. Here are two examples, one from the primary and the other from the upper elementary level.

We want the students to be convinced that $7 - 2 = 5$. We provide a wide variety of experiences, different in form and appearance, which illustrate this fact. Blocks and other concrete objects are used at first, then pictures and number-line models are used. Finally, all this is symbolized and the students are expected not only to *know* the subtraction fact

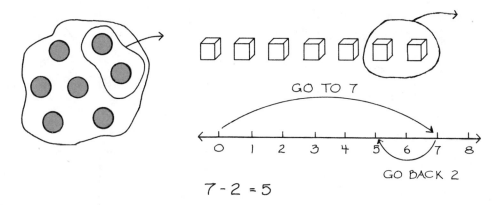

GO TO 7

GO BACK 2

$7 - 2 = 5$

but to believe it and to be able to demonstrate why it is true by using these models. Primary mathematics is rich in examples of the use of "raw" experience to support a statement.

When we want students to learn, know, and believe that there is only one way to express a number as the product of prime factors, we may ask them to try factoring a number in different ways and observe the results. See the diagram below.

We may now ask, "How are these answers different?" and later, "How are these answers alike?" We *try* to find a different way to factor 84 and find we cannot. This experience leads us to conclude that there is only one way to express 84 as a product of primes.

Sometimes "experience" is organized in a more formal and systematic way and

leads to conclusions that seem very strongly supported and that apply to a wide variety of examples. We refer to these systematic ways of organizing experience as plausible reasoning and inductive reasoning.

Plausible reasoning. "Plausible" reasoning can be used to support a variety of statements in elementary mathematics. This kind of reasoning is hard to describe; it is not strictly logical but so strongly rooted in common sense that the arguments and conclusions are almost impossible to deny. Organized experience and induction are sometimes included as ways to reason plausibly. Here is an example.

It is fairly easy to see why the area of a rectangle is found by multiplying base

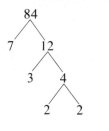

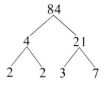

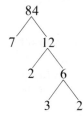

$84 = 7 \times 3 \times 2 \times 2$

$84 = 2 \times 2 \times 3 \times 7$

$84 = 7 \times 2 \times 3 \times 2$

times height. The area of a parallelogram is not so easy to see because the squares "don't fit" in the corners.

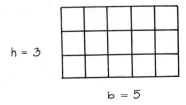

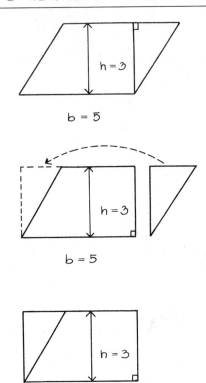

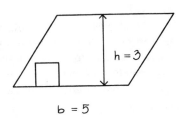

However, it seems plausible—sensible, reasonable—that if we cut up the parallelogram and piece it back together, the area will remain the same. If we can put it back together in the shape of a rectangle, we can then find the area.

There are many instances of an approach to a topic which, while not strictly logical in the mathematical sense, are believable, plausible, and which effectively convince students of the reasonableness of the conclusion.

In mathematics a number of nice conclusions can be obtained by looking at cases arranged in numerical order. This form of plausible reasoning is called "in-ductive" reasoning. It has strong appeal; most people look at several cases and feel that the principle they see *must* continue to be true in further cases. Sometimes, of course, it does not! Look at this table. Do you not feel certain you know what the sum of the first 6 or 10 or 100 odd numbers would be? The pattern seems to be so regular and so consistent that it cannot be a matter of chance!

Add the first 1 odd numbers.	$1 = 1 =$	1×1
Add the first 2 odd numbers.	$1 + 3 = 4 =$	2×2
Add the first 3 odd numbers.	$1 + 3 + 5 = 9 =$	3×3
Add the first 4 odd numbers.	$1 + 3 + 5 + 7 = 16 =$	4×4
Add the first 5 odd numbers.	$1 + 3 + 5 + 7 + 9 = 25 =$	5×5
Add the first 6 odd numbers.	The sum is _____.	
Add the first 10 odd numbers.	The sum is _____.	

Authority. When students accept a statement only because the teacher or the textbook says it is true, they have accepted it on "authority." There are some cases in which it is proper to rely on your authority or the authority of the textbook in presenting some fact. For example, in teaching symbolism, there *is no reason* why symbols are used as they are. Why do we use 3^4 and not 4*3 to mean $3 \times 3 \times 3 \times 3$? Symbols are a convention which students must accept and learn.

Teachers tend to use "authority" as justification for statements far too often and in situations in which plausible reasoning or explanations based on experience are possible. Try, as far as possible, to avoid such statements and to present a reasonable argument for the things you teach.

Summary

Before we close, let us step back and make a statement on what we see as the implications that theorists such as Bruner, Ausubel, Dienes, and Brownell have for teaching mathematics in the elementary school. We take the position that understanding can be developed through lessons that present mathematics as a reasonable subject. Children can be helped to see the sense of the mathematical symbols through a cycle of activities that progress in a lesson or through a series of lessons. A teacher can begin this cycle by having children manipulate or explore with concrete objects, such as rods, blocks, or geoboards, or with semiconcrete objects, such as number lines, picture drawings, or diagrams. It is not so important that the objects the children use are colorful and fancy. It is important that the students are familiar with the objects and the ways they are using the objects.

The cycle continues with the children using the objects in specified ways. They notice regularities or similarities, and use verbal and then symbolic statements to represent what they have been doing. This should help insure that the symbolic statements make sense to them.

After the teacher is sure that symbolic statements make sense to the children, formal practice or drill can begin on those procedures, algorithms, and facts the children need to be skilled in using. The teacher should be alert when children are doing practice activities and should check that children can take an exercise and use objects or pictures to explain what the symbolic statement means. Teachers should make it a habit to challenge students' answers. This should be done as often when the students' answers are correct as when they are in error. Students should have confidence in their answers and know that they may be called on to defend them with both logical answers *and* concrete or semiconcrete objects. The cycle of activities just outlined begins and ends with children using objects. However, at the beginning of the cycle children are using objects to explore a new topic. At the end of the cycle children are using objects and logic to explain what they are doing. The mathematics makes sense—it is reasonable.

Discussion Questions

1. In your own experience as a learner, what subjects were most "meaningful" to you? How did your understanding of those subjects develop?

2. What things have you learned by "authority"? Do you react differently to "authority" than you do to rational argument?

3. Ausubel points out three conditions which are necessary for verbally learned material to be learned meaningfully. Consider each of these and tell how the teacher might go about seeing that these conditions are met.

4. Consider the cycle of activities discussed in the preceding summary. Identify the place of Bruner's enactive, iconic, and symbolic modes of presentation. Where does Brownell's meaning theory come into the cycle of activities?

3. TEACHING FOR UNDERSTANDING

In teaching elementary mathematics there are many days when you are helping students with individual problems, following up and reteaching, or supervising and assisting students as they work on projects or activities. On some days, however, you plan activities that introduce a new topic, a new idea, or a new computational procedure. These lessons, in which the idea is first presented to the students, deserve our most careful attention. If a lesson is well prepared and presented, the students will have some ideas about the topic and about the subject of mathematics as well. We would like students to think of mathematics as sensible and enjoyable, related to experience, and an area in which the judgments of common sense are mostly correct. Students must be encouraged to think and reason for themselves. They must not be led to conclude that mathematics is a mysterious subject and, because their common sense and thinking are often wrong, that the only safe course is

to memorize what the teacher says. Developing a proper attitude lies not in what is taught but in how it is presented and explained and in how the child's ideas are received. As we go on to plan effective lessons, one of our major goals is to present topics so that students get the right overall picture.

The next topic will be a detailed description of the planning and development of lessons. You must be aware that most teachers seldom write out detailed plans such as these for every lesson they present in class. Normally you would do such detailed planning on paper only for purposes of a college course and during your initial teaching experience. We do not suggest that this degree of lesson planning is a standard which all teachers should meet. However, all teachers need to think out their development and presentation of important topics. The fact that experienced teachers rarely write out lesson plans cannot be used as an excuse for careless, inaccurate, or superficial lessons!

Preparing for the Lesson

It is important to prepare for the lesson you are about to teach. The better prepared you are, the better the lesson will be and the more the students will learn. Students soon recognize a teacher who is not well prepared.

Select the topic, state the objectives, and write sample test items. As we have discussed earlier, you need to decide on the appropriate topic and to state the objectives you wish the students to achieve. A few minutes spent here will eliminate confusion about what you want children to learn and will make it easier to select learning activities.

Study the textbook and teacher's edition and the guide or syllabus. Textbooks change and different textbooks will present topics in different ways. Do not assume that you can teach a topic the way it was taught to you or the way you taught it last year. Of course, if you are an experienced teacher, know your mathematics, and have taught the same textbook before, you have a right to feel secure in what you are doing! When you are taking up a major topic, study not only your textbook but the textbook for the grade above and the grade below yours. This will give you a picture of the students' progress and your place in it.

Look to the teacher's edition for suggestions. Normally these suggestions will include things to do before using the textbook pages and things to do to follow up the use of the textbook. You may find suggestions for ways in which to use concrete or semiconcrete material. If a local guide or state syllabus is used in your school, read it. These guides often contain excellent teaching suggestions.

Collect the material you will use in teaching the lesson. One reason most instruction in arithmetic is limited solely to the use of the textbook is that teachers are reluctant to take time to plan for use of concrete materials. When you plan a lesson that makes use of this kind of material, take the time to collect what you need beforehand. When the lesson is over, save it for use in the future.

Beginning the Lesson

When you are starting a lesson, you want the attention of all the children, you want them to be oriented to the topic of the lesson or to the activity, and you want them to be ready to learn. To ac-

complish this, spend a few minutes at the beginning of the period preparing the children for the learning tasks you have planned. You will get better results if you do this than you will by launching "cold" into the details of your lesson. Here are some suggestions.

Tell the students the general topic of the lesson. Knowing the topic should help students attend to the important parts of the lesson. Don't give the whole lesson away in your first sentence. This will take the excitement out of the lesson. It would be better to say, "Today we are going to look at the angles of a triangle," rather than, "Today we are going to learn that the sum of the angles of a triangle is 180°." The first statement tells the students generally what is important in the lesson; the second statement gives them so much that they don't need to follow the lesson.

Tell students the goal or purpose of a process or an algorithm. If students know why they are doing a calculation and what the answer means, they can often make sensible suggestions.

Poor:
> We are going to find square roots today. Here is how you find the square root of 36. . . .

Better:
> I am looking for a number. This number, when multiplied by itself, will give you 36 as the product. Can you find such a number?

After working similar examples in which the square root is a whole number, the teacher might ask, "Now can you find for me a number which, when I multiply it by itself, gives 50 as the product?" The students may be able to estimate and check, reasoning their way to a very acceptable answer to this question. Now they are prepared for the development of whatever procedure is to be used. "A number like that, one which when I square it will give 50, is called the *square root* of 50. Here's a way to find square roots. . . ."

In one case the teacher jumps right into the algorithm without any indication of what the square root "is" or why we might want to find it. In the second example, the teacher develops the notion of what a square root is and leads the students to see what they are looking for before presenting the algorithm.

Recall relevant information in the students' background. Students have had experiences that will help them understand mathematical concepts. You can make it easier for the students to learn a concept if you help them to recall these experiences. Suppose you are going to introduce fraction concepts in the first grade or in kindergarten. Many teachers assume that children have no information related to this topic. This is incorrect. You might ask, "Have you ever shared a chocolate bar with a friend? What is the best way to share it? Can you draw a picture and show us how you would share it?" Many children see nothing wrong with "taking the bigger half." Their idea of *half* is not wrong but it is incomplete; they think *half* means "divided in two parts." The concept is partly learned before you start to teach. You only need to add the notion that the parts must be equal in size.

You may recognize that this suggestion, to recall relevant information in the students' background, is related to an idea expressed by Ausubel—for an idea to be learned meaningfully and retained, it must be related to ideas already present in the learner's cognitive structure.

When you recall relevant parts of the students' background, you are helping them to fit the present idea into their cognitive structure. This will make it easier to learn the new idea and, in many cases, reinforce and clarify previously learned ideas.

If, at an upper grade level, you are working on an idea which requires several days of teaching time, students can be oriented if you start each day with a review of the big ideas that have been presented up to that time. This review brings them up to date and gives them a place to begin hooking on and fitting in new ideas to the existing cognitive structure.

Review briefly information the students will need to understand this lesson. In the course of a lesson you may need to rely on the students' understanding of some idea you have taught previously. If you are teaching division of fractions, you may want the students to be able to use the inverse relation between multiplication and division. If so, you should review this relationship, making sure it is clear and available in the students' minds. In this way it can be used smoothly and easily, fitting into the development without having to stop and reteach it in the middle of the lesson.

TO UNDERSTAND THIS,

$$\frac{2}{3} \div \frac{5}{6} = \square$$

$$\square \times \frac{5}{6} = \frac{2}{3}$$

REVIEW THIS,

$$12 \div 4 = \square$$

$$\square \times 4 = 12$$

BEFORE STARTING.

Developing the Lesson

Stating objectives, preparing the lesson, and reviewing prerequisite learnings all lead to teaching for the developing of understanding. If we prepare well and plan appropriate activities for the students, understanding will emerge. Now let us examine how lessons can be conducted to lead to the development of understanding.

One obviously cannot use all of the suggestions given in this chapter in a single lesson. The same applies to this topic. You will use only one or possibly two of these suggestions in any one lesson.

Use objects, pictures, or diagrams to illustrate the idea you are teaching. One vitally important way in which understanding develops and mathematical ideas are made meaningful is through concrete and semiconcrete materials. In Section 2 one can observe as a persistent theme the use of concrete and semiconcrete materials as "embodiments" of mathematical ideas used to develop meaning. In many cases it is a good idea to have students actually touch and manipulate material as the lesson progresses. In other cases it may be enough for you to "demonstrate" the use of the material as the children watch. In the latter case, the material should be made available later for those students who want or need to use it themselves. We turn now to examples of the use of concrete and semiconcrete materials in mathematics lessons.

As teachers teach addition facts, or the facts for other operations, they usually follow a concrete to semiconcrete to abstract teaching sequence and use the multiple embodiment principle. This development is suggested in textbooks; the material in the textbook is semiconcrete or abstract, and the suggestions for use of concrete materials are to be found in the teacher's edition. For example, it may be suggested that children form sets of small objects, count them, join the sets, and count again. This concrete activity would build understanding of the operation of addition and familiarity with specific addition facts.

The same ideas may be presented by using semiconcrete materials. In doing such exercises the children count pictures in two sets and then count all the pictures. They record the total number of pictures. Another sort of semiconcrete material used in exploring addition facts is the number line. Instead of counting discrete objects or pictures, the children count spaces to arrive at addition facts. "3 spaces and 4 more spaces gets me to 7, so $3 + 4 = 7$."

Concrete materials can also be used to explain the rationale of an algorithm; that is, to show why we perform the operation as we do. We want the students to understand the operation of regrouping in subtraction; we want to go beyond mere memorizing of the steps in the process. To attain understanding, manipulation of a concrete embodiment of the algorithm is effective. In the example on page 38, notice the close correspondence between the algorithm and the illustration. Each step performed in the algorithm is matched by a similar step in the illustration. When, for instance, 1 ten is renamed as 10 ones, giving 15 ones, the illustration shows a ten being traded for 10 ones and shows the 15 ones. This is certainly a powerful example of the way in which a meaning can be attached to an algorithm.

When you are preparing for a lesson, you may want sources of ideas for concrete or semiconcrete materials. Look in

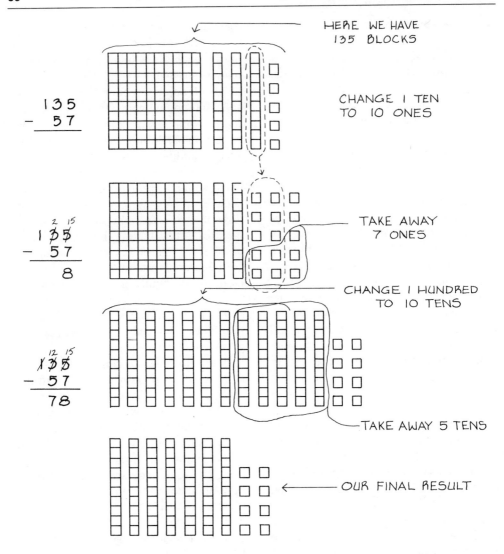

HERE WE HAVE
135 BLOCKS

CHANGE 1 TEN
TO 10 ONES

TAKE AWAY
7 ONES

CHANGE 1 HUNDRED
TO 10 TENS

TAKE AWAY 5 TENS

OUR FINAL RESULT

the textbook and the teacher's manual for pictorial material. If a picture or a diagram seems to explain something effectively, it is possible that drawing the same thing on heavy paper or cardboard and cutting it out will produce an effective concrete aid. (See page 39.)

Keep a supply of mathematics teaching material catalogs available. Even if your school does not spend much money on equipment, you may see pictures of ma-

terials which you or your students could make.

Present a new idea so that it is a logical extension or variation of an idea the students already know. Use logical or "plausible" reasoning to establish the new idea. This teaching technique is related to the discussion of verbal learning. Each new mathematical idea fits into the structure of previously learned ideas and is related to those previous ideas in cer-

PICTURE SHOWING THAT

$\frac{1}{3}$ IS THE SAME AS $\frac{2}{6}$

DRAW ON CARDBOARD

AND CUT OUT

tain ways. As you present new mathematical ideas, promote better learning by "fitting the ideas in" and "hooking them on" to the old ideas. Always try to show the relationship between what the student has learned before and what he is learning now. Here is an example showing how a new operation is an extension of previously learned operations.

Division is related to both multiplication and subtraction. The development of division may easily be done as an extension of subtraction; division is done by repeatedly subtracting the same number.

$$
\begin{array}{r}
24 \\
-\ 4 \\
\hline
20 \\
-\ 4 \\
\hline
16 \\
-\ 4 \\
\hline
12 \\
-\ 4 \\
\hline
8 \\
-\ 4 \\
\hline
4 \\
-\ 4 \\
\hline
0
\end{array}
$$

In the sample shown here, 4 is subtracted from 24 six times. We conclude that there are 6 fours in 24, so $24 \div 4 = 6$. A related idea that the students should already know is that multiplication is (among other things) repeated addition. Another way, then, to make the development of division more understandable is to show how its development from subtraction is analogous to the development of multiplication from addition.

Division is also the inverse of multiplication. The problem $24 \div 4 = \square$ may be related to $4 \times \square = 24$. The relation between multiplication and division aids the recall of division facts and, as the student progresses, makes the refinements of the division algorithm easier to learn.

$$
\begin{array}{r}
5\ \text{R4} \\
6\overline{)\,34} \\
-6\quad 1 \\
\hline
28 \\
-6\quad 1 \\
\hline
22 \\
-6\quad 1 \\
\hline
16 \\
-6\quad 1 \\
\hline
10 \\
-6\quad 1 \\
\hline
4 \\
\hline
5
\end{array}
\qquad
\begin{array}{r}
5\ \text{R4} \\
6\overline{)\,34} \\
18\quad 3 \\
\hline
16 \\
12\quad 2 \\
\hline
4\quad 5
\end{array}
\qquad
\begin{array}{r}
5\ \text{R4} \\
6\overline{)\,34} \\
30\quad 5 \\
\hline
4
\end{array}
$$

In the first example, above, division *is* successive subtraction, with no refinement. In the second example, the student "subtracts 3 sixes at once" and then finishes the problem by subtracting 2 more sixes. In the third example, the student may reason that $4 \times 6 = 24$, $5 \times 6 = 30$, $6 \times 6 = 36$, so I can subtract 5 sixes and no more from 34. In each case 4 is the remainder.

Let us examine the use of "plausible" reasoning to establish a conclusion, basing the conclusion on things the students already know. We begin by assuming students know the circumference of a circle is 2 times π times the radius ($c = 2\pi r$). We also assume they know the formula for the area of a parallelogram. We want to find the formula for the *area* of a circle. In the first diagram below, the figure formed from the sections of the circle does not look much like a parellelogram. By the third diagram, it does closely resemble a parallelogram. What are the dimensions of this "almost parallelogram" whose area *is* the area of the circle?

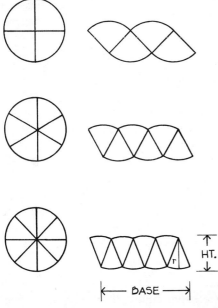

If you look at the drawing you will see that the height is very close to being a radius and, in fact, is slightly larger than a radius. The base is formed from "scallops" which were, in the circle, half the circumference. Because of the "scalloping" effect, the base is slightly shorter than half the circumference. But as we take thinner and thinner slices of the circular region, the result is closer and closer to a parallelogram.

Now we follow some calculations to get the formula for the area of the circle:

1. The base of the parallelogram is half the circumference of the circle. The circumference is $2\pi r$. Half of that is $\pi \times r$. So the base of the parallelogram is $\pi \times r$.

2. The height is one radius, r.

3. The area of the circle is the same as the area of the parallelogram, $b \times h$, which becomes $\pi \times r \times r$, or πr^2. Thus, $A = \pi r^2$.

But, you object, the height is not exactly the radius and the base is not exactly half the circumference. True. But the height is a little *more* than the radius and the base is a little *less* than half the circumference. These two errors tend to cancel and it is plausible that the result is at least "very close."

Begin a development with simple problems and introduce complications gradually; organize topics from simple to complex. If you are following a textbook or syllabus, you will find these guides are organized mostly in this way. If you examine the organization of multiplication of whole numbers, division of fractions, or almost any topic covering a significant span of time, you will see this simple-to-complex principle used. The organization places the easier aspects of the subjects first, as is appropriate for younger students. It also is easier to draw pictures or to use concrete material for the simpler aspects of a topic; presenting these first builds the students' understanding in concrete ways.

We can, for example, make diagrams to illustrate simple problems in division of fractions. The illustration shows that there are 8 halves in 4. We conclude that $4 \div \frac{1}{2} = 8$. There is no simple way to illustrate problems such as $2\frac{1}{2} \div 1\frac{4}{5}$. If we are going to provide a background of semiconcrete experiences for this topic, we must usually organize it so that the simple problems come first.

$$4 \div \frac{1}{2} = \square$$

Sometimes introduce a topic by presenting a problem to the students. This suggestion is, in reality, the opposite of the "simple-to-complex" organization of development. By first presenting the whole problem to students, you give them the complexity at the beginning. As the lesson progresses, you encourage and help students as they break the complex situation into simpler parts that they can handle, and finally reassemble the parts to achieve a solution to the problem.[1] This procedure might be called developing a topic from the complex to the simple.

Lessons resulting from this type of presentation are lively, open, full of discussion and even argument. The course of the lesson is not as predictable because students bring all kinds of material to bear on the problem. This is why topics are rarely presented in this fashion in

[1]For a more comprehensive discussion of problem solving see the chapter "Teaching for Problem-Solving Skill."

textbooks. Written examples cannot convey the open, exploratory feeling one experiences watching this sort of lesson. Nevertheless, we will outline an example and a probable course of development.

We are undertaking to teach the idea that "To determine whether a given number is prime, it is only necessary to divide it by primes less than or equal to its square root. If none of those divide the number, then it is prime." We assume here that students are already familiar with prime numbers.

Kickoff Question: Is 359
a prime number?

What may be expected now? Because the students know that a prime has no factors except itself and 1, we may expect that the first attempt will be to divide 359 by all numbers from 1 up to 358 to see if one of them is a divisor. It is not even certain that students will stop at 358. They may test even larger numbers. Here are the first few calculations. Frustration with this will build quickly and it is quite proper that it should. A seemingly simple question looks as if it will lead to several hours of dreary division. You may ask, "How long will this take?" to get students thinking about the enormity of the task.

$$1\overline{)359} = 359 \qquad 2\overline{)359} = 179 \text{ R}1 \qquad 3\overline{)359} = 119 \text{ R}2$$

$$4\overline{)359} = 89 \text{ R}3 \qquad 5\overline{)359} = 71 \text{ R}4 \qquad 6\overline{)359} = 59 \text{ R}5$$

A teacher always hopes that the students' understanding is such that a "flash of insight" will help them over a hard place. Sometimes you can generate such a flash with an appropriate question. To start students looking for more economical ways to work the problem, you might ask, "Is it really necessary to test *all* those numbers?"

The first economy they are apt to find is that it is not necessary to test any composite numbers. Suppose we check 14 to see whether it is a factor of 359. We ask whether there is a number (call it *n*) such that $14 \times n = 359$. But *if there is such a number,* we would already have found $2 \times 7n = 359$. If 14 is a factor, *so is* 2. But we tested 2 already and it is not a factor, so 14 is not a factor.

$$14 \times n = 359$$
$$(2 \times 7) \times n = 359$$
$$2 \times (7 \times n) = 359$$

Now, because we need test only primes and not composite numbers, we have a much shorter list to check. At the start, from 1 to 20, we find:

Primes: 2, 3, 5, 7, 11, 13, 17, 19.
Whole numbers: 1, 2, 3, 4, 5, 6, 7, 8, 9, 10, 11, 12, 13, 14, 15, 16, 17, 18, 19.

The second possible saving of work arises when one notices that factors must come in pairs and in each pair one factor will be larger than the other, except when the number is a perfect square. Look at 400. $20 \times 20 = 400$. Can you find two numbers which multiply together to give 400 and which are *both* larger than 20? Why not? Well, if both factors are more than 20, their product would be more than 400.

We might start the students thinking along these lines with a question like this: "Suppose I did find two numbers that would multiply together to give me 359, such as: $a \times b = 359$. How large could *a* and *b* be?" The hope here is that students begin to think, "Could they both be large?" or "Could they both be small?" Trying various numbers will, with guidance, lead to the result that if one factor is large, the other must be small and therefore easily found.

No doubt this lesson could be more quickly presented by the teacher; it could be well presented that way also. The lesson we have described here, however, is better than a direct teacher presentation because it is an exciting experience in a group search for ideas to solve a problem.

Encouraging Student Participation

Every teacher knows the frustration of planning a lesson, working hard to select good examples and organize them well, and having the lesson fall flat because students are just not participating. You want the students to follow the lesson, to anticipate the lesson, to be active participants in the development. Passive learners just sit there; active learners make suggestions, ask questions, answer your questions, and answer other students' questions. Here are some teaching procedures which will help develop active student participation.

Treat all student contributions with respect. Every student comment or question has some reasoning behind it. Be glad the child asked. Treat simple questions with tact; explain as simply and clearly as you can. Which one of these responses would you prefer, if *you* asked a question?

"Oh, Sara, are you still stuck on that? I thought we'd all learned that by now."

"I'm glad you asked that, Sara. That's important to understand before going on."

Even though a student's contribution or answer to a question is incorrect, it is still valuable. Both the question and the student deserve your respect. A teacher should never humiliate or disparage a student because of a poorly formed response or a careless question.

Accept and then challenge student contributions. The thinking behind a student's work is important to you. If a child's response is correct, you will frequently want to know whether the student was thinking in an appropriate manner or whether the answer was the result of a guess. Make a practice of being skeptical. Challenge, in a friendly way, correct and incorrect responses. You don't have to do this on every question, but do it often enough so that students are not surprised or defensive when you do challenge them. For example:

"Jenny, how did you get that?"

"I see you have been working hard, Jimmy. Tell me, why did you use division on this one?"

"Now, before you answer my next question, remember that whatever you say, I'm going to pretend not to believe you. You will have to show me why."

Listen to the student! Is there an error in the child's thinking process? Can you lead the child to find and correct the error? In explaining what was done, a child will *very often* find the mistake and correct it.

Do not expect a climate of openness and willingness to ask questions and express opinions to develop in the course of one lesson. You will have to show willingness to accept and value all contributions and questions consistently over a period of time. With older children, particularly, this takes time. Many students have had the experience of being ridiculed for asking a "simple" question or for making an error, and they are not easily persuaded to try again. Try to see the value of everything students contribute. Even if what a student says is dead wrong, it is valuable. You have discovered a topic that needs reteaching to at least one student and, more likely, to several. If you can treat all student contributions and questions as valuable and deserving of serious response, you will find that your classes are full of lively and stimulating student participation.

Plan questions which require higher-level answers. One way in which you can directly stimulate students to participate is by asking questions. To get the best results from your questions, to stimulate students' thinking, you should ask questions which require higher-level answers. Answers may be "higher-level" in that they require students to do more than just recognize or recall material; they may be "higher-level" in that they require longer or more involved answers. Frequently these factors go together but not always.

Perhaps the simplest way to ask higher-level questions is to use the "5 W's": What, When, Where, Why, and How. Answers to these questions nearly always call for a student to think out a full-sentence response, not just to recall information.

"*What* is the connection between multiplication and addition?"

"In a story problem, *when* do you use subtraction?"

"*Where* is the base of a trapezoid?"

"*Why* is every square also a rectangle?"

"*How* do you know 91 is a composite number?"

Lower-level questions are those which require the student to recognize or recall some item of information or which call for a short, simple answer. These questions do not stimulate much discussion but are better than no questions at all. For example, if the teacher says, "John, is 91 a prime number?" John may answer, "No." This question is a lower-level question. It calls for a one-word answer. The student is not asked to justify the answer or to explain how he obtained it. From the question and answer it is not clear whether John has memorized some primes and knows that 91 is not among them, or whether he has worked out the answer mentally. It is not possible to say whether John was simply remembering or performing on a higher level.

Suppose, however, the teacher asks, "John, tell us whether 91 is prime and tell us how you know." John then may answer, "91 is not prime because 7 is a factor of 91. Seven is a factor of 91 because $7 \times 13 = 91$." John gives and explains the answer. From the answer we are able to analyze his thinking and pose further questions or use his response to review the idea with the children.

A few cautions are needed in any discussion of questions. Teachers are sometimes surprised when they ask a very easy question and no student will volunteer the answer. The students may feel that to volunteer to answer such an easy question would be beneath them.

It is all right occasionally to use a question to bring back a student whose attention has wandered. However, remember that the main purpose of questions is to increase learning and promote discussion. If you frequently use questions as a disciplinary device, you may find students reacting negatively to all questions. For example, you ask a question designed to start a discussion and the student replies, "What was I doing wrong?"

It is certainly a good idea to match the question and the student of whom you ask it. If you direct a very hard question to a slower student, you virtually insure that the answer will be wrong. If you ask an easy question of a better student, the student will not profit much by answering. A certain sensitivity is required in directing questions to students. Try not to "point out" the slow students or emphasize their difficulties by always asking them the very simplest of questions. It is better sometimes to ask a bit harder question and to help the student to formulate the answer.

Use intentional errors. Another way to get students to participate in a lesson is to "play dumb." Make an error. Let the students catch you in the error and help you correct it by explaining why you were wrong and what the right answer or procedure is. Use this to elicit student discussion of the correct answer or procedure and to point out common errors to be avoided. Do not use this technique unless the material has been taught and you can reasonably expect the students to provide the correct procedure.

For example, in teaching addition of decimals you might put this on the board, and slowly start to add the first column.

$$
\begin{array}{r}
35.2 \\
1.67 \\
25.38 \\
+ \quad .96 \\
\hline
\end{array}
$$

When the children object, you may continue to play dumb and ask, "Is something wrong?" By replying, "Yes, you need to put your decimals in line," the students show they know the rule.

You might then ask, "Why must I do that?" This may bring out the explanation for the rule. The explanation should, of course, center around place value.

You may continue, "But I always put them this way before and it worked." The students may reply, "That works for whole numbers."

You may continue to probe. "Is the rule *really* different for whole numbers? Where is the decimal point in a whole number?" The answer to these somewhat more difficult questions will show the connection between the two forms of the addition algorithm.

Get mileage out of your questions. An excellent device to encourage participation and to ask higher-level questions is to get a number of students to respond to a question. Students should not be spectators. They should feel a responsibility to answer every question the teacher asks of the group. Consider the dialogue below.

Teacher:
Patti, what did you get for the area of the rectangle?

Patti:
26.

Teacher:
O.K. Let's see what Danny has — Dan?

Dan:
I have 40.

Teacher:
Oh, we had better look into this. Does anyone have an answer besides 26 and 40?

Teacher:
Now, let's have someone who has 26 show us why he thinks 26 is the area of our rectangle. Then we will let someone who has 40 try to convince us that 40 is correct. Then we will do the same for our other answers.

There are other advantages to using one question to involve a number of students. When students are mistaken, they can realize thay are not alone in their error. Discussion and debate will frequently involve a student far more intensely than a teacher's presentation.

Plan questions in advance. To get the best results from your questions, it is best to devise questions, at least key questions, when planning a lesson. This is especially true for higher-level questions. It is not always easy to think of stimulating questions on the spur of the moment when dealing with sometimes rambunctious youngsters. By planning questions at various levels in advance, you can help insure that lessons contain questions to encourage all students to participate and to stimulate thinking.

Use action to encourage participation. It is especially important for children in preschool and primary grades to express their understanding in physical action. For example, when teaching addition, you may have two groups of children come together to demonstrate an addition fact.

Older children enjoy action lessons, too. As simple a device as working problems at the board instead of doing seat work is a welcome change. Lessons which involve measuring, building, making things, and other forms of activity are frequently more effective than seatbound lessons. For a more complete discussion on activity in lessons, see the chapter on using concrete materials and laboratory activities.

Summarizing the lesson. When you have planned and started the lesson well, developed it effectively, and stimulated good student participation, there remains one thing to do: summarize the main point of the lesson. Many times, in a welter of examples, questions, discussion, and explanations, students can fail to distinguish the main point of the lesson clearly. At the end of a lesson you should briefly and directly state this main point and mention the most important supporting evidence.

Summary

The purpose of this section has been to help you plan and conduct lessons which will effectively develop understanding. The section includes ideas for preparing for the lesson, getting it started, presenting the main ideas clearly, encouraging students to participate, and, finally, summarizing the lesson. When you are planning lessons, review these ideas and use them!

Discussion Questions

1. Which of the ideas in the section, "Encouraging Student Participation," can you use in planning a lesson? Which ideas will you have to use according to your judgment as the lesson develops?

2. It was mentioned that a student can obtain a correct answer by guessing and that a teacher should check on the thinking behind both correct and incorrect answers. Besides guessing, how else might a student obtain a right answer and yet not be engaged in appropriate thinking?

3. In addition to those cited earlier, what are some advantages to getting mileage out of questions?

4. How could a teacher misuse the advice to get mileage out of questions?

5. Is "playing dumb" a way to generate higher-level questions? Defend your answer.

6. Make a case that lower-level questions have a place in teaching mathematics.

7. Why would it be a mistake to challenge only incorrect responses?

8. Consider the dialogue below. Identify the higher-level and the lower-level questions. Where could the teacher have challenged responses or gotten mileage out of a question?

Teacher:
We have been looking at fractions for some time now. We have been studying how to add fractions with like denominators. Now, let's see how we can add fractions with unlike denominators. Elsie, could you give us two fractions with unlike denominators?

Elsie:
Sure, one half and one third.

Teacher:
Fine, let's see how we can add $\frac{1}{2}$ and $\frac{1}{3}$. Now, we did add these the other day with rods. Does anybody remember what we got?

Tim:
I think it was five sixths.

Teacher:
Yes, that's right. So we know that $\frac{1}{2} + \frac{1}{3} = \frac{5}{6}$. Now, when we add two fractions, like one half and one third, we must find a common denominator. What might that be for these two fractions?

Kathy:
Six

Teacher:
Good. How many sixths does $\frac{1}{2}$ repre-

sent? (Students are not sure.) Well, how many times does 2 go into 6? Fred?

Fred:
Uh, 3 times.

Teacher:
O.K. Does that help us?

Frank:
Yes. That gives us $\frac{3}{6}$.

Teacher:
Why?

Frank:
Because $2 \times 3 = 6$ and $1 \times 3 = 3$, so $\frac{1}{2}$ equals $\frac{3}{6}$.

Teacher:
Very good.

9. Consider the ways in which students can demonstrate understanding: recognize and recall, application, seeing relationships, transforming, and transfer. Which of these ways are more closely related to lower-level questions, which to higher-level questions?

10. Before giving students a lesson in which they are to learn through reading, what could a teacher do to help insure that the children will understand what they read?

4. TEACHING FOR UNDERSTANDING BY DISCOVERY

Most of what children learn in school is not learned by discovery. Children learn most of what they know from imitation, observation, and being shown or told that something is true or that a task is done in a certain way. For example, children learn that the first President of the United States was George Washington by reading it in a book or being told that it is so. Likewise, most students learn that every rectangle is a parallelo-gram as a result of expository instruction, that is, by being told. We hope that, in teaching for understanding by exposition, many of the techniques suggested in this chapter are utilized.

School can be a more interesting experience if, in teaching for understanding, teachers sometimes provide activities where students can discover the knowledge to be learned. There is reason to believe that when students learn by discovery there is increased motivation on the part of the learner. Advocates of teaching by discovery also claim that knowledge learned by discovery is more likely to be retained by the students. Furthermore, it is hoped that learning by discovery promotes a problem-solving ability among students—a most important intellectual capability. At the very least, discovery lessons provide teachers with an alternative to expository teaching.

Some teachers mistakenly think any stimulating lesson that involves active participation by students must be a discovery lesson. If well planned and carried out, discovery lessons will be stimulating and they must necessarily involve students. However, these aspects of teaching are not unique to teaching by discovery. Expository lessons can also involve students and be interesting. What then is teaching by discovery?

Characteristics of Discovery

Teaching by discovery is arranging instruction in such a way that students come to know an item of knowledge not previously known to them without being told. There are two processes, *abstracting* and *generalizing,* that are basic to learning by discovery.

Abstracting. Abstracting is seeing (or realizing) the similarity in examples and their differences. To illustrate abstracting, consider a *wonk*. Oh, don't you know what a wonk is? Look at the following.

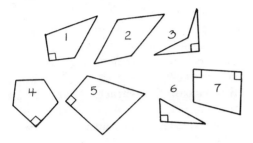

Figures 1, 3, and 5 are wonks; Figures 2, 4, 6, and 7 are not. What properties do Figures 1, 3, and 5 have in common that Figures 2, 4, 5, and 7 do not? How many sides does a wonk have? What statement can you make about a wonk's angles? The answer to these questions can be formulated on the basis of abstractions that you make from observing the drawings. Can you now formulate a definition of a wonk? Try it. A wonk could be defined as a quadrilateral with exactly one right angle. Why does this definition exclude Figures 2, 4, 6, and 7 from being wonks?

Children learn mathematical concepts by abstracting. Preschool children can learn the concept of *two* by realizing what property a pair of nails, a person's thumbs, a person's eyes, a couple of glasses, and other sets containing two objects have in common, namely, two-ness. Likewise, children learn what a triangle is by comparing triangles with circles, rectangles, and other figures and realizing that only the triangle has three sides and three "corners." That is, they abstract the common properties of triangles.

Generalizing. Another process that occurs in learning by discovery is generalizing. Briefly, generalizing is the formation of a conjecture, or guess, based on knowledge established by examining specific instances. For example, a person may observe that on four Fridays the Dow Jones average decreases. One might generalize, or form a conjecture based on four observations, that the Dow Jones average will always decrease on Fridays. Like any guess, it may be false.

Suppose you observe that the sums of digits of the numbers 117, 2,142, 97,281, and 16,803 were divisible by 9, that is:

$1 + 1 + 7 = 9$, and 9 is divisible by 9.
$2 + 1 + 4 + 2 = 9$, and 9 is divisible by 9.
$9 + 7 + 2 + 8 + 1 = 27$,
        and 27 is divisible by 9.
$1 + 6 + 8 + 0 + 3 = 18$,
        and 18 is divisible by 9.

Furthermore, the numbers 117, 2,142, 97,281, and 16,803, are all divisible by 9. Thus, for these four numbers, it has been established that if the sum of the digits of a number is divisible by 9, then the number itself is divisible by 9. Try this divisibility test with other numbers. Does it work? What conclusion might you reach concerning all whole numbers whose sum of digits is divisible by 9?

The reader may have noticed that generalizing necessitates the formation of two generalizations. The first is formed on the basis of the specific instances observed. In the two examples above, the first generalizations are, respectively:
A. For four Fridays, the Dow Jones average decreased.
B. The sum of the digits of each of the numbers 117, 2,142, 97,281, and

16,803 is divisible by 9 and the numbers themselves are divisible by 9. These are generalizations because they make claims for entire sets. In *A,* the claim is for the set of four Fridays being considered. In *B,* the claim involves a set of four numbers, namely, 117, 2,142, 97,281, and 16,803.

The second generalization that occurs in generalizing is more inclusive than the first. The second statement says something not only about the specific examples previously examined but also about all possible similar examples.

The second generalizations formed in the two examples above are, respectively:
C. On every Friday, the Dow Jones average will decrease.
D. Every number whose sum of digits is divisible by 9 is itself divisible by 9.

The subject of statement *C* includes the four Fridays and all other Fridays as well. The subject of statement *D* includes not only 117, 2,142, 97,281, and 16,803 but also all other numbers whose sum of digits is divisible by 9.

The importance of guessing. When a child abstracts a property common to a set of examples and then forms a generalization, he or she is formulating a conjecture, or guess. Sometimes the guess is clever, correct, and relevant to the intended discovery. In other cases, the conjecture may be wrong or irrelevant to the knowledge being taught. It is important that teachers encourage students to guess and make conjectures, regardless of accuracy or relevance. Students should be praised for venturing a guess and not be "put down" for incorrect or irrelevant conjectures. If students never

guessed, mathematics would become a rather boring subject.

To illustrate the importance of guessing and how a teacher might react to a student formulating an irrelevant generalization, consider the dialogue below in which a primary teacher is trying to get students to discover the following generalization: The sum of any two odd numbers is an even number.

Teacher:
Let's look at what happens when we add two odd numbers. John, could you pick some odd numbers for us to add?

John:
Maybe, 9 and 1, 1 and 5, 7 and 3.

Teacher:
Fine, let's write these on the board.

$$9 + 1 = \square$$
$$1 + 5 = \square$$
$$7 + 3 = \square$$

Now, who can tell me the sums? (Various students indicate the sums and the teacher completes the number sentences as indicated.)

$$9 + 1 = 10$$
$$1 + 5 = 6$$
$$7 + 3 = 10$$

Now, what do we notice about the sums when we added two odd numbers?

Mary:
None of them are bigger than 10.

Mary's statement is correct but is not really relevant to the knowledge in question. Nevertheless, Mary did abstract a property common to the three cases examined. Because of this, it is wise for a teacher to praise Mary for her discovery but at the same time redirect her thinking. The dialogue might continue as follows.

Teacher:
That's right, Mary. There are no sums greater than 10. Do you think this will always be true?

Mary:
I'm not sure.

Fred:
It won't be because, like $7 + 5 = 12$, and that's more than 10.

Teacher:
Very good. Mary was right for the numbers we looked at — but it won't work for the sum of *any* two odd numbers. Can anyone see anything else about the sums?

Alice:
They are all even.

Teacher:
That's an interesting observation. Do you think that will always be true when you add two odd numbers?

Mark:
I think so, because, well, it just works out that way.

Notice that the teacher accepted Mary's observation, and subsequently tried to redirect students in making other conjectures. A teacher should remember that the child is not privy to the knowledge being discovered and hence does not have a clear-cut basis for determining which guesses are relevant and which are not. Students' conjectures, therefore, should be accepted, examined, and, if necessary, redirected to other more relevant aspects of the discovery.

Determining If a Discovery Has Been Made

There are various ways a teacher can determine if a student has made a discovery. Sometimes, a teacher has an in-tuitive feeling that a student has made a discovery because of the student's facial expression. The most obvious proof that a student has made a desired discovery is that the student explicitly states the discovery.

Another indication of a student's making a discovery is the rapid answering of questions involving the knowledge to be discovered. For example, in discovering that a number is divisible by 6 if the number is both even and the sum of its digits is divisible by 3, the student can indicate the discovery by quickly stating which of the following numbers are divisible by 6.

$$40,142$$
$$33,615$$
$$5,904$$
$$56,911$$
$$904,218$$

When students quickly and correctly indicate whether a number is divisible by 6, it is likely that they have discovered the desired item of knowledge. It is not necessary to have them state a generalization to indicate that a discovery has been made.

Why does the rapid answering of questions indicate a discovery has been made? Because *use* of the discovered knowledge permits the student to avoid a long calculation. Without the use of the discovered knowledge the student would not be able to produce correct answers quickly.

This second indication is sometimes called *subverbal awareness*. The evidence is "subverbal" in the sense that a student is not explicitly stating the generalization to be discovered. Rather, he is utilizing the generalization to answer questions involving the particular item of knowledge.

Suggestions for Planning and Teaching Discovery Lessons

In teaching for understanding by discovery there are certain guidelines that can facilitate your planning and teaching of discovery lessons. We will suggest several here, discuss them briefly, and then illustrate them in the sample lesson that follows.

1. Have the item(s) of knowledge to be discovered clearly established in your mind.

It is essential that a teacher can state specifically the item of knowledge to be discovered. If the knowledge is clearly established, the appropriate learning activities can be devised to help students make the desired discovery. If a teacher is unclear as to what is to be discovered, then it is unlikely that the selected examples will be appropriate. Class discussion will likely drift with little chance of obtaining closure. As a result, students are more likely to become confused, frustrated, and hence develop a dislike for mathematics.

2. Carefully select your examples and present the easier examples first.

The sequencing of examples can be an important factor in leading students to make the desired discovery. In the lesson presented earlier involving the sum of two odd numbers, the children selected the numbers to be added. This helped insure that the children could find the sums themselves.

3. Don't force students to verbalize the discovery too soon.

Earlier, the concept of subverbal awareness was discussed as a means of determining if a discovery has been made. If some students are able to indicate their discovery by quickly giving correct answers, it may be desirable to delay the stating of the generalization. Some students have difficulty in expressing themselves. Requiring a verbalization may be frustrating and cause these students to lose interest in the lesson. Also, once the generalization is verbalized, the "cat is out of the bag" and other children are too late to make the discovery on their own. Teachers can take care not to force a premature verbalization by presenting students with additional examples to consider.

In the lesson presented earlier concerning the sum of two odd numbers, the teacher might have students indicate the oddness or evenness of the following sums: $19 + 7$, $21 + 35$, $23 + 5$. If students can respond correctly, they probably have the idea. If not, more examples could be presented rather than trying to probe for a statement of the generalization.

What should a teacher do if students don't make the desired discovery? First, decide if the lesson was appropriate for the students; that is, was the lesson appropriate considering the students' background and ability level? Perhaps the knowledge was too difficult for students to discover. If the lesson is judged to be too difficult, then it serves little purpose to force students to verbalize the discovery by continually providing hints. Don't continue and bring on frustration. Try another approach or wait until a later time to teach this knowledge.

However, if students fail to make a discovery, it is not necessarily the case that the lesson or knowledge to be learned was too hard. Check your examples. Are they appropriate? Are they easy for students to examine? Did you ask questions that caused students to compare and contrast the examples? If you feel the answers to these questions is "yes," then provide the students with additional examples for them to consider.

4. Have students verify their discoveries.

When the students make the desired discovery, how do they know it is correct? Of course, one way is for the teacher to tell them. Are there any other methods? Sometimes additional examples can be given to show that the discovery works. A plausible argument may be possible. In some cases, manipulative aids may be used to verify the discovery. For example, Cuisenaire rods could be selected which represent odd numbers. By placing the rods so that a sum is indicated, students could determine that the rod representing the sum also represents an even number. More mature students may be able to appreciate a logical argument using deductive reasoning or a plausible argument based on logic and sensory experience.

5. Provide students with opportunities to apply their discovered knowledge.

Any knowledge, regardless of how it is learned, will soon be forgotten if it is not used. Provide students with exercises that utilize the knowledge immediately after it has been discovered. This will help them remember what they have learned.

A Sample Lesson in Discovery

In this lesson the students are to discover the formula for the area of a triangle:

$$A = \tfrac{1}{2} bh$$

The objectives for this lesson are:

   a. The students can find the area of a triangle, given the lengths of its base and height.

   b. The students can state or recognize the formula for the area of a triangle.

Of course, other objectives could be stated, also. To enable students to make the discovery, the teacher can provide a series of triangles drawn on grid paper, as illustrated on the next page. To help students with the discovery, the table below should be completed.

	A	b	h
Triangle I			
Triangle II			
Triangle III			

The students should first determine the area of triangle I. Since students working this problem would not yet know the formula for the area of the triangle, they would have to find the area by counting unit squares, the small squares contained in the triangle. In accordance with the suggestion to present the easier examples first, the lengths of the bases and the heights of the triangles below are whole numbers, and in triangle I the fractional parts of the unit squares involve only the easier fractions. The students could determine by counting that there are 9 unit squares in triangle I. The base of this triangle is 6 units and its height is 3 units. Students should record these numbers in the table.

Now consider triangle II. How many unit squares are contained in this triangle? In this triangle the fractional square units are not so easily determined. However, consider rectangle DHFD'. What is the area of this rectangle? Triangle DFH contains what fraction of the area of the rectangle? What is the area of

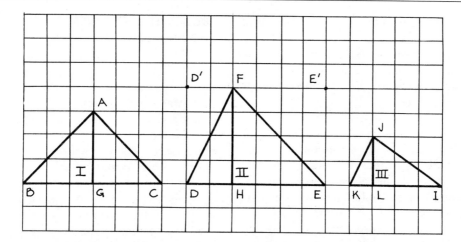

triangle DFH? What is the area of rectangle HEE'F? What is the area of triangle FHE? Then what is the area of triangle DEF? If $\overline{DE}$ is the base of triangle DEF, what is the height of the triangle? Students should record their findings in the table.

Finally, students could determine the area of Triangle III, the length of its base $\overline{IK}$, and the length of its height $\overline{LJ}$. Again, the results should be recorded in the table. The completed chart would look like the one below.

	A	b	h
Triangle I	9	6	3
Triangle II	12	6	4
Triangle III	4	4	2

From this chart it is hoped that students can make the desired discovery, namely, that the area of each of the triangles is measured by the product of one half the base times the height. For some students these three examples may be enough to formulate the correct relationship. However, for many students the relationship will not yet be realized. Rather than trying prematurely to state the desired formula $(A = \frac{1}{2} bh)$ it would

be best to provide additional triangles for consideration.

To determine if a discovery has been made, a teacher might present a triangle on grid paper and ask who can quickly find the area. Those responding quickly are probably determining the measures of the base and the height and using the formula. Others will try to count the unit squares. The former group will likely have made a discovery. For the latter, additional triangles should be presented and some guidance given as to what to look for. If some students have not found the short cut after many examples, it may be desirable to have a student verbalize the discovery so that all students can "know the secret." This helps alleviate any excessive frustrations that some students may experience. How many triangles should be presented and at what point it may be desirable to verbalize the generalization, i.e., $A = \frac{1}{2} bh$, will vary depending on the nature of the students.

Lastly, once everyone is aware of the generalization, exercises should be given using the formula. The exercises may be written statements, diagrams with measurements given, or simply statements of the measures of the bases and heights of the triangles. These exercises will help students remember the formula for the area of a triangle and will also help a teacher determine if the objectives have been realized.

Teaching by discovery is an exciting technique; more student interest and enthusiasm can be developed this way than by any other technique. No one advocates trying to teach totally by discovery. This would take far too long. However, when you come to a lesson that you could present in such a way that students *discover* the knowledge, try it. You'll like it!

Discussion Questions

1. Does using a discovery approach guarantee students will understand the mathematics being taught? Justify your answer.

2. What is the difference between abstracting and generalizing? Which comes first?

3. What can a teacher do to prevent one or two students from blurting out a discovery and thereby precluding others from making the discovery?

4. Consider all the mathematics lessons elementary teachers present. What percent of these lessons do you think are discovery lessons? Why do you think this is the case?

5. Examine two elementary school mathematics texts to estimate the percent of the lessons in these texts that are discovery lessons. Use a first- or second-grade text and a fourth- or fifth-grade text. Are there a greater number of discovery lessons in the higher-grade text? What kinds of things are presented in discovery lessons in these books?

SUGGESTED ASSIGNMENTS AND PROJECTS

Classroom Assignments

1. Select a chapter in a fourth-, fifth-, or sixth-grade text, list the topics that are covered in the chapter, and write objectives for the chapter. Include all five kinds of objectives which were discussed in Section 1, above. Based on your objectives, write a final test for the chapter. In class, compare these tests and discuss the differences in the kinds of items used. Try to reach agreement on the things a student must do to demonstrate understanding of the ideas in the chapter.

2. Select a chapter in a school mathematics textbook and list ideas presented in the chapter. For the five or six ideas you consider to be the *major* ideas in the chapter tell how the textbook develops or explains these ideas. How are the ideas presented, explained, exemplified?

3. Working in class through discussion, plan a single 30-minute lesson on a selected topic. Follow the suggestions given in Section 3. Include material and activities in your lesson which will start the lesson, develop the lesson, encourage student participation, and summarize the lesson.

4. Plan a five-minute lesson and present the lesson to your fellow students. When you do this, prepare and duplicate a sheet for each member of the class. On this sheet give your topic, your objectives, your brief lesson plan, and test questions you would use to determine whether the students comprehend the topic. After your lesson is presented, encourage discussion and critique of the objectives, the plan, the presentation, and the test items.

5. Select a major topic and plan five lessons of about 30 minutes each on the development of that topic. Try to make one of your lessons a discovery lesson. Use elementary textbooks and any other available resources to help in the planning. State the objectives you want students to attain, give sample test items, and describe in detail how you will proceed in class to teach these lessons.

Internship Assignments

Here are things you can do with children which will help you understand the ideas in this chapter. The things you do may be new *to you,* but you are learning *teaching methods* whose value is well known. If you learn to use a new method or procedure and find it successful, keep using it. The purpose of this experience is to permanently influence your teaching, not just to pass a course.

1. Observe the developmental teaching activities of a teacher over a one-week period. These "developmental teaching" activities would include discussion, teacher explanation, work with concrete or semiconcrete materials, and laboratory activities. If you are an intern, aide, or student teacher, you may observe the teacher with whom you are working. Keep a log of your observations, telling how many minutes were spent on all arithmetic activites and, of these, how many minutes were spent on developmental teaching. Describe the activities you observe and keep a copy of any materials which were used. Be prepared to report to your class.

2. Select a child who has completed the study of a chapter, make up a comprehension test, and give it to the child. Be sure to explain that you are trying out some new test questions and reassure the child that this special attention does *not* mean something is wrong. When the test is completed and you have read it, sit down and talk to the child about the test and the content of the items. Probe to discover the depth of his or her understanding. Thinking in terms of the five levels of understanding, can the child recognize and recall, apply, state relationships, transform, transfer?

3. Select a small group of children who need review and reteaching on some topic they have not adequately learned. Teach them the topic, following this series of steps.

a. Select the topic *you* are going to teach.

b. State your objectives. Try to have objectives of recognition and recall, application, stating relationships, transformation, and transfer. Write at least two test items for each objective, more if it seems desirable.

c. Pretest the group, using at least one item for each objective. Make a record of the success of each child on each objective.

d. Plan and teach the appropriate and needed material, using the principles of teaching outlined in this chapter.

e. Posttest on each objective, using the items not used on the pretest. Record the results on the same form used to record the results of the pretest.

f. Evaluate the students. What growth in understanding do you find? Evaluate your own teaching. For what objectives did you succeed in establishing understanding? What areas need improvement?

4. Select a group of children, the whole class or a smaller group, and present a new topic to them. Follow the steps in project 3, above.

SUMMARY: MAXIMS FOR TEACHING

1. "Understanding" is the most important objective in teaching elementary mathe-

matics. Teach for and test for all levels of understanding: recognition and recall, application, stating relations, transformation, and transfer.

2. To develop lessons from which understanding can emerge be sure to
   a. prepare yourself through study of the topic and adequate planning and
   b. prepare students by insuring that they have the necessary prerequisite knowledge.

3. Variety in your lessons will make teaching more effective and fun. Here are ways to conduct lessons:
   a. Use objects, pictures, or diagrams to illustrate the idea you are teaching.
   b. Present a new idea so that it is a logical extension or variation of an idea the students already know.
   c. Begin a development with simple problems and introduce complications gradually; organize topics from simple to complex.
   d. Introduce the lesson or topic by presenting a problem to the students.
   e. Encourage the students to learn by reading either the text or some material you have prepared.
   f. Occasionally plan for a discovery lesson, a lesson in which you do not tell or show the students the thing you want them to learn but you lead them to see, discover, it for themselves.

4. Students learn more and retain longer when they participate actively in the development of a topic. You can increase participation in several ways.
   a. Treat all student contributions with respect.
   b. Plan some easy questions to get the lesson off on a successful note and to involve some reluctant learners.
   c. Get mileage out of your questions.
   d. Make an error; let the students catch it and explain why it is an error and how to do it correctly.

5. Summarize your lesson, point out the important ideas and how they are related, so the students finish with the topic clearly in mind. If the summary is conducted through questions, you can partially evaluate the success of the lesson.

A Final Note

Some teachers, unfortunately, limit their teaching to showing the students how to do a computation and then assigning a page of problems for the students to do. Because all lessons are the same, students and teachers alike get tired of mathematics. In this chapter we have described a rich variety of possible lessons. If you are, or plan to become, a real "pro" in the teaching field, take it as a personal challenge to try all kinds of lessons, but not to find the one best because there is no one best. Try all kinds of lessons to provide variety for your students, to have alternate treatments when the first treatment fails, and to master the techniques of your profession!

3 · Teaching for Computational Skills

COMPETENCIES

Knowledge of Methodology

After studying the content of this chapter, the teacher will be able to

1. differentiate between drill and practice as defined in the chapter.

2. list the reasons why drill and practice are necessary and identify the most important reasons.

3. state objectives for drill and practice and describe evaluation techniques to determine whether these objectives have been achieved.

4. describe a procedure for determining when a student is ready for drill or practice on a topic.

5. describe some effective techniques for conducting drill and practice activities.

Preparing for Instruction

Given a topic in elementary school mathematics, the teacher can

1. state what computational skills are necessary to begin the study of the topic (prerequisites).

2. state what computational skills should be developed during study of the topic (objectives).

3. plan instructional activities appropriate for those objectives.

4. plan evaluation of the skills, including testing when appropriate.

Instructional Skills

For a child or for a small group of children, the teacher can

1. determine the content for which drill or practice would be appropriate.

2. plan appropriate drill or practice activities for short-term and long-term objectives.

3. carry out the planned drill or practice activities.

4. evaluate the degree to which a series of drill or practice activities have achieved the objectives specified.

INTRODUCTION

In the elementary mathematics curriculum some teaching methods are employed to develop or improve understanding, or comprehension; other methods are used to develop rapid, accurate computation. In this chapter teaching methods that result in rapid, accurate computation are described and the relation of these methods to comprehension is explained.

Observations indicate that the skill with which teachers handle drill and practice activities is closely related to their success in teaching arithmetic. Almost all teachers *want their students to achieve speed and accuracy in computation and to recall instantly the basic facts. If a teacher uses ineffective drill and practice activities, children are unlikely to achieve these goals. The teacher observes that many children are not making satisfactory progress in this area and may conclude the children need more drill and practice. It may soon follow that almost the entire arithmetic period is spent on ineffective drill and practice activities. Unfortunately, this can be observed in many classrooms!*

Effective drill and practice activities can result in speed and accuracy in computation even though a teacher uses only one third of the arithmetic period for such activities. The other two thirds of the period can be used for teaching meanings, explaining, laboratory activities, enrichment, and individualization. That is the way it ought to be: Highly effective drill activities save time for teaching arithmetic meaning and for developing understandings.

1. NEED FOR DRILL AND PRACTICE

Several words used in this chapter need definition. The definitions of *drill* and *practice* are not universally accepted but are needed to make a particular difference clear. Other words are given standard definitions.

Definitions

Drill. The words *drill* and *practice* are near synonyms in most instances. We will use these words in a slightly different way in order to emphasize a point. In learning the addition, subtraction, multiplication, and division facts, the child should be able to give each answer correctly and immediately. Responses are to be completely memorized. The high speed, memory-oriented, mainly oral activity which commits these facts to memory will be referred to as drill.

Practice. In working an exercise using, for example, long division, the child performs a series of steps to obtain the answer. The series of steps is memorized and can be done smoothly. The answer, however, is found by the process and not memorized. Activities that emphasize performing a process at reasonable speed but with emphasis on obtaining the correct answer will be referred to as practice.

Basic facts. The 390 addition, subtraction, multiplication, and division facts will be called collectively the basic facts of arithmetic, or just basic facts.

Habituated, memorized. A child who can give the answer to one of the basic facts from memory without counting or using other processes is said to have the fact habituated, or memorized. Note that a child may have learned a great deal about a basic fact, such as how to find the answer by counting or how and when to use it, and not have it memorized.

Maintenance drill. To establish a basic fact in memory, a fairly intense period of drill is required. Once this fact is memorized, only occasional review is needed to keep the fact in memory. This occasional review will be referred to as maintenance drill.

Overlearning. Psychologists use the term *overlearning* for drill or practice that is continued after the student has learned the response. This additional drill or practice after the student can do a process or has memorized a fact will make the learned fact or process more permanent in the memory.

Meaning. Frequently, in discussing the habituation of a basic fact or process, the point is made that habituation should occur after the acquisition of comprehension, or "meaning." A child is said to know a meaning of a basic fact if he can find the answer by using some process learned earlier. An illustration will clarify this statement. If we ask a child to divide 24 by 6, the answer may be found by using sets of objects, using a number line, or using a related multiplication fact. If the child can obtain the answer to $24 \div 6 = \square$ in one or preferably more of these ways, he is said to know one or more meanings of this fact. Other chap-

ters present a more complete analysis of the nature of meaning.

Algorithm. An algorithm, or algorism as it is sometimes called, is a procedure for finding the answer to a problem. It is characterized by a fixed set of steps which, when followed, will lead to the answer. An example is the process used to find the answer to a long-division problem. This process is called the long-division algorithm.

Developing Computational Skill

Drill on a fact or practice on a process is necessary whenever the fact must be recalled immediately, or when the process must be performed with speed and accuracy. To be skilled in anything, one

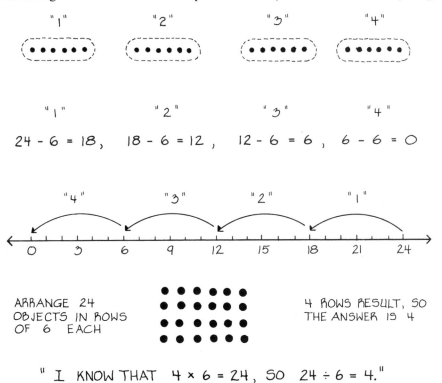

must practice or drill in that specific activity. One cannot become skilled solely as a result of understanding. There are basically two reasons for developing a particular computational skill—to be able to apply that skill in some practical situation, and to use that skill to make learning further mathematics more efficient.

Ability to apply skill. If a child fails to develop speed and accuracy in the basic facts and processes of arithmetic, he or she will have difficulty applying arithmetic in practical situations. Most practical situations call for the organization of information and the selection of processes to be used. In some situations an exact answer must be found, while in others an estimate is all that is required. In either case, knowledge of the basic facts and processes of arithmetic is essential. In estimating the area of a lot 390 feet by 78 feet, a person may say, "Well, it's about 400×80." It is still necessary to know $4 \times 8 = 32$ to continue the estimating process.

There is some evidence to indicate that a child who has not memorized the basic facts will not think of the appropriate operation in a problem situation. Given a set of chairs in the arrangement shown below, a child may count, add, or multiply to find the number of chairs.

□ □ □ □ □ □
□ □ □ □ □ □
□ □ □ □ □ □
□ □ □ □ □ □

A child who counts to find the answer will not see this as an addition problem, but only as a counting problem. A child who has memorized the additon facts may see this as a problem in addition:

$6 + 6 + 6 + 6 = \square$. The child who has memorized the answer to $4 \times 6 = 24$ is more likely to see this as a multiplication problem. We want children to associate the operations of arithmetic with situations to which they apply and to use the operations in those situations. To do this, children must develop enough skill in the operation so that it helps them find the answer in a practical situation.

The "social utility" argument for skill in calculation has been weakened by the widespread use of calculating machines in business applications. Hand-sized calculators also influence this issue. Currently, there is some insistence at the local school level that children learn to compute without being dependent on calculators. This will continue to be an important objective of school programs in the near future. However, the strongest argument for computational skill is that it is needed to facilitate the child's continued progress in arithmetic.

Making learning more efficient. If children lack speed and accuracy in the basic processes of arithmetic, it will seriously impede their progress in learning more arithmetic. Many children make marks on their papers to find answers to basic multiplication facts. An exercise worked this way looks like the example shown here.

$$
\begin{array}{r}
24 \\
\times\, 38 \\
\hline
192 \\
72 \\
\hline
912
\end{array}
$$

To find 8×4, the child has made 8 sets of 4 marks and finds the other answers in a similar way. This child knows what multiplication means and, if determined enough, will obtain an accurate result. But the future for this child is bleak. The process is so tedious and the child works so few problems that he or she will soon be frustrated. This frustration will arise whether the child encounters the problem 24×38 in an arithmetic class or in laboratory activities in science or some other subject.

Look at the multiplication skill needed in the problem $583 \div 7$. A student might reason as follows: One hundred times 7 is too big, so it is some number of tens times 7. Twenty times $7 = 140$, too small; $40 \times 7 = 280$, closer; $90 \times 7 = 630$, too big; $80 \times 7 = 560$, looks good! This reasoning occurs "in a flash" for some and at a painful crawl for others. But if the basic multiplication facts are not known, the child cannot perform this process with any reasonable speed. The child may work one or two examples but will soon be discouraged by the difficulty, frustration, and lack of results.

Consider the process of reducing a fraction to lowest terms, as shown here.

$$\tfrac{42}{56} = \tfrac{21}{28} = \tfrac{3}{4}$$

To do this, one may divide the numerator and the denominator by 2 and get lower terms. The next step should be to recognize at sight that $21 = 7 \times 3$ and $28 = 7 \times 4$ and to divide numerator and denominator by 7. Hence, skill in the reduction of fractions to lowest terms is dependent on mastery of multiplication facts.

Many other examples could be given, but the point is this: When a child fails to habituate a fact or process, the next process is performed with agonizing slowness. As speed drops and frustration rises, most children then are unable to continue to make satisfactory progress in arithmetic.

There have been suggestions that drill is unnecessary or undesirable. One suggestion is that necessary drill on one topic can be incorporated into the development of subsequent topics; another is that drill may be incorporated into problem-solving activities; a third is that drill is not necessary for a child who "really understands" the mathematics. These positions regarding the place of drill have not produced in practice the kinds of results that were expected. Drill remains a necessary ingredient in learning arithmetic.

Some say that drill is dull and uninteresting and leads to boredom in the classroom. There is no doubt that drill *can* be dull but it can also be stimulating and fun for the children. One of the objectives of this chapter is to show how to make drill stimulating and effective instead of boring and ineffective.

Discussion Questions

1. What knowledge of basic facts is needed to find a common denominator for $\tfrac{1}{30} + \tfrac{1}{25}$? Does the knowledge needed depend on the procedure you use?

2. In your daily life *other than as a student or teacher* how often do you use computational skills? How accurate are you in keeping your checkbook balance?

3. List some occupations in which computational skill is necessary.

4. List mathematical topics for which computational skill is necessary for efficient learning. Don't forget high school mathematics courses.

5. How do you do computation when the correct answer is very important? Do you own or use a calculator? What do you use it for? How do you check to see if it is working properly or to see if you have keyed in the correct entries in the proper order?

6. How could you use a hand calculator in an elementary school classroom to stimulate or reinforce drill and practice activities? Can you give answers to questions on just the basic facts faster from memory or by punching keys on a hand calculator?

2. OBJECTIVES AND EVALUATION

Here we will discuss the use of objectives for computational skill in an evaluation of students' progress. We will also discuss a way to write usable objectives.

Writing Objectives
for Computational Skill

Objectives should be clear and specific. A teacher should be able to determine whether or not a student has achieved an objective by assigning a task, watching the student do it, and listening to what the student says. Such objectives are frequently called "behavioral objectives." For computational skills, there are two kinds of objectives—one that indicates habituation of basic facts, and another that indicates computational skill in some algorithm.

Objectives for basic facts. For the basic facts the desired skill is habituation, the ability to recall answers without any internal or external processing. The following form is appropriate:

Given the basic facts listed below, presented verbally or on flash cards, the child will say or write the answers immediately from memory, with not more than 1 error in 20 exercises. [List the facts you refer to above.]

Note that this objective specifies without ambiguity what parts are to be used, how they are to be presented, how the student is to respond, and the acceptable error rate. Of course, this is just an example. You decide for yourself how many exercises to give and how many errors are allowable. This is fairly easy to do for objectives involving basic facts but not so easy for many other kinds of material. When you write an objective that is clear and specific, the objective itself tells you how to test it and what a "passing performance" will be. If I have been teaching a second-grade class twenty facts, I can say, "Number from 1 to 20 on your paper and write down the answers as I hold up these flash cards." I proceed to hold up 20 flash cards, each one only momentarily. A child has achieved the objective if he or she gets 19 or 20 correct.

Objectives for algorithms. The answers to more complex exercises are not memorized, of course, but are worked out through algorithms. We also want to have clear and specific statements of objectives for students' performance of algorithms. Here is an example:

Given exercises in adding columns of two three- and four-digit numerals, the student will perform the computations on paper and will solve 10 exercises in five minutes, getting 9 out of 10 correct.

There are several things that must be stated clearly: the operation and the kind of numbers to be used, how the computation is to be done, and the speed and accuracy of work to be attained. Note, too, that this objective states clearly what type of exercises are to be used, how they are to be presented, how the student is to respond, and the acceptable error rate. As before, this objective tells how to test itself.

The reader is sure to have noticed that these objectives related only to speed and accuracy of computation. There is no consideration here of whether or not the student knows what the computation means, why it is done as it is, or how to apply it. We assume that these goals are to a large extent reached before the development of computational skill, and we describe this relationship in detail in Section 3. When the student has previously attained appropriate meanings, objectives on computation need be stated only in terms of speed and accuracy.

Evaluating Computational Skill

Evaluation is done for many reasons — to find out where students are; to find out how far they have come; to decide where they should go next; and, frequently overlooked, to find out how effective our own teaching has been. Evaluation is a continuous process which most teachers do naturally and informally. They "keep track of where the children are" as they go through the year. Children also can keep track of their own progress and participate in setting their goals.

Some of the following steps in the process of evaluation will give a more precise idea of how students are progressing, and help you as a teacher to have a more precise knowledge of the effectiveness of your teaching.

Diagnose needs. Diagnose the need and readiness for drill or practice on a topic. After you have been teaching the meanings of an operation or the explanation of a computational procedure, ask yourself whether the students *need* drill on the topic and whether they are *ready* for drill. While this is explained in detail in Section 3, we may say here that students need drill if they need to improve in speed or accuracy. They are ready for drill if they know the meanings involved and the rationale for the computation.

State the objectives. Having determined the topic, you may decide what the students should attain in speed and accuracy on that topic. The objectives should reflect what you feel students can reasonably be expected to accomplish at their level.

Pretest objectives. Pretest your objectives, applying the same standards you expect to use on the posttest. In evaluation, pretesting is one thing teachers rarely do. Here are some reasons why you should pretest. First, it may confirm your judgment about the students' lack of speed and accuracy. Second, there may be some surprises — several students may already be fast and accurate enough to meet your objectives. You can let these students spend some of the practice time on something else or serve as leaders in some drill activities. Third, it gives you some specific data to compare to your final results and evaluate your own teaching.

Drill. Plan and conduct appropriate drill or practice activities. This is the topic of Section 4 of this chapter, Planning Effective Drill and Practice Activities, starting on page 69.

Posttest your objectives. Be sure that the exercises, time limits, and circumstances on the posttest are the same or very nearly the same as those on the pretest. Use the posttest data to give feedback to your students and to make decisions about the further progress of the students. Do they need more practice? Are they ready for a new topic? Does the group stay together or do students need to be regrouped?

Determine growth. Evaluate the students' growth in computational skill; evaluate your teaching effectiveness. Look at the changes from pretest to posttest. How many students made gains in speed, accuracy, or both? How many students now reach your objective who did not reach it at the time of pretesting? Are some areas of your teaching more effective, some less effective? Did accuracy improve? Did speed? Look critically at the pre- and posttest data to improve your teaching technique.

Pre- and Postassessment

We have talked about pre- and posttesting. However, the assessment of objectives need not be in the form of a traditional test. You may just hold up flash cards and have students write answers. You may test students individually to see whether they remember the answers to basic facts or are just counting to find answers.

In any case, remember that many students are test and grade conscious. You will want to explain to upper elementary students that the pretest is not to be graded but is for your use in planning what to do next. The posttest, of course, may be used for grading purposes in whatever grading system you use. With primary children simply say, "I want to see how well you can do on these problems to plan what to do next."

Discussion Questions

1. Many teachers do not pretest before starting a topic. How does this effect their use of student achievement for self-evaluation purposes?

2. Why is it necessary to give problems on a pretest that most children cannot work?

3. Suppose you set a goal for speed and accuracy and, on the pretest, all of your students meet or exceed the goal. What should you do then?

4. A student should pass on a unit of work if he or she
    a. attains 80% on the posttest.
    b. does as well as he or she can.
    c. is in the top half of the class.
    d. works hard.
    e. Other:_____.
List the responses you might write in for "other" and discuss.

5. How do you feel about an accuracy level of 95% for drill and 90% for practice? Should the levels be 100%? Should they vary according to the age and ability of the children? Should all children be expected to attain some minimum level of performance?

6. Evaluating student progress, using pretest and posttest data, can lead to evaluating teacher performance. Is student achievement data relevant to evaluating a teacher's performance? Is it possible for teachers to be using correct or acceptable methods and have their students' pretest and posttest scores register little improvement? Why?

3. DETERMINING READINESS FOR DRILL OR PRACTICE

As children move through the elementary school mathematics curriculum, they should achieve an understanding of each fact or process they encounter. After understanding has been achieved, they are ready for the drill or practice necessary to develop rapid recall and accurate performance of an operation.

Readiness for Drill

To determine when a child is ready to begin drill or practice on a particular topic, you must know whether he or she understands the process to be performed. You might ask, "Can the child, slowly and perhaps using some kind of model, correctly reason his or her way to the answer?" If the child *can* do that, the child is ready for drill. If not, more teaching of meanings is needed before drilling. Some examples will clarify the idea of "readiness" for drill.

Addition facts. A first-grade student, past midyear, is working on addition. The child has been taught sums less than 10 through concrete and semiconcrete examples. Our purpose is to find out whether or not the child "understands the meaning" of the addition facts studied and also whether or not the answers have been memorized. This is to determine whether to begin drill on the facts in question. We will present the child a problem, either verbally or on a flash card. It is presumed that the child can read the symbols and understands their meaning. If not, more work in that area would be indicated before drill on facts begins.

The problem presented is $3 + 4 = \square$

A. A child who has not acquired a meaningful knowledge of the addition process may respond in this way:

Child:
I don't know. (or silence)

Teacher:
Can you figure it out? Could you count to find the answer?

Child:
No, I can't do it. (or silence)

B. A child who has learned a meaning for the addition process will give the answer after going through one of these processes:

Child:
a. Counts objects or fingers
b. Draws and uses number line
c. Counts aloud or silently
d. Uses a known fact: $3 + 3 = 6$, so $3 + 4 = 7$

C. A child who has both meaning and habituation for the process will respond like this:

Child:
7 (responds instantly)

Teacher:
Very good. Suppose you forgot the answer. How could you figure it out?

Child:
Responds with one of the meaningful procedures in B.

A child who responds as in *A* is *not* ready for drill. The child clearly needs to be taught, through a variety of concrete and semiconcrete experiences, the various meanings for addition. For this child, our assumption that he or she "learned" the sums 10 and below was found to be false. The child has been "through the material" but has not learned meanings.

A child who responds meaningfully, finding the answer through one of the strategies in *B,* is ready for drill. This applies, of course, only to the addition facts the child has learned meaningfully. A child may be drilling on addition facts with sums less than 10 and may still be in the process of learning meanings for facts with larger sums.

A child who responds instantly and correctly has already habituated the fact. The teacher then probes for the meaning behind the fact. If the student can tell some meanings for the fact, he or she has both meaning and habituation and needs only limited maintenance drill.

Reading and writing numerals. One of the earliest topics on which drill is appropriate is the reading and writing of numerals. As before, the task should be meaningful before drill is appropriate to increase speed and accuracy. The numeral "6" can be meaningful to a child only after the spoken word has meaning. Before drilling a child on reading the numeral 6, the child should be able to do a variety of things showing that "six" has meaning for him. Among these are: Count a set of objects and tell if there are 6 in the set; get 6 pencils from a box when told to do so; state some numbers that are larger than 6 and some that are smaller; identify the 6th object in a line; tell what whole number comes before 6 and what whole number comes after 6.

When a child has this kind of command of the *idea* of 6, then it is reasonable to have the child learn to read and write the numeral 6. This can be accomplished by drill directly on the task.

The examples just presented have this in common: A child should know the meaning of the task he or she is to do before drilling to achieve speed and accuracy. Often, if a child knows the meaning of the task, e.g., to find the answer to 3×4, he or she will be able to do the task, working out the answer through counting or some other procedure. If a child cannot solve the problem in some meaningful way, he or she needs to be taught meanings before drill is undertaken. If a child has habituation and meaning, then only spaced maintenance drills are necessary to keep skills sharp.

Starting drill too soon. If drill is begun before meaning is firmly established, a variety of undesirable things will happen. The drill will be inefficient. Because a child memorizes a meaningless response more slowly than a meaningful one, drill started before meaning is established will take more time and achieve less than drill started after meaning is established. If a child forgets a fact (and some forgetting is inevitable), he or she has no way to work out the answer. If the child forgets it, it's lost. Drill on meaningless material is discouraging. It is hard for children to see purpose in the arithmetic curriculum even when it means something to them; without meaning, the task seems useless!

Starting drill too late. Starting drill too late or not starting at all is almost as bad as starting too soon. Here is a common example of the consequences of neglecting drill on addition and multiplication facts. This situation can be found in virtually any fifth-grade classroom. A boy of reasonable intelligence is having great difficulty doing multiplication problems. He makes some mistakes, but his basic difficulty is that he works at a very slow pace. In fact, he can't get the *practice* he needs on the multiplication process because in a half hour he works only three or four exercises. To work an exercise, say 37 × 6, he makes marks as shown here.

$$
\begin{array}{r}
37 \\
\times\ \ 6 \\
\hline
222
\end{array}
$$

ı ı ı ı ı ı ı   \ ı ı
ı ı ı ı ı ı ı   ı ı ı
ı ı ı ı ı ı ı   ı ı ı
ı ı ı ı ı ı ı   ı ı ı
ı ı ı ı ı ı ı   ı ı ı
ı ı ı ı ı ı ı   ı ı ı
ı ı ı ı ı ı ı

When he gets the 18 (from 6 groups of 3 marks), he counts on his fingers to add 4. Ask him, "Can you get 6 × 7 by adding up 6 sevens?" and you will find that he does all addition by counting. Even though all of the processes used are meaingful, this child is in serious difficulty in arithmetic. He can't keep up because habituation of addition and multiplication facts, which should have been done in grades one through four, was neglected.

It is now *more difficult* to achieve habituation for addition, and ultimately for multiplication, because the child has strongly formed habits of counting. It takes more time and more practice to replace one habit by another than to form the correct habit in the first place. Consequently, it must be emphasized that *drill on a fact should be started very soon after a child has learned the meaning of the fact.*

Readiness for Practice on a Process

Many of the same principles applying to drill on basic facts apply to practicing processes (algorithms) of arithmetic. We will review these principles and illustrate how they apply to practice on arithmetic processes. The basic idea governing the use of both practice and drill is the same: Understanding should precede the practice or drill that develops habituation.

Subtraction of fractions. Let us consider subtraction of fractions with regrouping. Considerable practice is usually devoted to this process early in the fifth grade. Before being assigned pages of practice exercises, students should know what they are doing and should know the reasons behind the procedures. How can you determine whether a child understands this process and is thus ready for practice? We concentrate our attention on the first step in the process, the step at which regrouping is done.

The student is given the exercise $3\frac{1}{5} - 1\frac{3}{5} = \square$ and rewrites it in column form.

$$
\begin{array}{r}
3\frac{1}{5} \\
-\ 1\frac{3}{5} \\
\hline
\end{array}
$$

Then the student performs the regrouping operation, or the first step in the computation.

$$
\begin{array}{r}
2\frac{6}{5} \\
-\ 1\frac{3}{5} \\
\hline
\end{array}
$$

When a student performs this step, we may ask, "Where did you get the 6 in $\frac{6}{5}$?" One common but unsatisfactory answer is, "You add the 1 and the 5." We might also ask at this stage, "Why did you change the 3 to a 2?" or "Where did the 1 go?" The explanations must add up to the idea that 1 is taken from the 3, leaving 2, and changed to $\frac{5}{5}$. Then $\frac{5}{5}$ and $\frac{1}{5}$ together are $\frac{6}{5}$.

A good question at this stage is, "Why did you do all that?" The answer must involve the convenience, bordering on necessity, of having something from which $\frac{3}{5}$ can be subtracted. If the child can give acceptable reasons for each step in the process, he or she is ready to practice the process to acquire smooth, reasonably rapid, and accurate performance.

Starting practice too soon or too late. The results of starting practice too soon or too late are not as serious as starting drill too soon or too late. If practice on an algorithm is begun too soon, progress toward understanding the reasons for the steps may be terminated in favor of rapid answer getting. Practice is rarely begun too late, since most texts or programs introduce ample practice soon enough.

Guidance from the text. Drill activities that help students learn the basic facts are, or should be, mainly verbal. Pages of written exercises are not very effective in promoting instant recall. Faced with such a page, most children will work slowly, finger counting when they wish, and will not really try to recall or work for speed. Verbal drill of the appropriate sort cannot be put in a textbook because it is *verbal,* not written. Consequently, a teacher who "follows the text," using pages from the text with no supplementary verbal drill, will have an *inadequate* drill program.

On the other hand, the algorithms of arithmetic are done mainly in written form. Adequate, in fact ample, practice on these algorithms is provided in most standard textbooks. A teacher who follows the text will usually have an effective practice program provided care is taken to develop meaning and understanding of the algorithms.

Practicing intermediate stages. Many of the algorithms of arithmetic are developed through a series of intermediate stages. These stages usually begin with the meaning of the operation explained in terms of the manipulation of objects.

There may be a stage in which the meaning of the operation is tied to another, previously learned, operation. Finally, the algorithm is taught in a way which emphasizes the meaning of what is being done and only then in the efficient form which adults use. (A teacher who "skips all that stuff and teaches them the right way first" has missed most of the meaningful mathematics teaching.) Let us look at a simple division problem, tracing the development from concrete objects to the final form of the algorithm.

The problem $46 \div 3$ is first solved by using objects, as shown below.

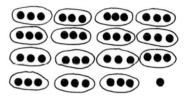

THERE ARE 15 THREES IN 46, AND 1 IS LEFT OVER.

The division problem is related to subtraction and the algorithm begins to emerge.

$$
\begin{array}{ll}
46 - 3 = 43 \ (1) & \quad 3\overline{)46} \\
43 - 3 = 40 \ (2) & \qquad \underline{3} \\
40 - 3 = 37 \ (3) & \qquad 43 \\
37 - 3 = \quad \vdots & \qquad \underline{3} \\
\vdots \qquad \vdots & \qquad 40 \\
\vdots & \qquad \vdots \\
7 - 3 = 4 \quad (14) & \qquad 4 \\
4 - 3 = 1 \quad (15) & \qquad \underline{3} \quad \text{3 is subtract-} \\
 & \qquad 1 \quad \text{ed 15 times.}
\end{array}
$$

"From 46 we can subtract three 15 times, and 1 is left over."

As the algorithm develops, place value concepts are used to make it more efficient.

```
   15  R1              15  R1
3)46                    5
   30    10 × 3         10          15  R1
   16                3)46        3)46
   15     5 × 3         30           3
    1    15            16          16
                        15          15
                         1           1
```

If we look at an elementary text series, we find that in grades three to six the children have considerable practice on intermediate stages. The purpose of this practice changes, however, as the child progresses. The manipulation of objects, the use of the number line, and the "scaffold" form of the algorithm are designed to teach the development of the meaning. Practice for *speed* at these stages is not necessary. At these stages, also, the students should be discussing, describing, and explaining the steps they are doing. They should not be merely going through the steps mechanically. All of this is background for the work on the "adult" form of the algorithm, at which time speed is desired along with meaning. To summarize, practice on preliminary forms of a process should be "thoughful practice," in which meanings are given careful attention; mechanical practice and an emphasis on speed are appropriate only for the adult form of the algorithm, after meanings are well established.

Discussion Questions

1. How would you determine whether a child is ready for drill on multiplication facts?

2. How would you determine if a child is ready for practice on addition of fractions with different denominators? Be specific—what must the child understand?

3. Why is the textbook a better source of practice material than of drill material?

4. What are the different effects of starting drill too soon and starting drill too late? Is it more difficult to motivate a fourth- or fifth-grade child to memorize basic addition facts than to motivate a first- or second-grade child to commit these facts to memory?

5. What "intermediate steps" for the column addition algorithm can you find in textbooks? In what way would you use these intermediate steps in practice?

4. PLANNING EFFECTIVE DRILL AND PRACTICE ACTIVITIES

Teachers differ considerably in the ways both in which they conduct drill and in the results they achieve. For some teachers, the learning of basic facts is a routine matter on which virtually all children succeed. For others, the learning, or nonlearning, of these facts is a year-long problem and a stumbling block to further progress. Successful teachers are involved with drill activities. They will be conducting drill with the whole class or moving from group to group during drill. They will use mainly verbal and mental drills that require their presence and participation. They will attempt to stimulate and encourage children to memorize and to respond as fast as possible. They will listen to individual children respond to determine if they are ready to move on to new material. Successful teachers consider drill an area for active participation in the teaching-learning process.

Teachers who are ineffective in their drill activities frequently present the opposite picture. They consider drill sessions to be "break time". They hand out ditto sheets of basic-fact problems and then observe or grade papers. Occasionally, a teacher who is otherwise very effective will have no drills at all on the theory that if children "really understand" mathematics, they won't need drill. Unfortunately, this is not so; for habituation to take place, drill is necessary.

We have two general pictures now, one of an effective teacher involved in a fast-paced drill program, the other of a teacher whose drill is ineffective and consists mainly of slow-paced ditto sheets and games. Let us look at the characteristics of *effective* drill activities and see what makes them successful.

Suggestions for Effective Drill

Explain carefully to the children the purpose of the drill. Many children do not know that the teacher wants them to memorize the answers to the arithmetic facts. Because they do not know what is expected, they think that "getting the answer quickly" is all that is required. Some children become marvelously quick at finger counting, on the assumption that this is what the teacher wants. Many teachers also do not really emphasize speed and memorization. Slow-paced drills, dittoed pages of basic facts on which the students work at leisure, and games in which the pace is slow will never promote proper memorization.

Drill should be based on "practicing remembering" an answer. Let us take as an illustration the situation in which children are to learn the fact $7 \times 8 = 56$. We begin by presenting the problem, either in written or verbal form, to the students.

"$7 \times 8 = \square$." Since we are just beginning drill, they will not know the answer immediately. They work it out using sets, by addition $(8 + 8 + 8 + 8 + 8 + 8 + 8)$, or by using a known combination $(5 \times 8 = 40$, so $6 \times 8 = 48$, so $7 \times 8 = 56)$. Now they have found the answer to $7 \times 8 = 56$, and we wish to fix this answer in memory. Repeat the question: $7 \times 8 = \square$. If they begin to work it out again, say, "You just worked that. Do you remember the answer?" If a child does not remember, say, "That's O.K. Work it out. This time try to remember." The child works out the answer again and tells you $7 \times 8 = 56$. Say, "That's right. Now, what is 7×8?" The child responds, "56". "Very good, you remembered it that time." Again say, "$7 \times 8 = \square$" At this stage, the child is now "practicing remembering," a far different activity from the "working it out" strategy used before. It will take a good many sessions over a fairly long period for this response to become permanently learned, but a start has now been made.

You need to work with children individually or in small groups to see how they are getting answers. Are they memorizing, trying to remember, or are they automatically counting to find each answer? This is very difficult to determine when you are using a textbook or ditto sheet, but it is easy to determine if you talk to a child and feed him or her verbal problems.

Activities for memorizing basic facts are mainly verbal. Practice is most effective when the task is performed in the same way it will be used. Since the use of basic facts will be mainly mental or verbal, the major part of the practice time on basic facts should be devoted to verbal and mental activities. This means either an oral presentation of the fact, or an oral response, or both. Let us look at the reason behind this suggestion. In almost every case, when a child is using the basic facts, he or she uses them in a "mental" way, not recording the answer as such, but retaining part of it in memory for regrouping. The process of long multiplication requires the child to remember sums and products, operate on them mentally, and record results in bits and pieces at various places. While this is called the "written algorithm," most of the work is done mentally. The problem shown here requires 17 mental additions and multiplications.

$$\begin{array}{r} 438 \\ \times 74 \\ \hline 1752 \\ 3066 \\ \hline 32412 \end{array}$$

Mental operations
in the order performed

$4 \times 8 = \square$	$28 + 2 = \square$
$4 \times 3 = \square$	$2 + 0 = \square$
$12 + 3 = \square$	$5 + 6 = \square$
$4 \times 4 = \square$	$1 + 7 = \square$
$16 + 1 = \square$	$8 + 6 = \square$
$7 \times 8 = \square$	$1 + 1 = \square$
$7 \times 3 = \square$	$2 + 0 = \square$
$21 + 5 = \square$	$0 + 3 = \square$
$7 \times 4 = \square$	

How can mental and verbal drill be done? Teachers may present facts verbally or on flash cards and have the children respond out loud or write the answer. The teacher must control the pace of presentation so that the child who uses counting processes will not be fast enough to keep up. Many other suggestions for drill activities are included later in this section.

Set attainable objectives. Avoid overwhelming tasks by concentrating your efforts on the memorization of a small number of basic facts. When a student, group, or class is ready to start drill, choose from 4 to 15 basic facts and work on these. Don't start with all 100 addition facts! This is overwhelming to the children and does not allow enough drill on any one fact to master it. Let us take a first-grade class working on addition as an example. The children may fully understand the addition facts with sums up to 8, be working on sums of 9, 10, 11, and 12, and not yet have thought much about higher sums. What should their drill activities include? Since they fully understand sums up to 8, they may be drilling on those. However, there are 45 facts with sums of 8 or less. To begin drill on all 45 facts at once is a mistake. Each fact will not be presented frequently enough for efficient learning. We may decide to begin with the 15 facts for sums less than 5. These include many easy facts, $0 + 0 = 0$, $0 + 1 = 1$, $0 + 2 = 2$, etc., which most children will learn quickly. When a few of these have been mastered, new ones can be introduced. Thus, children will progress through the addition table, having at all times a few facts on which they are drilling intensely and a group of other facts on which only maintenance drill is needed.

Present facts in random order during a drill session. When children are using facts, they occur in random order. Drill sessions should be planned the same way. Many students are drilled on their "times table" until they know it by heart *in order*. Most of these students cannot give the product of two numbers out of the order in which they occur in the table. That does not help them when they are faced with a problem like this one.

$$\begin{array}{r} 348 \\ \times 27 \end{array}$$

They must start out knowing 7 × 8, and next 7 × 4, and then 7 × 3. Clearly, there is no arrangement to the way in which the facts are used; hence, in the practice sessions the problems should be presented in random order. To do this, you may try these ideas. When you have selected the flash cards that are appropriate for an individual or a group, always shuffle them. This keeps the order of presentation random. When you are presenting exercises verbally, vary the problems you are using and do not fall into patterns.

Keep a record of each child's progress. This is a good suggestion for all children but it is particularly good for the children who have been working at a task for some time with little success. There are many ways to do it. Children might make their own decks of flash cards and keep them in three piles: those they have learned, those they are working on, and those they haven't started learning. As the children progress, the number in the "already learned" pile is a visible record of their success. Another way this may be done is to run off a blank addition table for each child. When a child masters an addition fact, that is, has memorized it, he or she records it in the table. Progress is obvious.

Learning all 390 facts of arithmetic is a very large and complex task. Children should focus on a few facts at a time and have visible evidence that they are making progress on those few. When some are mastered, several new ones may be added. This knowledge of success and progress is a strong motivation for students to continue.

Keep drill sessions short and frequent. Daily drill sessions are highly recommended. Many teachers also find that using those "odd minutes" during the day is a convenient way to work in a little extra verbal drill without taking the time from another subject. You should plan to spend no more than 15 minutes of your mathematics period on drill. Fifteen minutes of fast-paced verbal drill is exhausting for teachers and students. If you are doing it right, after 15 minutes you and the class will be glad to change to quieter and slower activities. Furthermore, using only one fourth to one third of your time on drill, and three fourths to two thirds of your time on developmental teaching, is a very effective division of class time.

Control the pace of the drill. If you have an opportunity to watch drill, you will see children do very different things, depending on the pace of the drill. When the pace is slow, the children can count fingers, count silently, or add to find the answers to multiplication facts. When the pace picks up, children really try to recall because they can't count quickly enough to find the answer.

When you conduct a verbal drill, you must be sensitive to pace and the way children are responding. Speed it up until counting will not work and the children are trying to remember the answers. When groups of children are drilling each other, encourage them to maintain the proper speed.

Provide a large number of responses by children. When a child has just memorized a fact or is trying to memorize it, he or she needs a large number of "question-answer" exposures to the fact. At the point of fixing the fact in memory, a large number of exposures in a few days, followed by some drill spread out over several weeks, is the most effective pattern. A five-minute flash-card drill during which the teacher flashes fifteen cards per minute, and the class responds verbally or in writing, is a very effective drill because it involves a large number of repetitions of basic facts.

Forgetting is as natural as learning. Expect normal forgetting and be prepared to reteach. During a period of disuse — over the summer, or even a short spring break — many children will lose habituation of facts you thought were secure. This is natural and, indeed, inevitable. Include these facts in your drills until habituation is established again.

Verbal Drill Activities

In the following paragraphs you will find a wide variety of suggested drill activities. When you have tried these, you can make up others like them. You can also get more drill games and activities from the references given at the end of this chapter. Because verbal drills and flash-card drills are the heart of an effective program, they are described first.

Oral drill. No material or equipment is needed. This is the most flexible of all drill activities. The teacher calls a problem to an individual, a small group, or to the whole class. The students respond orally. This activity can be used to fill in odd moments while waiting in line, or waiting for the music teacher. It can also be used as a "warm up" activity during the first two or three minutes of the mathematics period. When you give a problem to a small group or to the whole class, the students who get it right are reinforced by hearing right answers. Those who get it wrong also hear the correct answer. If many children get it wrong, reteach that fact. Keep the pace fast so that students are forced to respond from memory.

Sequential problems. No material is needed for this activity. A problem in which children perform operations mentally in sequence is a good form of drill. Many teachers who use this technique every day for two or three minutes report that they get outstanding results.

Each problem is presented like this: The teacher gives a starting number and then tells the students to carry on the operations mentally until the end, and then to say only their final answer. Here is an example that might be used with fifth graders.

Teacher says:	Students think:
Start with 37	37
Add 5	$37 + 5 = 42$
Subtract 2	$42 - 2 = 40$
Divide by 8	$40 \div 8 = 5$
Add 9	$5 + 9 = 14$
Subtract 6	$14 - 6 = 8$
What is your answer?	Students say, "8"

That was a hard one. You can, of course, make easier ones by using smaller numbers, or fewer steps, and by not getting into multiplication and division. Try *never to repeat;* repeating problems may encourage inattention. Strive for speed but don't run away from the class. Practice will help improve your own skills to the point that you don't need to prepare the problems in advance.

Flash cards. You will need several sets of flash cards in your room. In working with addition facts, there is not much reason to have missing addend flash cards ($3 + \square = 8$) because these responses do not need to be memorized. Get cards with arithmetic facts ($3 + 5 = \square$) only. In the upper elementary grades, flash cards for all four operations will be used. You should have one set of large flash cards for work with the whole class and several sets of small ones for individuals and small groups. The children, too, can make a few flash cards, especially for their personal hard facts, to carry around and use whenever they can.

Flash-card drill. For this activity you will need one or more sets of flash cards. You hold up flash cards one at a time while the students say the answers in unison. This sounds somewhat old fashioned, but it works! When the children all answer together, those who say the right answer are reinforced; they know they are right because they hear the same answer all around. Children who say the wrong answer are corrected in the same way. When many children give the wrong answer, you can stop the drill process and discuss the fact. Increase the speed until half the class has either dropped out or stopped saying answers, and then slow down until all are responding again. In this kind of drill, always encourage the children to respond as fast as they can; discourage them from counting or doing anything but practicing remembering.

To individualize drill, split the class into groups in which the students are working on approximately the same facts. Let the students in these groups take turns holding up the flash cards for the others. You can make groups as small as two children. Keep moving around from group to group to be sure the children are working on speed drills and not just "going through the motions."

Flash-card tests. For this activity you will need a set of flash cards. Have the children number from 1 to 20 down a half sheet of paper. Select the facts you wish to test and hold up the cards one at a time. As you hold up each card, count (to yourself) "1, 2, 3" and put the card down on the count of 3. It should take you less than one minute to go through 20 cards. For reviewing facts with students in upper elementary grades, take twenty-five each of addition, subtraction, multiplication, and division flash cards and present them in the same way. If you mix them up, it's harder, so go a little slower. You can give a 100-problem review quiz in five minutes using this technique.

Flash-card self-tests. A few sets of small flash cards will be handy for this activity. Children who are working on memorizing the additon facts may use a set of flash cards by themselves. They may go through the deck saying the answers and then checking each answer. Most flash cards have the answers on the opposite side of the card. The children can all do this each week and keep track of the number correct. Self-tests are a very effective form of motivation for children. They have a record of their progress from week to week, and can see themselves really "getting somewhere."

Using student-made cards. For this activity, several packages of 3 × 5 cards will be needed. Construction paper can be cut to size and used also. Each child should use a regular deck of flash cards to identify the facts he or she knows. Then the child selects a few (2 or 3 to 10 or 15) facts to learn in the next week. The child makes a flash card for each fact and carries it during the week, using it whenever there are a few minutes in school or at home. For the next week, the child will keep carrying the cards for the facts not yet learned and will make a few more. Cards for facts already learned may be kept in the desk for occasional review. Parents who want to participate in the child's mathematics can help effectively by working with the child on the weekly facts. Having just a few cards at a time will concentrate the drill on the desired facts.

Reading numerals. A chalkboard is all you will need for this drill. In Grade 1 some children need considerable drill in reading numerals. Write the numerals on the chalkboard in "scrambled" positions. Point to them randomly and have the children read them aloud as you point. When you do this again next day, write the numerals in different positions.

Games and Other Activities for Drill

There are a number of games for drill. These games provide a certain amount of practice and children usually enjoy games. It is a good idea to use such games occasionally for motivational purposes. It is not a good idea to attempt to run a drill program wholly on games because *games are too slow paced to provide effective drill.* In the first place, most games provide time for the children to count or to figure out the answer. As we have seen, that is not the intent of a drill activity. In playing a game most children are not "practicing remembering" the answers but are working them out. In the second place, the mechanics of playing most games, taking turns, keeping score, moving around, and so forth, slow up the drill, restricting the number of children who can respond.

Games can be used to provide relaxation, relief from the tension of a fast-paced drill, as a reward for good attention, or as a general motivator. Below are some good games for these purposes.

Bingo games. You can buy or make a variety of bingo-type games. Typically, these games will have cards with numbers in a bingo arrangement. The numbers are the answers to basic facts of addition, subtraction, multiplication, or division. The leader holds up a flash card, and the players find the answer on the board and cover the answer with a chip. When one player has a row of 5 chips (down, across, diagonal), he or she is the winner.

"Sport" games. Build a game around whatever sport is in season. Players will score or advance by giving a correct answer. In baseball the players may advance from base to base by getting a fact correct. Some teachers have the children actually move around a miniature baseball diamond in the room. The game may also be a reasonable rainy-day substitute for going outside. Other teachers have the children stay in their seats and keep track mentally of where they are. The children may be divided into teams and a score keeper chosen to determine the winning team. Of course, you and the children can make up your own rules and procedures as you adapt various sports to this purpose.

Dot-to-dot. A little drill or practice can be done using dot-to-dot pictures. Get a simple picture first. A child's coloring book is a good source of simple pictures. Write down about 30 problems you want the children to do. Place a blank, transparent paper over the picture and place the dots and answer numbers in sequence. Then draw in any other parts of

$\downarrow$ $4 + 2 = \square$ $20 + 1 = \square$ $40 + 2 = \square$ $20 + 4 = \square$

$6 + 3 = \square$ $2 + 5 = \square$ $10 + 9 = \square$ $20 + 20 = \square$

$7 + 4 = \square$ $1 + 3 = \square$ $4 + 4 = \square$ $0 + 23 = \square$

$9 + 5 = \square$ $20 + 7 = \square$ $20 + 2 = \square$ $0 + 0 = \square$

$4 + 8 = \square$ $9 + 6 = \square$ $30 + 1 = \square$ $40 + 1 = \square$

$7 + 6 = \square$ $10 + 10 = \square$ $30 + 3 = \square$ $24 + 1 = \square$

$2 + 3 = \square$ $0 + 3 = \square$ $1 + 1 = \square$ $9 + 8 = \square$

$8 + 8 = \square$ $9 + 9 = \square$

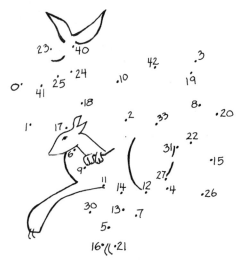

the picture that the dot-to-dot drawing will not produce. The children do the problems and connect the dots in the order of the answers. The example above shows this kind of exercise.[1]

Check my work. Write out a page of problems *with answers*. Make half of the answers *wrong*. Have the children mark each problem *X* or *C* and find the right answer to the problems marked *X*. This can be used in a race, either team or individual. Children love it!

---

[1]George Immerzeel and Donald Wiederanders, "IDEAS," *The Arithmetic Teacher*, Vol. 18, No. 1, (Jan. 1971). Copyright © 1971 The National Council of Teachers of Mathematics, Inc. p. 31. Reprinted by permission.

Suggestions for Effective Practice

Recall the definitions given at the beginning of the chapter. Drill is defined to be rapid, mainly verbal, and aimed at mastery of basic facts. Practice is the repetition of a process, such as the long division process, done mainly in writing, and in which speed is desired but not at the expense of careful performance and accuracy. We have discussed ways to plan effective drill and we now turn to ways to plan effective practice.

Use the textbook well. The textbook and collateral material normally provide sufficient practice and organize it well. The textbook may not be the best vehicle for verbal drill activities, but it is an excellent guide and source of material for practice on algorithms. Effective use of the practice materials in the text will go a long way toward developing computational skill. Some schools do not use a text. They rely on a combination of resources to develop their own mathematics program. In this case, there is an urgent need for teachers to understand how to design and to sequence practice exercises in order to have effective mathematics programs. The same principles also guide the authors of textbook series in the organization of the practice in the text.

Teach thoroughly. Practice on an algorithm comes only after the meaning of the algorithm has been thoroughly taught. We will examine the development of multiplying a 2-digit by a 1-digit number to illustrate this principle. What are the "meanings" that should be attached to multiplying 23 by 3 and to the algorithm for its solution? The problem has many different meanings. In the long run, children should know them all.

$$\begin{array}{r} 23 \\ \times 3 \\ \hline \end{array}$$

(1) 3×23 means "How many things are there in 3 sets having 23 things in each set?"
(2) 3×23 means "How many things are there in 3 rows having 23 things in each row?"
(3) 3×23 means $23 + 23 + 23 = \square$
(4) 3×23 means 3 jumps of 23 spaces each on the number line.

In addition to those four basic meanings of multiplication, the child should have meaning for the algorithm; that is, the child should know why the algorithm produces the correct answer. If we see 3×23 in two somewhat different ways as $(3 \times 20) + (3 \times 3)$, it is not surprising that the algorithm should be based on $(3 \times 20) + (3 \times 3)$. Note that $3 \times 2 = 6$ is not a part of the explanation at this stage. We are multiplying $3 \times 20 = 60$.

It is in this sense that the meaning both of the operation itself and the algorithm should be established before starting practice. You can find further examples of how algorithms are handled by examining various topics in any elementary school text series. For example, the development of division in Grades 2 through 6 shows an interesting sequence of meaning and practice lessons.

Practice regularly. When children are ready for practice on a topic, have a practice session every day until they attain reasonable speed and accuracy; after that, maintain the skill by periodic review and practice. When you are satisfied that children have acquired the appropriate meanings, they are ready for practice. At that point they need concentrated practice—a ten- or fifteen-minute session every day—to establish the skill and to fix the process in their minds. It is important that these practice sessions incorporate immediate feedback. Correct answers and correct displays of the algorithm must be available after each two or three exercises. Otherwise, we run the risk of having students practice some incorrect steps! When they have a reasonable level of skill, you can main-

(1) 3×23

$$3 \times 20 \qquad + \qquad 3 \times 3$$

(2) $3 \times 23 = 3 \times (20 + 3) = (3 \times 20) + (3 \times 3)$

tain that skill by having periodic practice sessions. Start with daily practice sessions on a topic; then reduce practice to perhaps two sessions a week. Finally, practice may consist of only the review exercises at the end of each chapter. This organization of practice sessions produces excellent results.

This organization is clear in textbooks. After the explanatory material you will find many sets of exercises, then a few, and finally the problem type will occur only in cumulative review sets. If you are following a text, this plan is built in; if you arrange your own practice, you should follow the pattern.

Motivate students. Getting the students to work hard to achieve speed and accuracy is essential for effective practice. When students work in a lackadaisical manner, without really putting forth effort, without much caring whether answers are right or wrong, very little improvement can be expected. Students must know what sort of performance is expected of them and must work hard and exert effort to achieve that level. The text provides exercises and guides the scheduling of sessions. But it is up to the teacher to stimulate and motivate the students. Here are some ways to keep motivation high for effective practice.

(1) Keep practice sessions short. Students cannot maintain intense concentration on practice problems. Understandably, repetitive problems become dull after a short time. Forty problems to be done in an hour is a terribly dull task. Ten problems in ten minutes is better. Provide the students with a challenge: How many can they get right in five minutes? This kind of race against the clock (get a kitchen timer with a loud bell) makes practice exciting.

(2) Use speed games, relays, and board work to keep the students interested and working to their maximum speed. Here is one good speed game: Divide your class into five or six equally matched teams. Give each team the same problems. Each student works one problem, but the second student can't *start* his problem until the first student has finished. This is a relay. The first team finished with no more than one error wins. Many of the games described for drill can be adapted to practice problems.

(3) Give the students immediate feedback on their work. Taking home a stack of papers to grade is no fun, anyway! Why not let the students use the Teacher's Edition to check their own work? Let them check their work with a calculator if one is available.

(4) Individualize your practice. Students should be practicing appropriate material. If a student is practicing something he or she doesn't really understand and is getting many answers wrong, motivation will be ruined. Likewise, if a student is made to practice something he or she has already mastered, the task will seem useless and motivation will fade. Make practice assignments suited to the needs of individuals or small groups to keep motivation high.

A Successful Drill Program

Mrs. Smith is planning a drill program for a group of second graders in her room. These children are working fairly well in addition by counting either verbally or on their fingers. However, they have not memorized many basic addition facts, and by midyear in the second grade they should be well on their way to

Name	PRETEST Number Correct, Remembered	Number Correct, Counted	Number Wrong	POSTTEST Number Correct, Remembered	Number Correct, Counted	Number Wrong
John	11	29	5			
Sam	18	23	4			
Bob	6	32	7			
Carol	8	35	2			
Ted	10	32	3			
Alice	5	36	4			

this goal. Mrs. Smith decides that her goal for February will be to have these children memorize all the facts with sums less than 9. She pretests them to see how many they have memorized. This takes only a few minutes with each child, using flash cards. There are 45 addition facts with sums less than 9.

The results of her pretest confirm her judgment about what the children know. They are pretty good at getting the answer right if they count, but they do not have very many of the addition facts memorized.

Mrs. Smith now plans her work with this group. She will concentrate on drill for 10 to 15 minutes each day. She will *not* devote the entire mathematics period

to this drill because 10 to 15 minutes each day is all the drill that can profitably be done. Each day she will review, orally or using flash cards, the facts these students already have memorized. Then she will introduce three or four that have not been memorized and work hard on those until the children give the answers from memory. Following that, she will gradually work in the facts formerly learned, mixing them with the facts just learned. She will use games the children like as motivators and to add variety to her drill activities, but her basic tools are verbal drill and flash cards.

During the month, Mrs. Smith has kept track of the number of facts the children have memorized, although she has

Name	PRETEST Number Correct, Remembered	Number Correct, Counted	Number Wrong	POSTTEST Number Correct, Remembered	Number Correct, Counted	Number Wrong
John	11	29	5	38	2	5
Sam	18	23	4	36	6	3
Bob	6	32	7	41	2	2
Carol	8	35	2	20	21	4
Ted	10	32	3	11	28	6
Alice	5	36	4	32	8	5

not written this down. Each day as she reviews the known facts and adds a few new ones she is reminded of the status of the children. Near the end of the month, she feels that her goals have been accomplished, and to verify this, she gives a brief test on the 45 addition facts she wanted the children to learn. Again, she tests each child with flash cards.

The results Mrs. Smith achieved are good but not remarkable. They are typical of what a teacher can achieve with a well-planned drill program that takes only a few minutes each day. You have probably wondered about Ted. There are always a few children who are not making progress as we would hope. The children who are not responding to drill should be checked to see whether they have learned the meaning of the facts they are to memorize. If this is the case, and in the absence of other problems, Ted will begin to commit these basic facts to memory. The children have memorized a great many basic facts. They still count when they forget one of them, and this is quite proper. They are not more accurate than they were at the beginning, but as they continue to work on these facts, accuracy will improve. Mrs. Smith decides that her work with this group has achieved her objectives; she was successful.

During the next month Mrs. Smith decides to add another 10 or 20 addition facts to the set on which this group is drilling. She will work them in gradually, two or three at a time, constantly reviewing the facts memorized earlier.

Planning a Drill and Practice Program

The activities discussed above and used in the example are effective in achieving long-term growth in computational skill only when they are organized into a drill and practice *program*. Even the best drill and practice activities will produce poor results if used occasionally, or on a "hit or miss" basis. In planning a drill and practice program we look at longer-range objectives, asking ourselves what we want the students to achieve in two weeks, in two months, in this year. We specify our objectives and evaluate growth over the long run. Here are steps for planning and carrying out a drill and practice program.

(1) *Diagnose needs.* From your previous knowledge of the children and from information gathered in informal discussion, attempt to determine their present status and needs in the area of computation. Do they need drill on subtraction facts? Do they need to practice the long-division algorithm? At this point you are trying to make a good guess. They seem to understand this particular topic but they have not yet attained appropriate speed and accuracy; therefore, this topic would be good for drill or for practice.

(2) *State objectives.* Thinking about what you can accomplish on your topic in two to six weeks, set objectives for your teaching. What should your students be able to *do* in two to six weeks? Write these objectives in clear, specific terms.

(3) *Pretest.* Give the students a pretest on the objectives. This may confirm your diagnosis (that they understand the topic but are slow and/or inaccurate), and will provide some data against which to compare your posttest data.

(4) *Plan and teach.* During a planned drill program the teacher must select the drill activities, schedule them, and, in addition, introduce new material into the

drills. The way this scheduling is done has a considerable effect on the success of the drill. Here is a summary of hints on the scheduling of drills.

a. Begin drill as soon as meaning is established. Don't delay. Once the children have acquired the meanings involved, move to establish speed and accuracy.

b. Have some drill every day but not too much. If you average about one third of your mathematics class time on drill and practice, you are about right.

c. Early drill on some facts may be quite concentrated. As the children get close to mastery of a topic, the drills on that topic may be spaced out and new material introduced. This is a continuous process.

d. Add new items gradually. Don't introduce 30 or 40 new facts all at once. Spread them out so you are bringing in two or three new ones each day.

(5) *Posttest.* Give the students a posttest to measure the learning that has taken place in the two to six weeks since the pretest. Record this data so that it is easy to compare the pre- and posttest performance of the students.

(6) *Evaluate.* Did the drill and practice program accomplish what you had planned? Was your teaching successful? What are the next steps for the students? What topics are they now able to begin practicing?

You must be aware that very few teachers presently teaching would write out all the steps in the above sequence. You are not likely to write out all these steps except perhaps as a class assignment. What *do* teachers do? All teachers diagnose needs of students in planning what to do next; all teachers *have* objectives whether they state them or not; all teachers plan and teach and posttest.

Two things are recommended here that are not routinely done by teachers — pretesting and self-evaluation. Without pretesting it is almost impossible to evaluate one's own teaching.

Discussion Questions

1. How does "practicing remembering" differ from finger counting in finding the answer to an addition fact exercise?

2. Why is it important to present facts in random order during drill on basic facts?

3. Describe some strengths and some weaknesses of games used as drill activities.

4. What are the differences in the objectives of drill on basic facts and practice on an algorithm?

5. How would the objectives of practice differ for these two algorithms?

$$
\begin{array}{rr}
34 & 34 \\
\times\ 26 & \times\ 26 \\
\hline
24 & 204 \\
180 & 68 \\
80 & \overline{884} \\
600 & \\
\hline
884 &
\end{array}
$$

SUGGESTED ASSIGNMENTS AND PROJECTS

Classroom Assignments

1. Use drill techniques to learn the names of your classmates. With a class of 20 you may be able to drill to the point of 90% – 100% mastery in 20 minutes. Test again in one week. What does this tell you about forgetting? about the value of periodic spaced review?

2. Learn each of these lists of words. Time yourself on the learning of each list. Which takes longer? Why? You have "learned" a list when you can say the words in order without a mistake. What does this tell you about meaning and organization in a task?

A	B
Centimeter	Garage
Inch	Horse
Foot	Radish
Yard	Aluminum
Meter	Pot
Kilometer	Dog
Mile	Book

3. Make a set of cards like the ones shown below. Use the cards to drill yourself to mastery on this task: Given a letter between K and $T,$ inclusive, state its position by number in the alphabet. For example, if I say $L,$ you say 12. When you have mastered this association, try it in reverse; that is, if I say 12, you say $L.$ What does this tell you about the reversibility of this connection? Test yourself on the task first thing tomorrow. Do you still have the mastery you attained?

4. Get a set of standard textbooks for elementary school arithmetic. Look for suggestions for drill and practice in the Teachers' Editions. Examine the development of the multiplication algorithm. Where are the practice exercises in relation to the lessons designed to develop meaning? What provision is made for "spaced review" and maintenance?

5. Using a set of standard textbooks, identify the approximate time at which the authors shift from meaningful developmental activities to drill for speed for each set of basic facts. The time will be different, of course, for the different operations.

Internship Assignments

1. Learn the names of the children in your group. If you have pictures of the children, write their names on the back and use them like flash cards. As you watch the children, mentally call their names over and over. How effective is your drill? Soon you should be able to call all the children in your class by name.

2. Observe the drill activities of a teacher over a one-week period. If you are an intern, aide, or student teacher, you may observe the teacher you are working with. Keep a log of your observations, telling how many minutes were spent on arithmetic and, of these, how many minutes were spent on drill. Describe the drill activities you observe and keep a copy of any materials which were used. Be prepared to report to your class.

3. Improve the speed and accuracy of one child on a selected computational skill. Follow these steps.

Diagnose. Select from your class *one* child and determine what topics would be appropriate drill or practice material for that

child. Select a child who needs drill on basic facts rather than one who needs practice on a long process. Use the diagnostic techniques described in this chapter to determine whether the child is ready for drill and on which facts.

Objectives. Now decide and state your goals. Exactly what facts do you want the child to learn over the next two or three weeks? Be sure to state the speed of work you want to attain and the specific facts you want the child to have memorized. Do not set your goals too high—a small number of facts *well learned* will give you a better idea of successful drill than a larger number only half learned.

Test. Verbally present the child the facts you want learned. Tell the child to try to remember but to count to find the answer if necessary, and tell the child to work as fast as possible. Record the number of problems, the number the child got correct by counting, the number the child got correct by remembering, the number wrong, and the time it took to finish.

Plan. Plan to work with this child for approximately ten minutes a day for two or three weeks. Do mainly oral work but also use flash cards and drill games. Through informal observation, keep up with the number of problems the child has memorized. Try to give this child ten minutes of your undivided attention each day. This may be very difficult to do, but try.

Teach. Follow your plan, but remember that situations change and plans must change with them. Don't follow your original plan if you think of other activities that would be more effective.

Test. Give the child the same problems in the same way as before. Record the information.

Evaluate. Was your teaching effective? What does your pre- and posttesting show? What do your observations show? Has the child now memorized some facts not memorized before? What can you do to prevent forgetting? What should the next steps be for this child?

4. Improve the speed and accuracy of children in a small group on one selected computational skill. Follow the steps in Activity 3.

SUMMARY: MAXIMS FOR TEACHING

1. Drill and practice are essential components of the mathematics program. Some appropriate drill and practice should be included every day.

2. Drill or practice on a particular task should begin only after that task has become meaningful to the student.

3. Drill activities are most likely to be successful if they follow these general guidelines:

Student	Before	After
Number of problems		
Number counted correctly		
Number remembered correctly		
Number wrong		
Time (Minutes: Seconds)		

a. *The children should know that the goal is to memorize the answer to each basic fact. Drill activities should be based on "practicing remembering" the answers.*

b. *Drill should be fast-paced, mainly verbal, and provide for a large number of responses by the children.*

c. *Concentrate drill on a small number of basic facts; as some facts are learned, introduce new ones into the drill.*

d. *Individualize drill so that children are drilling on appropriate material; keep records of progress or let each child keep his or her own record of progress.*

e. *Drill sessions should be short and frequent.*

4. *Practice activities are most likely to be successful when they follow these general guidelines:*

a. *The text usually provides very good organization and sequencing of practice activities.*

b. *Frequent practice sessions should be used to establish speed and accuracy; following that, occasional maintenance practice should be provided to maintain skill.*

c. *Motivation is the key to effective practice.*

   i. *Have short practice sessions.*

   ii. *Use games, relays, competitions.*

   iii. *Provide students with immediate feedback of results.*

   iv. *Individualize.*

AN ANNOTATED LIST OF PRACTICE AND DRILL ACTIVITIES AND GAMES

"Tricks of the Trade with Cards"

   Practice in basic operations and number concept development through a variety of games.

   The Arithmetic Teacher, February, 1977, pp. 104–111

"The Basic Fact 'Bug' "

   A geometric design which provides practice in addition or multiplication. Good idea for a spirit master.

   The Arithmetic Teacher, April, 1976, pp. 265–266

"Mystic Squares for Primary Pupils"

   Similar to but different from magic squares, this idea can be used with smaller numbers or larger depending on the age of children.

   The Arithmetic Teacher, December, 1976, pp. 592–595

"Magic Triangles and a Teacher's Discovery"

   A challenging game providing lots of addition practice.

   The Arithmetic Teacher, May, 1976, pp. 351–354

"Active Games: An Approach to Teaching Mathematical Skills to the Educable Mentally Retarded"

   Small group games which will provide teachers of younger children with an active break from seat work.

   The Arithmetic Teacher, December, 1974, pp. 674–678

"Tiger Bite Cards and Blank Arrays"

   Games for multiplication which do more than drill.

   The Arithmetic Teacher, December, 1974, pp. 679–682

"Mastering the Basic Facts with Dice"

   Some activities which can be used to vary your regular drill sessions on basic facts.

   The Arithmetic Teacher, May, 1973, pp. 330–331

"Elevator Numbers"

   A wonderful device for practice in addition for the younger child of both high and low ability. Highly recommended to teach-

ers of the primary grades.
The Arithmetic Teacher, October, 1971, pp. 422 – 424

"Diffy"

This game has several strong points. Among these are: it allows for individual differences, the exercises are constructed by the students, and it fits almost any grade level. It provides unique practice in subtraction, and its derivative, "Divvy," provides practice in division.
The Arithmetic Teacher, October, 1971, pp. 402 – 405

"Treasure Hunt" and "Through the Maze"

These games are geoboard activities that provide practice in naming points, checking points, writing the names of points, and organizing data.
The Arithmetic Teacher, May, 1971, pp. 327 – 329

"Mathematical Tag"

A game to review almost any of the notions and concepts about number. This game has many derivations.
The Arithmetic Teacher, May, 1971, p. 329

"Dominoes in the Classroom"

An effective vehicle for practice in addition and recognition of multiples.
The Arithmetic Teacher, January, 1971, pp. 53 – 54

"The Conversion Game"

Basically a bingo game, this activity is designed to help the student retain mastery of the various equivalencies among common fractions, decimal fractions, and percents.
The Arithmetic Teacher, January, 1971, pp. 54 – 55

"Multiplication Football"

A game to add excitement to flash-card drill in multiplication.

The Arithmetic Teacher, March, 1970. pp. 236 – 237

"Fraction Bingo"

A bingo-type game designed to provide practice in finding other names for a fractional number.
The Arithmetic Teacher, March, 1970, pp. 237 – 239

"A Game with Fraction Numbers"

A *unique* way to provide practice in the addition, subtraction, multiplication, and division of fractions.
The Arithmetic Teacher, January, 1970, pp. 82 – 83

"The Greatest – A Game"

The element of chance enters into this game that provides practice in any or all of the four operations.
The Arithmetic Teacher, January, 1970, pp. 80 – 81

"Bingtac"

This game provides practice in the four basic operations while capitalizing on the excitement of Bingo.
The Arithmetic Teacher, April, 1969, pp. 310 – 311

"War," a card game

This game enables the children to learn to recognize numerals and their ordered relationship. It promotes an understanding of the concepts *equal, greater than,* and *less than.*
The Arithmetic Teacher, December, 1968, p. 737

"Fish," a card game

Several games in one emphasize order relations and sums and differences in the set {1, 2, . . . 10}.
The Arithmetic Teacher, December, 1968, p. 737

"Number Trick," a card game

Provides practice in addition and subtraction over a wide range of sums and differences.

The Arithmetic Teacher, December, 1968, p. 737

"Number Scrabble," a card game

Similar to the commercial game of "Scrabble" in that combinations of numbers are sought whose sum is a specific number. The game is made more interesting by allowing other arithmetical processes besides addition.

The Arithmetic Teacher, December, 1968, p. 737

"Number Rummy," a card game

Provides practice in any one or all of the basic operations.

The Arithmetic Teacher, December, 1968, pp. 737–738

"Placo — a Number-Place Game"

This game emphasizes fun and the learning of positional and place value aspects of our number system while providing stimulating practice in computation. It has been used successfully in Grades 2 through 6 with as few as two children and as many as a whole class. It can be modified to include decimal fractions.

The Arithmetic Teacher, May, 1968, pp. 465–466

"Tic-Tac-Toe"

This game provides practice in using ordered pairs to name points in the plane. It can be used in Grades 4 through 9.

The Arithmetic Teacher, October, 1967, pp. 506–508

Solution, problem 4, page 97

One way to attack the problem is to consider suggestions 3, 4, 5, and 6 on pages 92–94. Take one man at a time, reduce the problem to 20 men and 20 lockers, make a table of every mans actions, and look for a pattern of open lockers. The first ten entries would give a table as shown.

After 6 men have passed, we can be sure that lockers 1 through 6 will not be changed again: 1 and 4 will remain open; 2, 3, 5, 6 will remain closed. What can we say about lockers 1 to 10 after 10 men have passed? Which lockers are open? Which are closed? What about lockers 1 to 20 after 20 men have passed?

A second way to attack the problem is to consider what happens to each locker. Only the "factors" of a given locker number open or close it. Lockers whose number has an even number of factors end up closed. Lockers whose number has an odd number of factors will wind up open. Most of the whole numbers from 1 to 1000 have an even number of factors since their factors come in distinct pairs. For example, 40 has 8 factors; they come in factor pairs: (5,8), (4,10), (2,20), (1,40). But there are others like 4, 9, 16, 25, 36, 49, 64, 81, 100 that have an odd number of factors. What are they and why?

	Lockers		**C: closed**			**O: open**			**−: left alone**											
	1	**2**	**3**	**4**	**5**	**6**	**7**	**8**	**9**	**10**	**11**	**12**	**13**	**14**	**15**	**16**	**17**	**18**	**19**	**20**
Start	C	C	C	C	C	C	C	C	C	C	C	C	C	C	C	C	C	C	C	C
1	O	O	O	O	O	O	O	O	O	O	O	O	O	O	O	O	O	O	O	O
2	−	C	−	C	−	C	−	C	−	C	−	C	−	C	−	C	−	C	−	C
3	−	−	C	−	−	O	−	−	C	−	−	O	−	−	C	−	−	O	−	−
4	−	−	−	O	−	−	−	O	−	−	−	C	−	−	−	O	−	−	−	O
5	−	−	−	−	C	−	−	−	−	O	−	−	−	−	O	−	−	−	−	C
6	−	−	−	−	−	C	−	−	−	−	−	O	−	−	−	−	−	C	−	−
7	−	−	−	−	−	−	C	−	−	−	−	−	−	O	−	−	−	−	−	−
8	−	−	−	−	−	−	−	C	−	−	−	−	−	−	−	C	−	−	−	−
9	−	−	−	−	−	−	−	−	O	−	−	−	−	−	−	−	−	O	−	−
10	−	−	−	−	−	−	−	−	−	C	−	−	−	−	−	−	−	−	−	O

4 · Teaching for Problem-Solving Skill

COMPETENCIES

Knowledge of Methodology

After studying the content of this chapter, the teacher will be able to

1. state the reasons why problem solving is an important objective in elementary mathematics.

2. name and describe the four phases of problem solving.

3. state and describe several "heuristics" which may be of use in each of the four phases.

4. describe the use of a heuristic in problem solving and distinguish between a heuristic device and an algorithm.

5. describe the essential features of a problem-solving program for (a) challenge problems and (b) story problems.

6. describe some ways of helping children solve problems. Relate these hints to the four phases of problem solving.

7. solve or attempt to solve problems, making conscious use of the four phases and heuristic devices suitable to each.

8. simplify a given problem in various ways to produce an easier problem.

Preparing for Instruction

Given a topic in elementary school mathematics, the teacher can

1. locate or write appropriate problem materials.

2. adjust the difficulty level of existing problems to the ability of the students.

Instructional Skills

For a child or a small group of children, the teacher can

1. present a problem and assist the children as they work it, giving constructive hints as necessary.

2. identify the problem-solving phase in which the children are working and suggest an appropriate heuristic to assist them in that phase.

3. plan and carry out an appropriate problem-solving program.

4. evaluate the success of a problem-solving program.

INTRODUCTION

Effective problem solving is a goal of the elementary mathematics curriculum. Problem solving, of course, is much broader than elementary school mathematics. It is vital and important in other areas of the school curriculum and in non-school activities. Elementary school mathematics, however, can be an important vehicle in the development and refinement of problem-solving skills. This development and refinement will be neither the beginning of students' problem-solving skills nor the completion. Problem solving in elementary school mathematics should have some payoff, in the long run, for problem solving outside of the mathematics classroom.

On the other hand, the nature of mathematics presents some demand for developing problem-solving skills in mathematics. Both specific and general problem-solving skills must be developed in the elementary school. Better problem solving in mathematics improves one's ability to use and apply mathematics.

In our view, problem-solving skills are actions that children do. This chapter is designed to convey the "action" view of problem solving. You will find these ideas consistent with other chapters, where we have sometimes utilized problem-solving situations to develop mathematical concepts and generalizations, to enhance understanding, or to provide for some type of drill. Such situations can also lead to learning potentially useful problem-solving strategies.

This chapter will present and help you organize some ideas about problem solving and the strategies for problem solving that children can be taught. You will become a problem solver and, we hope, experience some of the exploration, discovery, and challenge that is part of problem solving. You will engage in problem solving, explore what a problem is and what problem solving is, identify problem-solving strategies, and examine maxims for teaching problem solving.

More, perhaps, than any other topic in elementary mathematics, problem solving is viewed negatively by teachers and students. Many students believe they cannot solve problems, and many teachers feel that they have not been successful in teaching to this objective. The suggestions in this chapter have been tried many times and under most circumstances have been found to improve both student success and teacher satisfaction. The topic of problem solving is one in which we have the potential of markedly improving our success.

It is absolutely crucial that you work through this chapter with pencil and paper at hand. You will not come to an understanding of the ideas unless you work the problems and do the exercises as they are presented. Problem solving is doing, and you simply cannot learn to solve problems or to teach problem solving unless you do the problems presented.

Problems to Get You Started

You already have some concept of problem solving. Here you are asked to do three activities *prior to* study of the chapter. Write down all your work on notebook paper.

1. List three to six ideas that occur to you when you hear the term *problem solving*. How do your ideas differ from those of other students in the class?

2. Collect four observations of problem solving—two examples of mathematical problem solving and two examples of nonmathematical problem solving. For each example, your record should answer these questions:

A. *Who* was solving the problem? (Names, sex, age, level of intelligence, number in group, etc.)

B. *How* did the problem come up? (Teacher presented it, arose between the children, practice problem, etc.)

C. What was the *problem?*
D. Describe *unsuccessful* attempts to solve the problem.
E. Describe *successful* attempts to solve the problem.

You may record the observations by whatever means is available to you. If a tape recorder is available, you may wish to try having the problem solver (you, your roommate, or one of your students) talk aloud as the problem is attempted. Be prepared to discuss your observations.

3. Work the following five problems, keeping a record of all of your work, even false starts. Do not spend more than one hour on the five problems.
A. Find the sum: 13
                   +26
B. Find the maximum number:
    $3.\overline{3}$, $\sqrt{10}$,   3.3
C. Tom has exactly five coins. The value of his money is 50¢. How many of each coin does he have? Can you find more than one answer?

_____pennies   _____dimes
_____nickles   _____quarters
          _____half dollars

D. Arrange 10 points as shown. How

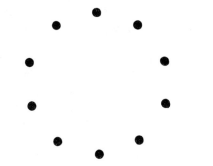

many line segments are needed to connect every point to every other point by a line segment? Work hard on this prob-

lem because it will be used as an example and studied thoroughly in a later section.

E. You have three containers holding 3, 7, and 10 quarts, respectively. The three containers are not marked to show how much is in them when they are less than full. The largest is full of water. Find a method of dividing this quantity of water into two equal amounts of five quarts each. Use *only* the three containers — no other measuring containers. Show your method.

What is an Appropriate Problem?

The fun and satisfaction in problem solving and the feeling of success that problem solvers get depend on attacking problems of just the right difficulty. The problem 3A, above, was probably not a problem for you. It was rather a routine exercise. Finding answers to such exercises is not a source of much fun or satisfaction because you already know exactly how to do it. Problem 3D, on the other hand, may have been too hard for some. If you worked and worked without visible progress, you probably did not find that fun. If you read problem 3D and said, "I don't want to bother with that," it was not a problem for you at all.

For a problem statement to be a problem *for some particular learner,* the problem must be unfamiliar in the sense that the learner has no "standard procedure," or algorithm, for solving it. If the learner has a standard procedure, then the so-called problem is merely an exercise. Yet the problem must be easy enough so that the learner can, with thought and effort, solve it or make some visible progress. Further, the learner must *decide* to try it, making a commitment of time and effort to the solution. As we shall see in detail in later sections, one of the teacher's main jobs in encouraging problem solving is to select appropriate problems and get students to attempt to solve them.

Discussion Questions

1. Was problem 3A really a problem for you? We may want to examine this example as we formulate a definition of "problem."

2. Is there any way you can organize your work on one of the problems to help in obtaining a solution?

3. Reflect on your solutions. Could you have solved any of the problems with an easier method?

4. Do you know what the bar over the tenths' digit in 3.3 means? Did you try to find out or did you think it was a misprint? The bar means that digit is repeated in the places to the right. So $3.\overline{3} = 3.3333 \ldots$, three repeating on and on. Perhaps now you wish to revise your work on problem 3B.

5. Did you try to draw a picture to represent one of the problems? Did it really help? Often, ideas for solving a problem come from trying a particular strategy.

6. Write a definition of "problem." Compare and contrast your definition with others in your class.

1. CHALLENGE PROBLEMS

Two kinds of problems most teachers want children to solve are challenge problems and story problems. Story problems are like the word problems that abound in mathematics textbooks. These will be discussed in a later section. Children are interested and can become more interested in challenging problems. Many children will work long and hard on problems posed by friends, parents, or puzzle books. You can develop this natural interest in problems and puzzles into an interest in mathematical problem solving.

A Challenge-Problem Program

When we list objectives we frequently include long-range objectives that are difficult to accomplish. An objective such as "to increase students' ability to think mathematically in solving problems" falls in this category. When we find that teaching the more routine topics takes much of our time and effort, we may abandon these long-range objectives. Sometimes we abandon them because we don't know what to do *today* that will help in achieving a particular objective. Long-range objectives require long-range planning and a program of activities that starts early and persists through the year. If you plan and stick to such a program, you will see that you are making real progress toward your objective.

In working on a challenge-problem program you have one built-in advantage: Children enjoy working on problems. They will look forward to problems and the problem-solving activities you conduct. Some will be "hooked" on problem solving and will become enthusiastic and expert problem solvers; others will be less enthusiastic but still enjoy problem solving. Realistically, you know that some will not really like it but will go along and work on a problem from time to time.

Collect problems. For a problem-solving program you will need a supply of problems. Collect them, starting with the problems in this chapter and in the references at the end of the book. Encourage children to find and bring in problems and puzzles. Save these problems and start a file of them. Note which students at which grade level like each problem best and what a child needs to be able to do to solve it. Be on the lookout for problems when you are talking with colleagues or listening to speakers talking about problem solving. Some professional and nonprofessional journals also contain interesting problems.

Present at least one "challenge" each week. Every week a challenge problem or two should be presented to the children. It may be part of every Monday's routine to have ten to fifteen minutes to present and to explain the challenge problems for the week and to post them on a bulletin board. Reserve space on the bulletin board for challenge problems and for posting the childrens' solutions. At some time later in the week have the children tell what they have done in trying to solve the problems. As children explain their ideas, they will stimulate each other in the problem-solving process. Remember to allow sufficient time for all or most children to try the problems. A smart student may spoil the fun for others by getting the answer ten minutes after you have presented a problem. Students who are smart enough to do that are also smart enough to understand the need to give others a chance. Have some more difficult problems in reserve for extra-smart students.

Encourage children to bring in problems. Be pleased when children start to bring in problems, puzzles, and even riddles. Encourage children by using their problems or by posting them in a special place *and* by working on them yourself. The fact that some of these problems will "stump" you can be used to advantage. When children see that you don't panic or give up but rather rise to the challenge and work on a problem for a relatively long period of time, they will be encouraged to persist in their own problem solving.

Helping Children Solve Challenging Problems

Effectively to help a child solve a problem, you must know "where he is" and "what he is trying to do." One way to do this is to divide problem solving into four phases and provide helps and hints related to each of these phases. To solve a problem, a child must (a) understand the problem, (b) devise a plan, and (c) carry out the plan. It is very helpful (d) to look back at your work. When working with children who are attempting to solve a problem, first decide what phase of problem solving they are in. Then provide the proper guidance to help them with that phase.

In this section we will list hints, strategies, and things to try. These suggestions are often useful and sometimes powerful means for accomplishing problem solving. Of course, they sometimes fail to help. In some literature on problem solving these suggestions are called *heuristics.*

Heuristics are rules, suggestions, guides, or techniques that may be useful in making progress toward the solution of a problem. They can be contrasted with an algorithm—a fixed procedure which, if followed, will guarantee successful completion of a task. *There are no algorithms for solving problems.* Heuristics are the best we can do. For this reason, we are very cautious about setting down a set of precise steps in problem solving—the problem solver has to internalize a flexible and adaptable *process.* Even the conceptualization of the problem-solving process into four broad stages is a heuristic. It doesn't work all the time, but it is frequently a successful organization for problem solving. Making a drawing is a heuristic—usually it helps with understanding the problem and in devising a plan, but sometimes it does not.

In this section we will discuss heuristics as they may be used in Grades 1–6 mathematics. The quotes are hints you may give to students. Obviously the form of the questions and hints will vary by grade level. These heuristics are organized to help students according to the phase of problem solving they are in.

The heuristics given below are stated in the form of suggestions or questions. When you solve a problem, ask yourself these questions and remember these suggestions. When you are helping students, *ask them* these questions and use the suggestions. *But most important, try to get the students to ask themselves these questions and remember the suggestions.*

Understanding the Problem

The first step is to be sure the students know exactly what the problem is.

1. "Say the problem in your own words." If the students can't read the problem well enough to extract the meaning, read it to them and then *read it with them.* Then ask them to rephrase the problem in their own words. If the students can read the words but don't understand the problem, *say it another way.* Try using short sentences, few prepositions, simpler words, and concrete objects.

2. "What do you know from the problem?" "What does the problem tell you?" "Look for other information that may help. Is there a picture with the problem?" If there is a picture connected with the problem, ask the student to explain what the picture means. He or she may be "misreading" it.

3. "What question does the problem ask?" "What are you supposed to find?" "Read the question again." "What are we looking for?"

4. "Is there anything else you need to know to solve the problem?" Many times common information like the number of centimeters in a meter will be needed but not given. Such problems are very difficult for students. "What do you want to find out?" "What questions must you answer?"

5. "Can you tell *about* what the answer may be?" "What would a reasonable answer be?"

Devising a Plan

Next, the students need to work out a plan of attack or a list of steps to follow in solving the problem.

1. "Have you solved a problem like this before?" In beginning to devise a plan, this is one of the most powerful lines of thought. The more problems you solve, the more ways you can recognize similar

problems. Think about the problems you have solved. When you recognize that some element in your present problem is familiar, try to remember where you have seen it before.

2. "Try to draw a picture." If the elements of the problem can be organized visually, a plan for solving the problem will frequently become clear. We use the problem about the number of line segments through 10 points as an example here. There certainly are a lot of lines — and we have not drawn all of them.

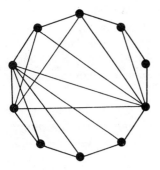

3. "Take one part at a time." In this case we take only one point and draw all the lines which go through that point. This is certainly "one part" of the larger problem. It appears that there are 9 lines going through this point. Do you think that will be the same for all points? Why?

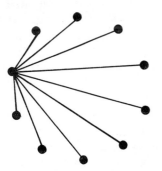

4. "Can you solve a similar, but simpler, problem?" We don't need to use 10 points. Why not a smaller number of points? It is certainly easier to look at 2, 3, 4, 5, or even 6 points, as we have here.

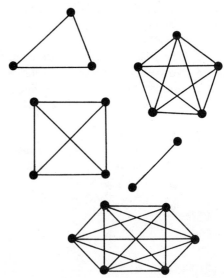

5. "Organize the information you have. Make a graph or table to help you see what's going on." If you study the table, you may be able to detect a relationship. As the number of points increases, the number of lines to each point also increases. Copy the table. In the middle column write in the number of lines coming to each point. Does that enable you to detect the relationship?

TABLE 1

Points	Lines to one point	Total number of lines
2	_____	1
3	_____	3
4	_____	6
5	_____	10
6	_____	15
7	_____	?
8	_____	?
9	_____	?
10	_____	?

6. "Look for a pattern. What regularities or relationships can you see?" If you completed Table 1 through 6 points, you found what is shown in Table 2. Do you see a relationship? For each line in the table, multiply the number of points by the number of lines to one point. Compare that product and the total number of lines. Do you see the relationship? Good! Now, can you use that relationship to find the total number of lines if there are 10 points? (The answer is 45.)

TABLE 2

Points	Lines to one point	Total number of lines
2	1	1
3	2	3
4	3	6
5	4	10
6	5	15
7	?	?
8	?	?
9	?	?
10	9	?

7. "Try to write a mathematical sentence." "Change the language sentences to mathematical sentences." If a student understands the problem but can't translate it into a mathematics sentence, write a problem with the same format but using smaller numbers. If you think a child *should* be able to write a mathematical sentence and can't, go back to further work on understanding the problem. It takes good understanding to be able to write the mathematical sentences.

8. "Let's try a new approach" or "Let's quit for a while." When a problem is really difficult and the plans do not seem to be working out, it frequently helps to take a completely fresh look at the problem or just to stop for a while. Sleep on it. If a problem is too easy, it's not much fun. Solving the hard ones gives a real feeling of accomplishment.

Carrying Out the Plan

Students who have been successful in the phases of understanding the problem and devising a plan do not usually have trouble carrying out the plan. However, at times some suggestions may be helpful.

1. "Keep a record of what you do." "If you guess, check it if possible." Trial and error procedures for problem solving can frequently be successful if each try is a little closer than the last. Encourage trial and error if the student cannot come up with a good plan. Above all, don't give up.

2. "Solve the mathematical sentence." "Can you find the missing number in that sentence?" Most often, a child who has written a mathematical sentence does not need encouragement to try to solve it.

3. "Complete your diagram." "Try to finish your drawing." "What do you need to add to the picture?" If a diagram represents the problem, perhaps the missing elements will represent the solution. Drawing in and counting *all* the lines is one way to solve the 10-point problem.

4. "Fill in the blank in your table." "Can you see a pattern in the table which will help you find the missing numbers?" In the 10-point problem we can see that the number of "Lines to one point" increases by one each time. There are several patterns in the "Total number of lines." One pattern to note is that the third column is one half the product of the first two columns. For example, for 8 points the total number of lines is

$$\tfrac{1}{2} \times 8 \times 7 = 28.$$

TABLE 3

Points	Lines to one point	Total number of lines
2	1	1
3	2	3
4	3	6
5	4	10
6	5	15
7	6	21
8	7	28
9	8	36
10	9	45

5. "Perform the steps in your plan. Do each step carefully." Encourage students to complete the plans they devise.

Looking Back

We learn a great deal when we study a problem we have already solved. Frequently, we are able to learn more by looking back than we learned through solving the problem.

1. "Can you check your answer?" This is a first and frequently neglected step. The check is not done by asking the teacher or by looking in an answer book. The check asks, "Does the solution fit all the conditions of the problem?" Students can check their own work by testing the answer against each of the conditions. Given the problem: I know 2 two-digit numbers that have the same digits. Their sum is 77 and their difference is 27. What are the numbers?
The answer must be
(1) 2 two-digit numbers.
(2) The numbers have the same digits.
(3) Their sum is 77.
(4) Their difference is 27.
When you have found the two numbers you can check each condition. You do not need someone to tell you if your answer is right or wrong; you will know.

2. "What does the result tell you?" "What is the answer to the question?" If you solve a problem and the solution is a number, this number is most always the answer to a question. How many lines are there? There are 45 lines. How far did John run? John ran $2\tfrac{1}{2}$ miles.

3. "Is there another answer?" "Is there another way to find the answer?" Considering these questions can lead to a deeper understanding of the problem.

4. "Can you now solve other problems like the one you just solved?" Often the solution of one problem has in it the solution of many others. Suppose you have 20 points. How many lines can be drawn through these 20 points? Having worked the problem with 10 points, this one seems perfectly easy—just another line in the table, really.

Points	Lines to one point	Total number of lines
20	19	?

Sometimes "like" problems are expressed differently. Try this one: Eight men enter a room and each man shakes hands with all the other men. How many handshakes occur?

5. "Can you now solve a more general problem?" For example, how many lines would go through N points? This problem is quite general; the solution is a formula rather than a number, but it can still be thought of as a line in the table.

Points	Lines to one point	Total number of lines
N	———	———

6. Teachers have some special concerns for problem solving. When you solve a problem, you may want to use it or one like it in class. "Can you make up a problem like the one you solved?" "Can you make up an easier problem?" or "Can you make up a harder problem?" "What mathematics did you need to solve the problem?" "Can I use this problem to introduce a mathematical topic?" "What age children can understand and attempt this problem?"

Discussion Questions

1. How important is problem solving as an objective in mathematics? in daily life?

2. How did you—and others in your class—feel about problems and story problems when you were in fifth grade? Take a vote and find out how many enjoyed story problems and felt successful in solving them? How many were neutral? How many disliked this activity?

3. What can you do to help children in your classes develop better attitudes toward problem solving?

2. PROBLEMS TO SOLVE

In the previous section, we described and illustrated some general phases of solving a problem. These phases are (a) understanding the problem, (b) developing a plan of solution, (c) carrying out the plan of solution, and (d) looking back. We have suggested many hints that are appropriate for *some* problems for each of the different phases. These phases were first described by Polya (1945) and we, as well as generations of mathematics students, have been influenced by his

ideas. Some of the suggestions in the preceding section were given to help students through these different phases. As you work on the problems below, try to watch yourself work and see yourself progress through these four phases.

We believe this section is important for another reason. One gains insight into teaching problem solving by being a problem solver. Obviously, you will not become a problem solver by just working a few problems in this section. Rather, this exercise is only a first step toward solving problems with your students for as long as you are teaching.

Problems

Solve as many of the following problems as you can. In each case record your solutions and analyze your method. You may join with a partner or a small group (up to four persons) to work one or two of these problems and analyze the methods used.

1. Solve the following code by finding the number that each letter represents. A letter always stands for the same number and different letters stand for different numbers.

$$\begin{array}{r} \text{SEND} \\ + \text{MORE} \\ \hline \text{MONEY} \end{array}$$

2. To number the pages of a bulky volume, the printer used 2989 digits. How many pages did the volume have?

3. Draw 6 lines so that (a) every line intersects all other lines and (b) 3 lines never intersect at the same point. How many intersections are formed by these 6 lines?

4. Imagine a row of 1,000 lockers, all closed, and a line of 1,000 men. Suppose the first man goes along and opens every locker. The second man goes along and closes every second locker, starting with locker 2. The third man goes along and changes the state of every third locker, starting with locker 3 — (if it is open, he shuts it, and vice versa). The fourth man goes along and changes the state of every fourth locker, starting with locker 4, and so on, until all the men have passed by all the lockers. Which lockers are open in the end?

5. A boy is five years older than his sister. The sum of their ages is 21 years. Find their ages.

Discussion Questions

1. Find one or two persons who have not solved the problems and present a problem to them. Watch each person work. Can you identify the four phases as they work? Observe whether their method of solution is similar to yours. Could you help them by using any of the hints in Section 1?

2. Find a small group of persons and compare solution methods for a problem. Identify activities you have pursued (a) to understand the problem, (b) to formulate a plan of solution (however tentative), (c) to carry out the plan, and (d) to look back at your solution.

3. STORY PROBLEMS

Solving story problems has long been regarded as one of the most difficult and most disliked aspects of elementary mathematics. This attitude on the part of children and teachers can be reversed.

Children and teachers can solve story problems and enjoy working them. This section is divided into several parts. The first presents some ideas for organizing your work on story problems. The second concerns *problem solving* and presents ideas on how to help children solve story problems, and the third suggests some problem-solving activities. A final part deals with evaluation.

A Story-Problem Program

The program described here is designed to reverse bad attitudes toward story problems and create good attitudes. It is designed to overcome failure and frustration and to promote success. This will not be done in one lesson or in several lessons, particularly at the upper grades where bad attitudes may be firmly fixed. You will have to think of your problem-solving program as extending over the year — but you can expect to see positive results much sooner than that. The whole idea of the program is to create a success-enjoyment-interest pattern to replace the failure-dislike-avoidance pattern that too often exists.

Do one each day. The most important element in the program is to assign, work, and explain at least one story problem *every day*. Story problems in textbooks tend to come in clusters. There may be no problems for a week or two, and then two pages to be done in a day. This approach is not effective because the procedures involved are not used frequently enough for skill to develop. You may wish to assign a few more story problems on some days. This will certainly not hurt. However, the

See page 86 for discussion of problem 4.

"story problem of the day" should become a regular part of your classroom procedure. *How* to handle the story problem of the day will be discussed later in this section.

Elementary school textbooks tend to present story problems in sets keyed to the topic being presented. The problems tend to be at the designated grade level of the text. In using these problems it is frequently desirable to use one or two each day rather than assigning them all at once. This is particularly true if your students are not up to their designated grade level. In that case they may find the problems difficult. You may also need to alter the problems to make them easier. Ways to do that are suggested below.

Start with very easy problems. To begin a success-enjoyment-interest pattern, you need *success* to start. This means choosing problems the students can read, understand, and solve. In the upper elementary grades this may mean choosing problems that are two, three, or four years below the students' grade level. You can go back to a second- or third-grade book for such problems or you can write them yourself. If you write the problems yourself, you can make the social context more interesting while keeping the difficulty level low.

Changing the story problem from one context to another is one way to make the easy problem more palatable to older children. For example, a problem such as, "On Thursday there were 125 people at the school concert. On Friday there were 175 people. How many people went to the concert?" becomes "On Thursday race driver Richard Petty drove 125 laps in practice. On Friday he drove 175 laps. How many laps did he drive on both days?"

When you have established success as a pattern in working story problems, gradually increase the difficulty level of the problems you assign. Approach the grade level on which the students are functioning. For example, if a class of sixth graders is working pretty much on a fifth-grade level, they will be able to work up to fifth-grade, not sixth-grade, problems.

Problems should also be "easy" to compute. The purpose of a story problem is to have the student analyze the situation correctly and to decide how to work the problem. When the student has analyzed the problem and has found what to do to solve it, the student should not be confronted with an operation that is too difficult to handle. Put another way, if a child can't divide, there is no point whatever in giving a story problem involving division. The success principle implies that the operations necessary to solve the problem should be ones the child can do fairly well. In that way the story and the problem are emphasized. As you teach, you can concentrate on problem solving, not on reteaching computation.

Use a variety of problems. When all the problems you assign can be worked in one way or by using one operation, children learn to "just look for the numbers and add" rather than to read the problem and think. If you are doing one problem each day, use different operations or combinations of operations each day. Even though you may be studying multiplication, if all your story problems are multiplication problems, the children will soon conclude that all they need to do is to multiply.

Another way in which to provide variety in problems is to use problems which make use of different situations. Try to mix numerical, geometric, and physical problems. Use a variety of different situations leading to the same operation. In the following three problems, the correct equation is $12 - 5 = \square$. (1) John had 12 marbles. He lost 5 of them. How many does he have now? (2) Kathy has 12 kittens, some gray and some black. Five of them are gray. How many are black? (3) Terry has 12 comic books. Sam has 5 comic books. How many more does Terry have? In each of these problems the physical situation is different. In Problem 1 the action of the problem is "take away," in Problem 2 it is "partition," and in Problem 3 the action is "comparison." Each of these situations leads to a subtraction sentence.

Helping Students Solve Problems

In the previous paragraphs we have discussed ways to plan and organize your teaching over a period of a month or more, pointing toward long-range growth in problem-solving skills and in the development of good attitudes. We will now discuss teaching procedures that are effective in helping children work on a particular story problem.

Teaching the "problem a day." You are going to spend five to ten minutes per day, each day, on a problem. What should you do during those five to ten minutes? As we present these suggestions you will recognize the four steps of problem solving that were described in detail in Section 1.

1. Read the problem. In so far as possible, the students should read the problem themselves silently. Then have sev-

eral students read the problem aloud. Help them as much as necessary. If necessary, act out the problem.

2. Ask questions to determine if the problem is fully understood. "What do you know?" "What did the problem tell you?" "What are you supposed to find?" "What action is going on in the problem?" The "action" is particularly important because the action in the problem *will* or should lead us to the kind of operation to be performed.

3. Plan the method of solution. Ask the students to select the operation and *explain why* the operation matches the action in the problem. Take, for example, the problem, "John has 12 marbles. Sam has 5 marbles. How many more marbles does John have?" A picture can be used to illustrate the problem and make clear why the equation fits the action in the problem.

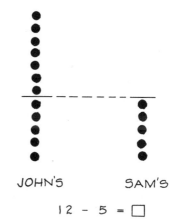

JOHN'S   SAM'S

$12 - 5 = \square$

4. Solve the problem. When the previous three steps have been completed, this should be the easiest step of all. Each student may work independently.

5. When a solution has been obtained, be sure to discuss what the answer means, that is, interpret the result in terms of the problem. Ask, "Does our answer seem reasonable?" In the problem above, the answer, 7, means that John has 7 more marbles than Sam. Check the computation in difficult examples where there is a significant chance for error.

6. It is particularly important for you to explain why the operation chosen *fits the action in the problem. Why* was subtraction the right operation?

7. As children work on a problem, there is a tendency for some to blurt out the answer. This spoils it for the rest. When a child has the answer, he or she may whisper it to you or write it on paper to show you.

Some days you will lead the students through this sequence in detail; other days you will simply give them the problem and let them work. Your objective, of course, is for students to be able to proceed through these steps independently. This does not happen automatically, however; you must teach students explicitly how to think their way through a problem.

Suggestions for helping. When a student is in the midst of solving a problem, there are some things you should do and not do to help him or her obtain a solution.

1. Try to determine which stage of problem solving the student is in and where the difficulty lies. Is he or she having trouble understanding the problem, devising a plan, carrying out the plan, or looking back?

2. Problems can be solved in many ways; be sure you understand what a child has done or has tried to do before commenting on it. You might ask, "How did you get that?" "What did you do?" "Why did you do it?"

Here is a problem presented to a fourth-grade student and her solution: There were 76 campers. 10 went hiking and 12 went fishing. How many stayed at camp?

$$
\begin{array}{r}
76 \\
10 \\
-12 \\
\hline
54
\end{array}
$$

When a student presents unusual work, be sure you understand how the child is thinking before you evaluate the work!

3. There are many good, intelligent, reasonable, frequently effective strategies that fail on a particular problem. Be sure you *praise a child for a good attack* even though it fails: "That's a good guess!" "That's an idea!" "I can see why you did that — it makes sense. Too bad it didn't work." "That was a good try. But let's try another way and see if we get it."

4. Wait for thinking; it takes time. Try not to feel nervous during a silent time while children think and work. Permit children time to work after a problem has been posed. Do not call on the first child who raises a hand. Allow time for many students to complete the problem. Children may say, "Oh, I see." "Hey, it works." "I got it." "I know mine's right."

5. Do not always tell children whether their answers are right or wrong. Ask the kinds of questions that will help them evaluate their own work: "Is your answer sensible?" "Can you check the answer?" "What would happen if you did that?" "Does it work?" "Let's check it." "How could we be sure it is correct?"

6. Be willing and ready to give hints on the solution of a problem before discouragement occurs.

Selecting and altering problems. Read each problem before you present it to the class. It may be that the problem needs to be changed to make it easier, or that there is an unfamiliar concept which will confuse students and prevent them from finding a solution. Consider this problem:

> While taking inventory in an auto dealer's parts department, George recorded 148 spark plugs costing $1.29 each and 237 plugs costing $.75 each. What is the total value of the inventory of spark plugs?

How can we make this problem easier to solve? Here are several ways.

1. Simplify the sentence structure and the vocabulary:

> George counted 148 spark plugs worth $1.29 each. He counted 237 plugs worth $.75 each. What is the total value of the spark plugs?

2. Change the situation to a more familiar one, one with which the students have some experience:

> George counted 148 baseballs worth $1.29 each. He counted 237 baseballs worth $.75 each. What is the total value of the baseballs?

3. Make the numbers *very small*. This will make the analysis of the needed operations the prominent part of the problem, reducing the importance of working with large numbers:

> George counted 6 baseballs worth $1.00 each and 8 baseballs worth $2.00 each. What is the total value of the baseballs?

Note that through all these changes the structure of the problem remains unchanged. The solution pattern is two multiplications, followed by an addition. The original was quite difficult; the final problem is much easier.

Don't use key words. There are a number of "key words" that occur in problems frequently enough so that some teachers are tempted to use them instead of analyzing the action in the problem. "Look, this problem asks 'how many are left,' so it must be a subtraction problem." or "When you see the words 'all together,' you know it's addition." You should *never* teach this kind of analysis. It is misleading. It prevents students from really making an effort to understand the problem. Moreover, it does not always work! Instead of using key words, analyze the action described in the problem and relate the action to the appropriate mathematical operation.

Consider the following problem: Mr. Smith has 53 doughnuts. He puts them in bags, 12 to each bag. How many doughnuts are left over? This problem uses the word *left*. Key-word analysis would identify it as a subtraction problem. However, it is clearly a division problem, the answer being the remainder.

Story problems for younger children. Children in kindergarten and Grades 1 and 2 are also expected to solve "story problems," such as: Jack put 2 blocks in the pile. Jill put 3 blocks in the pile. How many blocks are in the pile?

This story can be told to the children and then acted out by two children, and the answer found by counting blocks. In the first grade and after, a story problem may be incorporated into reading instruction. Children can be encouraged to tell about trips to the store or other experiences in which they deal with numbers. Use these opportunities to make experience charts that contain story problems. The degree of reading involved in a story problem will depend on the children's reading skill. Story problems, however, need not involve reading. For younger children, telling the story is the best way to present it. Here are some suggestions for working with story problems for younger children.

1. Use real situations and the names of your children in making up the stories.

2. Act out the situation in the story. Let the children take part, so the story tells about the action and the children see the actions performed. A play store and other similar settings will help.

3. Use real items, concrete materials, or such aids as play money to make the problem as realistic as possible. These aids should be available to help the children work out the answer.

4. As children increase in symbolic skill, both in language and number, gradually introduce reading as one way to understand the problem and writing an equation as one way to solve it. Make this a gradual transition to allow children to become comfortable with it. Different children will, of course, be ready for this step at different times.

5. Have the children make up their own story problems. You may find it helpful to structure their stories with directions such as: "Make up a story problem about buying candy. Make it fit the sentence $4 + 5 = 9$."

Story-Problem Activities

In presenting a story problem each day, have a variety of things to do. Here are some story-problem activities you can use to vary your procedures.

1. Oral reading or choral reading. Have the problem read aloud, perhaps several times. Sometimes have a student read the whole problem, sometimes have several students each read a sentence.

2. Silent reading. Simply assign the problem and have all students read and work it silently. Discuss it when most students have finished.

3. Use problems without numbers. For example, "John had some marbles. He lost a few of them. How many did he have left?" Ask the children to tell what you would do with the numbers if you had them. A correct analysis would be, "I would subtract the number he lost from . . . ."

4. Give the students a story problem but omit the question part of the problem. Then the task for the students is to decide what the question should be and answer it. For variety, you might challenge them to think up and answer as many questions as they can for the problem. Here is a numerical situation and several questions that could arise from it. "John had 8 cents and Alice had 12 cents. Who had more? How much more? How much did they have together? Could they put their money together and buy a 25¢ toy?"

5. Give problems in which some data is missing. Ask what is needed to solve the problem. Some problems lack a number that is unique to the problem, while others lack a number that is supposed to be common knowledge. "John ran 100 yards. How many feet did he run?" "John ran 100 yards in one race and much farther in another. How many yards did he run in all?"

6. Give problems with extra data, data that are of no use in the solution of the problem.

John ran 250 yards in one race and he ran 440 yards in another race. Ted ran 150 yards in one race. How far did John run in all?

Remember, these activities may be used occasionally, but understanding and solving a regular story problem is the main sort of activity for your "problem a day."

Objectives and Evaluation

In evaluating the success of your efforts in teaching problem solving, a number of factors are difficult to measure. Factors such as attitude and perseverance must be *judged* by your observations of the children as they work. These qualities will not show much change over a short period; a month or more of a carefully planned problem-solving program will usually be required for differences to be observable. The same is true for increases in problem-solving skill. It is difficult to show increases in a pre- and posttesting situation because so many factors are involved in problem solving.

To evaluate your overall success in teaching problem solving, we recommend that you use a check list of observations and some "soul searching" judgments of other factors. The "Problem-Solving Evaluation Check List," below, suggests a systematic way to evaluate students' success in problem solving. To evaluate success in story problems, record the approximate grade level of the problems each student is able to solve at the beginning, and again at the end, of the program. Record the student's attitude as good, fair, or poor. Some indica-

---

Problem-Solving Evaluation Check List

For each of the items below, estimate the average level of performance for your class (a) at the beginning of your problem-solving program and (b) at the end of the program. If you use a pre- and posttest, you can average the scores of students in your group.

1. Most students are capable of working problems at about what grade level?
   a. at the beginning of the program · grade: _____
   b. at the end of the program · grade: _____
2. Evaluate students' enjoyment of problem solving as good, fair, or poor.
   a. at the beginning · _____
   b. at the end · _____
3. Evaluate students' perseverance in problem solving as good, fair, or poor.
   a. at the beginning · _____
   b. at the end · _____
4. In the course of problem solving, have you seen students spontaneously use these problem-solving techniques?
   a. Reads problem carefully; makes an effort to understand problem.
      Yes _____   No _____
   b. Draws a picture.   Yes _____   No _____
   c. Organizes, makes a table, searches for patterns.   Yes _____   No _____
   d. Simplifies the problem or works on part of the problem.
      Yes _____   No _____
   e. Writes a mathematical sentence.   Yes _____   No _____
   f. Guesses, checks, tries new approach when stuck.   Yes _____   No _____
5. Average scores on problem-solving test.
   a. at the beginning · _____
   b. at the end · _____

tions of good attitude are paying attention, willingness to work on problems, bringing in extra "fun" problems or puzzles, working on the problems others bring, and good behavior during problem-solving sessions.

A student's attitude is also reflected in willingness to persevere. If a student is willing to work on a problem without success, if he or she lays it aside for a time and then returns to it, this student is on the way to becoming a good problem solver! Thus, we list one item, next to attitude, to indicate perseverance.

After the item on perseverance the other items in the evaluation refer to specific heuristics. You would not expect to observe all these behaviors as the student is solving one problem. Over the course of a problem-solving program you will see many students doing many of these things. Remember, the student has to try the heuristic *spontaneously*. If you suggest it, it doesn't count! A student who spontaneously at one time or another uses most of these heuristics in attempting to solve problems will be a good problem solver.

Another, very informal evaluation procedure is to get the sense of how the class as a whole is responding to the story problems and challenge problems you are using. If you feel that there is general interest in these items, and if you note that some students are very excited about problem solving, you have created the kind of class atmosphere in which good problem solvers develop their skills!

Discussion Questions

1. What is the advantage of doing one problem each day? of starting with rather easy problems?

2. How would you feel as a sixth grader if the teacher asked you to solve "John had 12 marbles and lost 8 of them. How many did he have left?" How could you make this problem more palatable to a sixth grader?

3. Did you ever use the "heuristic" of working all problems by using the operation presently being studied? "Since we are learning to add fractions, I bet all these problems are solved by adding fractions." How can that be avoided?

4. If a student is having trouble with a problem, should you tell him how to work it? What else could you do?

5. Why is problem-solving skill more difficult to evaluate than computational skill?

6. How would you evaluate a student's attitude toward problem solving?

4. PROBLEMS FOR GRADES 1 TO 8

The following problems can be useful in Grades 1 to 8. With any problem you, the teacher, must select and structure the material so that the problem-solving activity is appropriate for the child.

1. Place each of the numbers 1, 2, 3, 4, 5 in one of the circles in this figure so that no number is connected by a line to the preceding or following number. (For example, 3 must not be connected to 2 or 4.)

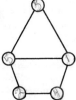

2. Pam told Sam, "If you give me 7 cents, we will each have the same amount of money." Who has more money? How much more? What is the smallest amount of money they could have started with?

3. Each of four people shakes hands once with each of the other three. How many handshakes will there be? How many handshakes will there be for five people? Is there an easy way of working out the number of handshakes for any number of people?

4. You have two equal rolls of pennies. You do not know how many pennies are in each roll, but you do know that on a balance scale, two rolls of pennies plus 3 loose pennies will balance 13 loose pennies. How many pennies in each roll? How many if 2 rolls and 5 loose pennies balance one roll and 17 loose pennies? Draw a picture.

5. Find a two-digit number which is equal to twice the product of those digits.

6. A special rubber ball is dropped from the top of a wall that is 16 feet high. Each time, it bounces up $\frac{1}{2}$ as high as it fell. The ball is caught when the top of its bounce is 1 foot high. Find the total distance the ball travels. Suppose this ball were to bounce forever. How far would it travel? (This is a hard problem.)

7. We wish to measure 4 quarts of water but we have only a 5-quart container and a 3-quart container. How can it be done if neither container is marked for measuring?

8. About $\frac{1}{20}$ of a person's weight is blood. How much do you weigh? How much does your blood weigh?

9. Since it takes the planet Mercury 88 of our days to travel once around the sun, a "year" on Mercury is 88 of our days. If a person were 10 years old, what is his age in "Mercury years"? Use 365 days for an earth year.

10. There are 6 more children in room A than are in room B. Five children move from room A to room B. Now there are twice as many children in room B as in room A. How many children were in room A before the move?

11. Find a four-digit number so that the number of hundreds plus the number of thousands is one, the number of tens is seven times the number of thousands, and the number of ones is five times the number of hundreds.

12. Notice that 17 and 71 are both prime. Find 3 other pairs of two-digit primes that have the same digits.

13. A dozen cookies and a loaf of bread cost $2.80. Half a dozen cookies and 2 loaves of bread cost $2.90. What is the cost of a loaf of bread?

14. John bought a bicycle for $20, sold it for $30, rebought it for $40, and resold it for $50. How much money did he make?

15. In a group of 50 women, 10 are neither pretty nor smart. 30 are pretty and 35 smart. How many are pretty and smart?

16. You have 8 sticks; 4 of them are exactly half the length of the other four. Enclose three equal squares with them.

17. Sue had a square piece of cardboard with a side measuring half a yard. Peg had a piece with an area of half a square yard. Which girl had the larger piece of cardboard?

18. In my carpenter shop, I make only three-legged stools and four-legged tables. One day I looked at my day's output and counted 31 legs. How many stools and how many tables did I complete that day?

19. The school band stood in a formation to play. The leader stood on the tip of the triangle. There were two people

Selected problems are discussed on pages ix and x.

behind the leader, three people in the next row, etc. Find the number of people in the band if there were 16 people in the last row.

20. Mr. Wilson and one man got on a streetcar. At the second stop, three people got on. At the third stop, two people got on and one got off. At the fourth stop, three people got off. At the fifth stop, six people got off and two got on. At the sixth stop, one half of the passengers got off and Mr. Wilson was the only passenger left on the streetcar. How many people were on the streetcar when Mr. Wilson got on?

21. What is the largest sum of money — all in coins and no silver dollars — that I could have in my pocket without being able to give change for a dollar, half dollar, quarter, dime, or nickel?

22. Would you rather work for a month (30 days) and get one million dollars, or be paid 1¢ the first day and double that, or 2¢, the second day, double that, or 4¢, the third day, 8¢ the fourth day, etc.?

23. A pilot and copilot for a space flight are to be chosen from a group of five people of different ages. If the older person must always be the pilot, how many different crews can be made up?

24. Magic squares:

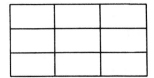

Arrange the numbers 1–9 in the squares so that the sums diagonally and the sums of every row and column are 15.

25. How many times between 4 A.M. and 2 P.M. will the minute hand of a clock pass the hour hand?

26. Visualize a three-inch cube painted red. Assume the cube is cut into 27 one-inch cubes, as shown.

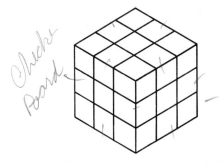

How many one-inch cubes will have red paint on none of the sides? on one face only? on two faces only? on three faces only? on more than three faces?

Visualize a two-inch cube painted red. Assume the cube is cut into 8 one-inch cubes. How many one-inch cubes will have red paint on none of the sides? on one face only? on two faces only? on three faces only? on more than three faces?

Answer the same questions for a four-inch cube painted red and then cut into 64 one-inch cubes. Can you arrange your work in a table? Can you find patterns in the table?

27. You have 6 sections of silver chain, each of 4 links. The cost of cutting open a link is 10¢ and of welding it together again is 25¢. What is the least you can pay to have the 6 pieces joined together in a single chain?

28. Five people, P, Q, R, S, and T, weigh as follows:

P and Q weigh 250 pounds
Q and R weigh 290 pounds
R and S weigh 275 pounds
S and T weigh 270 pounds
P, R, and T weigh 435 pounds

How much does each person weigh?

Selected problems are discussed on pages ix and x.

29. There are 16 girls and 14 boys in Mr. Gray's class. Twenty of the children ride the bus.

a. Is it possible that all the girls ride the bus?

b. What is the fewest number of girls that might ride the bus?

c. What is the fewest number of boys that might ride the bus?

30. Diane has 48¢.

a. What coins does she have if she has 9 coins?

b. What is the fewest number of coins she could have?

c. What is the fewest number of coins she could have and still have at least one quarter, one dime, one nickel, and one cent?

31. One morning a snail starts climbing up a board that is 10 feet long. Each day it climbs 2 feet. Each night it slips back 1 foot. On what day does it reach the top?

32. How many squares are in this figure?

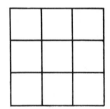

33. How many squares are in this figure?

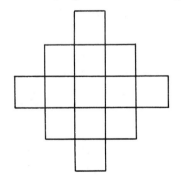

34. How many squares are in this figure?

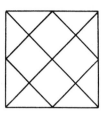

35. How many triangles are in this figure?

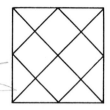

36. How many triangles are in each of these?

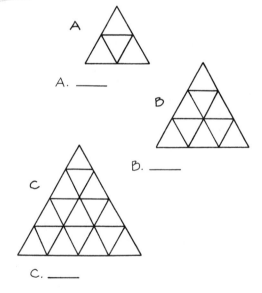

A. _____

B. _____

C. _____

37. What is the total number of squares, of any size, on a standard 8 × 8 checkerboard? (Hint: Consider a simple problem. How many squares in a 1 × 1 board? How many squares in a 2 × 2 board? Make a table.)

Selected problems are discussed on pages ix and x.

38. Place the digits 1, 2, 3, 4, 5, 6 in the circles so that the sum of each adjacent pair of circles (both horizontally and vertically) is different. There are *seven* adjacent pairs.

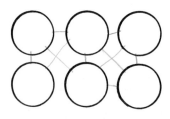

SUMS : __ __ __ __ __ __ __

39. A rectangular garden 15 meters wide and 20 meters long is to be fenced. Posts should be set no more than 5 meters apart. How many posts are needed? How many posts are needed if a gate 1 meter wide is to be built into the fence? How much fencing is needed?

40. Find a rectangle that has its area numerically equal to its perimeter.

41. Given a perimeter of 100 inches, what is the largest area you can enclose within a rectangular shape?

SUGGESTED ASSIGNMENTS AND PROJECTS

Classroom Assignments

1. Choose a grade level and practice *constructing* problems suitable for students in that level. For each problem, present the problem, give a solution, and discuss it.
a. What key mathematical ideas are needed in solving the problem?
b. What questions would you ask to bring about understanding of the problem? What heuristics actually help in obtaining a solution?

c. What hints would you give a student having difficulty with the problem?
d. What are some "looking back" activities you would lead students to do?

2. Select a chapter from a fourth-, fifth-, or sixth-grade textbook and note the topics that are covered in the chapter. Select or write problems for each topic. In class, or with a colleague, discuss the problems you have selected or prepared. Try to identify "looking back" activities for use with the problems.

3. Plan a five-minute problem-solving lesson around a given problem and present the lesson to your fellow students. Critique the lesson in terms of the phases of understanding the problem, developing a plan, carrying out the plan, and looking back.

4. Select a major topic and plan problem-solving activities to use in a sequence of five lessons. The lessons do not necessarily have to be devoted entirely to problem solving. State your objectives in each lesson, but over the course of the five lessons incorporate a suitable amount of problem-solving activities.

Internship Assignments

1. Observe the problem-solving teaching activities of a teacher over a one-week period. If you are an intern, an aide, or a student teacher, you may wish to observe the teacher with whom you are working. Keep a log of your observations, telling how many minutes were spent on all arithmetic activities and how many minutes were spent on problem solving. Describe the problem-solving activities you observe and keep a copy of any materials that were used. Be prepared to report your observations to your class, your instructor, or a colleague. You may wish to discuss your observations with the teacher.

Selected problems are discussed on pages ix and x.

2. Select a student for whom *individual* work on problem solving is appropriate and tutor this child on a set of problems related to the mathematics he or she has studied.

a. Assess the student's problem-solving abilities, using the Problem-Solving Evaluation Check List.

b. Prepare and execute a problem-solving program for the student.

c. Again assess his or her performance, using the Check List.

3. Select a group of students and plan and carry out a problem-solving program with this group. Follow steps *a*, *b*, and *c*, as in Exercise 2, above.

SUMMARY: MAXIMS FOR TEACHING

Problem solving is one area in which we can obtain much better results than we currently do. Working consistently on story problems and challenge problems can result in improved problem-solving skills and improved attitudes.

1. Begin a problem-solving program; organize it so that problem solving becomes a part of each day's work.

a. *Present one story problem to the class each day. Vary the procedure you use to present the problem but at some point always make clear why the mathematics used to solve the problem fits the situation of the problem.*

b. *Use a variety of problems: problems that involve different operations, different situations, one- and two-step problems, and so on.*

c. *Start with easy problems and work up to harder problems gradually. Choose problems easy enough so the children experience success from the beginning.*

2. Have a variety of interesting puzzles and enrichment problems available. Present one or two to the class each week. Encourage children to bring in puzzles and problems.

3. When children are working on a problem, keep in mind the four phases of problem solving:

a. *Understanding the problem*

b. *Devising a plan*

c. *Carrying out the plan*

d. *Looking back*

Look back to the specific hints which may help students in each of these phases and use these hints in problem-solving activities.

5 · Diagnosis and Remediation

Knowledge of Methodology

After studying this chapter, the teacher will be able to

1. discuss the nature of diagnosis and remediation.

2. diagnose and offer suggestions for remediation for learning problems involving concepts.

3. diagnose and offer suggestions for remediation for learning problems involving computational skills.

4. identify what knowledge is prerequisite to a given mathematical task.

Preparing for Instruction

Given a topic in elementary school mathematics, the teacher can

1. identify questions that can be used to determine the causes of misunderstandings.

2. develop activities that encompass a variety of experiences for students having learning difficulties.

Instructional Skills

1. Given a student with a learning problem, the teacher can conjecture the cause of the learning problem.

2. Given a diagnosis of a child's learning difficulty, the teacher can provide effective remedial instruction for the student.

INTRODUCTION

Most elementary school teachers are involved in group instruction when teaching mathematics. The group may be large or small but seldom does one find completely individualized "groups" of only one student. Because of this, teachers strive to develop teaching strategies that produce the greatest learning outcomes for most of the students. Even the best of these strategies, however, will not meet the needs of all students because students vary widely in their knowledge of mathematics.

In trying to help all students learn mathematics, teachers reteach some topics and develop supplemental activities to help students correct misconceptions. Diagnosis and remediation are processes that help discover a student's misconceptions or deficiencies and that identify teaching strategies to correct them. These processes represent important aspects of teaching mathematics. All successful teachers engage in diagnosis and remediation. Some students have misconceptions about numbers. Others do not understand algorithms for adding and subtracting fractions or for long division. Determining what students do not comprehend is essential for effective teaching. Without diagnosis, there is no basis for correcting misunderstandings. Remediation is vital to students' growth in mathematics. Once problem areas have been identified, instruction must be designed to alleviate learning problems and to provide a suitable basis for additional learning.

1. DIAGNOSING LEARNING PROBLEMS

Many of the errors that students make appear in paper-and-pencil activities. Such errors are observable and can be analyzed in an objective way. Sometimes a learning problem can be identified on the basis of a student's responses in class. Regardless of the means used to recognize the problem, the teacher should talk with the student about the problem. Communication can assist the teacher in obtaining additional information. It can also help the child cope with the learning problem in a way that fosters the development of confidence in his or her ability to learn.

Learning Problems and Self-Confidence

Children who continually make significantly more errors than their peers in trying to master an objective realize they are different in that way from other children. This, in itself, is not necessarily bad. But there is danger that these children will come to think less of themselves as persons. In short, a child's self-concept may be damaged. All children and all adults have their self-concepts threatened at various times in their lives. For most children the situation is only temporary. But for others, especially those who experience extensive learning problems, there is an increased likelihood that their self-concept will be severely damaged. A child's achievement in school and success later in life correlate highly with his or her self-image. What can teachers do to prevent students from developing a poor self-concept and to convince them they can achieve? We offer several suggestions in the context of diagnosing learning problems.

It is important for teachers to realize that everyone needs remediation at something. Adults can camouflage their shortcomings by avoiding certain situations. If adults are very poor at athletics, they tend not to participate — so as not to be embarrassed. If an adult is not interested in reading, he or she will likely watch television and not use spare time for reading. Similarly, if one feels inadequate in mathematics, he or she will avoid the subject.

Children do not have this option. One of the purposes of school is to help children acquire knowledge and skills in mathematics and other areas so that they feel confident in school and later in life. But schools are not always successful, and so some students do not make satisfactory progress. When unsatisfactory progress characterizes their mathematical learning, they need help. Unlike adults, they cannot escape by avoiding mathematics. A teacher must be sensitive to the plight of students. The teacher should strive to encourage students and to convince them they can improve and make progress. This can be accomplished by creating an aura of warmth and acceptance in discussions.

Discussing the Learning Problem
with the Student

An evaluation of a student's work (good or bad) does *in no way* indicate the worth and dignity of the child. Teachers must encourage and show acceptance of the child and at the same time be honest with the student in evaluating school work. The following statements exemplify a desirable relationship with the student.

Teacher:
> Mary, look how many you got right this time. That's much better. Let's see if we can figure out what went wrong on these other problems.

Teacher:
> Fred, I noticed you missed a lot of problems the last few days. We're having some trouble here, aren't we? Can you tell me what's causing it?

Compare the net effect of those statements with the ones given below.

Teacher:
> Mary, you are still missing too many problems. You will have to improve on this.

Teacher:
> Fred, last week you were such a good boy and got all of those problems right. But this week you made a lot of mistakes. It's not that hard. Pay attention and work harder.

What is likely to be the impact on a student like Mary if it is continually pointed out how many were missed rather than how many were right? What inferences might Fred make if the second approach was taken? If he is told he is a good boy because he solved problems correctly, is

he then a bad boy if he does not solve them correctly? What confusion could exist in his mind when such a statement is made?

Diagnosing Without Evaluating

In discussing a learning problem with a youngster, the teacher should play the role of an interested observer, one who is probing for additional information. The teacher should not be engaged in explicit evaluation or instruction, except when it is necessary to learn more about the problem. Consider the actions of a physician who is trying to determine the nature and extent of a medical problem. He or she asks questions relating to general health and about symptoms experienced by the patient. The doctor also tries to secure information from various tests.

When you discuss a problem with a student, occasionally ask the child what he or she understands and does not understand. This can be especially effective at the beginning of the conversation. Most children enjoy talking about themselves and will usually be happy to divulge information about themselves. Moreover, the student is less likely to be defensive or to view the teacher as a threat. The more the teacher listens, the more the student will feel comfortable in discussing the difficulty. Of course, at some point the teacher must interject some questions. But the questions should be in the vein of "Tell me what you know about this," rather than "Let me tell you about this," or "Let me show you how to do this." Ideally, all teaching should be diagnostic in nature. During group instruction it is not always possible to diagnose individual problems. We can strive to diagnose and remediate individual learning problems during group instruction by giving individual help as required.

Timing. When planning to discuss a problem with an individual student, try to select a time that does not involve an activity the student enjoys. Little will be gained by keeping a student from a favorite activity to discuss mathematical difficulties. The student will be less receptive and may even be hostile. The same might be true for keeping the student during lunch time or after school. If a student is kept during these times, make sure that the student is agreeable and that the child's parents are supportive.

Perhaps some time can be allocated during the mathematics period to work with individual children. While the other students are working independently, help can be provided to those who need assistance. Care should be taken, however, to see that the child still considers himself or herself part of the regular group. If class time is allocated to diagnosing individual learning problems, the teacher should be particularly sensitive to the student's plight. If the student perceives the discussion as an "interrogation" in front of peers, then surely the student's reaction will be negative. Extra care should be exercised to make the student feel secure, accepted by the teacher, and not threatened.

Discussion Questions

1. In what situations would you think it appropriate to tell a student that his or her learning problem is primarily caused by a lack of effort and that he or she needs to work harder?

2. Recall several times when you had some difficulty learning material. What was the teacher's attitude toward your difficulty? Was the teacher's attitude helpful or harmful when you tried to overcome the problem?

3. Identify several students in classrooms you are observing, or in which you are taking a course, who are experiencing some difficulty in learning. Note their behavior. Does their classroom behavior seem to differ in any way from that of students who are not having learning problems?

2. PROBLEMS IN LEARNING CONCEPTS

The word *concept* is used in many ways. In this chapter a concept will refer to a class of objects and the word denoting the class. The following are examples of concepts: fraction, square, obtuse angle, whole number, proportion, meter, and prime number. In each case, there are both a term associated with the concept, e.g., *fraction,* and the class of objects referred to by the term, e.g., $\frac{1}{2}$, $\frac{2}{3}$, and $\frac{5}{4}$. Students experience difficulty in learning mathematical concepts. In this section various problems that arise in learning concepts and means of remediating those problems will be considered.

Problems Involving the Use of a Term Denoting a Concept

One problem in learning concepts involves associating a term with the referent of that term. This problem is not serious, although it must be dealt with.

Diagnosis. Students may have difficulty in remembering which term is associated with a concept. An error of this type might include naming objects incorrectly or an inability to use the word associated with a concept. For example, a student might label numbers such as 14, 36, and 58 as odd. Or a student might continually misuse the terms *rays, lines,* and *line segments.* Perhaps a student is not able to give the proper word for an example of a concept. For instance, a student is unable to use the word *numerator* when asked to identify the number 2 in the fraction $\frac{2}{5}$.

When students mislabel items or cannot name objects, a teacher must determine what their problem is. Is it that they are unable to associate a word with an object? Or is the problem more complex? A child may have a fairly good idea about a concept but not know, or forget, the term denoting the concept. For example, a child may have a fairly well developed idea of what a trapezoid is but forget the word *trapezoid.* Similarly, a student may not be able to remember whether the top number of a fraction is called "numerator" or "denominator."

Remediation. Primarily, the student needs to establish an association between a word and the objects to which the word refers. Perhaps the student's attention should be focused on the definition of the word. In some cases the association can be acquired by some sort of mnemonic. If such remedies do not seem to resolve the problem, then the problem may be more serious. That is, there may be some basic misunderstanding rather than "knowing the concept" but "forgetting its name." Further diagnosis will be necessary and will probably reveal one of the other conceptual problems discussed in this section.

Problems Related to Not Recognizing Examples of a Concept

Sometimes the inability to use a word appropriately is due to a child's failure to recognize the unique characteristics of the concept. For example, the child may not be sure of those characteristics that distinguish a cat from a dog or a numerator from a denominator. This type of problem is not so easily resolved. Simply reminding students when it is correct to use a word will not likely solve the problem. Memory aids alone will not be enough. Unfortunately, teachers sometimes mistake a poor conceptual development for the simpler problem of misusing words.

Diagnosis. Many times the symptoms of this learning problem are similar to those identified with misusing words. To determine the source of the problem, additional evidence must be gathered. Imagine a student struggling with the concept of odd number. Consider the dialogue below, in which the class is considering various properties of odd and even numbers.

Teacher:
   And what do we call a number like 9, Jack?
Jack:
   An (hesitates) even number.
Teacher:
   Are you sure you mean that?
Jack:
   No—maybe it's odd. I have trouble remembering.

Alice:

Don't odd numbers end in 1, 3, 5, 7, or 9?

Teacher:

Well, that's one way to think of an odd number. So what is 15 — odd or even?

Jack:

Odd.

Teacher:

Good. And how about 24?

Jack:

Even.

Teacher:

I think you've got it.

At this point it would seem, at least in the teacher's eyes, that the problem is resolved. But such is not the case. Let us continue.

Teacher:

Now, let's see what the sum of two odd numbers is. Pick two odd numbers, add them, and what happens?

Jack:

Well, I got 14 — I added 5 and 9.

Teacher:

Based on this, what would you guess about what kind of number you get if you add two odd numbers?

Jack:

You get an odd number.

Teacher:

(Surprised) Why do you say odd? Alice said that an odd number has to end in 1, 3, 5, 7, or 9.

Jack:

Yes — and it does. 14 ends in 1 — it's odd.

Teacher:

Well, let's think of an even number as one that has 2 as a factor. For example, . . .

Jack's problem was not just a misassociation of a word. His problem was more complex than the teacher had originally diagnosed. He did not know the defining characteristic of even numbers, that an even number is a multiple of 2.

There are several questions a teacher might ask to ascertain whether a student has learned the conditions necessary for having an example of a concept. Several of these are illustrated below, using the concept of triangle.

1. How can we be sure if we have a triangle?
2. If I wanted to form a triangle with pencils, how many pencils would I need?
3. If I have a three-sided figure, will I have to have a triangle?
4. Can someone draw a figure that has three angles but is not a triangle?

The first and second questions require the explicit statement of the conditions necessary to have a triangle. The third and fourth questions require the students to determine which conditions are essential to ensure a triangle. These questions can serve as prototypes of questions you can ask students to determine their understanding of concepts. In general, the questions have the following form.

1. If we know _____,
   then are we sure we have a _____
   _____?
2. What must we know, in order to be sure we have a _____?

Remediation. The solution to this problem lies with teaching the student the conditions that must be known in order to have a concept. One means of doing this is simply to tell the student the needed information. In some cases this may work, but often more instruction is needed. One technique is to have the students examine the conditions in many different situations. To illustrate, consider the case of Rob in the dialogue below.

Teacher:

Remember what we said equivalent sets are—two sets that match, that contain the *same number* of things. Are these two sets equivalent?

Rob:

Well—I don't know. One contains blocks and the other bottle caps.

Teacher:

Do they have the same number of things?

Rob:

Four, I guess.

Teacher:

Okay, four. So that means the sets are equivalent, since they have four objects each. Now, how about these two sets? Are they equivalent? (Each set contains 10–15 elements.)

Rob:

No—because they have more than four things.

Teacher:

Well, okay—but do they have the same number—or can the two sets be matched?

Rob:

I don't know—I don't get this stuff.

Rob's problem is diagnosed as an inability to determine if two sets are equivalent. To resolve the problem, Rob must first be reminded that equivalent sets are two sets that have a one-to-one correspondence. This definition must then be reinforced by examining pairs of sets in which the numbers of elements in the sets are varied. Also, the sets could be arranged in a linear configuration, a circle arrangement, or in two piles where the student must construct the matching.

The point is that the crucial attribute—the matching—must be displayed in a variety of situations so that the student learns to ignore irrelevant attributes, such as size or configuration of the pairs of sets.

To illustrate further, suppose a diagnosis reveals that a student does not know how to determine if one triangle is congruent to another. To remediate this problem, the student must first be reminded what congruent triangles are. The student could be given one condition for ensuring congruent triangles, for example, "If two triangles have their sides respectively equal, they are congruent." Of course, this condition could also be the result of a discovery lesson. Next, the student could be given a variety of triangles in which the dimensions and positions of the triangles vary, as shown below. The student could find those triangles with the corresponding sides equal in length and then determine that those triangles are congruent.

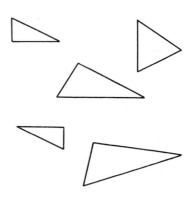

Again, the remediation procedure involves two steps. First, conditions providing examples of the concept must be identified. Second, these conditions must be displayed in a wide variety of contexts.

Problems Related to Not Knowing Information About Concepts

Sometimes students are not able to give information about a concept. Students with this problem are greatly limited in their ability to utilize and apply mathematics.

Diagnosis. Students making this type of error cannot associate meaning to a phrase or cannot state or use characteristics of objects named by a term. To illustrate, consider the dialogue below.

Teacher:
What do we call two fractions such as $\frac{1}{2}$ and $\frac{3}{6}$?

Rachel:
The same fractions?

Teacher:
Well, not really. We call them equivalent fractions. What do we mean by equivalent fractions?

Rachel:
They are the same.

Teacher:
Well, in a sense. What else can you tell me?

Rachel:
I'm not sure. Maybe we use them when we add fractions.

Teacher:
That's right. How can we tell if two fractions are equivalent?

Rachel:
I don't remember.

Teacher:
Can you tell me a fraction that is equivalent to $\frac{3}{4}$?

Rachel:
No, I don't know.

Rachel's problem may stem from not being able to identify any of the properties of equivalent fractions. If her inability to verbalize the properties is representative of her understanding of equivalent fractions, then she has a serious learning problem and will surely encounter difficulty in adding fractions with unlike denominators.

The problem no doubt is deeper than just not understanding the concept of equivalent fractions. Further investigation would probably reveal that Rachel does not have a very thorough knowledge of fractions. Usually when one problem appears, there are other more basic learning problems underlying the observable problem.

The following general questions can serve as a basis for diagnosing students' problems of not associating information with a term.

1. What are some of the ideas you have when I say _____?
2. If I wrote (drew) a _____ on the chalkboard, tell me all that you know about it.

Remediation. The first task is to make sure the student can identify objects named by the term. Once this has been achieved, then activities can be devised which emphasize properties of the objects. Here are several suggestions.

1. Properties of objects could be identified by having students measure the objects or by having them manipulate concrete objects which are examples of the concept. For instance, properties of parallelograms could be determined by measuring angles and sides of various parallelograms. Properties of odd numbers could be investigated by manipulating objects in an odd-numbered set.

2. Questions could be posed which compare and contrast various objects. For instance, students could be asked what property is true for a square and not for a rectangle (that is not a square). Or a meter could be compared to a yard; that is, what properties do they have in common and how do they differ? Or a factor of a number could be contrasted with a divisor of that number.

3. Games or activities could be devised that emphasized properties of objects. Clusters of students experiencing the same learning problem could participate. Perhaps each student could name a property of, say, the number 10. More elaborate games could consist of modified versions of "bingo" or "concentration," using concepts and associated properties. One such "concentration" card is given below.

One of the key considerations in devising remedial strategies for misconceptions is to utilize concrete objects which exemplify the concept. Remedial strategies, like any teaching strategies, are generally more effective for the struggling student if they involve materials that can be manipulated.

Discussion Questions

1. Identify and discuss what the learning problems below might be in terms of the preceding discussion on concepts.

a.

Teacher:
   Doug, do you have a prime number?

Doug:
   Yes, 15.

Teacher:
   Why do you think it is prime?

Doug:
   Because it is odd.

b.

Teacher:
   Kathy, would you please add $\frac{2}{3}$ and $\frac{3}{5}$.

Kathy, in solving the problem, does the following calculations:

$$\frac{2}{3} = \frac{4}{5}$$
$$\frac{3}{5} = \frac{3}{5}$$
$$\frac{7}{5}$$

Teacher:
   Now, would you please explain what you did.

Kathy:
   Well, first I had to get them so they had the same denominator. So I made $\frac{2}{3} = \frac{4}{5}$ by adding 2, and then I just added the fractions.

mixed number	exactly 2 divisors	multiple of 2	fraction more than one
numerator = denominator	even number	numerator > denominator	sum of whole number and fraction
fraction less than one	product of 2 or more primes	numerator < denominator	prime number
composite number	one	whole number	1, 2, 3, 4, 5, . . .

c.

Teacher:

Frank, how did you get the area of this figure to be 24 square inches?

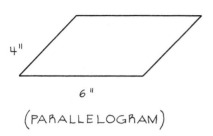

$$(\text{PARALLELOGRAM})$$

Frank:

Well, to find the area, you take length times width, or $6 \times 4 = 24$.

2. Identify possible learning problems you think students might have with the following concepts: percent, altitude of a triangle, least common multiple, equivalent fractions.

3. PROBLEMS IN LEARNING COMPUTATIONAL SKILLS

Computational skills play an important role in elementary school mathematics. An inability to compute is a great handicap to any mathematics student. In this section various problems students have in acquiring computational skills and suggestions for helping students overcome the problems will be discussed.

Problems Related to Incorrect Procedures for Performing an Algorithm

In this category we find the widest variety of errors and also the most serious and persistent errors. The errors are frequently based on a fundamental lack of understanding of the numbers and operations involved.

Diagnosis. Problems involving incorrect procedures are often characterized by errors that can occur in patterns. The pattern of the error will usually occur frequently — perhaps whenever a particular type of computational procedure is required.

Consider Becky, an average fourth grader. She was observed making the following errors in working with fractions.

$$
\begin{array}{r}
4\frac{1}{5} = \ 3\frac{11}{5} \\
-2\frac{2}{5} = -2\frac{2}{5} \\
\hline
1\frac{9}{5} = 2\frac{4}{5}
\end{array}
$$

$$
\begin{array}{r}
5\frac{1}{4} = \ 5\frac{3}{12} = \ 4\frac{13}{12} \\
-2\frac{1}{3} = -2\frac{4}{12} = -2\frac{4}{12} \\
\hline
2\frac{9}{12} = 2\frac{3}{4}
\end{array}
$$

Her pattern of errors was consistent. But the errors are *not* always consistent. The diagnosis is sometimes confounded by more than one conceptual error and also by mistakes in basic calculations.

Consider the case of Juan, who has a misconception similar to Becky's but who also makes other mistakes. Examine his work below and see if you can identify the types of errors he is making.

(a)
$$
\begin{array}{r}
5\frac{1}{3} = \ 5\frac{3}{5} = \ 4\frac{5}{5} \\
-2\frac{1}{2} = -2\frac{4}{5} = -2\frac{4}{5} \\
\hline
2\frac{1}{5}
\end{array}
$$

(b)
$$
\begin{array}{r}
6\frac{2}{5} = \ 6\frac{5}{9} = \ 4\frac{9}{9} \\
-2\frac{3}{4} = -2\frac{8}{9} = -2\frac{8}{9} \\
\hline
2\frac{1}{9}
\end{array}
$$

(c)
$$
\begin{array}{r}
5\frac{3}{4} \\
-2\frac{1}{4} \\
\hline
3\frac{2}{4}
\end{array}
$$
(d)
$$
\begin{array}{r}
10\frac{2}{7} = \ 9\frac{7}{7} \\
-6\frac{5}{7} = -6\frac{5}{7} \\
\hline
3\frac{2}{7}
\end{array}
$$

Clearly Juan has trouble finding a common denominator for two fractions having unlike denominators. In case (a), working with $\frac{1}{3}$ and $\frac{1}{2}$, a denominator of 5 was used. In item (b), Juan used a denominator of ninths for the fractions $6\frac{2}{3}$ and $2\frac{3}{4}$. How, then, did Juan make the conversions $\frac{1}{3}$ to $\frac{3}{5}$, $\frac{1}{2}$ to $\frac{4}{5}$, $\frac{2}{3}$ to $\frac{5}{9}$, and $\frac{3}{4}$ to $\frac{8}{9}$? One might conjecture that whatever number was added to the denominator, that same number was added to the numerator. This conjecture would seem to hold in three of the four cases but would not hold for the conversion of $\frac{2}{3}$ to $\frac{5}{9}$. Perhaps this was just a careless error and Juan meant to obtain $\frac{6}{9}$, in which case our conjecture would have additional support. Items (c) and (d) involve fractions of the same denominator, and hence we do not observe this same type of error.

Juan evidently has another problem. Notice that in three of the four cases, when a unit is converted to a fraction, the fractional part of the original number is dropped. For example, he converted $5\frac{3}{5}$ to $4\frac{5}{5}$, $6\frac{5}{9}$ to $4\frac{9}{9}$, and $10\frac{2}{7}$ to $9\frac{7}{7}$ and seemingly forgot the fractional parts of the numbers, $\frac{3}{5}$, $\frac{5}{9}$, and $\frac{2}{7}$. The fact that $\frac{3}{5}$ and $\frac{5}{9}$ represented errors in themselves does not change what appears to be a conceptual error on Juan's part. Of course, this conjecture does not account for Juan's converting $6\frac{5}{9}$ to $4\frac{9}{9}$. Was this another careless error? Probably so. This could better be determined by examining other instances of his work.

On the basis of these problems, one might conjecture that Juan has at least two misunderstandings involving the subtraction of fractions. He seems to understand the sequencing of the steps of the algorithm but makes mistakes when doing the steps. Specifically, he does not know how to find the lowest

common denominator nor how to convert mixed numbers to equivalent forms, as would be required in converting $6\frac{2}{5}$ to $5\frac{7}{5}$. To help verify our diagnosis, we could provide Juan with additional exercises and observe how he worked them.

Here is an example of another problem that is so common that it can be found in almost every class of students working on subtraction.

1. 84	2. 96	3. 82	4. 64	5. 43
$\underline{-8}$	$\underline{-7}$	$\underline{-9}$	$\underline{-9}$	$\underline{-7}$
84	91	86	65	44

What is the pattern? Describe it in words or work the problems below, using the same procedure the student used above.

$$\begin{array}{cc} 75 & 83 \\ \underline{-9} & \underline{-8} \end{array}$$

Which of the exercises 1 through 5 above does *not* follow the pattern? Can you suggest a reason why that exercise is different?[1] It is important to talk to the student. Ask how he or she does the problem and listen carefully to his or her explanation.

It is not enough to note that students are continually making mistakes in doing a particular calculation. To say that a student is weak in adding fractions is not much of a diagnosis. WHY do the mistakes occur? That question should be the primary emphasis in any diagnosis.

Remediation. Several suggestions are offered below for remediating problems involving incorrect procedures.

1. Teach students to watch for "reasonable" and "unreasonable" answers. Students should raise their hands

---

[1]Number 3 is different. It is a good guess that, in addition to the procedural error, the student made a mistake in a subtraction fact.

if they get an answer which is unreasonable. One way to begin this sort of checking is to use an estimate box beside the problem, as illustrated below. Before working the problem write a "reasonable estimate" of the answer in the box. If the answer and the estimate are not fairly close, the student should seek help.

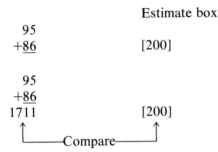

Estimate box

Of course, this alone does not resolve the problem but it does help make the student aware that errors are being made. Having the student realize that the procedure being used is incorrect is a good first step.

One word of caution is in order here. If a student is manipulating symbols with little understanding, he or she may not be bothered by an obvious difference between the estimate and the answer. Consider the case depicted above. While it is obvious to us that 1711 and 200 are incompatible, they may not be to an immature student. Such a student might reason as follows: 95 is a large number. 86 is a large number. When you add two large numbers, you get a large number. Both 1711 and 200 are large numbers. Hence, my answer seems reasonable and is probably correct.

2. Review any concepts or other algorithms that are prerequisite to the algorithm being learned. Consider the case of Becky. Most of her problem seems to stem from a misconception concerning

unity. Activities need to be devised to help her realize that $1\frac{1}{5}$ equals $\frac{6}{5}$, not $\frac{11}{5}$. Becky probably made this error because $3\frac{3}{10}$ equals $2\frac{13}{10}$ and she thought the same pattern held for all fractions.

Apparently Juan has a misconception regarding equivalent fractions. He uses the incorrect principle that

$$\frac{a}{b} = \frac{a+n}{b+n}$$

where n is some whole number. He needs help with conceptual development also.

3. Make sure the student understands each step involved in the process. To help students understand a procedure, you might have them perform the calculation using concrete materials representing the numbers. The problem with the estimate box, for instance, could be done using various embodiments of tens and ones. We refer you to the chapter on using laboratory aids for more extensive treatment on using concrete materials. By using physical objects students may be better able to associate meaning and symbols and hence have a better understanding of how to do an algorithm.

4. Have the students state how to perform the algorithm in their own words. This can not only help the student become more familiar with the procedure but it can also provide additional information on what the student does or does not know.

5. Provide reasons why the algorithm works. Most elementary students, particularly those having learning difficulties, will not profit from a deductive argument justifying an algorithm. But the algorithm may be justified by finding the answer with concrete materials or by alternative procedures. In either case, when the answer obtained by an alternative procedure is the same as the one obtained by the algorithm in question, it makes the procedure to be learned more reasonable.

6. Make sure students know when to use various computational techniques. In a way, this does not deal directly with remediating the problem of using an incorrect procedure. On the other hand, it can be helpful to a student to know when to use one technique, for instance, when to regroup and combine, and when not to. This can keep students from using an incorrect procedure which may seem justified because of its use in a previous context. This is illustrated below, where the first two problems are correct but the third is not, although it "appears" that the same algorithm is used.

$$
\begin{array}{ccc}
207 & 506 & 34 \\
\times 6 & \times 5 & \times 4 \\
\hline
1242 & 2530 & 1216
\end{array}
$$

Problems Related to Inadequate Mastery of Basic Facts

There is no question that a major factor in causing mistakes by students in elementary school mathematics is an inadequate mastery of facts. A lack of mastery in basic facts and skills greatly limits what can be achieved from studying mathematics.

Diagnosis. If students are uncertain of the basic facts, they may recall them correctly in one instance and incorrectly in another. Examples of such errors are commonplace and cause incorrect results in computations of all kinds. In the division example below we see the error

$9 \times 3 = 24$ as the cause of the incorrect result.

$$
\begin{array}{r}
29 \quad \text{R1} \\
3\overline{\smash{)}\ 85} \\
-60 \quad\quad 20 \times 3 = 60 \\
\hline
25 \\
-24 \quad\quad 9 \times 3 = 24 \\
\hline
1
\end{array}
$$

On the next problem the student may recall 9×3 correctly. Such errors often have a random character.

Remediation. When a student's performance is hampered by inadequate mastery, what can we do about it? We will not repeat here the techniques described in the chapter on computational skill, but we will reemphasize certain basic principles. It is important that students know the *meanings* of the facts. Following that, it is necessary to conduct effective drill activities to produce the speed and accuracy desired. Bear in mind that one should not expect perfection but only a reasonable degree of skill and accuracy. No one is perfect in mastery of the basic facts, as our experience in keeping a checkbook will attest.

Problems Related to "Irrelevant Rule" Errors

Sometimes students get problems correct but for the wrong reasons. They complete exercise after exercise correctly but the result may be only reinforcing an irrelevant rule. This is particularly likely to happen when a sample exercise is completed for the student and all other exercises are to be done in exactly the same way. For instance, a child is asked to complete problems like the following:

$$321 = \underline{3}\ \text{HUNDREDS} + \underline{2}\ \text{TENS} + \underline{1}\ \text{ONES}$$

$$417 = \underline{\ 4\ }\ \text{hundreds} + \underline{\ 1\ }\ \text{tens} + \underline{\ 7\ }\ \text{ones}$$
$$586 = \underline{\ 5\ }\ \text{hundreds} + \underline{\ 8\ }\ \text{tens} + \underline{\ 6\ }\ \text{ones}$$
$$397 = \underline{\ 3\ }\ \text{hundreds} + \underline{\ 9\ }\ \text{tens} + \underline{\ 7\ }\ \text{ones}$$

Examining the work, we may conclude that the student has a nice grasp of place value. The student, however, may be using an irrelevant rule in completing the exercise. It can be stated, "Copy the digits in order in the blanks." This rule will work as long as our practice materials are mechanical and routine.

Diagnosis. To diagnose whether in fact the student is focusing on a correct rule rather than an irrelevant one, exercises should be varied. In the above case, examples such as these could be given.

$$437 = \underline{\ \ }\ \text{tens} + \underline{\ \ }\ \text{hundreds} + \underline{\ \ }\ \text{ones}$$
$$296 = \underline{\ \ }\ \text{hundreds} + \underline{\ \ }\ \text{ones} + \underline{\ \ }\ \text{tens}$$

Cases where students are producing correct answers but using the wrong process are very difficult to diagnose. The best means of ascertaining the correctness of a student's thinking process is to make sure the exercises are varied and require a level of understanding beyond that of rote response.

Remediation. Any remedial steps must be based on providing an understanding for the correct process. This will mean reteaching concepts and skills underlying the procedure. Care must be taken that one rote method does not replace another one, however. For instance, instructions to "Write the digit to the left next to hundreds, the middle digit next to tens, and the digit to the right next to ones," will produce correct answers in a variety of situations. But the level of understanding may be no greater.

Problems Related to Affective Considerations

Sometimes students make mistakes for reasons other than not understanding the mathematics. In this section we will discuss the need for being aware of affective considerations as a cause of students' mistakes.

Diagnosis. To do an arithmetic calculation, particularly a long one, a student must do many steps, do each one correctly, and in the proper order. If motivation or interest is lacking, the child may easily make errors simply through carelessness. Fatigue, loss of interest, or distractions are other sources of errors.

Many teachers have made observations such as, "Helen can work them all right as long as I stand and watch, but when I move away she gets them wrong." While the teacher is watching, Helen will concentrate on the task; when the teacher moves away, Helen lets her mind drift. A child who gets the first few problems of a set mostly right but gets them mostly wrong by the end of the set is showing fatigue or loss of interest. Working a page of problems is not really very interesting, is it? Little wonder students become careless after twenty or thirty examples of the same type. Distraction or excitement may also cause errors in which no discernable pattern exists. You may conclude that a student's errors are due to these factors if the student can perform correctly under proper conditions but fails to perform correctly under other conditions.

Remediation. Dealing with problems of an affective nature is difficult. Providing a variety of learning situations and activities can do much to maintain interest and motivation. Keeping work periods relatively short so that students do not become bored is another suggestion. (*All* students will become bored with *any* activity if that activity is carried on long enough.) Furthermore, the work should be at a level that the students can understand. Nothing is quite as boring as performing a task about which you know little or doing a task when you do not know why you are doing it. Finally, and most important, you must be enthusiastic about your teaching of mathematics.

Discussion Questions

1. Consider the problems below.
   a. Can you detect a pattern in the errors?
   b. How much does the student "borrow"?
   c. Where does the student get the "borrowed" number from?
   d. What seems to be the misunderstanding behind the errors?
   e. What remedial instruction would you consider?

$$
\begin{array}{lll}
{}^{6\,2} & {}^{8\,1} & {}^{1}_{5\ \ 4} \\
\textbf{1. } 8\cancel{8}6 & \textbf{4. } 5\cancel{9}6 & \textbf{6. } 6\cancel{4}4 \\
\underline{-57} & \underline{-467} & \underline{-529} \\
811 & 120 & 020
\end{array}
$$

$$
\begin{array}{lll}
{}^{3\,6} & {}^{3\,2} & {}^{2} \\
\textbf{2. } 4\cancel{9}2 & \textbf{5. } 6\cancel{5}7 & \textbf{7. } 0\,0\,4 \\
\underline{-327} & \underline{-119} & 241 \\
111 & 520 & \underline{-127} \\
 & & 000
\end{array}
$$

$$
\begin{array}{l}
{}^{3\,5} \\
\textbf{3. } 5\cancel{8}5 \\
\underline{-329} \\
201
\end{array}
$$

2. Identify the pattern of errors in the examples below.

	a.			
	⁸¹	³²	³²⁵	¹¹
a.	596	657	644	427
	−467	−119	−129	−118
	120	520	200	300

	¹		¹	¹¹
b.	47	187	308	737
	+53	+632	+407	+296
	90	719	705	923

		¹⁶		
c.	40	160	108	500
	−16	−81	−36	−23
	30	080	102	500

d.	492	241	868	596
	−327	−127	−749	−467
	175	126	121	131

e.	23	59	71	98
	×12	×64	×28	×76
	46	22	568	588
	23	311	142	686
	69	333	710	1274

3. Discuss what might be the source of the difficulties as evidenced by the above errors.

4. Devise remedial strategies which might resolve the problems you diagnosed.

5. Make up a series of problems that have the same type of error. Give your problems to a classmate and see if your classmate can identify the pattern of errors.

6. Select an elementary school mathematics textbook and see if you can find a set of exercises that require only rote responses. Make up several questions you could ask the students to ascertain whether or not their thinking was rote in doing the exercises.

7. Suppose a student can perform the long division algorithm quite well but is repeatedly confused about when to use the algorithm in solving word problems. What simple situations that do and do not require division might you present to the student for consideration?

8. Repeat question 7 for the algorithm of subtracting whole numbers.

9. Suppose a student demonstrates that he or she knows how to bisect an angle, using a compass and a ruler, but does not know why the method works. Devise two ways by which you might explain why it works.

4. LOCATING GAPS IN STUDENTS' KNOWLEDGE

One of the primary tasks in diagnosing problems is to determine what "gaps" exist in a student's knowledge. By "gap" we mean an item missing from that body of knowledge — concepts and skills — that are prerequisite to the mathematics being learned. If a student is experiencing difficulty, assuming this difficulty is not based on emotional, physical, or other "nonacademic" problems, there must be some prerequisite aspects of mathematics that the student does not understand.

Locating a student's misunderstanding is, in part, a matter of analyzing a mathematical task to find the prerequisite knowledge that is needed. The relevance of determining prerequisite knowledge for diagnosis and remediation is clear. When students have not learned prerequisite knowledge, they are severely handicapped and perhaps prohibited from acquiring subsequent concepts and skills. Although most teachers would not do a detailed analysis of prerequisite

knowledge for a given task, a certain amount of analysis is necessary for use in diagnosing learning problems.

To illustrate how to determine gaps in students' knowledge by identifying prerequisite knowledge, an example will be considered which focuses on the task of adding fractions.

Determining the Prerequisite Knowledge for Adding Fractions

To determine the prerequisite knowledge for a task, "talk" your way through the procedure and record the subtasks or prerequisite tasks that a student must be able to do. Let us follow this suggestion by using the addition of fractions as our primary task. Let us assume that a problem such as the following is presented to the student:

$$3\tfrac{11}{20} + 4\tfrac{13}{15} = \square$$

The steps listed below are those a student would normally complete to solve the problem.

1. Rewrite the problem as shown here.
$$\begin{aligned} &3\tfrac{11}{20} \\ +\;&4\tfrac{13}{15} \end{aligned}$$

2. Find a common denominator for $\tfrac{11}{20}$ and $\tfrac{13}{15}$.

3. Change the fractions to equivalent fractions, using the common denominator.
$$\begin{aligned} 3\tfrac{11}{20} &= 3\tfrac{33}{60} \\ +\;4\tfrac{13}{15} &= 4\tfrac{52}{60} \end{aligned}$$

4. Add the fractional parts and the whole-number parts.
$$\begin{aligned} 3\tfrac{11}{20} &= 3\tfrac{33}{60} \\ +\;4\tfrac{13}{15} &= 4\tfrac{52}{60} \\ \hline &\quad\;\; 7\tfrac{85}{60} \end{aligned}$$

5. Change the improper fraction to a mixed number.

$$3\tfrac{11}{20} = 3\tfrac{33}{60}$$
$$+ \ 4\tfrac{13}{15} = 4\tfrac{52}{60}$$
$$\overline{\phantom{+ \ 4\tfrac{13}{15} =} \ 7\tfrac{85}{60} = 8\tfrac{25}{60}}$$

6. Reduce the fractional part of the answer to lowest terms.

$$3\tfrac{11}{20} = 3\tfrac{33}{60}$$
$$+ \ 4\tfrac{13}{15} = 4\tfrac{52}{60}$$
$$\overline{\phantom{+ \ 4\tfrac{13}{15} =} \ 7\tfrac{85}{60} = 8\tfrac{25}{60} = 8\tfrac{5}{12}}$$

At each point various questions could arise to identify a student's problem. For instance, at step 2 the following questions could be asked.

a. Does the student seem to have a conceptual problem, e.g., is the need for a common denominator recognized?

b. Does the student know what a common denominator is?

c. Does the student have an organized method for finding the lowest common denominator?

Questions could be asked for the other steps, also. The point is that by identifying the prerequisite knowledge, you can better determine the specific knowledge gap the student has which causes observed errors.

Discussion Questions

1. Design additional questions that could be asked relative to steps 3, 4, 5, and 6, above.

2. Identify prerequisite knowledge that a student must know in order to learn the following mathematics:

a. adding two-digit numbers with regrouping
b. determining which of two numbers (less than 100) is the larger
c. the distributive law

d. changing a common fraction to a decimal

e. long division

3. Examine each of the following errors and decide what prerequisite knowledge was lacking, causing the student to make the indicated error.

a. $\tfrac{31}{62} = .2$

b. $\tfrac{2}{3} \times \tfrac{4}{15} = \tfrac{1 \times 2}{1 \times 5} = \tfrac{2}{5}$

c. $4 + \square = 9$
$4 + 13 = 9$

d. Two supplementary angles $= 90°$
One is $40°$
Other is $90° - 40° = 50°$

4. Suppose a student's score on a standardized test is 4:3, meaning fourth grade, third month. Does this mean that the student knows all of the mathematics usually encountered at that level and knows no mathematics beyond the fourth year, third month? Are there any other possible interpretations? If there are, explain them briefly.

SUGGESTED ASSIGNMENTS AND PROJECTS

Classroom Assignments

1. Choose an elementary school mathematics textbook and select some topic from the text. Identify what you consider to be prerequisite knowledge for learning that topic. Verify your judgment as best you can by reviewing the sequencing of the mathematics prior to the selected topic.

2. Select a diagnostic or standardized test. If you were to use that test, what information might you hope to obtain relative to diagnosing learning problems? What information could the test not provide you?

3. Select a mathematical concept. Design a series of questions or activities you could use to ascertain if a student understood the concept.

4. Select a mathematical algorithm. Design a series of questions or activities you could use to ascertain if a student understood the algorithm.

Internship Assignments

1. Select a student who experiences difficulty in learning mathematics. What do you believe to be the cause of the learning problem?

2. Identify a child who is at least one grade level below expected achievement in mathematics. Through questions or tests determine what mathematical concepts or skills the child does not understand. Determine what gaps exist in the student's knowledge. Create objectives for the student, relative to your diagnosis. Design a remedial teaching strategy. Following your instructional program, design a test or a series of questions to evaluate the student's attainment of your objectives. Describe the extent to which your program was successful.

SUMMARY: MAXIMS FOR TEACHING

1. Make sure that both your curriculum and your instruction are appropriate for the students you are teaching. If a large number of students are experiencing extensive learning problems, you should review what you are teaching and how you are teaching.

2. Try to determine if a child has problems with concepts. Related to this is the child's ability to identify objects that are or are not examples of a concept and to discuss how these objects are the same or different. See if the child can identify conditions that must exist for an object to be an example of a concept, state a definition for a concept, and recognize characteristics of examples of concepts. These tasks can be used for diagnosis and as a basis to help remedy a conceptual problem.

3. Try to determine if the student does not understand an algorithm. Perhaps the child does not have a prerequisite concept or does not understand one or more steps involved in the algorithm. Once such difficulties have been ascertained, then develop an instructional technique to resolve the problem.

4. Determine the prerequisite knowledge for a given topic and utilize it to determine what gaps exist in the student's knowledge.

5. Look for patterns in the student's errors. If the student makes errors of a consistent type, the analysis of the nature of the errors can provide insight to the learning problem.

6. In divising remedial strategies, incorporate concrete materials whenever the child is unable to associate correct meanings with symbols or when the student makes errors in computations.

6 · Individualization of Instruction

COMPETENCIES

Knowledge of Methodology

After studying this chapter, the teacher will be able to

1. describe and discuss these questions: What is the role of intelligence and other differences among students? To what extent should individualization be attempted? How does individualization affect grading procedures?

2. describe and discuss various procedures for grouping students, citing strong and weak points of each.

3. describe and discuss a variety of techniques for individualization, including use of paraprofessionals and teaching aids and materials.

Preparing for Instruction

Given an appropriate topic in elementary school mathematics, the teacher can

1. specify how instruction on that topic may be individualized, using (a) concrete materials and (b) supplementary materials.

2. specify how that topic may be individualized through the use of a progression of algorithms from less mature to adult form.

3. devise or locate material for use in enrichment and/or remedial instruction.

Instructional Competencies

For a group of children the teacher can

1. diagnose the needs of the children for different modes or rates of instruction.

2. plan a program which will provide for individual instruction of the children and differentiated goals of instruction. Plan for both different modes of instruction and different rates of progress.

3. carry out the planned lessons.

4. using pre- and posttests and other data, evaluate the progress of each child toward his or her goals and the success of the unit in general.

INTRODUCTION

As teachers know, children are quite different from one another in their ability to progress in mathematics. They enter kindergarten and first grade with different background experiences and different readiness for learning. Differences become greater as children move into the upper grades. Their naturally differing rates of learning "pull them apart" in mathematics; the differences among children become greater as they grow older. It is also true that a good instructional program will make children more different, not less different. As each child is encouraged and helped to move at his own pace in mathematics, the gap between the slowest and the fastest students increases dramatically. We must accept differences among children as a fact and deal with that fact realistically in the instructional program.

We frequently talk about individual differences as a problem, and indeed they are a problem. We may wish that all children were equally superb in mathematical talent, but it seems that they will never be. The recognition of individual differences and the planning of instruction so that each child has the opportunity to achieve his or her maximum learning is a desirable, in fact, a necessary characteristic of good teaching. Any program or teacher who "does away with" individual differences does so by frustrating some students with work that is too hard and boring others with work that is too easy.

One approach to individualization is easily recognized because it is all-too-frequently used. This is the approach where every child in a class is given the same work. For example, every child in a fourth-grade class gets a fourth-grade mathematics text. ("Well, if that book isn't right for the grade, why did the company publish it and why did the school board buy it?") All students start on page 1 and work through the book together. All students study the same pages on the same days, and all have the same assignments. Students who finish early can do the extra exercises at the end of the chapter or book. ("I know they understand it but every student can profit from extra practice.") Students who "get it" slowly may do extra work or take work home. Students who can't "get it" will just have to do the best they can. At test time, the teacher of this class notes that some students excel. The teacher is proud. Their success proves the teacher's effective-

ness. Some students do average work, and some fail. Those who fail prove that the teachers in the first three grades are not doing their job. ("How can they promote into the fourth grade a student who can't even subtract?") By thus ignoring differences between children, this teacher provides an ineffective program for all—worse, of course, for the slower and faster students than for the average students.

While the existence of differences among children is a fact, it is a most difficult fact to deal with in planning an instructional program. When teachers discuss their most pressing problems, they will almost always ask questions such as, "In my third-grade class I have some children who are on the first-grade level and others who are on the fifth-grade level. How can I handle that?" The answer, unfortunately, is that handling individual differences, planning and teaching so that all these different children get appropriate instruction, is very hard work! This chapter has no suggestion that there is an easy solution to this difficult problem. Handling individual differences effectively will require time, effort, and hard work as long as you teach. Since we have no easy solutions, we will describe the origins and dimensions of the problem and we will tell you about techniques and materials that work for teachers who use them.

1. DIFFERENCES AMONG STUDENTS

We cannot, in this text, include detailed information about the basic human characteristics which make children different from one another. You may wish to review some of these details and, if so, a textbook in educational psychology will provide a great deal of information. The topics mentioned and briefly described here will outline the traits that most strongly influence a child's progress in mathematics.

Ways in Which Individuals Differ

Intelligence. Students vary considerably in the degree to which they can profit from instruction, learn, and solve problems. Some learn difficult material quickly; some learn easy material slowly. Essentially, these are the differences which are measured by "intelligence" or "mental ability" tests. While these tests are not perfect measures of intelligence, it is true that intelligence test scores are closely related to scholastic achievement, they are closely related to our observations of childrens' capacity to learn, and they are quite constant over a span of years.

Motivation. Motivation is the student's willingness and intention to exert himself to learn in the learning situation. Almost no learning takes place if the student lacks this exertion and intention, that is, if the student lacks motivation. Other factors being equal, a well-motivated student learns more than a poorly motivated student. Human beings *become* motivated when they experience success, recognition, and satisfaction. To increase the motivation of students, set tasks at which they can succeed and goals they can attain. When they succeed, recognize their accomplishments.

Preparation. Mathematical preparation for learning a topic is extremely important. By preparation we mean the possession of mathematical knowledge and skills that are prerequisite to the topic to be studied. One can hardly learn to di-

vide effectively without understanding subtraction and multiplication. Preparation, the knowledge of prerequisites, is one of the most individual, distinctive things about a student. As a student progresses through three, four, or five years of school, he or she learns some things, misses some topics almost completely, and probably learns some misinformation. The pattern of learned, nonlearned, and mislearned material is almost certainly unique for each student. Because of this, some of your teaching will be, in fact, must be completely individual.

Maturation. The "maturing" of the students, which presumably produces some changes simply because they grow older, is a factor that must be considered in working with children. Children in kindergarten and the primary grades are passing through stages, or levels, in their mental processing of information, and these stages certainly influence the kind of instruction that will be provided and the children's response to it. In the junior high or middle school years students experience the changes associated with adolescence. Some of these changes, while not directly related to mathematics, affect the students' social and emotional behavior and certainly influence their response to all school situations.

Behavioral factors. A student who is a slower learner does not necessarily cause discipline problems. A student whose behavior is disruptive, however, usually spends less time actually working than a student whose behavior is acceptable. In fact, this is almost the definition of acceptable classroom behavior: Good behavior is working on the task assigned; bad behavior is doing something else. Teachers must recognize that a student with behavior problems will not do as well in mathematics as he or she is capable of doing. Finding and correcting the cause of the behavior problem, or simply trying to promote more acceptable classroom behavior, are essential steps in helping the student do good work in mathematics.

Mathematical achievement. The factors discussed here account for differences among students. They help explain why some students learn more than others and why students learn at differing rates. Teachers and lay persons alike often say students may be "ahead" or "behind," they may be "fast," "average," or "slow." They may be "high" or "low" achievers. These terms suggest real differences in students' *achievement* and present *rate of learning*.

We will use these and other terms in this chapter to describe differences that exist among students. We mean no slur on a student when we say the student is "slow." We mean only that the student's rate of learning is not as fast as that of some other students. The constant adoption of new euphemisms does nothing to soften the reality of student differences and so we use fairly direct language in this chapter.

Individualized Rates and Modes of Learning

Because children are so unlike in their native capacity, willingness to work, and past mathematical learnings, they need mathematics programs suited to their individual requirements. We can vary the *rate* at which a student moves through a set of material—fast, average, or slow. Most attempts to individualize

instruction allow only for varying rates of progress.

We may also look beyond rate of learning, to the style, or *mode of learning,* and to the stage of mathematical development of the student. Look at it this way: Almost any student in first grade can comprehend and solve this problem: "Put these twelve bottle caps in piles so there are three in each pile. How many piles do you get?" This problem is essentially a division problem, $12 \div 3$. It is really fictional to talk of a fifth grader who "can't divide." All fifth graders (except the profoundly retarded) can solve the bottle-cap problem. It does make sense, however, to talk about a student's stage of learning in division. Does the student need to use concrete materials, or does he or she work abstractly? Does he or she understand the relation between multiplication and division? Does the student see the use of subtraction in doing division? What form of algorithm does the student use to solve problems? Selecting the proper style of teaching and mode of learning for a student is as important as varying the rate of progress, perhaps more so. We will look further at both these factors as this chapter progresses.

Discussion Questions

1. There is considerable discussion about whether the traits which make students different are changeable or unchangeable. Which of the factors discussed in this section do you regard as changeable? unchangeable?

2. If we conclude that students are quite different in their natural gifts, will that make a difference in our responsibility for educating these students?

3. Suppose a "slow" sixth-grade student is working hard and achieving the goals we set for him or her. What grade should we give the student? Why?

4. Suppose a "fast" student is loafing along but, through high ability, still scores at the top of the class. What grade should this student receive? Why? We will return to the question of assigning grades to students. This is a persistent problem for teachers, school systems, and parents.

2. GROUPING STUDENTS

Teachers have devised many techniques to individualize instruction. Some of these techniques require cooperation among teachers, but most are ideas you can use in your own class. You should try each of these techniques; using a wide variety of techniques will help you improve your teaching and will stimulate learning.

Because of the great differences among students in any grade level and the increasing differences as children grow older, admission to school by birthdate and grouping by age seem to be inefficient. Some problems in the first grade could certainly be reduced if students were admitted to school on the basis of social and intellectual readiness. Grouping by age, however, does keep children in groups in which they share common levels of social development and interest. A child in the sixth grade may need to learn some topics that were taught in the second grade, but to place the child in the second grade or to give him or her a second-grade book is clearly a mistake.

For many reasons, society has evolved a basic grouping pattern in which children who are assigned to a teacher tend to be all about the same age but are vastly different in scholastic performance. The difficulty of dealing with this range of scholastic performance is reflected in the variety of different systems which have evolved for grouping. "Ability grouping," "achievement grouping," "homogeneous grouping," "tracking," "streaming," "individual progress," "nongraded," "ungraded," and on and on—all attempts to arrange students in appropriate instructional programs.

Homogeneous Grouping Is a Fiction.

Sometimes a school divides a population of children among teachers so that the children are supposedly equal or nearly equal in achievement or in ability. This is referred to as "homogeneous grouping." At best, homogeneous grouping somewhat narrows the range of differences with which a teacher needs to deal. But, it is not perfect. No division of students is perfect; all groups have a wide range of differences. We have never met a teacher who was satisfied that the division of students "homogeneously" produced a class that could be taught as one group. It can't and it won't.

Currently, there is considerable objection to any scheme that tracks, or streams, groups of children on the basis of assumed measures of ability. Such systems tend to be quite inflexible. Once placed in the low track, it is often difficult for a student to move up, even though he or she may be found capable of doing better work.

To meet the need to group students for instruction while avoiding the injustice of schemes in which a student is more or less permanently grouped, a variety of systems have been devised for placing learners together on the basis of current performance and achievement. These systems are successful in creating reasonable groupings of students and in responding to changes in student performance. By providing for *frequent* review of progress, they allow greater flexibility in moving students from one group to another.

Grouping Within a Classroom

Just as primary-grade teachers normally group for reading instruction, teachers should group for instruction in mathematics. The class may be divided into two or three groups. Each group will progress at an appropriate pace. Because the groups are moving at different speeds through the material they are to cover, *they will be at different places in the program and doing different things.* If this is not the case, there is no point in having groups in the first place. For example, some groups of children will need more opportunities than others to explore and to manipulate objects before dealing with abstractions.

When the class is divided into groups, the teacher will need to spend some time with each group each day. Typically, the teacher will teach one group and leave the children with an assignment to do, and go on to the next group. As one might imagine, this requires more physical and mental effort than is needed to teach the entire class as a unit. More planning and organizing is required, more variety in concrete materials must be provided, and more "shifting of mental gears" will be needed to deal with groups of slower, faster, and average learners.

In such a program, students are easily moved from one group to another. When a student begins to perform differently from the other students in his or her group, the teacher, knowing the place and activities of all the groups, can decide whether or not to move the student. If the child is to be moved, the teacher will know what extra help will be needed. Establishing mathematics groups within the class is highly desirable. It provides for a fairly close match between a student's current achievement and progress and that of other students in the group. It provides easy access to placement in a different group. Most important, the teacher has a more personal knowledge of the student and can make more accurate judgments about proper placement.

Because of these advantages, grouping within a class is recommended *even though* the class may be grouped as part of a school-wide grouping system. As has been pointed out, any system of grouping will still result in classes in which the range of achievement is great. Grouping within a class is one way to individualize instruction to meet this range of achievement.

Flexible Grouping within a School

The advantages of grouping within a class can be increased if several teachers cooperate to form groups of children from all their classes. In some cases, all the children in the primary or intermediate unit may be divided into groups, and each group assigned to a teacher. If these assignments are permanent, however, all the problems associated with tracking will arise. Even though the groups formed were fairly compact in terms of achievement, the students will soon spread out to produce a much wider range of achievement, and the permanency of the placement will work an injustice on many students. Hence, the grouping of students should be flexible. The progress and group placement of a student should be reconsidered at frequent intervals—possibly every two or three weeks. If you have a student at the top (or bottom) of one group, you may want to move that student up (or down) to the next group. If you have frequent contact with the teacher handling the other group, it will be easier to determine how the student can adjust to the new group.

The commitment of teachers to such a system is essential because of the additional time required. Teachers must meet frequently to discuss the progress of groups and individuals and to plan for moves. They must decide how a student is to be helped to bridge the intellectual and social gaps when the student moves upward. In spite of the difficulties, when teachers become convinced that they want such a system and work together to plan and operate it, these arrangements work out satisfactorily and to the advantage of the students.

Completely Individualized Instruction

A number of programs are now available in which a student progresses on a completely individual basis. There are also some teachers who have evolved their own completely individualized styles for teaching mathematics. In one way these programs are ideal. Each student makes progress at his own pace, unaffected by the progress, or lack of progress, of other learners.

In other ways these programs are far from ideal. In completely individualized programs children frequently miss the discussion and interaction that characterize the best teaching and that enhance learning. Children are forced to work in isolation, making much or little progress as the case may be, but not talking about the mathematics they are learning. Achievement in mathematics is measured by the number of pages, booklets, or sheets completed and not by the quality of the student's thinking. The designers of these programs certainly did not intend for this to happen. This unfortunate result arises from other circumstances. One of these circumstances is the role of the teacher in the operation of an individualized program. The teacher is caught up in the demands of two very time-consuming roles: tutor and evaluator. Because all instruction is individual and because each child is usually at a different place, the teacher must teach the new material, diagnose errors, and provide appropriate assistance to the child individually. The teacher must move from child to child as help is needed, spending a few moments with each one. This takes more of the teacher's time, with the result that each child gets less instructional time than he or she would in a regular class. The teacher's function as evaluator and grader also requires a substantial block of time in each class period because students' work must be carefully checked to determine the next assignment.

There is another inherent danger connected with the teacher's role as evaluator. Children can obtain "correct" answers without understanding the mathematics of the problem. They can copy or get manipulative tricks from other children (or from aides or even teachers!).

They often figure out elaborate patterns that have no relation at all to the mathematical ideas, for getting correct answers. In some programs the answers are available. It the teacher does not probe childrens' thinking during development and accepts correct answers at face value, there is no way to gauge the student's understanding or to eliminate the "counterfeit" procedures.

A sensitive reader may detect some bias on the authors' part regarding this type of program. The picture of a teacher moving from child to child and spending only a few superficial minutes with each is far from our picture of ideal teaching.

Discussion Questions

1. What form of grouping was used in the elementary school you attended? How did it work? What were the social divisions between groups?

2. Compare the "high" and "low" groups in a fifth-grade mathematics class. What grades should be given to students in the high group? in the low group?

3. A teacher who maintains three groups of students within a fifth-grade mathematics class works substantially harder than a teacher who teaches the entire class at once. What should we expect of a teacher? In what way should extra effort be rewarded?

3. TEACHING TECHNIQUES FOR INDIVIDUALIZATION

Having discussed the grouping of students, what do we do with students when we get them grouped? What other techniques of individualization can we use

with classes and groups? Here are the important considerations in dealing with instruction of students in groups.

Encourage Multi-level Performance

In many mathematical topics individualization can be based on *how* an operation is performed. All students may be doing addition with regrouping, but they may be performing the operation, say, adding $125 + 37$, in a variety of ways. All of the students in your class may do the problem but some will use concrete, some semiconcrete, and some abstract methods. In this instance, grouping of students is not necessary for individual work; assignments can be presented to the whole class.

When this addition problem is presented, the variety of materials shown on page 136 may be made available for the students. The students must, of course, know how to use these aids to illustrate and solve the problem. When you *first* use them, you will have to show the students how. Those students who cannot yet work the problem abstractly will set up the problem in concrete or semiconcrete form and will use aids to work the problem. There are several advantages here—the child may experience success more easily, is learning more about the place value system, and will ultimately be able to work abstractly in the system. The child is working in a meaningful way with the mathematics rather than learning mechanical rules for the manipulation of numerals. Children do not need much encouragement to work a problem at the abstract level; it is easier and faster than using manipulatives. Consequently, children will progress from the more concrete to the more abstract (from top to bottom in the figure) as soon as they are able. They have the option, however, when understanding of the abstract fails, of going back to manipulatives to support their work.

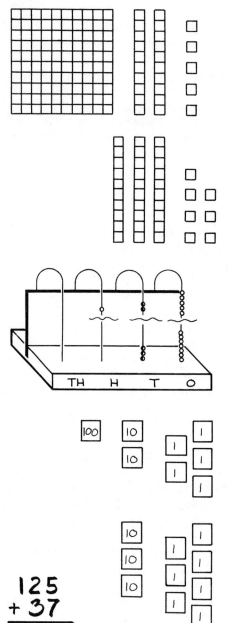

Almost any topic in the elementary school arithmetic curriculum has this characteristic: It can be developed from experiences with concrete materials, and the meanings of the abstract ideas are derived from these experiences. This means that the multi-level assignment, in which students have the option of working in a concrete, semiconcrete, or abstract mode, can be used with many topics. Some topics are also presented so that there is a gradual increase in the efficiency of an algorithm and a corresponding increase in abstractness.

Division is a good example of the way in which children progress from grade three to grade six through a gradual refinement of the algorithm. There is no reason why all children must be at the same level of refinement in division and use the same algorithm at the same time. In a class or in a large group studying division, some children may be using counting objects while others are working abstractly with one of the several algorithms available. Such a procedure would seem to be the highest expression of individualization, accounting not only for a learner's rate but also for his or her mode of learning and stage of development. It is also the most demanding on the talents of the teacher.

"Horizontal" Enrichment

If you visualize the mathematics curriculum as an arrangement of topics into strands that extend from grade to grade, two basic kinds of enrichment are possible: horizontal and vertical. Horizontal enrichment adds new or expanded topics at essentially the same level of difficulty. Vertical enrichment moves the student to topics at a higher grade level.

If you group your students, the "fast" group can be expected to make progress beyond that required to complete the work of the grade. You will have to decide: Do I give them enrichment in the form of extra topics to study, or do I let them go on to the next book?

In planning for horizontal enrichment you will need a variety of mathematical topics and activities. If you have more than average mathematics background, you may be able to guide and teach without outside assistance. More likely you will use some references to help you plan for interesting topics. As in many other instances, your textbook and teacher's edition are the the the most readily available source of ideas. Almost all textbooks now contain sections in each chapter that expand on material in the chapter. These sections, called "Extras for Experts" or "Try Something Harder," are an excellent source of ideas for horizontal enrichment. They are keyed to the topics in the text, often presenting the same idea from a different point of view or showing a different way to work a problem. See the enrichment topic on the next page. These sections are easy to use and fit in well with the regular program. Your faster group should do all of these items if you plan to use horizontal rather than vertical enrichment. In addition, the faster students should do all of the geometry, measurement, probability, and other items which teachers sometimes skip.

Beyond your textbook, there are a variety of materials for horizontal enrichment. Here are some sources which you may be able to use:

1. The National Council of Teachers of Mathematics (NCTM) publishes several helpful items. Your school (or you) should subscribe to *The Arithmetic Teacher*. This journal contains many ideas for activities to enrich or supplement the mathematics curriculum. The NCTM also publishes a yearbook series. Of interest to you will be the Twenty-seventh Yearbook, *Enrichment Mathematics for the Grades*. You may secure information on these items and other useful publications by writing to NCTM, 1906 Association Drive, Reston, Virginia, 22091.

2. The publishers of most textbook series have a complete line of enrichment problems, laboratory materials, and supplements. The publisher's representative would be glad to show these items to you.

3. There are two chapters in this book which in themselves contain some material you may use for enrichment. These are "Teaching for Problem-Solving Skill" and "Teaching Aids and Laboratory Activities."

4. The best suppliers of concrete materials have not only the materials list but supporting books, laboratory cards, and activity sets. For a list of these suppliers please see the chapter, "Teaching Aids and Laboratory Activities."

Thus armed with materials, topics, and suggested activities, you can develop a horizontally enriched program for your students. Under such a program, your fast group will complete the work of the grade they are in but will not do much work at the next grade level. Because they are a fast-moving group, they probably need fewer practice exercises to master an algorithm. The time saved will be used to present other topics at essentially the same level. This kind of enrichment is good. Its special value is that the extra topics introduced

Lattice multiplication   Multiply 436 by 25. Draw a lattice.

a. Make a 2 by 3 grid.

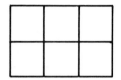

b. Draw diagonal segments.

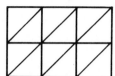

c. Place the factors.

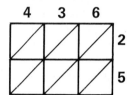

d. Multiply by 5.

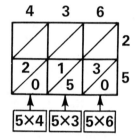

e. Multiply by 2.

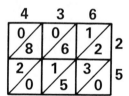

f. Add down each diagonal column.

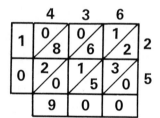

The product of 25 and 436 is 10,900.

For each exercise, draw a lattice and find the product.

1. 29 × 453   **2.** 98 × 612   **3.** 34 × 802   **4.** 19 × 356

5. 25 × 824   **6.** 91 × 375   **7.** 27 × 436   **8.** 35 × 439

can be selected to build interest and to develop a positive attitude toward mathematics. Topics of great interest and motivational value may be shared with all students. For all students, the time taken to build a positive attitude toward mathematics is time well spent! This sort of enrichment can be done by one teacher even where the school makes no provision for individualization. When you are reasonably certain that the school system will make no systematic provision for faster students, horizontal enrichment would certainly be best.

"Vertical" Enrichment

In contrast to horizontal enrichment, in which students stay essentially at their grade level, vertical enrichment allows students to progress through material in their own grade and then to begin work at the next grade level. Bright students who are permitted and encouraged to work at their own pace can make truly remarkable progress. It is not unusual for such students to complete two year's work in one year. This kind of progress is highly desirable as long as the proper provisions are made for the group. Here are some precautionary measures that should be taken to ensure an effective mathematics program for such students.

1. Progress should *not* be made by cutting out topics in the text. Some teachers look on geometry, measurement, probability, and even fractions in the primary years as "optional" topics. This is not true for faster students; these students should work all such topics.

2. Significant saving of time is possible by carefully deleting practice exercises. Faster students need fewer exercises

than are contained in the text to master a computation. A good deal of time can be saved by judicious deletion of unnecessary exercises. Be sure to include *some* practice exercises for skill development and maintenance. Just reduce the number of exercises assigned to the minimum number which will provide skill development.

3. It is essential that the subsequent material is available when needed. It serves no purpose to let a group work all the way through fourth-grade mathematics if the fifth-grade material is not available.

4. Many vertical enrichment programs fail to make a significant improvement in students' mathematical experiences because of a lack of coordination from grade to grade. If some fourth-grade students have worked ahead and are in the middle of fifth-grade work, the fifth-grade teacher must pick them up *at that point*. Otherwise, the work in Grade 5 will be repetitive and boring.

In comparing vertical and horizontal enrichment, we may conclude that horizontal enrichment makes more demands on the *teacher*. All of the necessary tasks—gathering material, studying new topics, and collecting references—take time and energy. Vertical enrichment makes more demands on the *system*. It does little good for a teacher to begin a program of vertical enrichment unless the materials needed are provided and the teachers of the next grade are willing to continue the program.

A final comment on "enrichment." All students can benefit from enrichment. The faster students have more time for it, but even the slower students will enjoy and profit from some extra, interesting work. Even though motivational activities will take some time from the regular program, it will be worth the time spent and will pay dividends in greater interest.

"Independent" Groups

Some teachers have designated their fastest group as an independent learning group. Independent groups work well from about Grade 4 up but not as well with younger children. An independent group of faster learners allows a teacher to spend more time with the less-gifted students. Independent learners can make far more use of the explanations in the textbook and should be charged with responsibility for helping each other. If you establish such a group, spend some time teaching them how to use the text as an independent learning aid. You may wish to use the chapter "Teaching Reading Skills and Using Textbooks" to help you do this. Students may use the teacher's edition as a source of answers and grade their own work when you feel they are ready for this responsibility.

Be prepared for bright students to make progress at a rapid rate! You will have to decide whether you want to enrich them vertically or horizontally and will have to provide appropriate materials. At times, a group of students in the upper elementary grades will "take off" on an advanced mathematical topic about which you may know little or nothing. Some children have an amazing grasp of mathematics. Don't panic; study along with the children and do your best. Call for help if you need it. It is usually possible to find a sympathetic supervisor or a high school mathematics teacher who will work with your group on an advanced topic.

Watch this group's work and progress to be sure they fully understand the topics they cover. Each day walk around the group and glance at their work. Question some students briefly about what they are doing. Teach this group once or twice a week to keep in tune with their progress. When you test, be sure to explore the deepest levels of understanding, as described in the chapter "Teaching for Understanding."

Using an independent learning group can be an eye-opening experience. When given responsibility for their own progress, many children respond with unexpected maturity and self-direction. Some of the techniques you learn while working with an independent group can be used with other groups to increase their self-direction, also. Try it; you'll like it!

Laboratories and Concrete Material

Although a later chapter discusses in some detail the use of laboratory activities and concrete material, we will now consider how these activities can aid you as you try to individualize instruction. The use of laboratory problem activities, *where appropriate,* will permit students to explore, develop, and apply topics with reduced teacher guidance, freeing you for more intensive work with other groups. Frequently, within the laboratory activity there are a variety of different jobs to do: measuring, counting, calculating, recording, or "just holding the other end of the measuring tape." As students work on these problems, you may encourage them to take on the most responsible job of which they are capable.

Whenever you use concrete materials to present a lesson or to develop a topic, you have an opportunity to individualize. There is a natural progression from more dependence on concrete material to more ability to deal with a topic abstractly. If you make the concrete materials available on an optional basis, children can individualize their own instruction by using the materials as they need to. In a way, some children have been doing this all along—they count on their fingers to find answers as long as they need to and ultimately give it up when they learn the facts.

Grading

No matter what program is used, there are basically only these choices in grading: One may grade students by comparing them to a "standard" for the class, by comparing them to others in the class, or by comparing them to an estimate of their potential achievement. When a program is individualized, comparison problems become even more complex. We cannot compare students to a grade-level standard because some may be working at other levels. We cannot compare them to others in the class because they may not be doing the same work.

There is no end to the dispute over how grades should be assigned, what they mean, for whom they are intended, and how they can be used and misused. Frankly, there is little a teacher can do about grading except to fit into whatever system is being used, no matter how poor the marking system is. It is better to have consistency in grading than to have each teacher grade differently. It is not remarkable that grading is a problem. We want that one little letter to report "progress," achievement, motivation, aptitude, and sometimes deportment.

The letter grade reports these things to the next teacher, the parent, the principal, the college, or a possible employer. What a marvelous letter it must be!

Let us look at some of the conflicts involved in grading by comparing a few students who have just completed fifth grade. Their teacher is trying to decide how to grade them. For convenience, their progress is expressed in grade-level equivalent scores.

1. Bob worked hard all year and moved from about 2.2 to perhaps 2.5 in grade level.

2. Carol worked hard and advanced from about 4.2 to about 5.8; she really bloomed this year.

3. Ted struggled from 4.8 to 5.6.

4. Alice did every bit of her assigned work and listened in class. She advanced from 5.3 to 6.9 during the year.

5. Ed never did any work at all, and he was on the 7.0 level at the beginning and at the end of the year.

Alice and Ed might get *A*'s because they are outstanding mathematics students—but is it right to give Ed an *A* for no work at all? On the other hand, his final test was the best in class. Even for no work and no progress, can we give him an *F?*

Carol and Ted are quite close in their final placement, but Carol gained about twice as much as Ted. Do they get the same grade?

Bob made little progress and has the lowest achievement but *he did his best*— can we really give him an *F* for his best work?

We would like to resolve these and other grading conflicts for you but we can't. Grading is a philosophical question, loaded with human values. It is not strictly an educational question. We cannot believe that a system that causes failure, anguish, and lowered self-esteem is a necessary one or the only one. Surely, human invention can triumph and invent a grading scheme that will reward Bob for his best efforts. Think about it!

Discussion Questions

1. Consider both horizontal and vertical enrichment strategies. Which would you prefer as a student? as a teacher? What are the advantages and the problems associated with both horizontal and vertical enrichment?

2. Do you think fifth-grade students can operate in an "independent group"? Why or why not? Would you be willing to try such an arrangement?

3. Reread the paragraphs on grading. Discuss the questions in those paragraphs. Assign grades to the five students described and defend your grades. What "philosophy" of grading did you employ?

4. USING HELPERS IN THE CLASSROOM

The number of classrooms in which more than one adult works with children has increased substantially in recent years. School systems are employing aides, parents are volunteering their time, and in some schools student teachers and interns are present in large numbers. This is an excellent trend; the more adults working in the classroom the better. However, it can create some problems. A teacher who went to school in classrooms having one teacher to 30 students and trained to teach under those circumstances may be dismayed by the variety of trained and untrained adults looking to him or her for direction. Managing the instructional program includes directing these adults; extra thought needs to be given to the task.

This is an opportunity to have far more effective individualization. It also means that you must be responsible for joint planning and *teaching these untrained adults how to teach.* If you just say, "Take that group and move them along," as too often happens, you are really saying, "All my training and experience are unnecessary; you can teach that group effectively without my help." It is your responsibility to do at least two things for these helpers: You must direct their teaching activities in detail at first through joint planning, and you must help them learn teaching skills. Following are some suggestions for each of the kinds of helpers you may have in the classroom. It is assumed that you will use these helpers to increase your individualization through putting these adults in contact with small groups of students.

Interns and Student Teachers

Interns and student teachers are an experienced teacher's most highly trained helpers. They come with recent experience in content and methods courses but lack classroom experience. Experienced teachers can learn from them the most recent thinking in elementary education. These students are looking for ways to apply what they have learned in college to the teaching situation. An experienced teacher can help them with suggestions based on his or her experience but must not try to turn each student teacher into a carbon copy of himself or herself. Because these students have the educational background to make a real contribution, teachers should involve them deeply in planning. Student teachers should have experience with a wide variety of tasks and a wide variety of children.

Paid Aides

Although they are not the most highly trained, paid teacher aides can be most consistent and dependable helpers. In many cases aides may have a high school education or less; on occasion one finds a college graduate or even a certified teacher employed as an aide. It is, quite frankly, not safe to turn over the mathematics instruction of a group to an aide without extensive preparation. The most prominent error made by aides and by parent volunteers, also, is to reduce a mathematical topic to a mechanical skill. For example, an aide may say, "Look, here is the easy way to do that, the way I learned it." This has devastating results on the continuity of meaningful development built into the program.

Teachers have the responsibility, in working with aides, to be sure the aide studies the program being used, understands the development, and can present it with meaning. This takes planning and time spent in making sure the aide understands the task. As you work with the aide to prepare him or her for taking on some teaching responsibilities, you may assign other instructional tasks, such as conducting drill and reinforcement activities, grading papers, supervising laboratory activities, or preparing instructional materials.

As a talented teacher, you are interested in the growth and progress of your aide as well as your children. If your aide shows that he or she could develop into a talented teacher, you will want to encourage him or her to take some academic work in college or junior college. Many aides have become excellent teachers through such encouragement.

Parent Volunteers

Parents and other volunteer aides, such as future teachers' groups, need training as much as do the paid aides. Usually, however, they are less available for training because they work only a limited number of hours. As with a paid aide, you will need to explore the capabilities and motivation of each of your volunteers. If a program involving volunteer parents is to make an effective contribution, two highly desirable features should be incorporated into the program. First, there should be some inservice training for the parents to prepare them, at least to some extent, for their task. A mathematics supervisor or a lead teacher, for example, should present a brief overview of the mathematics program and the ways that children have been taught to work problems and exercises. Second, there should be a parent in charge of the program. This parent can call and remind volunteers of their commitments, keep schedules, and coordinate teachers' requests for help. This is too big a job for a teacher to perform in addition to regular teaching duties.

Peer Teaching

Students are often remarkably effective in teaching other students *how to do* something. At times, teachers can use this to advantage by having better students teach those who are having difficulty. A word of caution is necessary, however. It is not always wise to assign some students extensive responsibility for teaching other students. Student tutors frequently review basics, but they themselves don't make progress or benefit from enrichment as they should. Furthermore, the students who are being tutored may receive only mechanical instruction in "how to do it," rather than a balanced program of meaningful instruction and drill. Use student tutors with close supervision and caution.

Discussion Questions

1. This section has been written mainly from the point of view of a teacher learning how to work effectively with other adults in the classroom. What do you think an aide, a student teacher, or an intern should expect from the teacher?

2. Some school systems have a regulation that "aides do not do developmental teaching." Under those circumstances how might you use an aide?

5. MATERIALS AND PROGRAMS

Systems for individualization are built into every series of textbooks and described in teachers' editions. Most publishers offer additional material to aid in individualizing. Some are management systems designed to keep track of pupil progress. Some are instructional materials to be used directly with students. In the last few years several "completely individualized" programs have been developed and are now being marketed. There are also a substantial number of teacher-planned and teacher-run systems of individualization in use.

Individualization takes time and effort on the part of the teacher even if a package program is purchased. No program can be effective without the cooperation of teachers and their willingness to make the effort to make the program work. Because of this, it is essential that teachers *believe in* the effectiveness of whatever system is used!

Individualization Within a Textbook Series

Textbook authors assume that a teacher will think about the program that will be most suitable for each student or group. When the teacher has made some decisions about appropriate programs, he or she will find a variety of helps in the text and in the teacher's edition.

The teacher's edition. Teachers' editions outline a planned program for groups of slower, average, and faster learners. The plan shown below, for example, reflects the fact that faster learners need less time and slower students more time to develop an understanding of basic concepts and related computational skills. The "minimum" course of study devotes more time to those skills and concepts considered essential for every student to master. The "maximum" course devotes less time to these essentials because faster students can master the skills in less time. The time saved is devoted to topics that go beyond the minimum essentials. The average class is between these extremes.

You will notice that in the minimum course for Chapter Six the students do not study all the concepts presented and

Concepts	Pages	Lessons	Class Periods per Course		
			Min.	Avg.	Max.
Reading and Writing Decimals	202-206	3	2	2	1
Decimals in Expanded Form	207	1	1	1	½
Decimals in Expanded Form, Using Exponents	208-209	1		1	½
Naming Equivalent Decimals	210	1	1	1	½
Decimals on the Number Line	211-212	1		1	½
Comparing Decimals	213	1	1	1	1
Adding and Subtracting with Decimals	214-222	8	7	6	5
Word Problems	223-224	1	1	1	1
Linear Metric Measurement	225-229	3	3	2	2
Word Problems	230	1	1	1	1

spend a total of 17 class periods on the chapter. The students in the maximum course cover more work in 13 class periods. The time thus saved may be used to provide enrichment or to move on to the next chapter. The students in the maximum course will probably cover the entire text, including the built-in enrichment activities. The general principle for planning these differentiated programs is that some students need more practice to attain mastery than do others. For those who need more time to attain mastery, some topics must be skipped; for those who need less time, enrichment activities are possible. This system provides the teacher with guidelines for different programs for three groups within a more-or-less normal class.

In addition to the suggested year's schedule, most teachers' editions contain chapter-by-chapter and lesson-by-lesson assistance in individualizing instruction. Chapter pretests can help you locate the topics on which some or all students will need extra emphasis and areas which some students can review rapidly and then go on. An analysis of the difficulties students may experience warns you about potential errors. Lists of minimum student requirements make clear what material a student must master before leaving the chapter. In many lessons you will find suggested materials for concrete approaches to the objectives. These suggestions can help you individualize the *mode* of learning, as discussed in Section 1.

The pupil's edition. There are always materials in the pupil's edition that assist in providing an appropriate program for each child. These items are planned with care and are designed for specific purposes. Some provide extra practice, while others provide for enrichment or challenge. If a teacher simply uses each page of the text with all students, he or she will *misuse* almost all of the items designed for individualization. Items are designed to be used with selected students, not with the whole class. The teacher must understand the authors' intent and assign these materials to students who need them.

Extra practice pages occur in almost every text series, grouped at the end of the text or at the end of each chapter. These pages concentrate on the most basic and important concepts and skills. As we have emphasized, the number of problems provided in the "regular" practice sets is generally ample. In fact, many students do not need to work *all* of the *regular* sets of exercises. Yet some students do need all the problems in the regular sets and more. When you have determined that a student needs additional practice on a particular skill, use these extra exercises. Do not assign all of these exercises to all students. For those students who have mastered the skill, these exercises can be a waste of time.

"Challenge problems," "extras for experts," and other similar phrases are used to designate material that extends the ideas in the text or that introduces a supplementary topic. This kind of material may appear within a set of exercises as "starred problems," at the end of a chapter, or in specially marked boxes on various pages. In one way, these are designed for the more capable student, and better students should try these enrichment exercises. At times, however, you will find material in these sections that is not quite so difficult but is more for fun and motivation. When you can, use these items to share the fun and excitement of mathematics with your less capable students. You and your students will more easily locate these and other items if you all learn the highlighting effects used in your textbook to designate more challenging problems.

Within your text series, pupils' and teachers' editions, you have a great many aids to assist you to individualize your teaching. Teachers' editions also describe materials that are available from the publisher of the textbook series but which must be purchased separately. Few teachers use the textbook as thoughtfully or effectively as they might. As we have said before, your textbook is the most readily available teaching aid and it should be used to best advantage!

Management Systems

There is a growing emphasis on individualization and on a careful accounting of students' progress. It seems a shame to have a student miss the development of an essential skill merely because he or she is absent for a week. Yet it happens. Management and accounting systems are designed to insure that in so far as possible all students acquire essential skills.

Most management systems are based on lists of performance or behavioral objectives or on check lists of skills. In some cases a system may simply list the skills (or objectives) the student is to master and provide a device for keeping track of which students have accomplished which objectives. In most cases the management systems are related to specific instructional materials. For example, a system may be based on a particular text series. In this case the objectives in the list would be consistent with the objectives in the text at all grade levels.

In some cases a management system is not related to any particular set of instructional materials. In this case the system presents an objective and keys that objective to the instructional material in each major text series. In that way the management system can be used with any textbook series or with a combination of several series.

In addition to lists of objectives, the management system will usually provide tests covering the objectives. These tests are to be used at the beginning and at the end of the school year or after a particular unit of work is completed. The purpose is to provide a continuous and up-to-date record of each child's progress and, cumulatively, of class and school progress. Management systems of this kind can provide valuable data if they are kept up to date and complete and are used to plan an appropriate program for each child.

A word of caution is in order here. When a student has been "checked off on a skill," the skill still needs periodic review and practice. All text series provide for this but some management systems do not. Even a well-taught and thoroughly learned skill will need review at the beginning of the year and periodically throughout the year.

Alternative Text Series

Some publishing companies now offer two text series in elementary mathematics, one for the average and above-average student and a second for the below-average student. There are advantages and disadvantages in using a second text series with below-average mathematics students. On the positive side, the alternative series will probably contain a more appropriate mixture of cognitive and social material. When it is necessary to review whole-number concepts at the sixth-grade level, the "social context" of the material—the examples, the pictures—should be of interest to a twelve-year-old, and not be the same as the material used for first and second graders. An alternative series also provides a slow learner with a different text, thereby eliminating embarrassment that can be created by having some students in Grade 6 using second-grade textbooks.

On the negative side, the alternative text series itself may identify those who use it as slow learners. The use of an alternative text makes it more difficult for a student to move with ease from group to group. Difficulty in changing texts may increase the tendency for students to become "locked in" to a group.

The use of an alternative text series *does not* eliminate the need for grouping within the classroom. No matter what book or what group of students, some will move ahead while others fall behind. To deal with this, alternative textbooks also contain a full range of aids to individualization. If the use of the alternative text series lulls teachers into believing they have no other responsibility for individualization, then the series has accomplished the opposite of its purpose. If the text is used with appropriate individualization in the classroom, as any text should be, then it may be of some advantage.

Completely Individualized Systems

There are a number of "systems" that are completely individualized in that each student works through the program at his or her own rate. Several of these systems have been published and may be bought by a school or a school system. In other instances, groups of teachers or curriculum specialists have devised their own systems. The steps in the process and the nature of the product seem to be very much the same for all of these programs.

First of all, the curriculum is analyzed and divided into topical strands. The strands are then subdivided into a sequence of topics. Specific, sometimes behavioral, objectives are written for each skill, generalization, and concept in the program. Understandably, there are a great many of these individual objectives. The objectives are placed in "levels" which, interestingly enough, do not usually correspond to grade levels. There may be eight or more "levels" covering the normal content of Grades K through 6.

A student beginning the program takes a placement test to assess his or her position in *each* of the strands. The student works through the strands, in most cases beginning with the strand in which he or she has made the least progress. At the start of each new topic the student takes a pretest; after studying the topic the student takes a posttest, which indicates what success has been achieved and what the next assignment should be.

Because students progress at their own individual pace and move from one topic to another in a potentially different order, the curriculum materials are produced in very small segments. Students work on only a single sheet or on one small, four-page booklet at a time. The work is usually graded immediately — sometimes by the student, sometimes by a teacher or an aide.

There are, of course, both positive and negative aspects of these completely individualized systems. No doubt, a dedicated and careful use of such a system can minimize the possibility that a student will miss a topic. These systems also increase the probability that each child will be working on mathematics topics that he or she has the background to master. Hence, students are likely to have successful experiences within the programs. Some evidence indicates that students in these programs will learn approximately as much as students in regular programs.

On the other hand, various observers have suggested that the quality of interaction between students and teacher is limited in these highly systematized programs. Because of the pressure of time on the teacher, critics also cite that the mechanics of the system tend to assume primary importance so that interaction with students suffers.

Robert B. Davis,[1] in a mimeographed paper, has identified several aspects of the programs that seem to lead students into difficulty. Working alone with paper

---

[1]Robert B. Davis, *Two Special Aspects of Math Labs and Individualization: Papert's Project and Piagetian Interviews.* (Urbana, Illinois: University of Illinois.) Unpublished, mimeographed.

and pencil is the principal way in which instruction is presented. The absence of physical materials (although some programs suggest their use) and the absence of discussion between teachers and students lead to somewhat mechanical learning of arithmetical procedures. Grading of answers by students or aides in terms only of "right" or "wrong" and the absence of probing or diagnosis of the depth of understanding can allow significant errors to remain undetected.

A recent analysis and summary[1] of the research relating to individualized programs suggests that these programs are no more effective, and in many cases are *less* effective, than traditional programs. They are expensive, require more effort from the teacher, tend to reduce the quality of pupil-teacher interaction, and require excessive time for testing. All in all, it would appear that in most situations such programs are not a good choice.

Discussion Questions

1. What are the advantages and the disadvantages of keeping all students together? of having each student work on his own? of having two or three flexible groups?

2. Read two articles from *The Arithmetic Teacher:* Harold L. Schoen, "Self-paced Mathematics Instruction: How Effective Has It Been?" *The Arithmetic Teacher,* Vol. 23, No. 2, Feb. 1976.
Joseph F. Lipson, "Hidden Strengths of Conventional Instruction." *The Arithmetic Teacher,* Vol. 23, No. 1, Jan. 1976. pp. 11–15

---

[1]Harold L. Schoen, "Self-paced Mathematics Instruction: How Effective Has It Been?" *The Arithmetic Teacher,* Vol. 23, No. 2. (Feb. 1976) pp. 90–96.

Be prepared to discuss the issues raised in these articles.

SUGGESTED ASSIGNMENTS AND PROJECTS

Classroom Assignments

1. Select teachers' editions from three different series or from three different grade levels of the same series. Read the authors' suggestions regarding individualization. In the corresponding pupils' texts, find examples of each of the aids provided to help you individualize instruction. Prepare a report for your class on the material in these textbooks; compare and evaluate the probable effectiveness of the material in each.

2. Select one textbook publisher and make a complete analysis of the material offered by that publisher for individualization. Attempt to get as much of the material as you can (possibly on loan from the publisher's representative) to display in class.

3. Locate one resource other than a textbook that will help you individualize instruction. Write a one- or two-paragraph description of this resource. Tell how it is used, how much it costs, and where it may be obtained. Make a copy of this for each member of the class.

4. You are teaching third grade. In a group of thirteen students you have three who know their addition and subtraction facts but who cannot do calculations involving regrouping; the other students can do regrouping. Describe how you would provide individualized instruction for the three. Explain when and how you will provide it; what material you will use; and what the other students will do.

5. Write a short paper identifying your three most serious concerns regarding individualization. Identify the problems and the ways you might try to solve them. Use this paper as a basis for class discussion.

Internship Assignments

1. Describe the ways in which you, or the teacher you are working with, now individualize instruction. How are your students grouped? What provision is made for changing a student from one group to another? What materials are used for individualization? Are students in your class working in different books? at different places in the same book?

2. Select one student in your class who needs help in mathematics and spend fifteen minutes per day alone with that student. Keep a written diary of your work with that student and include samples of his or her work. Try to understand how the student thinks about mathematics and why the student works as he or she does. Be prepared to report to the class on your goals and accomplishments with this one student.

3. Group your students into two or three groups for instruction on some mathematical topic. Plan and carry out the instruction with each group. Make use of the aids to individualization available in your text. Provide some enrichment activities for the faster students and some for all students. Provide diagnostic and remedial help for those who need it. Report to class on the material you used and the success of the unit.

4. Plan a topic in which you individualize by "mode of learning." This will involve (a) selecting a topic in which you can see a clear progression from concrete to abstract or through various stages of a process; (b) collecting the material needed; and (c) planning instruction so that students can make use of the material and progress through the process. As you teach the unit, observe the students' progress and their use of concrete materials. Be prepared to report to the class.

SUMMARY: MAXIMS FOR TEACHING

1. To be effective, grouping must be flexible. Students should be moved from one group to another as their current progress indicates. If teachers work together to operate such a system, they must meet regularly to discuss the progress and placement of groups and students.

2. Children are individual in the mode through which they learn and the rate at which they learn. Help children to learn through the mode which is most suitable to their present level of development: concrete, semiconcrete, abstract.

3. Extra topics may be included in a faster students' program without progressing to the work of the next grade (horizontal enrichment). A faster student may work ahead into topics normally covered in the following grade (vertical enrichment) if provision is made to continue his progress during the following year.

4. Teacher aides, student teachers, and others can be of great help in individualizing mathematics instruction. These people need the teacher's guidance and direction to work effectively in the classroom.

5. Study your textbook series, including the teacher's edition, pupil's edition, and extra material, to make optimum use of the aids to individualization that have been written into it.

7 · Teaching Aids and Laboratory Activities

COMPETENCIES

Knowledge Base

After studying this chapter, the teacher will be able to

1. state and explain the educational principles applicable to building meaning through concrete aids.

2. demonstrate the use of some common teaching aids.

3. describe the necessary conditions for operating a mathematics laboratory.

4. discuss his or her experiences in laboratory learning and relate them to present or future teaching.

Preparing for Instruction

Given an appropriate topic in elementary school mathematics, the teacher can

1. specify how some commercial teaching aid would be of value in presenting that topic.

2. construct a teaching aid which embodies some aspect of the topic.

3. select and/or design a laboratory activity that will contribute to the original learning of the topic or apply the topic to some realistic problem.

Instructional Skills

For a group of children the teacher can

1. select a topic appropriate for the children in light of their background.

2. state objectives for the topic and plan (a) lessons that make use of some concrete manipulative materials and (b) laboratory lessons.

3. carry out the planned lessons with the children.

4. evaluate the progress of the children on the topic and evaluate the success of the lessons.

INTRODUCTION

Using concrete materials in teaching and using laboratory techniques are closely related topics. When you use concrete materials in teaching, you are very close to a laboratory experience. Conversely, virtually all laboratory lessons require concrete materials.

Laboratory-activity teaching is one of many different techniques of teaching for understanding. It springs from the belief that most learning sequences should start with concrete materials and that a wide variety of concrete material is best; from the belief that active involvement of the learner in the learning activity results in the most effective learning; and from the belief that realistic applications are more interesting than textbook problems.

It is necessary to say, even as we advocate use of laboratory techniques of teaching, that use of the laboratory as the sole teaching technique is inadequate. When mathematics has been developed and a foundation of understanding has been laid, it is necessary to symbolize and organize the meaningful content, to draw out the connections between the present topic and former topics, to lay groundwork for future topics, and to provide practice for retention of learned material. Thus, in the task of teaching elementary mathematics, the laboratory can make a valuable contribution but it cannot do the whole job. You should balance enthusiasm for the laboratory approach with an appreciation for various methods of teaching, notably problem solving, directed practice, discovery, and other methods of teaching for understanding.

Some teachers have never themselves engaged in learning through laboratory experiences. If you have not, we recommend that you go first to Section 5, Experiencing Laboratory Learning, and work one or more of the laboratory problems in that section. Experiencing laboratory learning will help you appreciate how this method of teaching functions to promote learning.

1. USING TEACHING AIDS

In this section we will discuss and illustrate some general ideas about using concrete materials in the classroom. We will also give directions for using some commonly available items. The picture is one of a teacher working with a class or a small group, directing them as they manipulate materials, and questioning, discussing, and stating what they are to learn from this activity.

Building Meanings with Teaching Aids

For children, and for adults as well in many cases, thorough understanding of a topic is obtained by starting with concrete objects, using these objects to represent the concepts and operations to be learned. Gradually the children are able to increase the use of abstract operations in solving problems. They finally use only abstract operations to solve problems but, when they encounter a difficulty, they are able to go back to the concrete materials through which they first learned. Here we present some suggestions for effective use of concrete aids in teaching and learning.

Exploration and play. When you introduce a new teaching aid, let the children play with it for a time without direction. Children are fascinated with a new aid just as they are with a new toy. It is a lot easier to get them to engage in structured activities after they have become familiar with the materials. Furthermore, children can also learn a great deal through unstructured exploratory activities.

Relate teaching aids to the curriculum. Teaching in a school in which a variety of materials are available is certainly an advantage. The teacher, however, has the additional responsibility of coordinating the materials so that the mathematics program has coherence. If only a textbook is available, then the text *is* the program. If other materials are available, the teacher must decide who should use what, for how long, and for what purpose.

Take, for example, the introduction of subtraction facts for 6 through 10 in Grade 2. You will find in the text a variety of suggestions for work with concrete and semiconcrete materials. A few days before you are ready to begin the chapter, you might begin to explore subtraction, using rods or bars, counting objects, or other aids. The children should be shown how subtraction facts can be modeled in the concrete materials. Then as you introduce the chapter, explore subtraction facts for 6, 7, and so on. Make up your own activities as well as using the suggestions in the text. Finally, as the children begin working in a more abstract mode, leave the materials out on a "math corner" table. Children may take their problems to the math corner and use concrete materials to work out answers if they wish.

The teacher's edition of the textbook provides guidance in the appropriate use of concrete materials. It is unfortunate that many teachers use only the pupils' pages and do not utilize the other suggested activities. A first step to a well-coordinated program in which materials, activities, and textbook function effectively together is to use the suggestions in the teacher's edition.

Meanings through concrete materials. When you are ready to introduce mathematical symbols, equations, processes, or algorithms, you should try to make these meaningful by using concrete materials. Concrete materials and the operations we perform on them model, or "embody," the numbers and operations; that is, the materials show what the numbers "are" and how the operations "work." In the chapter "Teaching for Understanding" is a discussion of the use of concrete and semiconcrete materials to develop meanings. Most learning begins with experiences of this type. Without such experiences, abstractions may be difficult to understand.

In the same chapter is also a description of the "multiple embodiment principle." This principle says that you should use a variety of different concrete materials to illustrate a particular mathematical concept. Doing so will lead to more effective learning.

Explore various levels of abstraction in working with numbers. As you develop an operation or an algorithm, you will find available not one but several levels of abstraction. Different children will be able to function effectively on different levels. A child should always have the option of moving back to a more concrete level to solve a problem. Looking at the ways in which children deal with regrouping presents a striking progression from concrete to abstract thinking. On the next page you can see several stages in progression from completely concrete, in which a "ten" is an actual bundle of 10 ones, to abstract work with place value. Where you can see a progression of this sort from concrete to abstract, follow it, permitting the children to function on various levels of abstraction.

Using Some Common Teaching Aids

Using counting objects. Counters have many uses at the primary level. Described below are some typical activities in which counters are used. We assume that counters of various colors are available.

Ask a child to show a set of blue counters that matches a set of 1 to 10 red counters. Place sets of 3 red counters and 5 blue counters side by side. Ask the children which set has more counters or less counters. Repeat with other sets of

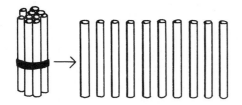

A BUNDLE OF 10 STICKS OPENED
TO PRODUCE 10 ONES

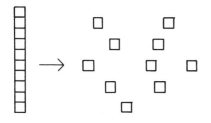

A CARDBOARD 10 TRADED
FOR 10 ONES

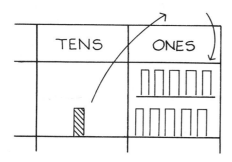

A 10 REMOVED
AND 10 ONES INSERTED IN
A PLACE VALUE POCKET CHART

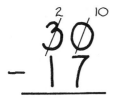

A 10 REGROUPED AS 10 ONES
IN THE TRADITIONAL ALGORITHM

counters. Have the children count sets of counters from 1 to 10 or more. The children may make color patterns with the counters. For example, start with 1 yellow, 1 blue, and 1 red. Then have the children reproduce and extend the pattern.

Allow the children to use the counters when solving an addition or subtraction sentence. Have the children use the counters to illustrate and compare 2 two-digit numbers. For one of them, show 37 as 3 groups of 10 counters each and 7 counters. Then have the children compare and decide which is more. Show the children how $6 + 7$, for example, can be renamed as $(6 + 4) + 3$. Place 6 red counters in your right hand and 7 red counters in your left hand. Then move four of the counters from your left to your right. The total is the same.

Multiplication may be introduced by showing 3 sets of 2 counters each. Ask the children how many counters there are in all. Division facts, such as $20 \div 4 = \square$, may also be shown with the counters. Group subsets of 4 counters each from a set of 20 counters. How many subsets are there? Show a set of counters. Have the children find $\frac{1}{4}$, $\frac{1}{3}$, $\frac{1}{6}$, or $\frac{1}{2}$ of the counters.

Using the number line. The number line is one of the most useful devices in teaching mathematics. It can be used at all levels of instruction from kindergarten to graduate school. While most children will not use counting objects much after third or fourth grade, they will continue to use the number line as long as they study mathematics. The number lines below indicate some of the various kinds of numbers that can be graphically illustrated on the number line. In the elementary school we are mainly concerned with whole numbers, fractions, and decimals. It appears possible that decimals and negative numbers will be increasingly prominent in the elementary curriculum of the future.

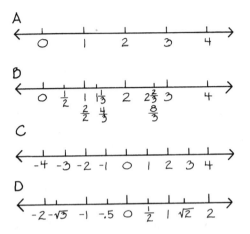

A number line can be made on the floor by using masking tape and cards for the numbers. Floor number lines may also be purchased. These are, of course, for the primary grades. With a floor number line children can investigate cardinal and ordinal number concepts, reinforce their reading of numerals, and solve addition and subtraction problems. The size of such a number line invites exploration and encourages its use in various games.

Here are some activities using a floor number line. Have each child step along the floor number line as the rest of the class count the steps. The child starts on 0. The first step is 1, the second step is 2, and so on. Have a child stand on 0 and toss a bean bag to a selected numeral. She or he then walks to that numeral by stepping on each numeral, counts the steps, and picks up the bean bag. Ask several children to stand on 7, 4, 12, 1, and 5 to help them recognize those numerals. Allow the children to trace the

numerals with their fingers. Have one child stand on 5 and another on 8. Cut lengths of heavy yarn 5 units and 8 units long. Compare the lengths of yarn and relate the lengths to the ideas that 8 is greater than 5 and 5 is less than 8.

Number lines on the floor may be used to solve addition and subtraction sentences. For $3 + 4 = \square$, the child stands on 0, walks to 3, takes 4 more steps, and tells the sum, 7. Allow two or more children to experiment with the number line and solve sentences such as $5 + \square = 8$, and $9 - \square = 4$.

Children may also use number lines drawn on paper or on the chalkboard to represent numbers and operations. Number line A, above, shows how the whole numbers are represented. The spaces between the numerals should be equal. Number line B shows how various fractions may be represented. This provides an embodiment of equivalent fractions. To take a simple example, we can show that $\frac{1}{2}$ and $\frac{2}{4}$ are equal because they are the same point on the number line. The number line shows that $\frac{4}{4} = \frac{2}{2} = 1$. Decimal fractions can also be represented on the number line.

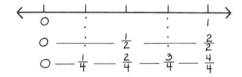

The number line can be used to illustrate addition and subtraction problems involving whole numbers and fractions. When you work with fractions, care must be taken that the denominators are not too large; it is very difficult to draw 36th's on the number line! Starting at 0, addition is represented as a sequence of moves to the right on the number line, and subtraction is shown as a move to the right followed by a move to the left. The strategy can be used to represent addition or subtraction of whole numbers, fractions, and decimals.

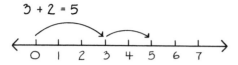

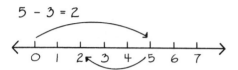

Using rods and bars. Various rod and bar devices are useful aids in teaching many mathematical topics because they come in lengths that are multiples of the shortest bar. By calling the shortest bar the "one-bar," the other bars become the "two-bar," "three-bar," and so on, up to the "ten-bar." When these relationships are established, the bars can be used by the children to solve problems and investigate number relationships.

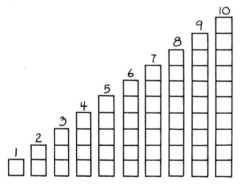

When you introduce the bars, provide ample time and opportunity for the children to explore their potential uses. At first the children should be encouraged to explore and make discoveries on their own with a minimum of direction. It is desirable to go through exploratory activities first, at all grade levels, since familiarity with the bars is helpful before more structured problems are attempted. After the children have had adequate free play, you should then direct the use of the bars in specific ways.

First, make a pattern for the children to reproduce or extend. Then have them create their own patterns, make squares or rectangular designs and enclosures, cubes, staircases, or other designs. Use a sorting box or a table. Have the children sort by color, naming the colors. What do they notice about all the bars that are the same color? Mix the bars and have the children sort them by length. What can they say about all the bars that are the same length? The children should use the words *long, longer, longest, short, shorter, shortest,* and *the same length* to describe and compare the bars. Sorting the bars while wearing a blindfold is an activity which many children will enjoy.

By Grade 1 the children should name the bars by their number names rather than by colors. The children should refer to them as the one-bar, the two-bar, and so on. The bars can now be used for problem solving.

Have the children build a staircase with the bars by starting with the shortest bar and placing the next shortest bar alongside. As they count the steps, have them name the bars. The first step is the one-bar, the second step is the two-bar, the third step is the three-bar, and so on.

Select any bar and make a line of one-bars as long as the selected bar. The number of one-bars is the number of the selected bar. Repeat with other bars.

Place a seven-bar and a two-bar side by side. The children should recognize that $7 > 2$ and $2 < 7$.

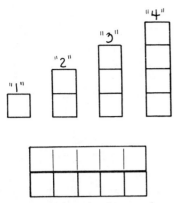

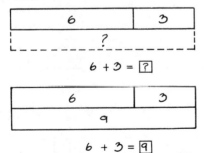

The longest bar is the ten-bar. Any number larger than 10 is represented as one or more ten-bars plus a bar less than 10. Our decimal system is based on this fact and can be visualized with the bars. To show 16, for example, use 1 ten-bar and 1 six-bar. The children may also use 1 ten-bar and 6 one-bars.

Addition and subtraction. The children can solve addition and subtraction facts with the bars.

If you are introducing the fact $3 + 6 =$ □, for example, the children get a three-bar and a six-bar and place them end to end. Then they find a bar, the nine-bar, that is equivalent to that length. Addition with three or more addends can be solved in the same manner.

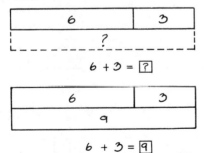

The children can also solve missing addend examples, such as $5 + □ = 8$, with the bars. Have them place the five-bar on top of the eight-bar. Then have

them find a bar to place next to the five-bar so that both are equivalent in length to the eight-bar. In this case they would choose the three-bar.

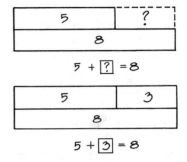

Families of facts can be shown with the bars. To show the facts for 7, first choose a seven-bar. Below it, place combinations of bars that have lengths equivalent to the seven-bar. Encourage the children to verbalize or write the facts they show. For example, $7 + 0 = 7$, $6 + 1 = 7$, $5 + 2 = 7$, $2 + 2 + 3 = 7$.

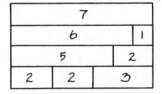

To solve subtraction problems, such as $9 - 5 = □$, use a procedure similar to solving missing addend examples. Place the five-bar on top of the nine-bar. Only the four-bar, when placed as shown, forms a length equivalent to that of the nine-bar, and solves the sentence.

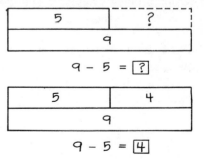

When the children can demonstrate the addition and subtraction facts for 0 to 10, allow them to work exercises for the sums and differences for 11 to 18. The bars can be used to show how the addition facts for 11 to 18 can be renamed as tens and ones. Place an eight-bar and a nine-bar end to end. Their sum, 17, is equivalent in length to a ten-bar and a seven-bar.

Multiplication and division. To show the multiplication fact $3 \times 4 = \square$, choose 3 four-bars. Place these end to end. The product may be found by placing ten-bars and one-bars below the set until an equivalent length is formed. On paper or on the chalkboard, write the number of bars, 3, the number of units in each bar, 4, and the total number of units, 12, as $3 \times 4 = 12$.

4	4	4
10		2

$$3 \times 4 = \square$$
$$10 + 2 = 12$$

To help children find the quotient for $15 \div 5 = \square$, place a ten-bar and a five-bar end to end. Then ask, "How many five-bars can be placed on top of those bars to form an equivalent length?"

5	5	5
10		5

Division problems having remainders can be nicely illustrated using bars. The problem $27 \div 4$ can be set up and solved as follows. First, 27 is 2 ten-bars and 1

seven-bar. Then we ask, "How many four-bars would it take to make 27?" We see that we can line up 6 four-bars along 27. The seventh would go beyond. So there are 6 fours in 27 and 3 ones left over. Thus, we have a visual representation of each part of the division shown here.

$$4\overline{)27} \quad \begin{array}{c} 6\ R3 \end{array}$$

Fractions. Bars can be used to teach fraction concepts and addition and subtraction of fractions. Representations of various fractions can be formed by using different bars as the "unit," or "one." We will take an example using sixths and follow the same example through this procedure. Although this takes only a few paragraphs here, it represents a span of three or four years in the elementary mathematics curriculum.

If we select the six-bar to represent "one," fractions as small as sixths can be illustrated. A bar can be found that represents one half. We recognize it because it takes 2 of these bars to equal "one." Similarly, we can represent one third and one sixth with the bars. Looking at the bars grouped in the diagram, it becomes visually obvious that $\frac{1}{2} = \frac{3}{6}$, $\frac{1}{3} = \frac{2}{6}$, $\frac{1}{2} = \frac{1}{3} + \frac{1}{6}$, and, of course, $1 = \frac{2}{2} = \frac{3}{3} = \frac{6}{6}$. We have observed students,

ONE					
$\frac{1}{2}$			$\frac{1}{2}$		
$\frac{1}{3}$		$\frac{1}{3}$		$\frac{1}{3}$	
$\frac{1}{6}$	$\frac{1}{6}$	$\frac{1}{6}$	$\frac{1}{6}$	$\frac{1}{6}$	$\frac{1}{6}$

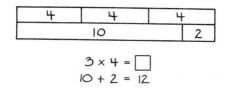

4	4	4	4	4	4	1	1	1
10			10			7		

27 = 6 FOURS AND 3 ONES

27 ÷ 4 = 6 R 3

quite slow students as a matter of fact, look at this kind of display and observe, "One half is the same as one-and-one-half thirds, isn't it?" This would certainly cause most adults to stop and think, "Is it?"

When we wish to add, say, $\frac{1}{3} + \frac{1}{3}$ or $\frac{1}{6} + \frac{2}{6}$, we can use this representation with no difficulty: $\frac{1}{3} + \frac{1}{3} = \frac{2}{3}$ and $\frac{1}{6} + \frac{2}{6} = \frac{3}{6}$. We can also find another, simpler way to write the answer to $\frac{1}{6} + \frac{2}{6}$. The answer is $\frac{1}{2}$ as well as $\frac{3}{6}$, $\frac{1}{2}$ being "simpler" because it uses smaller numbers in numerator and denominator.

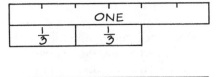

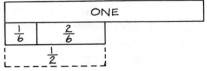

When we add $\frac{1}{2} + \frac{1}{3}$, we find a problem that we have not encountered before. We can't use either halves or thirds to express the sum. To solve this problem, we may line up various bars until we find a length that works, and we will find the answer is $\frac{5}{6}$. We may also go back to the original diagram, in which we studied the relations between 1, $\frac{1}{2}$, $\frac{1}{3}$, and $\frac{1}{6}$. There we search for some way to express $\frac{1}{2}$ and $\frac{1}{3}$ as fractions we know we can add, that is, fractions with the same denominator.

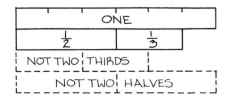

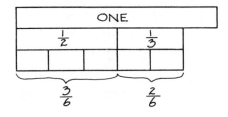

We find that sixths will work because $\frac{1}{2} = \frac{3}{6}$ and $\frac{1}{3} = \frac{2}{6}$. This leads us to a symbolic translation of the problem—to one that we know we can solve.

$$\tfrac{1}{2} + \tfrac{1}{3} = \square$$

$$\tfrac{3}{6} + \tfrac{2}{6} = \square$$

We also have introduced a common denominator concept as an aid to adding (and subtracting) fractions. A great deal of developmental teaching needs to be done to develop the procedure for finding any common denominator. However, a start has been made, and we can see in this overview how fraction concepts and fraction operations can be firmly rooted in concrete materials.

More techniques for the use of rods or bars in teaching particular topics can be obtained from the manuals for those materials. In other chapters in this book, particularly those on teaching whole numbers and fractions, there are more specific instructions for using these aids.

Using Place Value Materials

Place value materials provide a concrete representation of our base ten system and also of systems in other bases. Materials for this purpose include place value cards, multibase arithmetic blocks, the abacus, and place value pocket charts. Commercial sources are listed at the end of the chapter, and many of these items can be made by teachers or pupils.

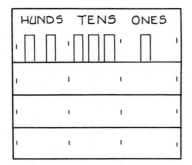

PLACE VALUE POCKET CHART
SHOWING 231

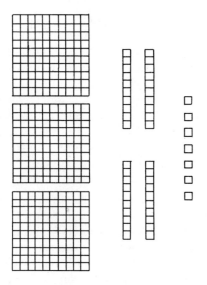

PLACE VALUE CARDS
SHOWING 347

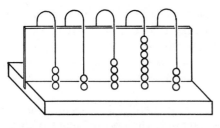

BEAD ABACUS SHOWING 32,473

Number concept development. The concept of numbers through hundreds or thousands, or even higher, can be developed by using place value materials. A student may be asked to represent a given number or to state a number represented by a collection of material. The figure shows numbers represented by various kinds of place value materials.

Counting can be done with place value materials. This helps students understand the orderly progressions of 1, 2, 3, . . ., 10, 20, 30, . . ., 100, 200, 300, . . ., and so forth. It also gives an appreciation of the size of 1,000 or 10,000 compared to 1. Each time the children count a number, they move a one. When they get to a multiple of ten, 10, 20, 30, and so on, they move a one, pick up the 10 ones, and replace them with 1 ten. When they get to a hundred, they pick up the 10 tens and replace them with 1 hundred. These steps may be done with any of the items shown in the diagram.

Use the materials to compare 2 two-digit numerals or 2 three-digit numerals. For example, represent 37 and 73, or represent 201 and 199. In each case, have the children tell which is the greater and the lesser of the two numbers.

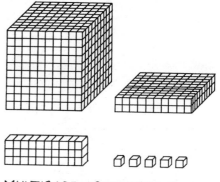

MULTIBASE ARITHMETIC BLOCKS
SHOWING 1,235

Renaming. Have children practice renaming by exchanges of materials, such as 1 ten for 10 ones or 1 hundred for 10 tens. If 241 is represented, the 2 hundreds, 4 tens, and 1 one may be renamed as 1 hundred, 14 tens, and 1 one.

Addition and subtraction. The operations of addition and subtraction and the regrouping which is sometimes necessary can be illustrated by using these types of material. A complete explanation is included in the chapter on whole numbers.

Fractional Parts of Shapes

A "tried and true" device for teaching fraction concepts is the use of fractional parts of various geometric shapes. These are pictured in textbooks, are easily made from cardboard or construction paper, and can be drawn on the chalkboard. A quick sketch on the chalkboard or a paper-cutting activity may contribute immeasurably to students' understanding by relating abstractions to familiar relationships between objects. We may use these diagrams, or objects cut out in a similar fashion, to teach fraction concepts. If an object is divided in half, do the halves need to be the same shape? (No, they may be different shapes.)

These objects may also be used to illustrate relationships between fractions, as shown below.

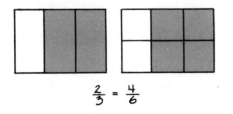

$$\frac{2}{3} = \frac{4}{6}$$

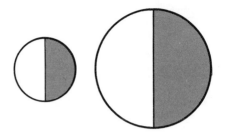

Are the halves of different objects all alike? Of course not, as we can clearly see when we compare half a small pizza to half a large pizza. When we talk about fractions, we have, stated or understood, some unit or "one." All fractional parts are taken to be parts of that unit. If we change the unit or if we use fractional parts of different units, then the parts are not comparable.

Diagrams and cut-outs are useful for illustrations of operations. As an example, we will use a problem in subtraction with regrouping. The problem illustrated on the next page will help to clarify regrouping and the operation itself. If the textbook contains such diagrams, you may refer to them and explain how they relate to the steps in the symbolic operation. If such illustrations do not appear in the textbook, you may draw them on the chalkboard. Students will also benefit from having a collection of circles, halves of circles, and fourths of circles and actually performing these manipulations while they work the problems. Again, they are using objects to give meaning to the manipulation of symbols.

Discussion Questions

1. Can you tell, from your own experience, why exploration and "play" are a necessary step in using a new aid?

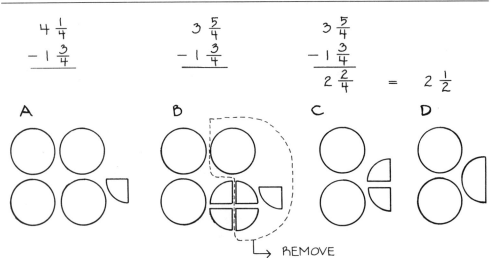

$$4\frac{1}{4}$$
$$-1\frac{3}{4}$$

$$3\frac{5}{4}$$
$$-1\frac{3}{4}$$

$$3\frac{5}{4}$$
$$-1\frac{3}{4}$$
$$2\frac{2}{4} = 2\frac{1}{2}$$

A   B   C   D

↳ REMOVE

2. Think of examples of exercises that can be worked at different levels of abstraction. Could you have the whole class "doing division," even though some students are working concretely and others abstractly? Tell how.

3. Do you yourself learn best through concrete or abstract experience? Can you remember your third- or fourth-grade mathematics program? Did you have much concrete work? How would you improve on your own elementary school mathematics experience?

2. A MATHEMATICS LABORATORY

Mathematics is an abstract subject. Of all the subjects that children encounter in school, it is the most abstract and the most symbolic. The statement "2 + 3 = 5," for example, is not about *anything* in the same way a statement in social science might be about government. In another way, the statement "2 + 3 = 5" is about *everything* because combining any set of two things with any set of three other things will produce a set of five. Because mathematics is an abstract sub-

ject, we seem to experience swings of opinion from the position that "mathematics should be taught as a beautiful abstract system, worthy of study in its own right" to the position that "mathematics should be taught through and for its applications." Both of these positions are correct. It is, however, the second position that stimulates the development of mathematics laboratories.

Laboratory Experiences and the Mathematics Curriculum

Laboratory lessons have two basic uses. First, the laboratory is a place where children have experiences that help them learn mathematics. Most often these experiences involve concrete or semiconcrete materials and real physical situations. The children use these materials and learn some mathematics they did not previously know. Second, the laboratory provides situations in which children use the mathematics they already know to solve real or realistic problems. They learn, from these laboratory experiences, how to apply the mathematics they know.

While these two functions seem to be distinct, in practice they are not always separated. Students may learn some mathematics and see its applications in the same laboratory experience; or they may learn some new mathematics while attempting to solve a problem. However, it is a good idea for you to know whether you are planning a laboratory lesson mainly for teaching new mathematics or for applying previously learned mathematics. As we will see, this will make some difference in the way you structure the lesson.

Even though many textbook series, several "individual progress" programs, and a number of local and state curriculum guides are in use, the topics covered and the grade placement of the topics do not vary widely from one program to another. The laboratory learning experiences should be planned *in relation to* that general curriculum. This does not mean that laboratory programs must slavishly follow the text or that no new topics should be introduced. It does mean that each laboratory learning experience should be planned and conducted so that it makes a contribution to the curriculum. A laboratory problem related to some topic in the curriculum may be scheduled to introduce the topic, to help develop the topic, or to summarize it. A problem for which the students need certain prerequisite learnings should be scheduled after students have had those topics. In any case, it seems ill-advised to have mathematics laboratory experiences without considering the purposes they are to serve and the contributions they will make to the students' overall mathematical development.

Remember, there are many kinds of topics and many kinds of objectives in the elementary mathematics curriculum.

No one instructional method will serve to teach them all. Select those topics and those objectives that can best be taught through laboratory techniques and use laboratories for those. Do not try to teach all topics through laboratory lessons!

Laboratory lessons can be used to provide individualization in the mathematics program. There are two sorts of individualization, "vertical" and "horizontal." In vertical individualization, children move "up" to higher grade levels or stay on grade level or move "down" to lower grade levels. In horizontal individualization, children who are more capable will explore other topics not normally included in the program; they will learn more topics and learn them to a greater depth rather than advance faster. For the able students, laboratory problems can provide exposure to topics they would not ordinarily learn at any stage in the curriculum. For the less able students, the mathematics laboratory offers an opportunity to increase their understanding of the mathematics of the regular program or to review some topic missed earlier. That can be done in a small group setting through work with concrete materials.

Laboratory problems can be used for all students to preview topics which will be taught later in a more formal way. This will create a good background of understandings and will facilitate later learning of the topics. Mathematics is used not only in mathematical study and physical science but also in a wide range of occupations in social science, business, and education. Laboratory problems prepare students to understand how mathematics is applied to problems in various fields. Thus, for all students, laboratory problems prepare the way for new areas of mathematics and illustrate the nature of mathematical applications.

Many topics can be treated at several levels of difficulty. When working on subtraction with regrouping in fifth grade, for example, some children may be working with place value cards or an abacus to solve the easier problems in the text. These students are catching up on concrete background which they should have acquired in the second and third grades. Other students may be working the problems in the text by using the standard regrouping algorithm, as they are expected to do at that grade level. More able students, who have mastered the subtraction algorithm, may be working with materials for base four or base five. These students are extending their knowledge of subtraction and their understanding of place value. Here we see a single topic, subtraction with regrouping, treated in three different ways for children of different ability. In this case, horizontal individualization is made possible by laboratory activities.

Objectives and Evaluation

In other chapters we have gone into detail on stating objectives and evaluating cognitive outcomes of instruction. Laboratory activities have the general objectives of understanding and problem-solving skill. When you plan a laboratory lesson, you should have in mind the objectives you want the children to achieve. As the lesson progresses and at the conclusion of the lesson, you should determine whether they have been achieved. You can do this in a formal way by having a test on the laboratory lesson. You may also assess informally: As you walk around the classroom su-

pervising the laboratory activities, ask questions of the students to determine whether they know what they are doing and why they are doing it. Have they grasped the point of the lesson? Can they carry through the laboratory activities? Can they draw conclusions from what they have done? Can they solve the problem posed in the laboratory? Can they solve a related problem? If you can continually inquire in this way, you will get a good sense of the success of the laboratory lesson.

There are other objectives of laboratory lessons, which are just as important as the cognitive objectives: motivation and attitude, problem-solving persistence, independence from the teacher, and group cooperation.

Motivation and attitude are difficult to measure but teachers believe, probably correctly, that they can "get the feel" of the children's attitudes toward school or toward a particular subject. Do the children like laboratory activities? Do they enjoy the freedom that comes with laboratory work? Do they use that freedom to direct their own work or to play around? Motivation is another aspect of attitude. Teachers can assess children's motivation, that is, desire to work, by watching their behavior. Do they keep working on the problem? Do they ask for other laboratory problems? Has their interest in mathematics in general increased?

Persistence in problem solving is the willingness of a child to keep working on a problem, even though he or she does not seem to be getting a solution. An interesting phenomenon is often observed when a difficult problem is presented in an upper elementary class. The bright children, because they are accustomed to getting answers immediately, sometimes give up when a solution is not easy to obtain. Children who are accustomed to *working* on a problem will keep working on it, even though frustrated. Laboratory problems (some of them) should be hard enough to cause difficulty. Children should be encouraged to stay with a hard problem, organize their resources, and fight it through to a solution.

Independence from teacher direction is also a highly desirable outcome of laboratory work. You will find that most children, when first exposed to a laboratory lesson, are somewhat at a loss as to what to do. Children see school as a place where you follow directions; thinking for yourself only gets you into trouble. Questions such as, "How are we supposed to do this?" often come up in response to a laboratory problem. The answer, "That is part of the problem, so try to figure it out for yourself," is a shock to children who are accustomed to highly directive teaching. Encourage children to become independent thinkers and self-starters in laboratory problem work.

Group cooperation and division of a task into parts or assignments can be encouraged by having laboratory problems that require different people to do different things. When children are measuring, for example, there is the job of measuring and there is the job of recording the measurements. Group cooperative effort can make the task easy.

If you watch four children build a hut in the woods, you will see all the elements of good laboratory learning. There is a problem, and a variety of material, appropriate and inappropriate, is available. You will see motivation and interest and a positive attitude toward the task. Persistence in solving the problem in the face of many obstacles is obvious.

Independence from adult direction is important; an adult may only spoil it. Group cooperation is assured. Laboratory learning should be as natural and enjoyable as the projects children invent and undertake for themselves.

Starting a Mathematics Laboratory

Most teachers, even teachers who would like to use laboratory activities, never begin to use the laboratory method. Some teachers start to use laboratory techniques without adequate preparation and, consequently, fail where they could easily have succeeded. Here we want to give some practical suggestions for starting laboratory activities in such a way that they will be not only successful but also orderly and under control.

Prepare the students. Many students, particularly in the upper grades, are accustomed to teaching in which the main activity is to sit still and follow directions. In laboratory activities students move around the room and have a great deal of responsibility for planning and directing their own activities. Like all student behavior, self-direction in planning purposeful activity is *learned,* and it is not learned all at once. Prepare the students for laboratory activities by explaining to them that more self-direction will be required. However, you may expect that when students first experience this degree of unaccustomed freedom, there will be some inattention to the task, some noise, and some playing around. Don't expect more dedication to tasks from children than we normally expect from adults! Try to work persistently but good naturedly to increase the skill of your students in self-direction. After all, that is one of our main objectives in education, regardless of the teaching method we are using!

It is a truism that good teaching will prevent many discipline problems. It is also true in using laboratory activities. The more interesting and challenging your activities, the more your students will concentrate on the task and work hard and persistently (though not necessarily quietly) on the activity.

Students are also prepared for laboratory activities by a gradual introduction to such work. If your students are not accustomed to laboratory work, you will probably want to introduce it gradually. You can try these ideas: Start with one small group doing a laboratory problem, while the rest of the class docs seat work. In time, everybody should get a turn to do laboratory work. A different procedure is to start with the entire class doing the same problem, while you give specific directions as to how it is to be done. Start with a limited time for laboratory work. If you start with a 30-minute laboratory period each week, the students can graudally get used to the new format. Start with "structured" laboratory problems in which the directions for work are clear and specific. Then you can move toward more exploratory problems as you and the students are ready for them.

Prepare the materials. When you have used laboratory techniques for a time, you will find that almost every object in your room, the room itself, and the people in it can be "materials" for mathematics laboratory experiences. At first, though, to increase your enjoyment and your confidence in using laboratory activities, you should collect beforehand all of the materials you will need for a particular problem and have them ready and organized before you begin. When you are done, you should box the materials used in that laboratory problem so they can be used again conveniently.

Prepare the room. The room arrangement may need to be different for the laboratory activity. If you are planning to begin with a small group working on a laboratory problem, you may find it desirable to block off a corner of the room, using a bookshelf or screen. This will create a "lab corner," with a different feeling from the rest of the room. It will also prevent the laboratory students and the others from bothering each other. If all students are doing a laboratory activity, you may want to create clusters of four to six desks in the corners of the room.

Prepare the activity. As you have prepared the students, the materials, and the room, you will want to prepare the activity itself with great care. In your first laboratory activities, there should be considerable guidance in the activities: very clear, specific directions, definite things to do, and a very clear "conclusion" to the activity, when the problem has been solved. As you and the students become more familiar with laboratory work, you can introduce open-ended exploratory activities. When the activity is concluded, or when the time for laboratory activities is over, tell the children to put the room back in its regular arrangement. This signals a clear end to that activity and saves you from having to put the room in order. Plan enough time so that the children can finish the activity. It is frustrating and disappointing to have to leave a task just when you can see you are "getting it." Also, be prepared to fill some time with an alternate activity in case the children do the laboratory problem much faster than you expected.

Advance preparation for your first few laboratory sessions is essential. Of course, some advance preparation is *always* needed for laboratory work. However, if you are extra careful with your first few laboratory sessions, you will have better results both for the students and for yourself. Many teachers, when the use of laboratory activities is suggested, say, "I tried that and the kids just ran wild." All we can tell from that statement is that the teachers expected results without careful preparation. *Begin gradually and plan with care and you will have successful laboratory activities.*

Running a Mathematics Laboratory

When you have started using laboratory lessons and found them to be a practical and effective technique, you may want to use the technique frequently. There are some practical problems in using laboratory lessons. Therefore, we suggest here how to keep your laboratory in operation.

Laboratory problems. Where do you get a collection of laboratory problems that will supply one good lab a week for a year? Let us begin with sources close at hand: This chapter has a section of sample laboratory problems (Section 3), complete with notes for you on how the laboratory might be expected to proceed. In other sections of this chapter you will find activities described as examples of some particular technique.

You may use all of these. The suggestions in the teacher's edition of your textbook are a good source of ideas for using concrete materials. These suggestions often make good group laboratory activities. Enrichment materials in your textbook can very often be used as laboratory problems. At the end of this chapter, in the section Suppliers of Teaching Aids, is a list of suppliers where you can obtain laboratory problems, laboratory kits, and sets of laboratory exercises. It is suggested that you write for several catalogs in order to get a good idea of the kinds of materials available.

In all of this, we have neglected two sources: you and your students. Think up a laboratory lesson on some topic and try it out. If it works well, keep it! If not, discard it. In that way you can build a file of workable laboratory problems of your own design. Your students can sometimes ask the best questions: "I wonder how tall that tree is?" "Are boys, or girls, taller in the fifth grade?" "How fast are those cars going past the school?" Any good question can turn into a laboratory lesson!

Materials. There are two problems with the concrete materials needed for laboratory lessons: getting them and storing them once you have them. A successful mathematics laboratory can be run on the materials found around school and things children can bring in. A somewhat wider range of materials is available if a little time is spent in construction of the things to be used. The materials of construction are mainly things found in school. See Section 4 for a wide variety of teaching aids and laboratory materials which teachers and students can make.

It is not impossible, however, to get some money for materials. The first rule is to know what you want, where it can be obtained, and how much it will cost. The only way to know those things is to have catalogs available. A catalog makes it easy for the principal to place the order! Write for some catalogs listed at the end of this chapter. Always know what your "first choice" item is and be ready to ask for it. Know when money for teaching aids is most likely to be available. Is it in the spring or some other time of the year? Be ready with your list and your catalog.

Now that you have something, where do you keep it? Mostly, on shelves and in boxes. The boxes that mimeograph paper comes in are good for storage of larger items. Smaller items can be put in shoe boxes. If you do not have shelves, make a stack of cartons or crates. Mark on each box what it contains. The teacher who has a big closet or a big storage cabinet has it easy; the rest of us have to improvise.

Room arrangements. Your room arrangement will depend on the furniture you have available. Tables are best for laboratory work. If you are going to do small-group laboratories, you may use a table and chairs in the back of the room. Try to create a laboratory corner by separating the table from the rest of the room. If you can do that with a book shelf or cabinet, it will also help solve your storage problem. If the whole class is to do laboratory work at one time, you may group desks in circles or move the desks out of the way and work on the floor.

In some schools there is enough interest in laboratory teaching to designate a room as a mathematics laboratory. If your school has a vacant classroom which can be used in this way and if

there are enough teachers interested in it, you are fortunate. In such situations materials and good laboratory problems can be shared. It is even possible to team with a colleague. If one teacher would *rather* teach laboratory lessons in mathematics and another would *rather* teach something else, they can switch for laboratory lessons.

Discussion Questions

1. Students in a mathematics laboratory setting must be largely self-directed. What problems do you foresee? How can you prevent problems from arising?

2. Laboratory lessons require extensive preparation. Evaluate the preparation and the possible benefits. Is it worthwhile?

3. In your elementary school education, did you have experiences in laboratory learning? How well organized were they? how effective? Are you inclined to try laboratory teaching? under what circumstances?

4. Do you believe that learning to be self-directed is a major goal of education? Is it more important for students to follow directions or to think for themselves? How does this relate to consideration of laboratory learning?

3. SAMPLE LABORATORY PROBLEMS

These problems are provided for you to use in getting started on a mathematics laboratory. Not enough problems are provided at any grade level for you to use them as your whole laboratory program. But the problems will at least get you started. The grade levels indicated on the problems are approximate. You should scan through the problems and pick those you think your students can do and might enjoy. The equipment needs are minimal and include only things you can collect, or buy in local stores.

Laboratory Problem No. 1. Grades 1–2

Teacher: "Let's make a chart to tell visitors when our birthdays are. How can we do that?" (For children in the lower grades the teacher will usually introduce laboratory work verbally. For upper-grade children "Lab cards" can be used to present these problems.)

"How many birthdays are in each month? Let's write that number above the names." "Which month has the most birthdays in it?" "Which month has the least?"

This activity is interesting to children because it is about themselves. Children enjoy showing the chart to visitors. The activity provides for discussion of how to make charts in general. Many numerical questions can be asked about the graph, and the idea of reading a graph to obtain information can be introduced. Other graphs and tables to show the same information can be constructed. For children in higher grades a wide variety of similar graphs may be made.

Laboratory Problem No. 2. Grades 1–6

Problem: Find out how many _____

For upper-grade children a "Lab card" format may be used to introduce each laboratory problem.
Materials: Common measuring instruments.

Notes for Teachers
Prerequisite knowledge: Ability to count; ability to compute proportions; for some problems a knowledge of area or volume formulas may be helpful.

Well, you ask, how many *what?* A good question—the only limit is your imagination. Here are some suggestions: How many bricks in our building? How many panes of glass in our building? How many squares of sidewalk in a mile? How many erasers (shoe boxes, basketballs, ping pong balls, you name it) would fit in our classroom? How many drops in a bucket? What difference does a "drop in a bucket" make? How many beans in a jar? How many grains of sand in a quart of sand? As you can see, there

1	2	1	4								
			CAROL								
			TED								
	FRED		BOB								
SAM	MARY	JOAN	ALICE								
JAN	FEB	MAR	APR	MAY	JUNE	JULY	AUG	SEPT	OCT	NOV	DEC

(THE CHILDREN WRITE THEIR NAMES ON SQUARES OF PAPER AND PASTE THEM ON THE CHART)

is no end of "how many" questions. Most such questions involve numbers too big to count and we will make use of approximations.

Let's look closely at "How many shoe boxes will fit in our classroom?" We could find this by calculating the volume of the room in cubic inches and the volume of a shoe box in cubic inches and dividing. We might also see how many times a shoe box would fit along the dimensions of the room. Then multiply these numbers together.

"How many grains of sand are in a quart of sand?" We might try to find out how many grains of sand are in a thimble first. Have fun with this one.

Laboratory Problem No. 3. Grades 4–8

Problem: To find a relationship between the numbers of vertices, regions, and segments in figures.

If you look at drawings that can be drawn with dots and lines on a sheet of paper, you will find something interesting. In such figures each dot is called a *vertex* (plural: *vertices*), the lines are called *segments,* and the areas (such as the shaded one) are called *regions.* The first drawing shown here has 5 vertices, 7 segments, and 3 regions. Figure 2 has the numbers of vertices, regions, and segments shown in the table.

Figure	Vertices	Regions	Segments
1	5	3	7
2	7	5	11
3			
4			
5			
6	5		6
7	6	3	
8		5	11

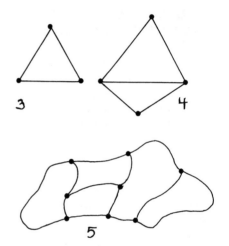

3   4

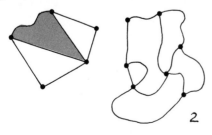

5

Fill in the numbers of vertices, regions, and segments for Figures 3, 4, and 5. Try to see a pattern in the table that will help you fill in the missing numbers in lines 6, 7, and 8. Try to draw figures having the numbers of vertices, segments, and regions given in lines 6, 7, and 8.

See if you can make a drawing which has 4 vertices, 2 regions, and 6 segments. Draw several figures having 4 vertices and 2 regions. What do you find in any drawing having 4 vertices and 2 regions?

Notes for Teachers

Work this laboratory exercise yourself before reading further.

The relation the students are asked to find is that the sum of the numbers of vertices and regions is one more than the number of segments. In an equation, v, r, and s are related in this way: $v + r = s + 1$. There are several other ways to express the relation, such as $v + r - 1 = s$. All are equivalent, however.

When the students have found this relation, they fill in the missing numbers in lines 6, 7, and 8 without actually having drawings to work with.

The last paragraph before Notes for Teachers asks for a figure having 4 vertices, 2 regions, and 6 segments. In that case, $v + r \neq s + 1$, so it is not possible to draw such a figure!

Laboratory Problem No. 4. Grades 4–7

Problem: Can you always find one missing part of two equivalent fractions? Or, How can you tell if two fractions stand for the same point on the number line?

Notes for Teachers

Prerequisite knowledge: Students should be able to multiply and divide whole numbers, to reduce fractions, and to generate some simple equivalent fractions, such as: $\frac{1}{2} = \frac{2}{4} = \frac{4}{8}$, $\frac{2}{3} = \frac{4}{6}$, and $\frac{2}{5} = \frac{4}{10} = \frac{6}{15}$.

Directions for students: Look at these fractions. $\frac{5}{10}, \frac{40}{50}, \frac{25}{30}, \frac{2}{8}, \frac{2}{4}, \frac{3}{9}, \frac{10}{5}$

How are they alike? _____
Can they all be reduced? _____
Let's reduce them. The first one is done for you.

$$\frac{5}{10} = \frac{1}{2} \qquad \frac{40}{50} = \square \qquad \frac{25}{30} = \square$$
$$\frac{2}{8} = \square \qquad \frac{2}{4} = \square \qquad \frac{3}{9} = \square \qquad \frac{10}{5} = \square$$

Now look back at each pair and draw a loop around it. Study each pair of equiv-

alent fractions. Look at them like this: ↗, then like this: ↘. Do you see anything that is always true? _____
Think *multiplication*. Try to multiply the top of one and the bottom of the other, like this: ↗ and ↘. Now do you see something? _____
What? _____

_____

It should be true that the products (we call them *cross products*) are always the same in each pair of equivalent fractions. Why do you think we call them cross products? _____
Now reduce $\frac{20}{30}$. $\frac{20}{30} = \frac{\square}{\square}$
Are the cross products the same? _____
Make up three fractions that can be reduced. Then reduce them and check the cross products. The cross products should be _____.
Now let's try some that look even easier. We will do part of the work for you. Here's one: $\frac{6}{8} = \frac{3}{\square}$. Here's another: $\frac{12}{18} = \frac{\square}{6}$. Can you find the missing parts? If so, put them where they belong. Check by cross multiplying.

Here are two harder ones: $\frac{24}{40} = \frac{3}{\square}$ and $\frac{20}{28} = \frac{\square}{7}$. You can do part of a cross multiplication on each one. For the $\frac{24}{40} = \frac{3}{\square}$, you can say $40 \times 3 = 120$. But what do you do with the 24? Hint: Try dividing the

$$120 \text{ by } 24. \text{ What do you get? } 24\overline{)120}^{\,5} \text{ Try}$$

the 5 in the fraction. Does it work? Does $\frac{24}{40} = \frac{3}{5}$? Check by _____ multiplying? Try this on $\frac{20}{28} = \frac{\square}{7}$. Cross multiply the 20 and 7 and then divide by the _____. Do you get 5? Check: Does $\frac{20}{28} = \frac{5}{7}$? Are the cross products equal? Remember this way of finding the missing number. We will use it again.

Now these: $\frac{4}{10} = \frac{\square}{5}$, $\frac{6}{14} = \frac{3}{\square}$, $\frac{10}{\square} = \frac{2}{3}$, $\frac{\square}{20} = \frac{3}{4}$, $\frac{6}{8} = \frac{30}{\square}$, $\frac{36}{72} = \frac{1}{\square}$.

One more question: Take the fractions $\frac{1}{2}$ and $\frac{3}{4}$. Check the cross products. Are they the same? _____

Why? _____

_____

Laboratory Problem No. 5. Grades 1–2

> Problem: Let's explore the geoboard!

Materials: Geoboards and rubber bands of assorted colors and sizes. Geoboards can be purchased or constructed. To construct a 5 × 5 (5-nail by 5-nail) geoboard, divide a square piece of $\frac{1}{2}''$ or $\frac{3}{4}''$ plywood into a grid of 25 smaller squares—each the same size (congruent). Drive a $1''$ to $1\frac{1}{4}''$ flathead nail securely into the center of each small square. Leave most of the nail exposed. Then erase or paint over any lines you drew to construct the squares. Your finished product should look like the geoboard shown below. You may also look at the "geoboard cards" described in Section 4. Of course, 6 × 6, 7 × 7, and 8 × 8 geoboards can also be constructed. You may also ditto pages containing square arrays of dots. The dots play the role of the nails, and children use pencil lines instead of rubber bands.

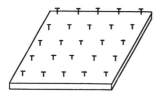

Prerequisite knowledge: Since the activities that follow can be used either to introduce certain geometric shapes or to reinforce previous learnings, no mathematical knowledge is required beyond the ability to count.

Notes for Teachers

Initially, children should be allowed to explore the geoboard on their own. They should be encouraged to make any shapes and designs they can by stretching rubber bands around the nails. At least one entire lab period can be used in this way. Children can compare their shapes and designs and try to copy one another's work. In addition to art designs, students can form some letters of the alphabet, numerals, figures, faces, and imaginary characters.

In another lab session children can practice forming and naming some of the standard geometric shapes: squares, rectangles, segments, and triangles. Be sure to construct triangles of different shapes—short and fat, tall and skinny, tiny, large, and right. Properties of these shapes can be discussed. One way to approach this activity is to give children models of triangles, rectangles, and squares, either drawings or shapes made of plastic or wood. Challenge them to make similar shapes with the rubber bands on their geoboards. Two or four children can push their geoboards together and then make even larger, taller, thinner, or fatter figures. Be sure to use the mathematical names of these figures in all conversations.

Another simple laboratory problem is to figure out how many nails are on the geoboard. Encourage the children to find three or four ways to convince you of the correct number by using the rubber bands. Ringing all the nails and counting is only one way. In the following figure two other ways are shown.

At this level geoboards are also useful in illustrating the concepts of open and closed curves, area, perimeter, and intersecting curves. Children do not have to compute areas or perimeters to deal with

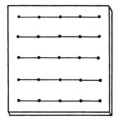 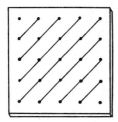

these concepts. They can estimate relations between the areas and perimeters of figures (Which is larger? smaller?), and then cut up paper shapes and use string lengths to compare the areas and perimeters of the figures.

Laboratory Problem No. 6. Grades 3–8

> Problem: Some neat things to do using a geoboard. Try them!

Notes for Teachers

Suggestions for making geoboards or using grid (dot) paper are given in Laboratory Problem No. 5 and in Section 4.

Prerequisite knowledge: If the following activities are going to be used to introduce various geometric concepts and generalizations, then the ability to count and a reasonable knowledge of the terms *area, perimeter, congruent triangle, rectangle, square,* and *perpendicular* are needed. If the activities are intended to have children apply their geometric knowledge concerning area, perimeter, diagonal, congruence, size, and shape, then knowledge of these concepts is necessary.

Activities for students

1. Ring the outside nails with one rubber band making a large square. Take another rubber band and divide your geoboard into *two* identical (congruent) shapes. One shape must be exactly the

same size and shape as the other. We have done three for you. Draw a picture of each pair of shapes you find. You should try for at least five more. Now try

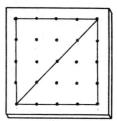

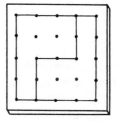 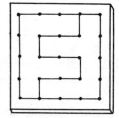

to make *four* congruent shapes on your geoboard. You will need to use another rubber band. We have done one for you. Make drawings of three more.

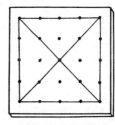

2. If you like one of the designs you have made in Exercise 1, you might try this: Using stiff paper, carefully cut out one shape exactly like any of the congruent shapes on your geoboard. Use this cut-out piece as a pattern. From it, trace about 16 more—just like your pattern. Color both sides of each piece any way you want. Now all of your pieces will fit together, like a puzzle. Make some fancy and colorful designs. Tape them together and show them off.

3. Play "Last one home" — an elimination game. Stretch a rubber band on the geoboard so that it does not cross itself. Make one end the goal *(G)*. Place three markers *(A, B, C)* on any three nails. Always stay on the rubber band and do not put two markers on the same nail.

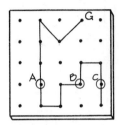

Each player in turn moves *any* one marker any number of nails toward the goal *(G)*. No backing up or staying put. When a marker reaches the goal, it is removed from the board. The player who moves the *last* marker to the goal wins. This is a good activity for two or three players. It requires a lot of thinking ahead.

4. Finding perimeters. On a separate piece of paper make a number line using the horizontal or vertical distance between any two nails as the unit. (Have the children do this.) Then give the children drawings of various shapes — squares, rectangles, triangles, even pentagons and hexagons — and ask them to create the shapes with rubber bands on their geoboards. Then, using lengths of string, have them find the perimeter of each shape, compare the string to the number line, and record their answers. In some cases, they will have approximate lengths that do not come out to be whole numbers.

Also, give the children specific lengths, either numbers or lengths of string, and have them construct various

shapes from the given lengths. Remember not all perimeter lengths can be made into every geometric figure on your geoboard. For example, you can't construct a square with a perimeter of 6 on your geoboard, or a rectangle with a perimeter of 11 or $15\frac{1}{2}$.

5. Finding areas. Show students a unit of area — the 1×1 square will probably be the best one to use on a geoboard.

ONE UNIT OF AREA,
ONE SQUARE UNIT

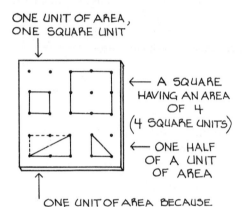

← A SQUARE HAVING AN AREA OF 4 (4 SQUARE UNITS)

← ONE HALF OF A UNIT OF AREA

ONE UNIT OF AREA BECAUSE IT IS ONE HALF OF A RECTANGLE HAVING TWO UNITS OF AREA

Find the area of these shapes:

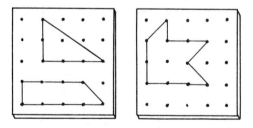

An interesting discovery concerning a relationship between the areas of rectangles having a fixed perimeter can be set up as follows:

a. Make as many rectangles as you can having a perimeter of 12 units (Larger geoboards, such as 6×6 or 8×8, or dittoed arrays of dots, work much better than the small, 5×5 geoboards.) Record the length and width of each rectangle.

b. Make as many rectangles as you can having a perimeter of 14 units. Record the lengths and widths.

c. Make as many rectangles as you can having a perimeter of 10 units. Record the lengths and widths.

d. Then find the areas of the rectangles and record them, as in the following chart:

Rectangles with perimeter 12 units	Area of each rectangle (sq. units)
1 by 5	5
2 by 4	8
3 by 3	9
Rectangles with perimeter 14 units	
1 by 6	6
2 by 5	10
3 by 4	12
Rectangles with perimeter 10 units	
1 by 4	4
2 by 3	6

e. Look at the numbers for the perimeters. Look across to the areas. Do you see a quick way to find the area? Try your idea on a few rectangles. See if it works.

f. Now look at all the rectangles having a perimeter of 12. Which one has the largest area? Look at all the rectangles having a perimeter of 14. Which one has the largest area? If the perimeter of a rectangle is always the same, when does the rectangle seem to have the largest area? Does your idea work when the perimeter is always 10?

Draw some rectangles having perimeters of 20 and 30. Does your idea still work?

Suppose you had 100 inches (or centimeters) of string. What would be the lengths of the sides of the rectangle having the largest area and a perimeter of 100?

How could you use your idea to fence in the largest area for a garden if you already had the wire for a fence?

Laboratory Problem No. 7. Grade 6

> Problem: Use a rule to find the thickness of a sheet of notebook paper. Check your answer with a micrometer if you have one.

Notes for Teachers

Prerequisite knowledge: Students will need to know how to count and measure accurately. Computation with decimals will come up, and the use of a micrometer may be learned during work on this problem.

Materials: Common measuring instruments, micrometer optional, and a stack of notebook paper.

This laboratory will give you the opportunity to generate a discussion of an "appropriate" measuring instrument. Of course, a ruler is not very appropriate for measuring the thickness of *one* sheet of paper.

Don't be quick to tell the children the solution to this problem. The solution is clever. How clever it is becomes apparent when you try for a while to solve the problem. You *can* measure the thickness of one sheet of paper if you make a stack of, say, 500 sheets, measure the thickness of the stack, and divide by 500.

If you can get a micrometer, you may check the accuracy of the "stack" method against the micrometer.

Laboratory Problem No. 8. Grade 6–8

Problem: How fast can_____

_____

_____

Notes for Teachers

Prerequisite knowledge: If students have worked Laboratory Problem No. 4, they have sufficient background to tackle this problem. If they have not, then the ability to compute with whole numbers and to find a missing term in a proportion will suffice. If you are teaching ratio and proportion, then this laboratory exercise is an application of that content.

In using proportions to find speed, a reference ratio is necessary. Guide students in forming any one of the ratios in the table below.

Your students will be able to use any of these. However, the ratios for 60 mph and 90 kph will probably be the easiest to remember and to use in computations.

Now, how fast can what? Again, the limit is one's imagination. Some suggestions: How fast can you run or walk? How fast can you throw a softball, football, ping pong ball? How fast is the creek flowing today? How fast can you ride your bike? How fast are the cars going past the school?

Students can use a stopwatch and a measured distance to gather data. Then ask, "If you run 200 feet in 10 seconds, how fast are you running in one second?" The answer is:

$$\frac{200 \text{ feet}}{10 \text{ seconds}} = 20 \text{ feet in 1 second}$$

The following proportion can then be set up:

$$\frac{88 \text{ feet per second}}{60 \text{ miles per hour}} = \frac{20 \text{ feet per second}}{\square \text{ miles per hour}}$$

$$\frac{88}{60} = \frac{20}{\square}$$

To find missing numbers in proportions, students need to multiply and then divide. In this case, $(60 \times 20) \div 88$.

$$\frac{10 \text{ miles}}{1 \text{ hour}} = \frac{10 \times 5280 \text{ feet}}{60 \times 60 \text{ seconds}} = \frac{14.7 \text{ feet}}{1 \text{ second}}$$

$$\frac{30 \text{ miles}}{1 \text{ hour}} = \frac{30 \times 5280 \text{ feet}}{60 \times 60 \text{ seconds}} = \frac{44 \text{ feet}}{1 \text{ second}}$$

$$\frac{60 \text{ miles}}{1 \text{ hour}} = \frac{60 \times 5280 \text{ feet}}{60 \times 60 \text{ seconds}} = \frac{88 \text{ feet}}{1 \text{ second}}$$

$$\frac{30 \text{ kilometers}}{1 \text{ hour}} = \frac{30 \times 1000 \times 100 \text{ centimeters}}{60 \times 60 \text{ seconds}} = \frac{833.3 \text{ centimeters}}{1 \text{ second}}$$

$$\frac{90 \text{ kilometers}}{1 \text{ hour}} = \frac{90 \times 1000 \times 100 \text{ centimeters}}{60 \times 60 \text{ seconds}} = \frac{2500 \text{ centimeters}}{1 \text{ second}}$$

$$\frac{30 \text{ kilometers}}{1 \text{ hour}} = \frac{30 \times 1000 \text{ meters}}{60 \times 60 \text{ seconds}} = \frac{8.3 \text{ meters}}{1 \text{ second}}$$

$$\frac{90 \text{ kilometers}}{1 \text{ hour}} = \frac{90 \times 1000 \text{ meters}}{60 \times 60 \text{ seconds}} = \frac{25 \text{ meters}}{1 \text{ second}}$$

Laboratory Problem No. 9. Grades 4–8

> Problem: Let's go on a scavenger hunt!

Materials: Various measuring instruments depending on the items in the hunt. You need rulers, string, yardsticks, mastersticks, scales to weigh pounds or grams, a stopwatch, compasses, and protractors.

Notes For Teachers

Prerequisite knowledge: Scavenger hunts are probably best used as practice in estimating and making direct measurement. More efficient practice will occur if children are familiar with the measuring instruments and use them to check their work.

Students can work individually or in small groups. Teams can compete in scavenger hunts by working at the same time. Scavenger hunts can also be one of several activities children choose to try.

Directions for students: Here is a list of hints about things in this room. Try to find at least one thing that fits each hint. Keep a list of your answers. All measurements are rounded off to the nearest unit.

Hint

1. My length is 25 cm.
2. My diagonal is 8 feet 4 inches.
3. My diameter is 30 cm.
4. My area is 64 square inches.
5. I weigh 2 pounds.
6. My radius is $\frac{1}{4}$ of a meter.
7. My perimeter is 14 feet 7 inches.
8. My circumference is 44 cm.
9. I'm hiding — I weigh 10 kg.
10. Betcha can't find me — my volume is close to 37,000 cubic cm.
11. I'm hard to find. I weigh 2.5 grams.
12. I'm twice as wide as your math book.

Answers, as well as the numbers used in the hints, will vary according to the objects you choose to use. Use the lengths, areas, perimeters, weights, etc. Use the doorway, desktops, items on the bulletin board, the waste basket, books, drawers, boxes, clocks, pencils, erasers, jars, animal cages – almost anything.

Children will enjoy creating scavenger hunts for others to work. A group of children from one classroom could visit another room and construct a scavenger hunt for other classes using the room.

4. AIDS MADE BY TEACHERS AND STUDENTS

Many items can be made by teachers or by teachers and students working together. Constructing a teaching aid is a laboratory activity itself, and frequently children benefit as much from making it as from using it. For this list, we selected items that can be made with material normally found in school.

Ones, Tens, and Hundreds

From stiff paper, about the weight of a file folder, cut squares $5'' \times 5''$. Then cut strips $5'' \times \frac{1}{2}''$ and small squares $\frac{1}{2}'' \times \frac{1}{2}''$. Draw lines as shown in the figure. Easier than that is to draw two of the "hundreds" on a ditto sheet (it will just fit) and run on "card stock." Then cut up several of the hundreds into tens and several of the tens into ones.

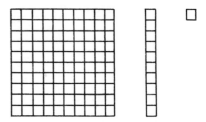

As a variation for upper grades, make ones, fives, and twenty-fives and use them to teach the base five system.

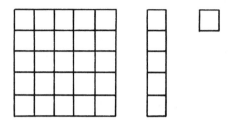

Place Value Pocket Chart

Begin with a file folder which is approximately $12'' \times 18''$, unfolded size, or another fairly stiff paper of that size. Use a ruler and a ball-point pen to draw the lines, as shown below. Press down HARD to dent the paper so it will be easier to fold. You may staple the folds down and also use staples to create pockets. There may be three pockets, as shown, or four pockets, from ones to thousands. Use this for work in place value and addition and subtraction with regrouping.

Use poster paper to make a ones-tens-hundreds chart, as shown below. This is arranged to look like the algorithm for adding and subtracting three-digit nu-

merals. Glue a styrofoam cup in each location marked "*." One is shown. Use to work addition and subtraction problems, particularly with regrouping.

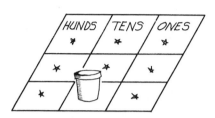

Counting Objects

Collect several hundred small objects to use for teaching number concepts, making sets, counting sets, comparing sets, and so forth. Objects which are small enough to swallow are too small. Beans and marbles are not recommended. Bottle caps are excellent.

Number Sticks

Using a paper knife and poster paper, cut out strips 1″ wide in lengths of 1″ to 10″. You may mark them off in 1″ sections or leave them blank or write a numeral indicating the length. Use these as you would rod or bar materials, de-

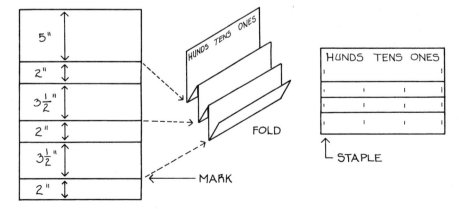

scribed in Section 1. Do not make sticks longer than 10″. To represent the number 13, use a 10 stick and a 3 stick. Use these for teaching number concepts, addition and subtraction facts, measurement, length comparison, *greater than, less than,* and a host of other concepts.

Number Cards

On small cards, about half the size of a 3 × 5 card, write 1, 10, 100, and so forth. Make cards to represent the numbers your group will be working with. You will need 20 of each kind of card to do addition and subtraction problems. Use these cards to represent numbers, as shown below. By adding or removing cards, illustrate addition and subtraction. Regrouping is done by trading cards; for example, 1 hundred-card for 10 ten-cards and vice versa.

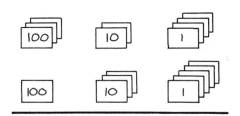

Giant Number Line

This teaching aid, almost a class project actually, is appropriate for upper-grade levels, particularly Grades 6, 7, and 8. Use a 20-foot- long piece of wrapping paper at least two feet wide. Begin the year by drawing on it the numbers you study first. As the year progresses and different sets of numbers are intro-

duced, these may be added to the number line. You may add common fractions, decimal fractions, negative numbers, and irrationals, such as square roots. Color coding may be used, and some children may wish to add historical information about the numbers. The number line may be kept on display or rolled up until something new comes up to add to it.

Fraction Pies

These are easy to make, and making them can be used as a laboratory lesson for the children. Using a compass, the children should draw some circles on construction paper, all the same size. Some of the circles are then marked and cut into fractional parts. Folding, measuring, and cutting out these parts can be a laboratory problem. How do you get fourths? Easy. Fold a half in half. How do you get thirds? Measure 120° because the whole circle is 360° and 360° ÷ 3 = 120°. For greater understanding, use these circles and fractional parts to illustrate computations with fractions.

Geoboard Cards

Use cardboard to make geoboard cards, such as the one shown below. The dots should be placed carefully in straight lines one inch apart. Laminate or cover with clear contact. You can use the card with a grease pencil or crayon to do the geoboard laboratory exercises in Section 3. An alternative way is to run the pattern of dots on a duplicating machine. Run the paper on both sides. Then, when one page of dots is used, it can be discarded.

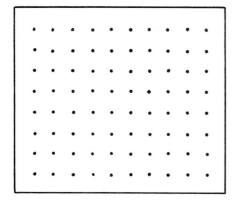

5. EXPERIENCING LABORATORY LEARNING

Many inservice and preservice teachers have never experienced learning in a "mathematics laboratory" setting. If you are to use laboratory learning activities with your students, you must experience how laboratory learning takes place. This section illustrates different sorts of laboratory activities. Take the time to work through these laboratory lessons, following directions carefully.

Laboratory Lesson 1

For this lesson you will need a tape measure or ruler, string, and a collection of circular objects of different sizes. These objects may be as small as a coin or as large as a waste basket. Taking each circular object, measure the distance around (circumference) and the distance across (diameter). You may find it easier to wrap the string around the object and measure the string with the ruler. Make a table like the one below and record your results as decimal fractions. Do not change the measures to fit what you think they "should be." Re-

cord exactly what you measure! You may wish to use metric units for all or some of your measurements but always measure diameter and circumference of any object in the same units.

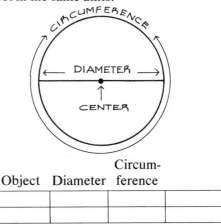

Object	Diameter	Circum-ference	

What relationship do you see between the diameter and the circumference? In the fourth column write the heading "C ÷ D," circumference divided by diameter. Do the divisions and fill in that column. Use a calculator if you have one. Now what relationship do you see between the diameter and the circumference?

Average the numbers in the last column. Now look up the value of *pi* (π) and the definition of pi in an encyclopedia, dictionary, or mathematics text.[1] What value for π did you find? Did you obtain exactly that value for any of the circles you measured? Why or why not? Did you obtain exactly that value for the average of numbers in the last column? Which was closer to the actual value, the numbers in the last column or the average of those numbers? Why? Was the ratio of C to D usually closer to the true value of pi for larger objects or for smaller objects? Why?

---

[1]References may certainly be part of laboratory work!

Look back at the laboratory lesson you have just completed. Notice that it was highly structured through directions and questions. There were specific learning outcomes to be derived from the lesson and you were guided toward those objectives. These objectives are at the upper elementary level, and you may use this laboratory activity at that level if you wish.

Laboratory Lesson 2

Find the area of this figure.

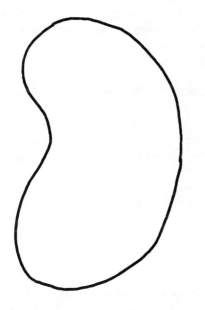

Laboratory Lesson 3

This lesson depends on the circumstances in which you are using this chapter. If you are working in an elementary school as a teacher, teacher aide, intern, or student teacher, you can do the following problem:

How much will a student grow between fourth and fifth grade? Will this be the same for a boy and a girl?

If you are in a college class, you may prefer to work on the following problem:

Are girls (boys) today taller or shorter than their mothers (fathers)? How much?

The reaction to this kind of laboratory lesson is frequently, "How in the world would I know?" When you get over that reaction, you will see that you can develop your own plan for finding the answer. Good luck.

As you think back over the laboratory problems you have just worked, be aware of these things: Each of these problems was focused on *learning* or *using* some important mathematical topic. Each of these laboratory problems could easily be used in the mathematics program at some level. These laboratory problems differed principally in the amount of direction given for doing the activities. You may have very "closed," carefully directed laboratory activities or much more "open," exploratory labs. Keep these distinctions in mind as you plan laboratory activities for your students.

Discussion Questions

1. What new content did you learn from these laboratory lessons?

2. What is your opinion of the methodology? What potential advantages or disadvantages do you see in this technique?

3. Did you enjoy doing these laboratory lessons?

4. Have you done any work in a mathematics laboratory setting before this? Describe it.

SUGGESTED ASSIGNMENTS AND PROJECTS

Classroom Assignments

1. Select a lesson for which a homemade teaching aid would be effective. Build the teaching aid and teach the lesson to your fellow students. After the lesson, briefly tell how you felt the aid improved the lesson. Encourage group discussion of the lesson. If possible, select an aid which you can use later in an internship or a student-teaching situation.

2. Make one or two of the teaching aids described in Section 4. In a textbook find a picture which suggests a useful concrete aid; make one and tell the class how you found the idea and made the aid.

3. Select several laboratory problems and duplicate enough for the class. Divide the class into learning centers, with a different laboratory problem at each center. Start a file of laboratory problems; when you use them with the children, you can keep those which work well and discard the others.

4. Go back to each of the laboratory problems in Section 3. State the possible purposes of each problem. Would the problem be used to review, or to introduce, a topic? Give at least two objectives of each problem.

5. Write for several of the catalogs of companies listed at the end of the chapter. You may write as a class, requesting one for each member of the class.

Internship Assignments

1. Select a child who needs help on some fundamental topic. (A child can almost always be found who needs help on subtraction with regrouping). Make a teaching aid for the topic and work with the child as a tutor. Set objectives and evaluate the progress of the child's learning.

2. Teach a lesson to two groups of children. Teach one group using a teaching aid you have constructed; teach the other group without using the aid. How do these lessons differ in the way children respond? in the way learning progressed? in the degree of attention? If you think one group missed something, go back and reteach that group.

3. Plan and conduct a laboratory lesson with a small group of children. Use one of the laboratory problems contained in Section 3 or one of the laboratory lessons developed by a member of your class. Evaluate the lesson by setting objectives and checking to see whether the objectives were attained.

SUMMARY: MAXIMS FOR TEACHING

1. Use manipulative materials and pictures or diagrams — concrete and semi-concrete materials. They contribute much to effective teaching.
a. Use these materials for demonstrations in which you use the material while the children watch.
b. Use these materials for active lessons in which the children handle the material.

2. Relate the use of manipulatives to the curriculum. Use them to help children attain specific understandings. Sequence the use of manipulatives so that their use fits in well with the text and other resources.

3. To find ideas for making and using manipulatives, look into your text, teacher's edition, catalogs, journals, and other references.

4. Using concrete teaching aids requires careful planning. Even experienced teachers need to plan carefully how manipulative materials are to be used.

5. Try laboratory teaching; it is effective and a stimulating change from regular instruction, but —

6. Always prepare with extra care for a laboratory lesson. You should prepare the laboratory activity, including the materials you will need, prepare the students for the new experience, and prepare the room. If you start slowly and carefully, you will find laboratory activities a successful and interesting form of teaching.

A Final Note

There are always, at the end, some things which need to be said, or said again, for clarity or emphasis. In advocating strongly the use of manipulative materials and laboratory activities, we do not mean to say that all lessons should be of these kinds. A balance of manipulative, exploratory lessons, expository lessons, and drill activities is necessary for a successful program. A real "pro" should be able to use all kinds of instructional techniques and know when to use them.

All use of manipulatives and laboratory activities should be carefully related to the curriculum. To use some concrete materials just because they have arrived or to have a laboratory activity that contributes nothing to the overall arithmetic program is useless, perhaps worse than useless because the teacher may conclude that the teaching aid or the laboratory activity is of no value. For manipulative materials or laboratory activities to be successful, their use must be related to the goals of the curriculum and contribute to the attainment of those goals.

SUPPLIERS OF TEACHING AIDS

All manipulatives should come with instructions, at least a teacher's manual telling how to use the items. Most, but not all, do provide this assistance to the teacher. In addition, some manipulatives come with "student activity materials." These may be laboratory cards, problem cards, or a book of activities for children to read and do. In most cases these materials are sold separately. Many manipulative materials are not well used because nobody knows what to do with them. When you order an item, get at least a sample of the student activity material and insist on getting the teacher's manual for the item.

American Seating
354 Nelson St. S. W.
Atlanta, Georgia 30313

The American Seating catalog contains the catalogs of a number of companies selling educational equipment and materials. In addition to a wide variety of manipulatives, you can get ideas for room furniture and arrangement.

Beckley-Cardy Company
114 Gaither Drive
Mt. Laurel, New Jersey 08057

A large catalog covering all subjects, furniture, aids, and manipulatives.

Creative Publications
P. O. Box 10328
Palo Alto, California 94303

Their catalog contains a comprehensive, well-illustrated selection of manipulatives, laboratory cards, other student activity material, and references.

Creative Teaching Associates
P.O. Box 293
Fresno, California 93708

An expanding array of materials for elementary mathematics, including manipulatives and student activity cards. Material offered separately and in kit form.

The Cuisenaire Company of America
12 Church Street
New Rochelle, New York 10805

The Cuisenaire Company has expanded its offering to include a variety of manipulatives, laboratory activities, books and games. The familiar "Cuisenaire Rods" continue to be their most prominent product.

Gel-Sten, Inc.
P.O. Box 2248
Palm Springs, California 92262

This catalog is a compilation of catalogs of suppliers of elementary materials for mathematics and other subjects. A wide variety of material is described and illustrated.

Ideal School Supply Company
Oak Lawn, Illinois 60453

A good selection of materials, mainly for the younger child.

Judy Company
250 James Street
Morristown, New Jersey 07960

A variety of manipulatives for the elementary mathematics program, some in kit form and also separately. Instructions accompany items and manuals come with kits. Laboratory cards are available separately for many items.

Math Media, Inc.
P.O. Box 1107
Danbury, Connecticut 06810

Manipulative materials and student activity cards for elementary mathematics.

Math Shop, Inc.
5 Bridge Street
Watertown, Massachusetts 02172

An excellent selection of manipulatives and reference books, organized by topic. Most manipulatives have student materials, work cards, or laboratory cards, either accompanying the item or available separately.

Selective Educational Equipment (SEE), Inc.
3 Bridge Street
Newton, Massachusetts 02195

The SEE catalog describes and illustrates a wide variety of mathematics manipulatives. The emphasis is on material for the elementary grades. For many items, work cards or laboratory problem cards are available. A few publications are offered.

E. H. Sheldon Equipment Company
Muskegon, Michigan 49443

This company supplies larger items— desks, storage facilities, and specialized centers for mathematics and science. Their catalog contains a variety of suggestions on room arrangements to facilitate laboratory work and, at the same time, to accommodate all the children.

8 · Teaching Reading Skills and Using Textbooks

COMPETENCIES

Knowledge of Methodology

At the conclusion of this chapter, the teacher should be able to

1. argue for the importance of being able to read mathematics.

2. identify and give a rationale for the guidelines of previewing and slow, careful reading.

3. identify and distinguish between procedures to teach the meaning of a term or symbol and procedures to help children become skilled in reading mathematical terms and symbols.

4. give suggestions for helping children read graphs and tables, computations, exercises, and problems.

5. discuss the use of a diagnostic reading skills check list.

6. identify and discuss features of teachers' editions and students' texts that can be useful in planning and teaching mathematics lessons.

Preparing for Instruction

Given a topic in elementary school mathematics, the teacher can

1. identify mathematical terms and symbols used in teaching it.

2. create procedures designed to teach the meaning of a word or symbol and procedures intended to help children acquire skill in reading mathematical words and symbols.

3. create questions on other procedures to help a group of children read a given computation, graph, table, or problem.

4. create a diagnostic reading skills check list.

5. use features of teachers' editions and students' texts in planning a mathematics lesson.

Instructional Skills

For a child or a group of children, the teacher can

1. diagnose their ability to read mathematics, using a given check list of reading skills.

2. design and conduct lessons on the basis of the above diagnosis to (a) teach meanings of terms and (b) develop reading skills.

3. guide the children in previewing and carefully reading a lesson.

4. *help them read a computation.*

5. *guide and ask questions to help them read a graph or a table.*

6. *guide and ask questions to help them read and understand a problem.*

INTRODUCTION

Words and symbols are parts of the language of mathematics. Children must learn to read this language for they will meet it in newspapers, periodicals, travel schedules, owner and repair manuals, building instructions, cooking and sewing guides, and in every school subject and textbook. If students cannot read mathematics with understanding, they will be handicapped whether they are reading to carry out a task, for information or enjoyment, or to further their academic knowledge.

Reading mathematics is not easy. The reader of mathematics must
1. *possess a specialized vocabulary.*
2. *know the meaning and various uses of special symbols.*
3. *follow notational agreements and abbreviations.*
4. *be aware of the sequence of steps recorded when computations are displayed.*

Consider, for example, the specialized term rhombus *and the common and mathematical meanings of the terms* base, set, foot, *and* face. *Consider also the different meanings of the symbol* · *in 3.5 and 3 · 5. In adding and subtracting whole numbers, children must learn to read and use special notational agreements concerning regrouping, and they must learn to read from right to left in vertical jumps instead of following the usual left-to-right, horizontal procedure you are using now.*

To be able to read mathematics, children must acquire some special skills. While every teacher teaches reading, the mathematics teacher has the special responsibility of teaching children to read mathematics. We will try to help you do this by identifying problems and offering suggestions. We begin by considering two general techniques for reading mathematics.

1. GENERAL GUIDELINES FOR READING MATHEMATICS

We have probably all heard claims that individuals can read at what appears to be an amazing rate. While we do not wish to dispute these claims for certain individuals and certain kinds of material, we want to emphasize that such claims are not made for reading mathematics books.

Reading Slowly for Detail

One may claim to have read *Gone with the Wind* in an evening or two. A similar assertion would not be made for mathematical or other technical material. Mathematics should be read slowly and carefully — usually more than once. Often, students are not aware of this. As children develop their ability to read, they are encouraged to read as rapidly as they can. When reading stories, they seldom reread. In reading mathematics, however, speed is only a minor concern. Comprehension of every detail is so important that rereading is a highly recommended procedure. For example, the following statements can be found in many first- and second-grade mathematics textbooks.

$$3 + 5 = \square$$
$$3 + \square = 5$$

While the symbols are the same, the statements are not. The detail of the placement of the □ is important, and the child is expected to discriminate between these two equations and act upon them differently. Such careful discrimination may not be as necessary in the general reading program. Repetitive material still characterizes beginning reading material. The child can miss a word or miss several words and still get the essential meaning. In mathematical equations, missing a symbol or interchanging two symbols may change the meaning entirely.

Why is it necessary to read slowly and carefully and reread passages of mathematics? The answer lies in the compactness of the symbolism, the precise meaning of most terms, and the need for the reader to reason and recall relevant and previously learned information. For example, a statement such as:

$$362 = 300 + 60 + 2 = 300 + 50 + 12$$

is much shorter than the written statement, "three hundred sixty-two equals three hundred plus sixty plus two, which equals three hundred plus fifty plus twelve." Understanding the statement demands at least recall of place value and of the rules for applying this concept in our numeration system. In mathematics instruction, it is so important that the student grasp the relationships in the statement that rereading to insure clarification of all details is essential.

Children must be taught to read mathematics slowly and carefully and to reread to be sure they understand. Reasons for using this technique should be discussed with children. They must be *convinced* of the need to reread. One way to do this is for teachers to ask questions about the mathematics children read. Referring to the equation above, questions such as

"Linda, where does the 60 come from?" or

"Wes, how did the 2 become a 12?" are examples of questions students should ask themselves as they read.

Since rereading is extra work, teachers must emphasize its importance. In addition to asking questions, a teacher may, after assigning a passage to be read, have the children close their books and write down everything they remember from the passage. The children can be asked to reread and to write down anything they may have omitted the first time. The new notations serve as evidence of the benefits of rereading. As a variation of the technique, the teacher can write the children's statements on the board. If the statements are in conflict with, or leave out, points in the passage, have the children reread. The benefits of rereading should be discussed with the group.

Reading Quickly for an Overview

In various situations it can be advisable to have children practice a reading technique called *skimming*. That is rapid reading to obtain a general impression.

Skimming to preview. Skimming can be useful in previewing a chapter in a mathematics textbook. It can be done by examining the chapter title, the table of contents, and page titles. This should be done with the teacher, who points out the important topics coming up. Skimming is a good practice to begin as early as the third grade. As long as the teacher leading the preview is enthusiastic and expresses confidence in their ability, children are likely to benefit by "peeking ahead."

Previewing can be done in several ways. A teacher can ask the children to see how many new words, or how many different mathematics symbols, they can find in the chapter. The teacher can lead discussions about the meanings of the terms and/or the symbols and can have the children use the textbook's glossary or a dictionary. The children can read passages containing the words or symbols to extract meanings from the context.

Another variation of the activity is for the teacher to list new words or symbols in a chapter and to ask the children to find the first page where each appears. The children can then try to ascertain meanings.

One technique for previewing a printed lesson is to make copies of the page or pages and cut them up. Then the students can be asked to arrange them by putting the "puzzle" together.

Previewing a printed mathematics lesson alerts students to the main ideas of the lesson, to new terms, new phrases, or new principles. These ideas are usually highlighted. Previewing may also help recall related knowledge or encourage a review of forgotten material. Many mathematics texts guide students in observing patterns and in discovering relationships. A preview can help the student become aware of this.

Reviewing a unit. Skimming may also be used to look back over a unit of study. Under the guidance of the teacher, children can rapidly read through section headings and page titles of material, noting the topics they have studied. For example, a fourth-grade teacher, in leading a review of a chapter dealing with the addition and subtraction of fractions, could have children skim through the chapter and list the topics studied. The teacher writes the list as the children mention topics. Then the students are challenged to sequence the topics as they think they should appear in the book, perhaps as follows:

1. What are fractions?
   a. Fractions as parts of things
   b. Fractions on the number line
2. When are fractions the same?
   a. Families of fractions
   b. Reducing fractions
3. Adding fractions
   a. with the same denominators
   b. with different denominators
4. Subtracting fractions
   a. with the same denominators
   b. with different denominators
   c. in problems

This sequence can then be compared to the textbook. After constructing the list with students, the teacher could ask for page numbers of topics on the list, or call out page numbers and have students write the numbers beside the appropriate entries on the list.

Skimming to understand the organizational pattern of a book. Skimming may be useful in helping children recognize the organizational pattern of their textbook. Most mathematics textbooks follow some organizational pattern. Ideas or algorithms are usually presented in one or two ways and are followed by exercises and problems. Distinct lessons may be constructed to fill one or two pages. Color coding, boldface type, cartoon characters, and other highlighting devices usually follow a consistent pattern in a given textbook series. Teachers become aware of this. Students often do not. Teachers should have children skim material before they begin slow and careful reading. When children have become familiar with the organizational and highlighting patterns of their text materials, they can preview each lesson and obtain some idea of what to expect.

The two general guidelines presented above are, on the surface, somewhat contradictory. One advises rapid reading; the other a deliberate approach. However, there is no conflict when these guidelines are applied. Students should be instructed and helped to preview material rapidly and then to read and reread slowly and carefully, making sure they understand every line. Students will not do these things naturally. It is your responsibility to help them see the wisdom of these guidelines and to provide practice in following them.

Discussion Questions

1. Which of the two general guidelines do you think will be harder for children to follow? Why? Do you employ either of these guidelines when you read a mathematics text? Why?

2. Consider two different one- or two-page lessons in a child's mathematics text. The first lesson presents and explains some mathematics and then provides practice. The second displays data from which the child is asked to discover a mathematical principle. Exercises are provided. Discuss the importance of previewing each lesson. Which of the two lessons is more important to preview?

3. Why will children need to be convinced of the need to preview and skim mathematics reading material?

4. Think back to your high school and college mathematics courses. How much did you learn from reading the textbook? How much help (of the kinds suggested here) did you get in learning how to use the textbook?

2. READING SKILLS IN MATHEMATICS

There are several specific skills which are necessary in order to read mathematics efficiently. In some cases these are extensions of the skills taught in language arts; in other cases the skills are quite different. Teachers who are planning to help children learn to read the textbook need to incorporate these skills into their instruction.

Knowledge of Vocabulary

Mathematics has its own vocabulary. While many mathematical terms are borrowed from everyday English, a reader of mathematics must be skilled in knowing both the mathematical and everyday meanings of words.

Words have many meanings. Teachers should be careful to introduce each new mathematics word and to help children learn its special meaning. The importance of this is underscored when one realizes the large number of mathematical words that have a "common" meaning and a mathematical meaning. A list of many such terms in elementary school mathematics is given in Table 1. It is surprisingly long!

Teaching the meaning of a word. What can you do to help children become skilled in the vocabulary of elementary school mathematics? First, you must call the students' attention to *every* new

TABLE 1 • A List of Words in Elementary School Mathematics Having an "Everyday Meaning" and a Mathematical Meaning

acute	commute	invert	property
add	compass	irrational	radical
alternate (interior angle)	complement	lateral (area)	rational (number)
altitude	concave	law	ray
angle(s)	cone	leg	real (number)
array	convex	less	right (angle)
associate	correspond	like (fractions)	(square) root
axes	count	lowest (terms)	round (off)
balance	cross (product)	major (arc)	row
bar	curve	map	ruler
base	degree	mean	scale (drawing)
between	distance	minor (arc)	second
borrowing	distribute	mixed (number)	set
boundary	divide	natural (number)	sign
braces	element	negative	similar (figures)
cancel	even	odd	simple (closed curve)
cardinal	exterior	opposite	simple (form of fraction)
carrying	face	origin	solution
casting (out nines)	factor	perfect (number)	space
check	foot	place	square
chord	greater	plane	term
clock (arithmetic)	intercept	plot	twin (primes)
closed	interior	point	union
column	intersect	power	unit
common (denominator)	intersection	prime	volume
		product	yard

mathematical term they meet—every term, not just those that have dual meanings. Before and after a term has been identified, give *examples* of objects to which the term refers, examples of objects that have the property denoted by the term, or examples of actions the term signifies. A variety of examples is probably the most powerful teaching technique for teaching the meaning of a word. Don't only give examples; explain to the students *why* they are examples. To explain the term *acute angle,* the teacher can generate examples by drawings, by pointing to acute angles indicated by lines in pictures, and by holding two pencils or similar objects in appropriate positions. The teacher can also indicate why a particular object illus-

trates an actue angle—either by using a protractor or by relying on the children's intuitive notions of whether or not the angle is "opened up" more or less than 90 degrees.

It is also useful sometimes to provide a few *nonexamples,* explaining why the object is not an example of the term you are teaching. In teaching the term *acute angle,* the teacher can refer to drawings or physical embodiments of angles that are not acute angles.

You should be careful to tell why an object or drawing is an example of the word you are explaining. You may state that an angle is an acute angle because it is less than 90 degrees or because it is smaller than a right angle. In this way the students become aware of the specific conditions for an angle to be an acute angle.

In addition to examples, nonexamples, and pointing out the conditions implied by a word, teachers can also compare or contrast a word with related words. *Acute angle* can be contrasted with the terms *angle, obtuse angle,* and the word *acute.* Sometimes comparisons can be made when a word has a root or prefix in common with another word the students know. The roots *equi* and *equa* are found in many mathematics terms *(equilaterial, equivalent, equal, equation),* as are the prefixes *bi* and *in.*

All of the techniques just discussed pointing out the conditions a word implies help students understand the meaning of a term. Students will indicate that they understand a term when they can identify and justify examples and nonexamples, when they can make comparisons with other terms and use the term correctly in written and spoken sentences, and when they can paraphrase the definition of the word. All of these indicate that an association, or link, has been established in the child's mind between the word and those things to which the word refers. For reading purposes, however, understanding is not enough. Students must be *skilled* in knowing meanings of mathematics terms: The students' associations between the words and their referents should be immediate.

Teaching for skill in knowing meanings.
Being *skilled* in knowing the meanings of mathematical terms requires *practice.* Short vocabulary drill sessions two or three times a week are necessary. Here are some sample vocabulary practice techniques. Practice is essential in building a vocabulary because it strengthens the link, or association, between the term and the objects the term signifies. Without practice everyone forgets.

1. *Matching exercises* — Present children with a list of terms and a list of statements or pictures. Have the children match the appropriate items in each list. Use the vocabulary list at the end of each chapter in your text and the glossary. Be sure to review terms from other chapters.

2. *Guess the word* — Give a succession of hints about a mathematical term. Allow each student one guess. Hints can include objects illustrating the term, rhyming words, anything you think is related to the term, such as conditions needed for it to apply.

3. *Fill in the blank* — Give a partially completed term and a partially completed statement about the term. Students fill in the blanks. Examples:

    a. l__w__st t_____s: a _____
       that cannot be _____
       any more.
    b. pl_____: a flat _____.

4. As a humorous activity children enjoy making up or figuring out nonsense meanings for certain terms. Here are some examples:
acute — a very nice looking boy or girl
polygon — a parrot that has flown away
meter — you get together with a girl
protractor — someone who likes tractors

5. *Flash word* — Hold up a flash card for a moment. If the card has a term on it, have the students give the meaning of the word, use it in a sentence, or draw a picture of an object related to the term. If the card contains a picture, children are to write the word or words they think the picture represents.

6. *Password*—This can be played in the same way as the commercial game. One player tries to get another to say a particular term by giving one-word hints. In the mathematical version the students may use symbols.

Using root words. In teaching reading and in practice sessions, include discussions and exercises on root words, prefixes, and alternate forms of words. For example, *add* serves as a root, or stem, for at least six mathematical terms *(add, addition, adding, addend, additive,* and *adds). Measure, measuring,* and *measurement* all share a common root, as do *multiple, multiplier, multiply,* and *multiplication.*

Other roots include:

equa—equal, equation, equality, equate

equi—equivalent, equiangular, equidistant, equilateral

circum—circumference, circumscribe, circumcircle

divi—division, divide, dividend, divisible, divisor

sub—subtract, subtraction, subtrahend, substitute, subset

sum—sum, summation

Roots can be important clues as to the meaning of a word. Students are not always aware of this. A national study of seventh- and eighth-grade students revealed that 98 percent knew the meaning of *sum* but only 17 percent knew the meaning of *summation;* 92 percent reported knowing the meaning of *equal* but only 24 percent knew the meaning of *equate.*[1] One exercise involving root words is to ask students to write as many words, mathematical and nonmathemat-

ical, as they can using the same root. Another exercise is to have them compare and contrast the meaning of various words based on the same root. Root words are important aids in building a general vocabulary. There is no reason why mathematical vocabulary drill cannot be included in general word-attack practice sessions.

Using prefixes. Prefixes, too, play a role in the development of vocabulary. In elementary school mathematics the prefixes below are common.

bi—binary, bisect, bisection

ex—exterior, extract, extreme, expand, exponent

in—interior, inscribe, incenter, internal, intersect

in—infinite, inequality

mid—middle, midpoint

non—nonsimple, nonnegative, nonterminating, nonmetric, nonlinear

poly—polygon, polyhedron

re—rename, replace, regroup

trans—transversal, transform, transitive, translate, translation

tri—triple, trisect, tripod

un—unequal, undefined, unknown, unlimited, unlike

Prefixes behave much like roots and can be incorporated into practice sessions involving root words.

Different phrases having the same meaning. In addition to helping children with roots and prefixes, you should also alert them to different forms of the same terms or phrases. The following set of terms or phrases—*associative, associative principle, associative law, associativity*—mean essentially the same thing. Similar sets of terms and phrases can be constructed for *commutative, distributive,* and *transitive.*

---

[1]R. B. Kane, M. A. Byrne, and M. A. Hater, *Helping Children Read Mathematics.* (New York: American Book Company, 1974) pp. 75–90.

Sometimes the form of a word changes but the meaning remains nearly the same. For example, look at the following sets.

equal, equate
line, linear, collinear
radius, radii
circle, circular
approximate, approximation
bisect, bisection
calculate, calculation
combine, combination, combining
compare, comparing, comparison
construct, construction
estimate, estimating, estimation
factor, factoring, factorization
percent, percentage, percentile
relation, relationship
solve, solving, solution

Common mathematical meanings of terms, roots, prefixes, and different forms of terms need to be discussed with young readers of mathematics. Plenty of practice should be provided in all of these areas.

Here are some additional exercises for providing practice in using mathematical terms.

1. Match the word with the symbol having the same meaning. Some may not match.

meter	cm³
milliliter	m²
cubic centimeter	ha
dekameter	m
kilogram	mg
square meter	k
miligram	dam
hectameter	ml

2. Write the words or phrases that are related in the same rectangle.

times	equal	add	hour

add	multiply	times
equal	equation	second
time	instant	addition
total	balanced	equality
factor	addend	product
sum	watch	plus
hour		

3. Write as many words or phrases as you can that begin with:

dist_____
num_____
add_____
multi_____
sub_____

4. Write a sentence using each of these words in a mathematical way. Then write a sentence using each word in a way that has nothing to do with mathematics.

yard   power   law   odd
borrow   count   degree

Knowledge of Symbols

In addition to being skilled in recognizing the meaning of words and phrases, children must also be skilled in recognizing the meaning of mathematical symbols. Symbols are the shorthand of mathematics. Children learn the meaning of symbols and their pronunciation by means of explanation, demonstration, advice, and usage. A list of some of the symbols used in elementary school mathematics is given in Table 2.

TABLE 2 • A List of Symbols Used in Elementary School Mathematics

0, 1, 2, 3, 4, 5, 6, 7, 8, 9, 10
$+, -, \times, \div, \cdot, :$
$<, >, \leq, \geq, =, \neq$
%, º, $, ¢, ', "
I, II, III, IV, V, VI, VII, VIII, IX, X
$\Delta, \pi, \rightarrow, \leftrightarrow$

Use of symbols. Many mathematical symbols are used in more than one way. Consider the following different uses and *pronunciations*.

Different uses of "3":	3, 34, 342, 2^3, p_3, 25.3
Different uses of "—":	-4, $\frac{5}{2}$, $18 - 12$, $-\frac{4}{2}$, $\overline{AB}$ .2463$\overline{4}$
Different uses of ".":	.333 . . ., $\pi \doteq 3\frac{1}{7}$, 3 · 5

Note also how 3, —, and · can all be used together.

$$3 \cdot 3 \qquad -3 \cdot 3$$
$$3 - 3 \qquad -3.3$$

Because even in elementary school mathematics the use of symbols is extensive and complex, students need a great deal of practice using and recognizing them. Here are some skill builders.

1. Match each symbol with the correct word or phrase. Some may not match.

{6}	six
"	the set with nothing in it
VI	perpendicular
⊥	decimal point
(3,4)	a right angle
.	multiply
∅	the set with 6 as its only member
	inches
~	a point 3 over to the right and 4 up
	not equal
	four

2. Some of the words and phrases in Exercise 1 didn't match any symbol in the list. Write them below and give their correct symbols.

3. Here is a list of statements made with mathematical symbols. Beside each one make other symbols that mean the same thing. For example, $4\overline{)12}$ means $12 \div 4$.

$$4\overline{)12} \qquad\qquad 4 < 10$$
$$8 + 2 = 10 \qquad\qquad 6$$
$$3 \times 5 = 15 \qquad\qquad .333 . . .$$

$$\begin{array}{r} 14 \\ \underline{-9} \\ 5 \end{array} \qquad \begin{array}{c} \frac{10}{12} \\ .5 \end{array}$$

$$4 \cdot 4 \cdot 4 \qquad\qquad \emptyset$$

4. Make a set of flash cards. On one side of each make a math symbol. On the other side write the word or phrase. Use these cards to practice, and add new ones as new symbols are introduced. Right now you should know at least 30 symbols. See if you can remember them all.

5. Make up a story by using math symbols for some of the words. For this story you can use math words and symbols to mean something besides math. Here are some examples.

$$\{ \ \} \ \text{THE} \quad \text{(table)} .$$

Set the table.

$$\text{MY} \quad \text{(12" ruler)} \ \text{HURTS} \ \frac{6}{3}.$$

My foot hurts, too.

$$\text{THAT} \ \pi \ \text{DESERVES A} \ \text{(compliment)} .$$

That pie deserves a compliment.

$$(\ ) \ \text{RATES COST} < \longrightarrow \text{SAID}.$$

Group rates cost less than Ray said.

Reading computational exercises. Reading mathematical computations requires eye movements different from the normal left to right movements used in reading English. To read a computation, the eyes may need to move up, down, diagonally, and to the left as well as to the right. Consider how the eyes must move to read these sample computations as they might be presented in a textbook.

$$\frac{3}{4} = \frac{9}{12}$$
$$+\frac{2}{3} = \frac{8}{12}$$
$$\overline{\frac{17}{12} = 1\frac{5}{12}}$$

COULD
BE READ

$$47 = 40 + 7$$
$$+\ 26 = 20 + 6$$
$$\overline{60 + 13 = 70 + 3 = 73}$$

COULD
BE READ

The complexities of eye movement in reading mathematics are surprising to most adults! We have learned them in conjunction with standard reading eye movements without realizing how confusing they must seem to children. Children need practice in reading computations. One type of exercise is to have children do what we did above: Have them draw eye-movement diagrams. You might write a computation *large size* on the board and have a child draw the eye-movement arrows in a different colored chalk. Make a ditto sheet with an oversize computation—have each child draw the eye-movement arrows. Discuss with the children how reading computations is different from normal reading.

Using Skills Together

Teachers should be careful to discuss the meaning of each new mathematical symbol, the words used to indicate the symbol, and the eye movement required to read each symbol in the context in which students will read it. Symbols will usually be accompanied by mathematical words and phrases, and the word-use skills discussed earlier should be used. Teachers must help children relate objects, words, and symbols. Understanding suffers when children do not see the relationships between a drawing and the words and symbols they read. For example, the diagram, words, and symbols below are all related. If this relationship is not perceived, a child will not understand this reading material.

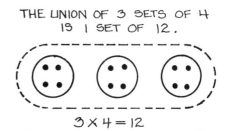

THE UNION OF 3 SETS OF 4
IS 1 SET OF 12.

3 × 4 = 12

The object of instruction is the relationship between the terms *union* and *set*, the symbol 3 × 4 = 12, and the diagram. The teacher must ask questions to bring out this relationship. More important, children must be encouraged to look for such relationships every time they read. They should always check to see if the diagrams, words, and symbols are working together like a team. If there is no picture, the words and symbols must team together. Practice in coordinating pictures, words, and symbols can take many forms. Students can be given a diagram and asked to construct appropriate words and symbols explaining it.

Children can be asked to draw a number of diagrams to accompany verbal or symbolic statements. Here are a few such exercises.

1. Draw a picture that helps you explain $40 \div 5 = 8$.

2. Finish and give an example of this rule:

   To add two fractions with the same denominator, just add the numerators and _____

   _____.

3. Finish this picture by putting in numbers. What is this picture saying? Write your answer in words only. Then write what the picture says using only mathematical symbols.

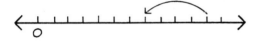

Discussion Questions

1. Consider the statement, "For reading purposes, understanding is not enough. Students must be *skilled* in knowing meanings of mathematics terms." Defend this statement. Then take issue with it.

2. Is the above statement in conflict with positions taken in the chapter entitled "Teaching for Understanding"? Explain.

3. Are there differences in the teacher's role and behavior when teaching the meaning of words—helping students understand words—and when helping students become skilled in knowing the meanings of mathematical terms? Explain.

4. Is there a difference between teaching the meaning of a word and teaching the meaning of a symbol?

3. SPECIAL READING PROBLEMS

Three situations pose special problems in reading mathematics: reading a computation or algorithm; reading graphs and tables; and reading story problems. In each of these situations, as in any other reading of mathematics, the skills of recognizing mathematical words and symbols are facilitated if a rapid preview is followed by slow, careful reading and rereading. However, these situations pose special difficulties that require additional attention on the part of teachers.

Reading Computational Exercises

There are several reasons why computations are difficult to read. The first has to do with eye movement. Eye movement in reading a computation is seldom left to right. Children have to learn many different eye-movement sequences—practically, one for each different algorithm. Earlier, we sketched possible eye-movement diagrams for reading two algorithms. Teachers must demonstrate the order for an algorithm and get students to practice following it.

Having children construct eye-movement arrow diagrams is one form of practice. Having students construct a series of instructions for reading or working a particular computation is another. This does not have to result in a written list. It can take place when one student gives directions to another, telling step by step how to read or perform the computation. Try this by placing two students back to back in a simulated telephone conversation. Let one give directions to the other, who pretends to be confused. This exercise can result in enjoyable and worthwhile practice. Let's "record" the beginning of a conversation.

Clare:

Hi, Andrea, I forgot how to do those addition problems we learned today. You know, the new, fast way.

Andrea:

Oh, that's easy! Want me to come over and show you?

Clare:

Let's try to do one right now.

Andrea:

On the phone?

Clare:

Yeah

Andrea:

O.K. I'll try. First, you line them up—you know, put them over each other.

Clare:

Wait a minute. Let's do it with 743 and 126. Now, which one goes on top?

Andrea:

Either one—just be sure to line them up so that 6 is right over or under the 3. Then line the 4 and 2, and the 7 and 1. O.K.?

Clare:

O.K. Now what?

Reading Graphs and Tables

Learning how to read a graph or table is an essential skill in reading mathematics and in reading periodicals, newspapers, and other printed material. Although tables and graphs can take many forms, reading them is easier if done in two steps. First, have the students skim the table or graph for the topic. Have them identify all the categories reported. Let them obtain a general impression.

Then, ask for a detailed study. This is best accomplished by systematically extracting enough details to make the reader familiar with the graph. If teachers encourage students to follow these two steps in reading tables and graphs, and have them *practice* reading and constructing various types of tables and graphs, this important skill can be acquired. To illustrate these two steps, a teacher might proceed as follows:

1. Let's all look at the graph over on the wall — I clipped it out of last night's paper. (See the graph below.)

2. Kathy, what kind of graph is it? What does it show?

3. Dan, what is recorded along the horizontal side of this bar graph?

4. Jennifer, what categories are given on the vertical side?

5. O.K.—we have years ending with 1975 along the horizontal and the population of our county in thousands along the vertical. Now, without giving me any specific numbers, what do you think will happen in 1980? Can we be sure?

6. Now let's get some details. Everyone write the population for these years— 1950, 1965, 1975. What do you think the population was in 1964? I know that is not right on the graph but I think you can use the graph to make an estimate.

7. Up on the board I have written some data about the population of our state capital. Make a bar graph out of it right now.

Reading Word Problems

Word problems, whether they are simple applications of previously learned computational procedures or challenging

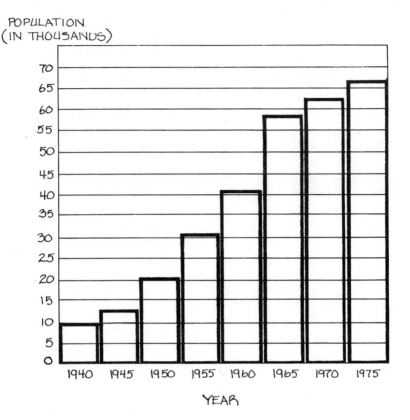

POPULATION OF CLARKE COUNTY, GEORGIA

POPULATION
(IN THOUSANDS)

YEAR

"mind benders," are an important part of a mathematics program. Problems must be read and understood before they can be worked. Children are often taught to read a problem for key words or phrases, such as "how many more" or "altogether." This is a *very poor* way to analyze problems—it ignores understanding the problem. Sometimes children look at the numbers given in the problem and try to determine the appropriate operation on the basis of the size of these numbers or on the number of numerical quantities given. Both of these strategies run counter to the development of reading comprehension and of problem-solving ability. They should not be encouraged. Chil-

dren who add every time they have a problem with three or more numbers, or who divide when they have one "big" number and one "small" number, do not benefit from solving story problems. They are not applying their knowledge of mathematics.

When children are faced with reading a story problem, they should first follow the two guidelines for reading any mathematical material. Skim the material to obtain a general idea, and then read and reread the problem carefully. This reading is directed toward getting the children to state the problem situation correctly in their own words and to identify what the problem is asking them to find.

Once they can do this, they can then move on to the algorithm needed to solve the problem. We have more to say about problem solving in the chapter on problem solving. Here we are concerned with reading and understanding the problem.

Students can be aided in stating a problem in their own words by acting out the situation and by drawing a diagram. They can analyze or complete verbal or pictorial models of the problem. Students can also write their own problems. When children are constructing problems, you may have to start them by supplying them with a general context. For example, have them build a problem around two friends with a certain amount of money buying candy in a store.

One way to model the reading techniques we have been discussing is to take up problems children construct, reproduce them so they can be read by the entire group, and then let the children observe you skimming, reading carefully, stating the problem in your own words, drawing a sketch, and telling them what it is you are to find out. You may wish to have children, other than the problem's author, help you in these tasks.

Diagnosing Mathematics Reading Problems

One way to measure a child's ability to read mathematics is to test his or her knowledge of the mathematical terms and symbols he or she reads. Most textbooks or teachers' guides contain vocabulary lists for this purpose at the end of each unit of study. Another method is periodically to complete a reading-ability

check list on each child. This can be done by observing a child read a selected passage and respond to directions in the passage, and by talking with the child about the material that has been read. The following sample items might serve as a guide to compiling the check list.

I. Basic Techniques
   1. Usually skims a passage and obtains a valid general impression of the main topic
   2. Is able to skim a passage and obtain a valid general impression of the main topic
   3. Reads at an appropriate pace for the difficulty of the material and his/her ability to understand
   4. Usually rereads material to insure understanding
   5. Is aware of the need for skimming, careful reading, and rereading
II. General Skills
   1. Realizes terms can have mathematical and nonmathematical meanings
   2. Can give a valid explanation of the mathematical terms being read
   3. Can use the meaning of the roots and prefixes previously studied to explain the meaning of a term
   4. Can pronounce terms being read
   5. Can pronounce names given to symbols being used
   6. Can explain the meanings of the symbols being used
   7. Can relate words and symbols to a picture in a given situation
III. Special Skills
   1. Computations
      a. Can read an algorithm in

the proper order
  b. Can relate a given algorithm to a previously understood and more detailed algorithm or to the manipulation of real or pictorial objects
2. Graphs
  a. Can skim a graph to obtain the topic, main categories, elements in each category, and the general relationship expressed in the graph
  b. Can extract details from a graph
3. Word Problems
  a. Skims a problem to obtain a general impression; then reads and rereads the problem
  b. Can restate a given problem in own words and identify the question to be answered

When you listen to children read, note the skills in which they are weak. Plan instruction in those skills, using the suggested activities in this chapter and others you may devise. Apply your knowledge of the teaching of reading directly to the reading of mathematics. This may be done on an individual basis or as a class activity.

Discussion Questions

1. Think of computations where each of the following eye movements are used:

Write the computations and the eye-movement arrows.

2. In this section a bar graph was illustrated. What other kinds of graphs are used in elementary school mathematics?

3. How is a table different from a graph? What kinds of tables are used in elementary school mathematics?

4. Apply the check list to your own reading of mathematics. Do you use all the skills?

4. READING AS A TEACHING TECHNIQUE

A primary reason why children have difficulty reading mathematics is that reading is rarely taught or utilized in mathematics classes. Children quickly learn that the most efficient way to study mathematics is to listen carefully, watch the teacher work sample problems, then go directly to the problems in the text and work them the same way. They see no need to develop reading skill until it is too late. It is "too late" when an eighth-grade teacher says, "Read pages 37, 38, and 39 and work the exercises on page 39," and the child has no idea how to proceed to get the meaning from the mathematical explanations on the pages.

If we are to change this, we must make reading the mathematics text a frequent part of in-class and out-of-class activities. We must strive to teach children skills they need to read mathematics, and we must make sure these skills are used. Having listed and explained techniques and skills that are used in reading mathematics, let us suggest some ways in which reading mathematics can become a regular part of your instructional program. These activities also give you an opportunity to diagnose problems your students are having in reading mathematics.

Have students read the mathematics book aloud in class. Pick a page from the textbook that gives a clear explanation of the topic you want to teach. Have the students skim and state their general impression. Then have the students take turns reading portions of the page aloud. When graphs, tables, examples, pictures, or other explanatory material are referred to in the text, examine them carefully. Encourage the reader and the other students to pay attention by asking questions: "What does that sentence mean?" "Can you tell us in your own words?" "What does [mathematical term] mean?" When the textbook explanation has been read and discussed, give the assignment without further explanation. Make it clear that you expect the students to learn from what has been read. When the students are doing fairly well at this, try the next suggestion.

Have the students read the text silently and begin working the assignment. While the students are reading and beginning to do the assignment, you should be available to answer questions. Use this time to ascertain which students have difficulty reading silently and what their specific problems are. If you are going to do some topics not covered in your text, you might type up a ditto sheet explaining the new material. This procedure has advantages: The students get an accurate record which they may keep (note taking is often incomplete), practice in reading is provided, students can use the material at different times when they are ready, and the material can be kept for future use.

Give a homework assignment in which the students learn by reading how to do the work. This procedure should be used only after students are doing well on the assignments above. Make sure the students understand that they *read first* and work the problems second. Prevent this exchange:

Parent:
How are you supposed to do these problems?

Child:
I don't know. Mrs. Smith hasn't taught us that.

Be sure the children know that they are to learn by reading!

We hope you will use a variety of different lessons as you teach. Lessons that emphasize independent learning by reading are only one type. How often should you use such lessons? If you have a lesson once a week which emphasizes reading in one way or another or if you give one reading-oriented homework assignment each week, you will make good progress in this area. Most teachers do so little about reading mathematics that any organized work is bound to produce improvement.

Perhaps the main reason why most teachers do so little in helping children read mathematics has been the failure of mathematics educators to be sensitive to the problems involved in reading and to offer assistance to teachers. We hope this chapter is a step toward meeting that need. Much of the material in this chapter was influenced by the pioneering work in reading in mathematics by Kane, Byrne, and Hater, mentioned earlier. We refer readers to their comprehensive treatment of reading in mathematics and to their workbook series designed to help teachers teach reading in mathematics.

Discussion Questions

The following three pages are reproduced from pupils' textbooks at the first-, third-, and sixth-grade levels. Refer to these pages in discussion of the following questions.

1. What reading skills identified in Sections 2 and 3, above, are needed in reading these pages?

2. What vocabulary and symbols do students need?

3. What are the advantages and disadvantages of using each of these pages in a reading lesson?

4. Is it reasonable in each case to ask a student, assuming that the student is reading on grade level, to read the text material and then work the exercises? Explain.

5. If the answer to Question 4 is No for any page, what other help would the student need to work the exercises?

5. TEXTBOOKS—HOW CAN THE TEACHER'S EDITION HELP YOU?

Teaching mathematics to children calls for a variety of teaching behaviors, not merely assigning pages of exercises and problems to be worked in some prescribed way. Teachers are responsible for explanations, demonstrations, conducting exploratory investigations, and encouraging, diagnosing, and evaluating learning. A textbook is one of the tools used in these activities. Textbooks are valuable because they contain an organized and comprehensive treatment of the basic mathematical concepts, principles, and skills that society expects children to acquire.

Making Full Use of the Textbook and Teacher's Edition

You should expect to use textbooks from two or more grade levels in your classroom. Groups of children working with the same textbook will frequently be at different places. You should also supplement any textbook with an assortment of manipulative materials, models and teaching aids, various extra practice items, and ditto masters designed for specific occasions. The suggestions given for each lesson in your teacher's edition will frequently suggest the use of such supplementary materials.

As we have emphasized in the first part of this chapter, you should help children learn to read their mathematics text. Begin by reading the text *with* the children and helping them understand what the authors are saying. That is not accomplished when a teacher merely summarizes the discussion in the textbook and assigns exercises for students to complete. Reading lessons can be followed up by students' paraphrasing what they have read, demonstrating their understanding through working problems, and answering or asking questions.

The textbook and teacher's edition are carefully planned to provide you with help in teaching. Many teachers do not take full advantage of the features in either the text or the teacher's edition. In the next few pages we present a summary of the materials included in the teacher's edition and some suggestions on their use. The basic and most important suggestion is to read the text and teacher's edition *before* planning a lesson. The teacher's edition is a rich source of both mathematical background and activities for students. Use it!

(Text continues on page 206.)

NAME

2 + 1 = 3
IN ALL

3 - 1 = 2
IN ALL

1 + 3 = ___
IN ALL

4 - 3 = ___
IN ALL

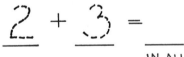 

2 + 3 = ___
IN ALL

5 - 3 = ___
IN ALL

  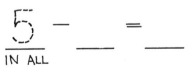

4 + ___ = ___
IN ALL

5 - ___ = ___
IN ALL

To use patterns to add hundreds

addition fact	adding tens	adding hundreds
3 + 5 = 8	30 + 50 = 80	300 + 500 = 800
5 + 4 = 9	50 + 40 = 90	500 + 400 = 900
6 + 8 = 14	60 + 80 = 140	600 + 800 = 1 400

What addition fact was used to find the sum for this example?

$$\begin{array}{r} 700 \\ +\ 200 \\ \hline 900 \end{array}$$

skill check   Find each sum.

1.	2.	3.	4.	5.
200 + 300	300 + 300	500 + 900	800 + 800	500 + 600

EXERCISES

Copy, and find the sums.

1.	2.	3.	4.	5.
300 + 700	400 + 400	200 + 500	600 + 300	700 + 600

6.	7.	8.	9.	10.
900 + 300	800 + 700	600 + 600	400 + 700	900 + 900

To tell the value of each digit in a numeral

millions			thousands			units		
hundreds	tens	ones	hundreds	tens	ones	hundreds	tens	ones
	7	0	1	4	6	9	8	4

The position of a digit in a numeral determines its value.

digit x place = value of digit

$7 \times 10\ 000\ 000 = 70\ 000\ 000$

$0 \times\ \ 1\ 000\ 000 = \ \ \ \ \ \ \ \ \ 0$

$1 \times\ \ \ \ \ 100\ 000 = \ \ \ 100\ 000$

$4 \times\ \ \ \ \ \ 10\ 000 = \ \ \ \ 40\ 000$

$6 \times\ \ \ \ \ \ \ 1\ 000 = \ \ \ \ \ 6\ 000$

$9 \times\ \ \ \ \ \ \ \ \ 100 = \ \ \ \ \ \ \ 900$

$8 \times\ \ \ \ \ \ \ \ \ \ 10 = \ \ \ \ \ \ \ \ \ 80$

$4 \times\ \ \ \ \ \ \ \ \ \ \ 1 = \ \ \ \ \ \ \ \ \ \ \ 4$

---

skill check   Tell the value of the red digits in **451 829 709**

EXERCISES

Tell the value of the digit 4 in each numeral.

1. 407 233 861
2. 914 703 121
3. 389 478 501
4. 28 702 564
5. 56 384 097
6. 72 140 538

Answer these questions about the numeral 571 429 086.

7. What is the value of the digit 1?
8. What is the value of the digit 2?
9. What digit is in ten millions' place?

An Explanation of the Program

Scope and sequence. The first ten to twenty pages of a teacher's edition are usually given to a complete explanation of the mathematics program in that particular series. The mathematics in the entire series is usually summarized, topic by topic (often called strands), grade level by grade level, in a *scope-and-sequence chart*. These charts frequently run across three or four pages. We have reproduced one part of a scope-and-sequence chart below.

One series may highlight a special topic, such as "Applications" or "Number Theory," as an additional strand, but upon close examination you will likely find the material in those strands to be incorporated in other series under different strands. For example, material appearing in one series under "Applications" will appear in another under "Problem Solving." The importance of a scope-and-sequence chart lies in its usefulness in answering such questions as:

What exactly is covered in this particular book?

What mathematics has been studied in previous books in this series?

What mathematics is coming up in future books?

Where do we find addition and subtraction of fractions?

Where is area presented?

What should my students have had in geometry by now?

What will I be teaching in geometry this year?

Do not be overly concerned if some of your students have been using a different textbook series. A check of the scope-and-sequence charts for a number of series will make you think, "All scope-and-sequence charts look pretty much the same." Textbooks differ much more in the way material is presented than they do in mathematical content.

The authors' beliefs. In explaining their program to teachers, authors do more than present a scope-and-sequence chart. Frequently, they state how they intend the text to be used and also their beliefs about teaching and learning.

In reading the introductory remarks of a teacher's edition, look for the authors' stated beliefs on issues such as problem solving, applications, drill and practice, and the relative importance of the various strands in the scope-and-sequence chart. An understanding of these matters can assist you in making instructional decisions. For example, suppose the authors state that much tiresome drill and practice can be avoided by giving students a variety of explanations and by having them discover the rules for certain operations. You can expect this text to have lots of good ideas for presenting mathematics and an abundance of leading questions but only a modest amount of exercises and practice material. If you believe the acquisition of skills requires careful attention to drill and practice, then you must plan to construct such activities or find them elsewhere.

In similar vein, look for the authors' philosophical position on the issues of the "why" of a procedure and the "how" of the same process. Do they believe both are important or is one going to be emphasized in this book more than the other? The hypothetical position stated in the previous paragraph would indicate these authors place more emphasis on "why" and less on "how."

	1	**2**
OPERATIONS AND PROPERTIES	Addition: sums to 5 Subtraction: differences from 5 Addition: sums to 9 Subtraction: differences from 9 Addition: vertical form Subtraction: vertical form Related number sentences Add tens: sums to 90 Subtract tens: from 90 or less Add tens and ones Subtract tens and ones Commutative and associative properties of addition Find a missing addend Addition: sums to 18 Sums of doubles Subtraction: differences from 18 Multiplication readiness	Write addition sentences Use number line: sums to 5 Write subtraction sentences Related number sentences Use number line: differences from 5 Addition: sums of 6-10 Use number line: sums of 6-10 Subtraction: differences from 6-10 Use number line: differences from 6-10 Add and subtract tens Add and subtract with 2-digit numerals Add with 3 addends Associative property of addition Commutative property of addition Addition and subtraction facts: 11-18 Add and subtract tens and ones Multiplication: 2-6 as factors Multiplication: as repeated addition Relate multiplication and division Addition: rename 10 ones as 1 ten Subtraction: rename 1 ten as 10 ones
SETS, NUMBERS, AND NUMERATION	Identify sets of 2, 3, 4, 5, 1, and 0 Write numerals 0-5 Write numerals for one more, one less Identify sets of 6, 7, 8, and 9 Write numerals 6-9 Identify and mark sets of 10 Write numerals 0-10 in order Write numerals to complete sequences Match ordinal numbers and words Mark halves, fourths, and thirds Identify half, fourth, and third Order the numerals 1-12 Select sets of 10 Recognize sets of 19 or less Write numerals 10-19 in order Recognize and record sets of 20-49 Write numerals in order to 50 Count by twos and fives to 50 Write numerals, sets of tens Odd and even numbers Write numerals, sets of tens and ones Write numerals 100-150 in order Join sets with same number of members Write numerals in order through 200	Match members of two sets Match a numeral with a set Zero: as numeral for empty set Write numerals 0-9 and 10-19 Write numbers as tens and ones Write standard numeral: tens and ones Write numerals to 100 in order Group into tens and ones Ordinal numbers: *first* through *tenth* Count by tens Place value: 2-digit numerals Write numerals: hundreds, tens, and ones Write numerals in sequence to 200 Place value: 3-digit numerals Identify halves, fourths, and thirds Rename hundreds and tens as tens Count in order to 1000 Ordinal numbers: to *twentieth* Rename 10 ones and 1 ten Odd and even numbers Complete sequences Union of sets Different names for the same number

SENTENCES AND PROBLEM SOLVING	Write addition sentences for number
	   stories
	Write subtraction sentences for number
	   stories
	Interpret number stories
		Read and solve number stories
		Solve number stories: facts, 11-12
		Solve number stories: facts, 13-16
		Solve number stories: facts, 11-18

Special features. In explaining their program, authors usually elaborate on the special features of their textbooks. The use of boldface type, color, photographs, cartoon characters, and other points will be explained. Another feature, appearing in most recent series, is the identification of performance (behavioral) objectives for each chapter and/or lesson in the text. Some series give these in a particular place in the teacher's edition. Other series display them on each page of the students' text. Knowledge of the authors' intent for a particular lesson can assist you in planning your explanations and in forming questions evaluating the effectiveness of the lesson. Frequently, only a single performance objective is given for each lesson. This should not prevent you from establishing additional objectives to measure students' understanding. (See the chapter on "Teaching for Understanding," Section 1.)

Other features of a textbook series may be discussed in the introductory pages of the teacher's edition. Many authors incorporate reviews, challenging puzzles, games, and even units on special topics into their series. Some of these features appear in the students' books. Others are only in the teacher's edition. It is a common practice for teachers' editions to include estimates of the amount of time teachers should spend on various chapters or lessons.

Suggestions for Implementing the Program

Chapter overviews. Teachers' editions should contain an overview for each unit or chapter. The mathematics is summarized, and in some cases the teacher is given some background material for further understanding of certain topics. In addition, the overview often lists prerequisites and gives sample test items to use in checking on students' knowledge of these prerequisites. The authors frequently outline expected outcomes of studying the chapter. This can be done with a list of performance objectives and by identifying difficulties and errors students are likely to make.

The information contained in a chapter overview can serve as valuable background information as you preview a chapter with students. Use of this fundamental reading technique can help teachers and students in setting their expectations for the unit of study. There is little doubt that setting realistic objectives in a positive way can have a positive effect upon learning.

Time schedules and individualization. Almost all teachers' editions address the issue of individualizing instruction. The authors make the point that different groups of children progress through the text at different rates. This discussion appears where a timetable is presented. Suggestions for spending more or less time on certain topics and the omission of certain groups of lessons may be given for both high-ability and low-ability groups. Places in the text where teacher-directed remedial and enrichment activities are presented are also identified.

Examine one part of an individualized course and time schedule, below, noting in particular that the *minimum* course spends the *most* time on each lesson while covering the fewest topics. The approach is to learn a few things well. The maximum course spends fewer days on each lesson and covers all topics. Presumably, more able students can learn many things well.

The Individualized Course and Time Schedule is designed to assist you in planning a minimum, an average, or a maximum one-year course in mathematics. The minimum course (Min.) includes all the basic skills and concepts and is for students who need extra time for drill, practice, and the mastery of new ideas. It concludes with Chapter Eight. The average course (Avg.) uses somewhat less time for the basic skills and concepts and includes additional work in geometry and measurement. It is completed at the end of Chapter Nine. Students who assimilate mathematics quickly and who need less than the normal time to master new skills and concepts should be given the maximum course (Max.). This course allows time for the study of probability, statistics, graphing, integers, and other enrichment topics given in Chapter Ten.

Since students seldom progress precisely according to a predetermined time schedule, this schedule is offered merely as a suggestion. To master any given topic, students may need more or less than the recommended number of class periods. If minimum- or average-course students have the time, topics from the last two chapters can be included in their programs.

Concepts	Pages	Lessons	Class Periods per Course		
			Min.	Avg.	Max.
Rounding	17-18	1	1	1	1
Base Six	19-22	2		2	2
Addition Facts and Patterns	23-24	2	2	1	1
Properties of Addition	25	1		1	1
Roman Numerals	26	1		1	1
Addition and Subtraction of Whole Numbers	27-33	4	4	3	2
Number Sentences	34-36	2		2	1
Word Problems	37-40	4	1	1	1

Suggestions for each lesson. The most useful information in any teacher's edition is contained in the suggestions for each lesson in the text. These suggestions are usually made in the margins, alongside the replicas of each page of the student's text. The suggestions are usually made under a set of headings. A typical set of headings is as follows: Background Material, Purpose of Lesson, Presenting the Lesson, Key Questions, Follow-up Activities, For Low Achievers, For Advanced Students. Here the authors draw upon their knowledge and experience to make specific, down-to-earth suggestions. Suggestions are made about chalkboard displays and overhead displays, on points for elaboration and discussion, and on demonstrations and uses of manipulative materials.

Discussion Questions

1. One of the most notable features of a teacher's edition is its provision of answers. Discuss ways in which a teacher could use answers. Could they be used to individualize instruction? Could having answers help you in diagnosing conceptual problems? in preventing discipline problems? in other uses?

2. Are authors likely to overstate the merits of their series? Why?

3. Some teachers eliminate geometry and measurement for students who are of below-average ability. Is this proper? Are these topics important? practical? Which is more important, knowing how to measure area or knowing how to divide fractions?

4. Many of the suggestions in this section relate to understanding the curriculum as presented in the text. How important do you believe it is to follow the authors' approach? Can or should each teacher be free to teach in his or her own way?

6. THE STUDENT'S TEXT AND OTHER MATERIALS

Explanation, Exercises, and Problems

The vast majority of space in the children's text is given to explanations, exercises, and problems. The explanations are the principal reading material in the text. They are intended for students. Helping children in learning to read the sentences, pictures, graphs, symbols, and computations that make up these explanations is an important instructional responsibility.

The exercises and problems in the students' books are a valuable resource. Mathematics is not for spectators. Children must *do* it. Working the exercises and problems in their textbooks and workbooks and creating and solving their own problems are essential in learning mathematics. Such work can be overdone. The assignment of large numbers of exercises and problems, particularly as a device to keep children quietly occupied, is a poor teaching practice. Tedious assignments cause children to dislike mathematics and to believe it is a boring subject. Short written assignments of five to ten minutes in length, accompanied by help, encouragement, and knowledge of results, are very worthwhile. Assignments taking thirty minutes or longer to complete, without guidance and encouragement, and waiting until the following day for knowledge of results are likely to produce inaccurate work and a dislike of the subject.

Spread out practice sessions, keep them short, check the work as soon as possible.

Review Exercises

Review exercises appear in various places but almost always at the completion of each unit. One way to use these exercises is to have children work them and grade their own papers. Call this a "practice test" if you like. Then extra practice and/or additional explanations can be designed for individual students. Review exercises can also be used for an oral review and discussion of a unit.

Frequently, review exercises are placed in the middle of a unit. Such exercises are usually intended as a review of material in other, previously studied units. They are scattered through the textbook to maintain skills. Skills become "rusty" without practice. Half a page of review exercises for every ten pages of text is about right. If your text does not include frequent reviews of previously studied material, you should construct your own.

Enrichment Problems

Most textbook series incorporate some kind of "extra credit" problems. Sometimes these are displayed in special inserts on pages in each unit. They are frequently captioned with titles such as "Brainbuster" or "Mind Puzzler."[1] Suggestions for projects and demonstrations are sometimes made in problem sets. Quite often, such problems are marked with a star or an asterisk.

Many teachers feel that puzzles, hard problems, and projects are only for their advanced students. This is not true. A hint, or being allowed to work with a partner, can sometimes help a slower student to experience the pleasure of resolving a brainbuster and then trying it on friends or parents. Tell your students, "Puzzles are supposed to be tricky. You should not feel badly about being unable to solve them. Try them for fun."

Glossary

Most student textbooks contain a glossary. This alphabetical list of definitions and illustrations of the mathematical terms in the text can be used in constructing and conducting vocabulary drills. The glossary can serve as a source of items for many reading skills exercises. For example, in playing "Password," players can obtain words and ideas for hints from the glossary. The glossary can also be used to construct vocabulary tests. Students should often be encouraged to use the glossary when they are reading mathematics and come across a term they think is new or one they have forgotten.

Material for Extra Practice Offered by Publishers

In addition to the pupil's text and the teacher's edition, publishers generally offer a wide variety of other materials related to their text series. No teacher is able to use all of these items, but a carefully selected set of supplementary mate-

---

[1]Here is an example of a Brainbuster—try it!

A man has 20 coins consisting of dimes and quarters. If the dimes were quarters and the quarters were dimes, he would have 90 cents more than he has now. How many dimes and quarters does he have?

rials can be an aid to learning. We list here and discuss the items most frequently offered as companions to the text in a complete program, or system.

The most common items for extra practice in computation are workbooks, practice pads, boxed sets of skill cards, and duplicating masters. It is unlikely that one would use all of these items. A teacher should select those which she or he can use most effectively.

Boxed sets of skill cards are designed to be used in a diagnostic setting or in a program with emphasis on individual progress. Normally, the students first complete an inventory test; then their errors direct them to certain cards for practice on appropriate material. Care must be taken in using the cards that adequate instruction is given on the topics to be covered. The cards are designed to assist individualization but they are *not* a substitute for the teacher in explaining the material. Because of this and because of a lack of attention to topics other than computation, the cards do not by themselves comprise a suitable mathematics program. Skill cards are designed to be used as an aid for individual computational practice.

Duplicating masters can be used in about the same ways as the boxed sets of skill cards. Different students may work with them on different topics at the same time. Of course, the same caution applies to the use of duplicating masters that was discussed for skill cards. The duplicating masters have the advantage that children do not have to copy the exercises before working them.

Workbooks and practice pads tend to be used in a less individual way than skill cards and duplicating masters. Using a workbook or practice pad, with its pages keyed to pages or objectives in the text, is a good way to provide extra practice for students who need that extra practice for most lessons in the text. Workbooks and practice pads, being consumable write-in items, can also be used to save children the completely unnecessary labor of copying problems. This is extremely desirable in cases where the law states that all textbooks must be hardbound and reusable.

Many publishers and other educational suppliers have audio tapes or slide presentations for practice activities on the basic facts of addition, subtraction, multiplication, and division and such topics as time, counting, and money. They are of variable quality and effectiveness. Audio tapes often are too slow to provide effective practice on basic facts and it is impossible to speed them up. Many slide projectors, however, can be adjusted for speed to meet the present rate of response for various groups of children. Slide presentations can be used for both large and small group drills. A fast-paced slide drill, perhaps in the form of a contest, can be an exciting drill.

All in all, there are enough materials for extra practice to "choke a horse" or to stun a student. A child whose arithmetic program is one page of exercises after another will become bored with arithmetic. The majority of class time should be spent on developmental teaching and explanations designed to build understanding. Use extra practice materials with discretion and only after you have carefully considered what kind and amount of drill the student needs.

Supplementary Topics

In various programs and systems, some material will be presented through an extra booklet or on duplicating masters. Often, material which is "extra" in one series will be "standard" in another. These supplements can be found on a wide variety of topics: The metric system is widely offered as a supplement; independent student investigations or laboratory exercises are popular; and enrichment topics sometimes considered too difficult for the regular text may be offered this way. Material which either supplements the text or reinforces the text is frequently available on films, film loops, or audio tapes. As with the text itself, you should evaluate supplementary material with care before you buy it in quantity. A good plan is to begin with a small quantity until the value of the item can be determined.

Teaching Aids and Laboratory Material

Many publishing firms are now in the business of supplying concrete teaching aids and laboratory materials. Laboratory activities are frequently designed for a kit of materials, containing either laboratory task cards or an instruction booklet. Because of the necessity of having equipment of various kinds (e.g., scales, tape measures, stop watch), these materials are always supplementary rather than being an integral part of the mathematics program.

Concrete materials are used to illustrate concepts and operations. The range of materials available for this purpose has increased substantially over the past few years, and the problem, for a school with money to spend, is not finding materials but selecting from this abundance the items that will be most effective.

It is not a good idea to order a large quantity of any teaching aid at first. A better procedure is to order small quantities of different materials and to try them in the classroom. At this stage, learning how to use the materials is essential. If you are experimenting with a variety of materials, you may profit from discussing with other teachers how each item is used and what each is designed to help teach. When you have decided which items are most effective for you, you may then wish to get a more complete set of these materials.

Discussion Questions

1. How can a teacher determine the need for extra practice? How can you detect the need for more practice as opposed to the need for more explanation?

2. Enrichment problems are supposed to be enjoyable. Did you find them so when you were in school? How can you make them enjoyable for your students?

SUGGESTED ASSIGNMENTS AND PROJECTS

Classroom Assignments

1. Using general materials suitable for children reading at a third-grade level, cite a dozen instances where children are reading the language of mathematics. In each case, identify the mathematical words and symbols. Use materials such as *My Weekly Reader,* current events, newsletters, magazines for children, and other materials designed for children.

2. Obtain two textbooks from courses you have taken in high school or college. One of these should be a mathematics text. The other should be in some other subject. Time yourself in reading a three-page passage in each text. Be sure to skim the mathematics text first and then read at a pace that permits you to understand the material.

3. Using a child's mathematics textbook, read a series of about 20 lessons. As you read, make a list of words and symbols that are likely to be new or difficult for children to understand. Also note, on the basis of your reading, those lessons that ask children to observe a pattern and figure out, or discover some relationship.

4. Without glancing at Table 1, construct a list of 20 words that have both a mathematical meaning and a common, or everyday, meaning. Then check your results against Table 1.

5. Is there a difference between knowing the meaning of a word and being *skilled* in knowing the meaning of a word?

6. a. What teaching procedures could you use to teach the meaning of these mathematical terms: millimeter, centimeter, decimeter, meter?

b. What different teaching techniques should you use to help children acquire skill in knowing the meanings of these same words?

7. Without checking Table 2, construct a list of at least 30 mathematical symbols used in elementary school mathematics. Did you list any that were not in Table 2?

8. With another adult simulate a conversation between two fifth-grade students. The students are discussing how to perform algorithms, such as the following:

$$\begin{aligned} \frac{3}{4} &= \frac{9}{12} \\ + \frac{2}{3} &= \frac{8}{12} \\ \hline \frac{17}{12} &= 1\frac{5}{12} \end{aligned}$$

One student knows the procedure and is telling the other how to read and do the algorithm. The second student keeps asking questions, such as: "How did you get that?" and "Why do we do that?"

9. In Section 4 three different kinds of reading assignments were discussed. In addition, three pages from students' textbooks were displayed. For each of the three student pages, outline how you would conduct the first type of reading assignment, that is, how you would read it aloud with the children. What would you do? What would you have the children do?

10. Select teachers' editions of mathematics textbooks from three different publishers. Compare the scope-and-sequence chart and the introductory remarks of each. Are they basically the same? What appears to be the major difference in these series? Is it the grade placement of topics, the selection of topics, eye appeal, or the way the reading material is presented? How do the authors claim to have provided for children of varying ability in mathematics? Do all series present enrichment problems? Are the suggestions for teaching individual lessons more comprehensive in one series than in the others?

11. Without glancing at the scope-and-sequence chart in Section 5, predict the grade placements of the following topics. Then check your predictions—some may appear at more than one grade level.

Addition: sums to 5

Add and subtract 2-digit numerals

Addition: sums to 18

Multiplication readiness

Mark halves, fourths, and thirds

Write numerals to 100 in order

Internship Assignments

1. Use the check list in section 3 — for diagnosing mathematics reading problems — to construct a diagnostic reading test for some child. On the basis of your diagnosis, plan and conduct a series of reading lessons for that child over a two- or three-week period. Posttest, using the same diagnostic test. Discuss your results and outline a new series of lessons either to further develop or to maintain that child's reading techniques and skills.

2. Depending upon which is the most appropriate for a given group of children, conduct two reading lessons, using two of the techniques described in Section 4.

3. From either the glossary, a list of terms at the end of a chapter, or by examining a chapter being studied by a group of students, plan and conduct a lesson designed to improve the students' skills in knowing the meanings of these words and symbols. Assume the meanings of the terms and symbols have been acquired. Remember, skills are developed through practice. Be sure to incorporate feedback. At the conclusion of the lesson, identify words and symbols the meanings of which are apparently not clear to the children. Then design and conduct a lesson to reteach these meanings. Use the ideas presented in Section 2 for teaching the meanings of words.

SUMMARY: MAXIMS FOR TEACHING

1. In teaching children to become skilled at reading mathematics, help and encourage children by having them
a. skim first for an overview.
b. read slowly and carefully for detail.
c. note and ask about new terms, symbols, phrases, and diagrams.
d. realize the different mathematical and nonmathematical meanings of many of the words used in mathematics.
e. practice recognizing the meaning of mathematics vocabulary words and symbols.
f. realize the order in which computations are performed and recorded.
g. read word problems carefully to be able to state the problem in their own words before they attempt a solution.

2. If a child is having difficulty in reading mathematics, a teacher should consider using a diagnostic scheme (see Section 3) to determine whether the child is lacking in Basic Techniques, General Skills, or Special Skills in reading mathematics.

3. Occasionally, use reading as a teaching technique — have children depend on their reading skills to participate in a mathematics lesson.

4. Use your teacher's edition! It can help you realize the intent and objectives of the authors, provide the scope and sequence of the curriculum, and offer suggestions for particular lessons.

5. Make use of all the features in the student's text — the review exercises, enrichment problems, and glossary.

6. Consider supplemental publications by the publisher of your textbook series. These include: extra practice materials, games, diagnostic and achievement tests, manipulative materials, and enrichment activities and topics.

TWO · CONTENT

9 · Teaching Whole Numbers

INTRODUCTION

The purpose of this chapter is to review the content of the elementary mathematics curriculum in the area of whole numbers. This includes developing number concepts, relations between whole numbers, and operations performed on whole numbers. Emphasis will be placed on understanding the material children are to learn and on sample activities through which that material may be taught. The activities frequently involve the use of concrete materials to explain and illustrate the processes and concepts of arithmetic.

1. DEVELOPING WHOLE-NUMBER CONCEPTS

The first set of numbers that children learn is the set of whole numbers, 0, 1, 2, 3, and so on. It is frequently suggested that learning to count and to say number names are the first step in this developmental process but that is not the case. There are many things children can and should learn before they learn to count. To emphasize this, we will refer to these as "precounting objectives."

Precounting Objectives and Activities

Children should be able to do many things involving number concepts before they learn counting and number names. While some children already possess these skills when they come to kindergarten, other children do not have them upon entering first grade. These children are frequently placed in a "readiness" group. This group will do kindergarten-level work until they are ready for first-grade work.

Number is a complex concept. It has two major characteristics—cardinality and ordinality. Consider the number *five*. A group of five objects, such as ∴, is a cardinal representation of the number *five*. It is a property of the entire set, not just one member. Compare this cardinality, or totality, aspect of *five* with the notion of the fifth object in a sequence. To say a person is fifth in line is a specification of the ordinal aspect of fiveness. This ordinal aspect is associated with one element of the set, not with the set as a whole. These two aspects of number —cardinality, or totality, and ordinality, or position—are complementary and, of course, are closely related. Both need to be taught. We now consider developing these two aspects of number.

Matching Relations—Cardinal Number Readiness

Children should be able to compare sets by matching. This comparison is done by pairing the elements of the sets to be compared. When the elements have been paired, the result is either a one-to-one correspondence (Figure *A*), or one set has one or more elements left over (Figure *B*). If there is one-to-one

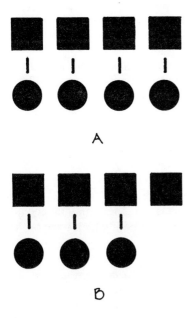

A

B

correspondence, the phrases "same number as" and "as many as" are used to compare the sets. Recognition of this relation will lead children to an understanding of *equality*, which will be studied later in mathematics. In the case where one or more elements are left over, the children may say there are "more" in one set and "less," or "fewer," in the other. This will lead in later mathematics to the relations *greater than* and *less than*.

Note that children do not need to count or to know any number names to make these comparisons through matchings. Matchings are, or should be, learned before the introduction of counting.

Typical matching exercises involve a natural connection between objects.

This helps children do the matching. There may be as many rabbits as carrots or there may be more dogs than dog houses in pictures that children match.

Children should recognize the matching relations "as many as," "more than," and "fewer than" and further should recognize that these relations are independent of the size or position of the objects. Young children frequently make comparisons based on the size or position of the elements. They also *change* their judgment of the relationship if the position of the objects is changed. Consider the squares and circles in the drawing below. A child who says "same number" when the objects are in position *A*, may change the response to "more circles" when the objects are moved to position *B*. This child has not yet recognized that the relationship is independent of changes in position. A child who recognizes that the relationship is independent of position is said to "conserve" the relation. Such a child will continue to assert that there are the same number of objects, even though they are moved to position *B*.

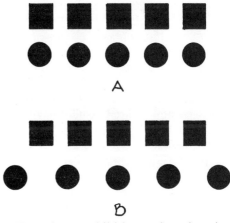

A

B

How does a child learn that changing from *A* to *B* does not change the relation between the sets? We are not sure. We know it requires many experiences by the child with sets of objects over a period of time. Providing a few examples and a verbal explanation is not effective. The child may learn to "respond" correctly but be responding to you or your explanation rather than to the relation exemplified by the sets. It is through the child's *own* organization of experiences that he or she comes to recognize and understand that changing the position of elements in the sets does not change the relation between the sets. You could ask questions designed to help the child reflect on number conservation and ask the child to try to match sets that have been changed from position *A* to position *B* or to put them back the way they were.

Don't verbally force conclusions on children. Let the physical situations dispose them to reorganize their thinking. A child should have substantial experience working with concrete objects. In particular, a child should form one-to-one correspondences as in *A*, move to position *B*, and back to *A*. Pictures of sets can also be used to develop this understanding.

Children should use matching to create a set of objects or draw a set of marks so that the set created has as many members as a given set, has more than a given set, or has fewer than a given set. Concrete examples should come first, of course. Examples indicate the performance desired. Children may be asked to draw a set of marks that matches a set of pictures. Children may also be asked to draw more or fewer marks than are in a set of pictures.

All of these tasks can be done successfully without any mention of number names or counting. These comparisons are made entirely on the basis of matching sets.

Order Relations—Ordinal Number Readiness

Just as sets and pairing of elements were used to develop readiness for cardinal number, so a variety of ordering and comparison (premeasurement) activities can be used to develop readiness for ordinal number.

Children should be able to compare two objects and tell which is longer or shorter, fatter or thinner, or larger or smaller in some other sense. In some cases this is easy. When objects or pictures are presented with the ends lined up conveniently, there is not much difficulty in selecting the longer or shorter object. When the ends are not lined up conveniently, there may be considerable discussion about which object is longer.

Children should be able to place collections of objects in order from longest to shortest or from largest to smallest. This objective is an extension of the previous objective. It involves sequencing and comparing and ordering three or more objects. Children may make various lengths and place them in order from longest to shortest or shortest to longest. The lengths do not have to be graduated

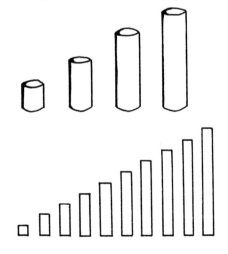

in "one-step" lengths. Children can also sequence collections that have irregular intervals.

One of the first activities recommended in the use of rod or bar devices is to make a staircase by arranging the rods from shortest to longest. The rods come in graduated one-step lengths. There are 10 rods, having lengths proportional to the numbers 1 to 10. They are arranged in a staircase, as shown above. The staircase shows a connection between the cardinal and the ordinal aspects of number. The fifth rod in the row is as long as five of the first rod; thus, the fifth rod represents *five* in both a cardinal and an ordinal sense.

Children should be able to follow and construct patterns based on ordering and number sequences. Patterns are important in learning mathematical generalizations. Often, it is far easier to see the pattern of a mathematical idea than to learn a verbal expression of that idea. Pattern recognition starts early and can be developed through practice. The display shown below is used to practice pattern recognition. Each of these patterns has numerical elements: 1 dark, 1 light; 1 *x*, 2 *0*'s; 3 dark, 1 light; 1 *0*, 1 *x*, 2 *0*'s, 1 *x*, and so on.

The ordering and number sequences can be used to introduce the number line. In the illustrations on the next page children make hops along the number line and see both sets and numerals, associating the cardinal and the ordinal aspects of number.

Counting — The Introduction of Number Concepts

In the preceding sections we have seen how children can build readiness for the development of cardinal and ordinal number. We now look at some ways in which numbers can be introduced.

Pattern and rote counting. *Children should be able to say the number names and recognize numerals in order*—first to 10, then to 20, and then to 100. Children can learn to say by pure memory the number names and to recognize numerals up to 20. It is desirable for them to learn this because they use rote counting in learning to count rationally. Counting beyond 20 or 30 to 100 or more is not a rote, or pure memory, performance. If it were, few children could do it! Counting to 100 and above requires memorizing decade names and the recognition of patterns all based on the pattern of 0-1-2-3-4-5-6-7-8-9-10. Multiples of 10 (10, 20, 30, . . .),

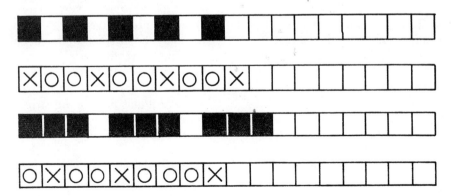

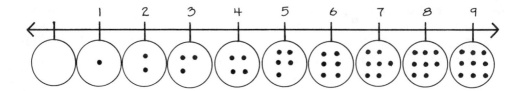

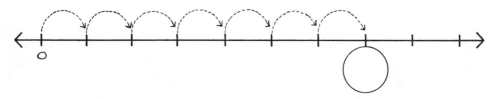

multiples of 100 (100, 200, 300, . .), etc., all follow the 1 – 10 pattern.

1–	10–	100–1,000
2–	20–	200–2,000
3–	30–	300–
4–	40–	400– and
5–	50–	500–
6–	60–	600– so
7–	70–	700–
8–	80–	800– on
9–	90–	900–
10–	100–	1,000–

From one multiple of 10 to the next multiple of 10, counting from 1 to 10 is repeated, as, for example, in 70, 71, 72, 73, 74, 75, 76, 77, 78, 79, 80. Children could not possibly count to 100 or beyond without a recognition of these patterns. This patterned counting is far more important than the phrase "rote counting" suggests. Patterned counting to 100 is an important objective of first-grade mathematics.

One device that can be used in teaching pattern counting to 100 is a hundred board or a hundred chart. A hundred board or a hundred chart is a rectangular arrangement of the numbers from 1 to 100 or from 0 to 99.

0	1	2	3	4	5	6	7	8	9
10	11	12	13	14	15	16	17	18	19
20	21	22	23	24	25	26	27	28	29
30	31	32	33	34	35	36	37	38	39
40	41	42	43	44	45	46	47	48	49
50	51	52	53	54	55	56	57	58	59
60	61	62	63	64	65	66	67	68	69
70	71	72	73	74	75	76	77	78	79
80	81	82	83	84	85	86	87	88	89
90	91	92	93	94	95	96	97	98	99

You may wish to construct a hundred board from wood using nails to hold tags with numerals on one side. Children can practice pattern counting starting with the blank sides of the tags facing out and turning the tags over. They can proceed in order horizontally at first. Then they can be asked to make vertical as well as horizontal predictions.

It may be helpful to have children construct hundred charts from a number line drawn on a long sheet of paper. Do this by cutting the number line at 9, 19, 29, . . . 99 and placing the strips in the rectangular pattern displayed on a hundred chart.

Rational counting. *Children should be able to count the elements of a set by* *ones and state the number in the set.* Rational counting, in contrast to rote counting, is more than repeating the number names in order. In rational counting the children begin with a set and as they say each number name, they identify an element of the set; every element of the set is noted and no repetitions are allowed. This forms a one-to-one correspondence between the set of number names and the set of objects. The last number named is the number of things in the set, and the set will have the same count regardless of the order of counting. This is usually the first and, at the elementary school level, the most frequently used model of number. As we shall see, sets are combined and separated in various ways to model each of the basic operations. Correctly forming this matching is not easy for some young children. The required hand-eye-voice coordination is difficult, as is keeping track of which elements have been counted. When the counting process is completed, the number in the set is the last number named. Some children do not know this! If they count a set and you then ask, "How many?" they will count the set again. They think the question "How many?" is a direction to count.

The activities of rote and pattern counting and rational counting are not strictly sequenced. Children may be counting rationally sets of 5 or 10 while still learning pattern counting to higher numbers. Children will increase gradually in their ability to count to higher numbers.

Children should recognize that the number of elements in a set remains the same regardless of rearrangements of the elements. This is similar to the conservation of one-to-one correspondence between sets. The recognition that the number is not changed by a different order of counting is also involved. As with several other objectives, gradual accumulation of counting experience finally accomplishes this objective; direct teaching is not very effective unless the child has accumulated the counting experience.

Understanding Number Concepts

The concept of six. Teachers frequently say they want children to *really understand* number concepts. A student who really understands the concept of *six* can do the things listed below. Of course, the student doesn't learn them all at once but gradually over the primary grades. It is particularly important for students to acquire a complete understanding of the numbers 0 to 10 because larger number concepts are built on such understandings.

The Concept of Six

The student:
1. counts a set of six objects and responds "six" or writes the numeral "6" in answer to the question, "How many things are there?" and conserves the answer when the set of six objects is rearranged.
2. knows that any set in one-to-one correspondence to a set of six also has six elements.
3. when told "Get six____from the box," can do so.
4. can state some numbers that are larger than six and some that are smaller than six.
5. can compare, in varying perceptual situations, a set of six objects to sets containing five and seven objects and state the correct matching rela-

tion *(more than, fewer than)* between the sets.

6. can read and write the numeral "6."
7. in a sequence of things, can identify the sixth one.
8. can arrange things in a series so that a specific one will be sixth.
9. can tell the ordinal number (position) of a specified element in a series when the specified element is sixth.
10. can identify at sight a set of six in comparison to a set of three or a set of twelve.
11. given a number line with only the points for 0 and 1 labeled, can identify the point to be labeled 6.
12. can tell what whole numbers come before and after six.
13. can express six as a sum, e.g., five and one more, and as a difference, e.g., two less than eight, in a variety of ways.

Representing larger numbers. We now proceed to the modeling of concepts of larger whole numbers and the introduction of numerals for these numbers. Children and adults, too, have limited ability to deal with large numbers of objects in an unorganized form. You can see in the figure that it is far easier to find the number in the organized set. The collections both contain almost 50 objects. Yet in set *A* it is difficult to estimate the number and next to impossible to tell the number exactly without tedious counting. In set *B*, when the organizing principle is understood, one can tell at a glance that there are between 40 and 50, nearly 50, and with a little counting, exactly 47.

Our numeration system uses a grouping principle that groups 10 ones into 1 ten, 10 tens into 1 hundred, 10 hundreds into 1 thousand, and so on. *Children*

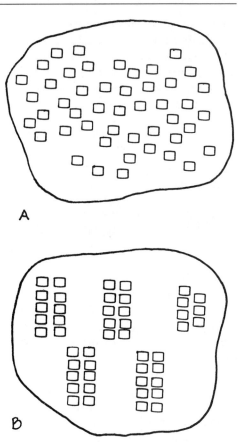

must understand this grouping principle if numerals and the ways numerals are used in the algorithms of arithmetic are to make sense to them! For example, as first-grade children learn about numbers from 10 to 100, they group them by tens. This means that 52 *must* be thought about as 5 tens and 2 ones as well as 52 ones.

Concrete models. A variety of concrete materials are used to help children understand numbers larger than 10. The pictures of ones, tens, and hundreds commonly used in textbooks are not effective for numbers much larger than 200. Sets of loose counting objects cannot be used effectively in instruction for numbers much larger than 50. The time taken to count out sets simply consumes the instructional time available. Because of these problems, teachers use a variety of concrete aids which are structured to represent, or model, numbers organized on the same principle as our numeration system, that is, as ones, tens, hundreds, and so forth. You will observe in these models a progression from a "real" representation, in which the units are actually there and available for counting, to a more abstract representation. These models, in addition to their use in teaching number and numeration concepts, are used to present and explain the algorithms for whole numbers and decimal fractions. Consequently, they will be used frequently as we present those topics.

Counting objects, used extensively to teach small whole-number concepts, are also used to introduce grouping. Children count sets, grouping the objects in sets of ten. They can quickly learn that it is easier to count sets grouped by tens and then whatever loose ones may be left over than it is to count by ones. They can learn to associate the tens and the ones with the spoken and written forms of the numeral.

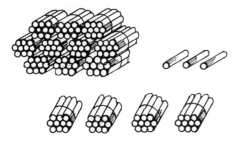

Many exercises in Grade 1 are designed to make the process of grouping by tens automatic for children. The teen numbers are organized as 1 group of ten and some more ones. Unorganized sets

are grouped by tens in order to count the sets more easily and to write the numbers. Multiples of ten are recognized and children count by tens, as "ten, twenty, thirty, . . ." or "1 ten, 2 tens, 3 tens, ..." Sets of objects are organized into groups of tens and ones, and the grouping is associated with a 2-digit numeral on a tens' and ones' grid.

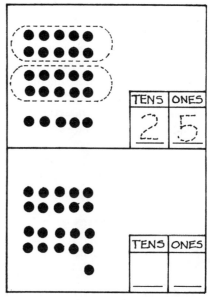

A hundred chart mentioned earlier is another way to depict the decades up to 100. Try to get children to see the horizontal and vertical relationships in a hundred chart. Each horizontal row is a decade. The vertical columns show increases and decreases by tens.

The number line can be labeled with numerals in various ways, depending on the concepts children are learning at the time. The number lines below show 0 to 10, a decade between 10 and 100, and counting by tens from 300 to 400. The number line shows the order of the numbers and, in a measurement sense, their magnitude. It is also used extensively to model various operations.

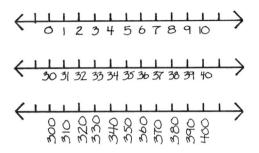

Place value cards and base ten blocks are "preorganized" or constructed to represent ones, tens, hundreds, and thousands. Base ten blocks, especially, give children experience in the size, weight, and feel of numbers from 1 to 1,000 in a way no other material does. A strong association can be seen between the material and the numeral. This builds the number concept and also makes the numeral more meaningful by providing an exact parallel in both structure and value between the concrete material and the numeral.

Devices that represent numbers and the numerals in a semiconcrete form include the counting frame and the place value pocket chart. Note that in place value cards and in base ten blocks you can *see* the 100 little squares on a hundred card or block and count them if you wish. The hundred is actually there in a sense. On a counting frame or a place value pocket chart, the 1 hundred is not actually there but is represented by a bead on the frame or by a slip of paper in the hundreds' pocket. This moves the student one step closer to a symbolic representation. Both these devices, also, are extremely useful in teaching the algorithms for operations.

The concrete materials shown here represent large numbers quite effectively. Because this is the case, drawings of

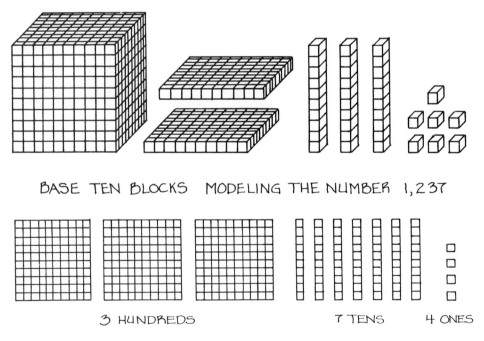

BASE TEN BLOCKS MODELING THE NUMBER 1,237

3 HUNDREDS   7 TENS   4 ONES

PLACE VALUE CARDS MODELING THE NUMBER 374

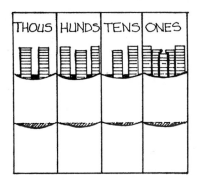

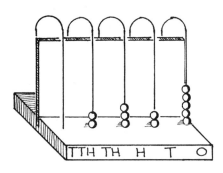

PLACE VALUE POCKET CHART

COUNTING FRAME

these devices are frequently used in text-books to suggest meanings for larger numbers.

After using concrete and pictorial materials to represent numbers, children should understand the standard form of the numeral. A device frequently used to call attention to the values of the places, particularly in operations, is the place value grid. The values of the places are identified at the top, and the numerals are placed in columns under these values. Grids begin in the first grade with the words used to identify the places and, after gradual refinement, are used

	HUN-DREDS	TENS	ONES
TH	H	T	O
1000	100	10	1

THREE FORMS
OF A PLACE VALUE GRID

with powers of ten in the upper grades. When decimal fractions are introduced, the grid is used again.

Looking Back

There are many objectives related to counting which students should master through the primary grades. This mastery is essential in using counting to understand larger numbers and to investigate operations. These objectives include the reading and writing of numerals, skills that we assume children will also learn. The objectives represent the conceptual background, based on counting, for numbers 1 to 1,000. We present a list as a summary to this point.

Children should be able to:

1. Count 1 to 100 by ones.
2. Count 1 to 100 by tens.
3. Read and write the numerals from 1 to 100.
4. Count from a given number by ones, forward or backward.
5. a. Given a set, count by ones and state the number of elements in the set.
   b. Given a number, count by ones to make a set having that many elements.

6. a. Given a set containing a multiple of ten, organize the set in groups of tens and count by tens.

   b. Given a multiple of ten, count objects in groups of ten to create a set having that many elements.

7. a. Given a set $10 \leq N \leq 100$, organize the set into tens and ones and count first tens and then ones.

   b. Given a number $10 \leq N \leq 100$, count objects by tens and ones to make a set with that many elements.

8. a. Given a multiple of ten, tell how many tens are in the number.

   b. Given a number of tens, e.g., "6 tens," tell the regular name for the number.

9. a. Given a two-digit number, tell how many tens and how many ones make up the number.

   b. Given a number of tens and ones, e.g., "5 tens and 4 ones," tell the standard name for the number.

10. Count by hundreds, by tens, or by ones starting at any point between 0 and 1,000.

11. Read and write the numerals from 1 to 1,000.

12. Count the number of elements in a set up to 1,000 elements by first counting sets of 100, then counting sets of 10, and finally counting the ones.

13. Create a set having up to 1,000 elements by first making sets of 100, then constructing sets of 10, and finally adding ones.

14. Order sets of numerals representing the numbers from 1 to 1,000.

15. a. Given a 3-digit number, tell how many hundreds, tens, and ones make up the number.

   b. Given a number of hundreds, tens, and ones, tell and write the standard name for the number.

Discussion Questions

1. How could a teacher use the list of behaviors given above or the list given for the concept of six in

a. planning instruction?

b. diagnosing and assessing learning?

2. Examine a kindergarten and a first-grade mathematics text. How much emphasis is given to

a. ordinal number readiness?

b. cardinal number readiness?

3. Does the phrase "Conservation of Number" as it is usually used refer more to ordinal or more to cardinal number?

4. Suppose a child comes to school for the first time and you are told "Jenny can count all the way to 100. She really understands her numbers." What is your reaction?

5. Design a game that could be played on a hundred chart or board. What is the purpose of your game?

6. When the hundred chart was first mentioned, it was noted that it might be wise to have children construct their first hundred chart by cutting up a number line. Why do you think this was advocated?

7. Design an activity or game using base ten blocks and two or three different colored dice or spinners. Have the children first roll the dice or spin and then construct a representation of a number. What is the purpose of your activity or game?

8. In what ways does the mathematical knowledge presented to this point in this chapter form a basis for explaining and helping children understand addition, subtraction, multiplication, and division of whole numbers?

2. ADDITION

We now turn to a discussion of operations on whole numbers. Each operation is presented in essentially two ways. First, the fundamental meaning of the operation is illustrated, using a variety of models. Second, both concrete and abstract explanations of the algorithm are presented.

Models of Addition

Addition is usually introduced as the joining of two sets, as jumps on the number line, and as lengths of rods or bars. After this concrete introduction children learn to think of addition as a successive counting operation. The problems may be written in horizontal or vertical form. The act of counting each set, writing the numerals, and finally completing the sentence is designed to associate the action and the symbolic representation. As children learn to use the number line to represent numbers, it can be used to give another meaning to addition. At first,

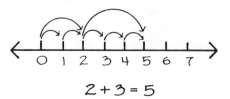

$$2 + 3 = 5$$

children counts "hops" of 1. This illustrates the close relation between counting and measuring. Later, the children will represent the numbers by arrows of lengths 2 and 3. In order to establish these meanings firmly in the minds of the children, teachers spend considerable time in kindergarten and Grades 1 and 2 working with counting objects of all kinds, with number line exercises, and with rod or bar devices. Please refer to the chapter "Teaching Aids and Laboratory Activities" for a description of the uses of rods and bars.

Children can understand and work with story-problem situations, if the numbers used are small, before they can work abstractly with the addition operation. A simple story problem, such as "John has 3 marbles. Ted gives him 2 more. How many does he have?" presents a situation children can act out, or they can use real marbles to find the answer. This kind of story problem *clarifies* the nature of the operation. The story itself can be read to children or put on an experience chart used in a reading lesson. See the chapter on "Problem-Solving Skill" for further ideas on using problems.

The missing addend problem, $3 + \square = 7$, is more appropriate for second or third grade than for first grade. A story is a very useful device for introducing this problem. "John has 3 cents. He wants to buy something that costs 7 cents. How much more does he need?" Children will understand this far more easily than the symbolic form. Another effec-

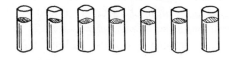

tive way to teach the missing addend is to use two different sets. Using the figure, we may say, "Every child is to have milk and a cookie. How many more cookies do we need?" Eventually, children will solve such problems by subtraction, but the missing addend form, "How many more do we need?" should be retained as long as possible. Teachers find that most first graders and many second graders have difficulty with this kind of problem. Teaching the topic to older children, second or third graders, is far more successful.

You may notice that there are two different ways to represent addition, just as there are two for whole numbers. These are the *counting* model, using sets of discrete objects, and the *measuring* model, using the number line or rods or bars to represent the operation.

As children become familiar with meanings of addition, they will have less need to use concrete and semiconcrete models for the operation. They will internalize the operation, take it into themselves, as a counting operation. When this happens, the child will solve example *A* by counting aloud or silently, "1, 2, 3, 4, 5 (pause), 6, 7, 8."

$$\text{A. } 5 + 3 = \square$$
$$\text{B. } 8 + 2 = \square$$
$$\text{C. } 2 + 8 = \square$$

Notice that after counting to 5 the child has to count "6, 7, 8 *and* keep track of the number of counts. A more efficient process, which children will adopt as their understanding increases, is to "count on" from the first addend rather than to count both numbers. Then they will solve the problem saying, "5 (pause), 6, 7, 8" or just "6, 7, 8." You can tell whether a child is using this process by giving two problems such as *B* and *C*. If the child is counting both numbers, he or she will solve both problems in about the same time. If the child is starting with

the first number and counting on, he or she will solve *B* more quickly than *C*.

In addition to these concrete models and counting procedures, children may, at various times, use many meaningful procedures for finding answers to addition problems. Making one addend a 10 is common. The associative law is at work in example *A*, below. The child thinks, "Take 3 from the 8 and give it to the 7." In example *B* a known fact can be used to find an unknown one. In this case, because $7 + 7 = 14$, $7 + 8$ must be 15. "Eight is 1 more than 7, so the answer must be 1 more." In example *C* "you can add numbers either way," the commutative law of addition, and here again a known fact is used to find an unknown one.

$$\text{A. } 7 + 8 = (7 + 3) + 5$$
$$= 10 + 5 = 15$$

$$\text{B. } 7 + 8 = \square$$
$$\text{I know } 7 + 7 = 14, \text{ so}$$
$$7 + 8 = 15$$

$$\text{C. } 6 + 9 = \square$$
$$\text{I know } 9 + 6 = 15, \text{ so}$$
$$6 + 9 = 15$$

It is perfectly acceptable, and at some stage desirable, for children to find answers by counting their fingers. These are the discrete objects which are most readily available. As children progress through Grades 1 and 2, they should first learn counting procedures described above and then learn the addition facts for automatic recall. Use the techniques in "Teaching for Computational Skills."

Explaining the Addition Algorithm

When children have learned the meanings of the addition operation and have achieved some success in automatic recall of the basic facts, the standard column form of the addition algorithm is introduced. This is done gradually as the child's knowledge of the place value system increases. We will present concrete and semiconcrete models of the algorithm and also logical explanations based on the child's knowledge of addition and of the place value system.

When using a model to explain an operation, it is important to maintain very close association between the model and the problem. As *each* action is performed on the model, the corresponding operation should be done to the written problem. The model and the problem should be close, side by side, so the connection between what is done to the model and what is done to the problem is clear. This is illustrated on the next page as various models of addition are presented.

You will note that these models vary in abstractness. Counting objects and base ten blocks are concrete; a child can actually see and count the numbers. The counting frame is representative of the numbers but there are no actual objects to count. Finally, the algorithm itself is completely abstract, taking its meaning from the representations.

Rational explanations. As children begin to perform the addition algorithm abstractly, without reference to concrete models, the operations can be explained by referring to the properties of the place value system. All our numbers can be written on a "grid" such as this one, which identifies the values of the places.

Thou- sands	Hun- dreds	Tens	Ones
1000	100	10	1

Most often the grid is not actually written, but it can and should be written out as the addition algorithm is explained. Consider the problem $187 + 76 = \square$ and the variety of ways of explaining the algorithm used to solve it.

We may write out the values of the places in words.

$$
\begin{array}{l}
1 \text{ hundred} + 8 \text{ tens} + 7 \text{ ones} \\
\underline{\hspace{3em} 7 \text{ tens} + 6 \text{ ones}} \\
1 \text{ hundred} + 15 \text{ tens} + 13 \text{ ones} \quad (A) \\
1 \text{ hundred} + 16 \text{ tens} + 3 \text{ ones} \quad (B) \\
2 \text{ hundred} + 6 \text{ tens} + 3 \text{ ones} \quad (C) \\
\phantom{2 \text{ hundred} + 6 \text{ tens} } 263 \phantom{+ 3 \text{ ones}} \quad (D)
\end{array}
$$

The first step is to add *(A)*. We find that the number is not grouped properly; in our system we never permit more than 9 in any place. We first regroup 10 ones as 1 ten *(B)*, then 10 tens as 1 hundred *(C)*. Finally, we may write the numeral in conventional form *(D)*.

A shorter form, progressing toward the standard algorithm, follows.

$$
\begin{array}{rll}
187 = 100 + 80 + 7 & \\
\underline{ 76 = 70 + 6} & \\
= 100 + 150 + 13 & (A) \\
= 100 + 160 + 3 & (B) \\
= 200 + 60 + 3 & (C) \\
= 263 & (D)
\end{array}
$$

Here the values of the digits are written out and the addition performed on ones, tens, and hundreds. The first form of the answer *(A)* presents us with the same problem: There are 13 ones in ones' place and 15 tens, 150, in tens' place. First we regroup 10 ones as 1 ten and combine the tens *(B)*, then regroup 10 tens as 100 and combine hundreds *(C)*, and finally write the answer as a standard numeral *(D)*. Children should do a few problems this way until they "get the idea," and then more efficient forms

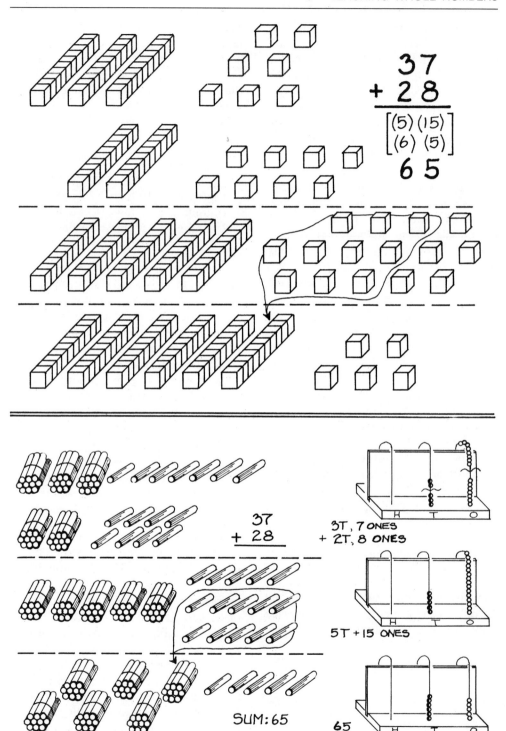

$$\begin{array}{r} 37 \\ + 28 \\ \hline \left[\begin{array}{cc}(5)&(15)\\(6)&(5)\end{array}\right] \\ 6\ 5 \end{array}$$

$$\begin{array}{r} 37 \\ + 28 \end{array}$$

3T, 7 ONES
+ 2T, 8 ONES

5T + 15 ONES

SUM: 65

65

(such as the following) should be introduced. Long sets of practice exercises on the algorithms above are not productive.

An efficient and meaningful form of the algorithm results from representing the problem on a grid.

H	T	O
	8	7
1		
+	7	6
	1	3
1	5	0
1	0	0
2	6	3

Each column is added separately and the result recorded as a standard numeral. Thus, in adding the tens column the student would think "80 plus 70 is 150" and write 150 in the normal position on the grid. In some problems further regrouping is necessary when the resulting columns are added.

To move students from this form to the adult form of the algorithm, only the placement of the regrouped numbers need be changed.

HTO	HTO	HTO	HTO
1 87	1	1 1	1 1
+76	1 87	1 87	1 87
13	76	76	76
1 50	3	63	2 63
1 00			

(A)	(B)	(C)	(D)

We see in *(B)* that the 1 ten is recorded in tens' column still, but above the 8. In *(C)* the 1 hundred is recorded in hundred's column above the 1. The final form is displayed in *(D)*.

Beyond this, children rapidly learn to add larger numbers and longer columns of numbers. It is done mainly as a repetitive process by analogy with the operations performed on smaller numbers. You could add 10 20-digit numbers if asked, even though you may never have done so before.

Proficiency in column addition is dependent in a considerable measure on the students' proficiency in mental arithmetic. As they add the ones' column, they must add mentally, recording the answer only at the end of the column. This is a mental skill. For other techniques for achieving computational proficiency, see the chapter "Teaching for Computational Skills."

Discussion Questions

1. Consider the ordinal and the cardinal aspects of number. Consider addition as the joining of sets, where each set is counted. Then consider addition as "counting on," where the child counts on from the first addend. Do you see a relationship between these aspects of number and these two models of addition?

2. In working the addition problem $5 + 3$ by "counting on," it was indicated that a pause should be used, e.g., "5 (pause), 6, 7, 8." Why do you suppose this was the case?

3. In this section it was stated, "It is perfectly acceptable, and at some stage desirable, for children to find answers by counting their fingers." At what point do you think it would become undesirable for children to add by counting their fingers? Does your answer relate to advice given in the chapter "Teaching for Computational Skills"?

4. Show how the regrouping (or carrying) marks in the problems below represent physical regroupings using base ten blocks.

$$\begin{array}{r} {\scriptstyle 1} \\ 37 \\ +25 \\ \hline 2 \end{array} \qquad \begin{array}{r} {\scriptstyle 1\ 2} \\ 468 \\ 29 \\ +37 \\ \hline 534 \end{array}$$

5. What do all of the following have in common?

$$37+5=42 \qquad 17+5=22 \qquad 7+5=12$$

What does this have to do with column addition?

3. SUBTRACTION

In this section we will describe and illustrate the basic models used to give meaning to the subtraction operation and the procedures of the subtraction algorithm. You should observe that these closely parallel the models for addition.

Models for Subtraction

As addition can be illustrated through the joining of sets, subtraction can be illustrated through the separation of one set into two. The separation of sets usually conforms to one of two models — the "take-away" model and the "partition" model. In the take-away model we designate a set and actually remove a subset, as indicated in *A* in the illustration below. In the partition model we designate a set such as that in *B* and indicate a subset. We ask for the number in the other subset.

Another model, closely associated with the partition model, is the comparison model. Here we compare two sets, e.g., "How many more circles than squares?" Note that there is no separation of one set into two, as in the take-away and the partition models.

The number line is a useful visual illustration of subtraction. We show the subtraction operation for the problem

$$6-2=4.$$

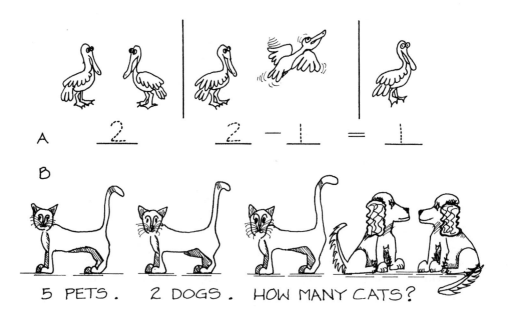

A   2   2 − 1 = 1

B

5 PETS .   2 DOGS .   HOW MANY CATS?

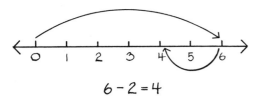

$$6 - 2 = 4$$

Any of the set models—take-away, partition, comparison—can be used in a story problem. A story problem may be used to clarify the meaning and use of the operation. Children can model the problem by using objects or they can act it out in class.

John has 2 marbles.
Alice has 5 marbles.
How many more does Alice have?

The models presented thus far (except comparison) all suggest that subtraction "undoes" what addition does. Because of this, addition and subtraction are called inverse operations. If sets of 3 and 2 elements are combined ($3 + 2 = 5$), they can then be separated by removing the set of 3 ($5 - 3 = 2$) or by removing the set of 2 ($5 - 2 = 3$). Thus, every addition sentence leads to two subtraction sentences.

We saw in the section on addition that after children have internalized the operation of addition, they utilize a "counting on" strategy to find sums. Similarly, a "counting back" procedure can be used to solve subtraction problems. The problem $8 - 3 = \square$ can be solved by counting. It is necessary for the child to keep track of the number of counts: "7, 6, 5" is 3 counts, and fingers are often used for this. "Eight (pause), seven, six, five, so 8 − 3 = 5." This strategy can also be used in conjunction with the number line, using hops.

Besides using sets, the number line, and "counting back" procedures, there are other procedures for solving simple

subtraction sentences. These usually come into play before the child memorizes the subtraction facts. Use of the inverse relation between addition and subtraction and known addition facts is one procedure. Another is to subtract parts of the subtrahend successively, usually subtracting enough to get back to 10, then subtracting the rest of the subtrahend.

A. $8 - 3 = \square$ B. $13 - 8 = \square$
   I know $5 + 3 = 8$ $13 - 3 = 10$
   So $8 - 3 = 5$ $10 - 5 = 5$

Children find subtraction more difficult than addition for a number or reasons. Static illustrations of subtraction do not convey the procedure involved very well. For this reason, a great deal of work with sets of objects and number lines should be done when subtraction is introduced.

In working with larger numbers, principles of grouping are applied, using groups of ten as the standard. To solve a problem such as $35 - 12 = \square$ we could use bundles of sticks or strips, as shown.

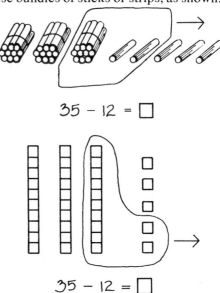

$$35 - 12 = \square$$

$$35 - 12 = \square$$

As the child becomes familiar with the base ten place value system, place value pocket charts and the counting frame are also used.

Another procedure is to write the numbers in their expanded form – 35 as 3 tens, 5 ones; 12 as 1 ten, 2 ones – and to place them in vertical form.

$$\begin{array}{rr}
\text{3 tens, 5 ones} & 35 \\
\underline{-1 \text{ ten, } 2 \text{ ones}} & \underline{-12} \\
\text{2 tens, 3 ones} & 23
\end{array}$$

Notice that a transition has been made from the grouping into tens with blocks or strips to the writing of the numbers in vertical, expanded form. We have gone from the concrete to the semiconcrete to the abstract but in such a way that each step follows naturally from the previous step. When children use the expanded form procedure, they are learning a subtraction algorithm.

Explaining the Subtraction Algorithm

$$\begin{array}{rl}
23 & \text{MINUEND} \\
\underline{-8} & \text{SUBTRAHEND} \\
15 & \text{DIFFERENCE}
\end{array}$$

The vocabulary associated with subtraction, while it *is* desirable, seems to be used less frequently now than formerly. It is still better to say "minuend" than "the number on the top." The minuend will not always be on top; in $23 - 8 = 15$ it is not.

All of the semiconcrete models lend themselves to developing the subtraction algorithm for problems in which no regrouping is needed. We have already seen illustrations of addition using bundles of sticks, the counting frame, and base ten blocks. We will write all problems in vertical form.

To subtract numbers in which one digit of the subtrahend is greater than the corresponding digit in the minuend, regrouping, or borrowing, is necessary. We will emphasize here the use of concrete and semiconcrete models of the algorithm and ways to explain it. Despite extensive practice, children still make many errors in regrouping; better explanations are urgently needed! In this example note how the steps in the algorithm follow and draw meaning from the manipulation of the model.

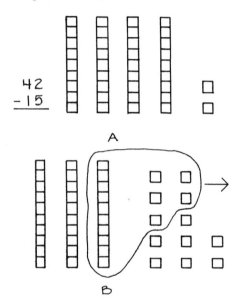

When we saw *(A)* that there weren't enough ones from which to remove 5, we exchanged a 10-strip for 10 ones *(B)*. One 10-strip and 5 ones were then removed. It is frequently said that we "borrow" 10, but "regroup" is a more descriptive as well as a more accurate term.

Using the expanded word form, the same problem appears as

$$\begin{array}{rl}
42 & \text{4 tens, 2 ones} \\
\underline{-15} & \underline{-1 \text{ ten, } 5 \text{ ones}}
\end{array}$$

$$\begin{array}{r} \text{3 tens, 12 ones} \\ -\text{1 ten, 5 ones} \\ \hline \text{2 tens, 7 ones} \end{array} \qquad \begin{array}{r} \overset{3\ 12}{\cancel{42}} \\ -15 \\ \hline 27 \end{array}$$

H	T	O
2	11	14
−	3	5
2	8	9

An approach taken after the expanded word form is to use the place value grid. The key to success with this approach is the extent of the children's understanding of place value. They must realize what "borrowing" from the next digit to the left actually means.

H	T	O		H	T	O
2	3	5		2	2	$\overset{15}{\cancel{5}}$
−	2	6		−	2	6
				2	0	9

For more complicated problems, where regrouping must be done more than once, each intermediate step is shown. By showing the intermediate steps and following the rule that each digit of the minuend must be greater than or equal to its corresponding digit in the subtrahend, the problem is transformed into a "solvable" form. This process is shown below.

3 hundreds, 2 tens, 4 ones
−   3 tens, 5 ones

H	T	O
3	2	4
−	3	5

3 hundreds, 1 ten, 14 ones
−   3 tens, 5 ones

H	T	O
3	1	14
−	3	5

2 hundreds, 11 tens, 14 ones
−   3 tens, 5 ones

An example that merits special attention is the solution to a problem where one of the digits from which we must "borrow" is zero. In expanded word form, the problem appears below. In order to put the problem into workable form, 10 tens are first "borrowed" from the hundreds. We then proceed according to the previous algorithm.

3 hundreds, 0 tens, 4 ones
−   3 tens, 5 ones

H	T	O
3	0	4
−	3	5

2 hundreds, 10 tens, 4 ones
−   3 tens, 5 ones

H	T	O
2	10	4
−	3	5

2 hundreds, 9 tens, 14 ones
−   3 tens, 5 ones

H	T	O
2	9	14
−	3	5
2	6	9

The transformation of subtraction problems on a single grid or in expanded form to the ordinary form of the algorithm simply involves dropping out the helping extras in the problem. The objective of the use of concrete materials and explanations has been to guide the children's thinking process. They should be thinking of the values of the places, or at least *able* to think through the values of the places, as they work a problem. To check on this, you should periodically have children think out loud — talking as they work — to see if they can explain what they are doing.

Discussion Questions

1. Do you see a relationship between the cardinal and the ordinal aspects of number in considering subtraction as "take-away," "partitioning," and "comparing"? For example, is cardinality more closely related to one of these three models of subtraction than to the others?

2. Which of the three models of subtraction is used when the number line is used to illustrate subtraction?

3. Make up a story problem for each of the three models of subtraction.

4. Can you sketch one illustration using sets of objects and one using the number line to show the inverse relationship between addition and subtraction, as shown in these three sentences?

$$5+3=8 \qquad 8-3=5 \qquad 8-5=3$$

5. Discuss the use of a pause in doing subtraction by "counting back." How can ignoring this pause lead to errors?

6. Children frequently make the following kind of error in working subtraction exercises:

$$\begin{array}{r} 36 \\ -28 \\ \hline 12 \end{array}$$

a. Discuss how this error might be related to reading the digits in each column in different order — that is, by reading the ones' column like this ↓ and the tens' column ↑.

b. In verbalizing and reading subtraction sentences, children can read $8 - 6 = \square$ as:

8 take away 6 is $\square$ or
6 from 8 is $\square$ or
8 is how much more than 6?

Associate each of the three ways to read $8 - 6 = \square$ with the three models of subtraction.

c. Can each of the three ways to read $8 - 6 = \square$ above, be used (by primary-age children) in reading $6 - 8 = \square$?

d. In view of your deliberations in a to c, above, discuss the merits of the following advice to teachers:

Have your children read each column in subtraction exercises such as $\begin{array}{r}3\,6\\-2\,5\end{array}$, $\begin{array}{r}3\,6\\-2\,7\end{array}$, $\begin{array}{r}2\,4\,3\\-1\,7\,2\end{array}$, from top

to bottom (↓). Have them use the "take-away" vocabulary when doing this.

7. Show how the regrouping (or borrowing) marks in the following exercises can be related to physical manipulations of base ten blocks.

$$\begin{array}{r} \overset{2\ \ 17}{\not{3}\ \not{7}} \\ -2\ 8 \\ \hline 9 \end{array} \qquad \begin{array}{r} \overset{3\ \ \ \ 9\ 12}{\not{4}\ \not{10}\ \not{2}} \\ -2\ \ 4\ 5 \\ \hline 1\ \ 5\ 7 \end{array}$$

8. Show how base ten blocks and a place value grid can be used to work subtraction problems like the ones below, where the minuend has two or more zeros.

$$\begin{array}{r} 3\,0\,0\,5 \\ -\ \ 1\,1\,7 \end{array} \qquad \begin{array}{r} 4\,0\,1\,0 \\ -2\,5\,3\,2 \end{array}$$

4. MULTIPLICATION

Models for Multiplication

We have used multiplication several times previously as an example of development of meanings. Meanings of multiplication are developed through concrete and semiconcrete materials and also abstractly. There are two concrete representations which are used extensively — sets of sets and jumps on the

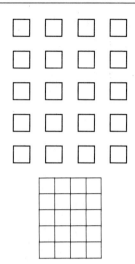

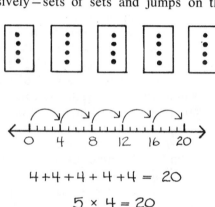

$$4 + 4 + 4 + 4 + 4 = 20$$

$$5 \times 4 = 20$$

number line. Five sets of 4 things and 5 jumps of 4 spaces each on the number line both suggest the addition of 4 as an addend 5 times. This is one abstract meaning, thinking of multiplication as repeated addition or as a short cut to addition, which is taught and learned successfully.

Related to the set of sets idea, we have the "array," or row and column representation of multiplication. Five rows and 4 columns make 20 squares. If the squares are put together, we have a 5 by 4 rectangle. Its area is 20 square units.

Each of these models is used in elementary school textbooks to present multiplication. Each of these models has important functions in problem solving and further mathematical learning. You

will note that several concrete meanings are developed and one abstract meaning. It would be possible to give some meaning to multiplication by the repeated addition (abstract) model only. As Bruner suggests, however, if the concrete and semiconcrete stages are omitted from the teaching sequence, there is no way for children to proceed if their abstract problem-solving techniques fail.

Another model of multiplication, which is included but not emphasized in elementary mathematics, is the Cartesian product. It is quite different from the other models. In each of the other models one has 20 objects (elements of sets, squares, spaces on the number line) and the *arrangement* of these objects shows the association with 4×5. Twenty objects could also be arranged so as to be associated with 2×10. The Cartesian product model begins with two sets, P and Q, P having 5 elements and Q having 4. Using elements from the two sets, make pairs as follows: Pick *any* element from set P (say A) and pair it with *each* of the elements from set Q in turn. List these pairs. Now select another element from set P and repeat.

P = {A, B, C, D, E}
Q = {a, b, c, d}
(A,a) (A,b) (A,c) (A,d)
(B,a) (B,b) (B,c) (B,d)
(C,a) (C,b) (C,c) (C,d)
(D,a) (D,b) (D,c) (D,d)
(E,a) (E,b) (E,c) (E,d)

When you have used all of the elements from P in this way, you have formed all the possible pairs; you have 20 pairs and, in general, the number of pairs formed will be the product of the number of elements in each of the sets. This model of multiplication is included in most textbooks but as an enrichment topic or a sidelight.

Children use all these models in two different ways. The first we have explored: The models give meaning to the operation and can be used to recover a forgotten fact. In this case the student is given the fact and must recall a model and use it to find the answer. The second use is in the solution of problems. In the typical story problem shown below the student must recognize the set of equivalent sets in the problem and must recall a multiplication fact to find the solution.

A baker packs 6 buns in a small box. He sold 7 boxes one morning. How many buns did he sell?

The more models a student knows for an operation, the more problem situations will be recognizable. Learning a variety of models of an operation increases the usefulness of the operation for problem solving.

While we have this problem in mind, let us look at the operations that can be used to solve it: It can be solved by counting, by adding, or by multiplying. Children who find answers to multiplication facts by counting will see this as a counting problem. It does not help them to think of multiplication in connection with the problem because they revert to counting to solve multiplication problems anyway. A child who solves multiplication exercises by repeated addition will interpret this as an addition problem and write an addition sentence to solve it. As before, there is no point, for that child, in thinking of the problem as a multiplication problem because "multiplication does not help you solve the problems. You have to add anyway." This is another argument for memorizing multiplication facts and learning the multiplication algorithm to the point of smooth efficient operation. Only if multiplication is an effective problem-solving tool, will it seem worthwhile to a child to interpret problems in terms of that operation.

We have looked at the models or representations of multiplication of whole numbers, using 5×4 as an example. There is some evidence that students learn meanings for multiplication "all at once" in the sense that if a student knows a meaning for 5×4, he also knows that meaning for any other problem involving *one-digit numbers other than zero and one*.[1] Multiplication by 0 and by 1 are not automatically included within these meanings and need special treatment.

Multiplication by 1 can be interpreted in terms of the models we have used for 5×4. If you interpret 4×1 as repeated addition, you can obtain the answer easily; add 4 ones: $4 \times 1 = 1 + 1 + 1 + 1 = 4$. Using the same interpretation, 1×4

[1]Dennis L. Fordham, "An Investigation of Third, Fourth, and Fifth Graders' Knowledge of the Meanings of Selected Symbols Associated with the Multiplication of Whole Numbers." Unpublished doctoral dissertation, University of Georgia, Athens, Georgia, July 1974.

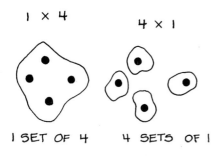

I × 4   4 × 1

I SET OF 4   4 SETS OF I

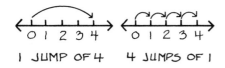

I JUMP OF 4   4 JUMPS OF I

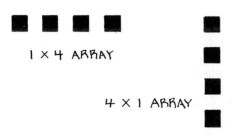

I × 4 ARRAY

4 × 1 ARRAY

should be obtained by adding 1 four. This is not possible because addition is a binary operation, which simply means that we must have *two* numbers in order to add. Children do not need to worry about this, since the models in the drawing enable us to find the answer to 1 × 4.

When confronted with 4 × 0 = 0, children frequently ask, "But what happened to the 4?" You can tell them that a dragon ate it or you can look back to the models used previously! The problem 0 × 4 presents some difficulty because there are no sets, no jumps, no elements in the array, and repeated addition has the same problem encountered earlier—

you can't have an addition problem with no addends. The problem 4 × 0 is easier because four sets with 0 in each, four jumps of 0 on the number line, and 4 × 0 = 0 + 0 + 0 + 0 are plausible interpretations.

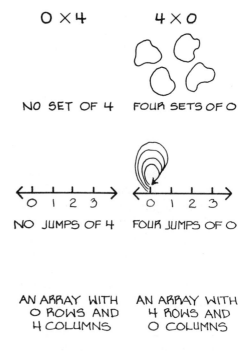

0 × 4   4 × 0

NO SET OF 4   FOUR SETS OF 0

NO JUMPS OF 4   FOUR JUMPS OF 0

AN ARRAY WITH   AN ARRAY WITH
0 ROWS AND   4 ROWS AND
4 COLUMNS   0 COLUMNS

$0 × 4 = \square$ $4 × 0 = 0 + 0 + 0 + 0$

An action-oriented, set-of-sets interpretation can be used. First, establish that if I give 4 things to each of 3 children, the number of things given is 4 × 3 = 12. Several examples establish that interpretation of multiplication. Now, if I give 4 things to each of 0 children, how many do I give? Or if I give 0 things to each of 4 children, how many do I give? In any case, be alert that multiplication meanings involving 0 and 1 are not learned as readily as others; they should receive special attention.

Explaining the Multiplication Algorithm

The purpose here is to relate the basic models for multiplication described above to multiplication problems involving larger numbers and then to trace the course students follow in learning the final form of the algorithm. For meaningful performance of the multiplication algorithm, children need to have developed a reasonable understanding of the place value system and some skill in addition. These are important prerequisites in the development of multiplication.

An array model is frequently used to illustrate problems such as 3×23. The array and the repeated addition problem both show clearly that 3×23 must be found by multiplying 3×20 and 3×3. The number line does not show this as clearly and is not really convenient for problems involving numbers this large.

A very important application of the distributive property of multiplication over addition is its use in explaining the algorithm for multiplication. Obviously, if this is to be successful, the students must first understand the distributive property. In this case, understanding means that they must know what it does, that they are able to use it, and also that they *believe* that these manipulations can be done without changing the number represented. The distributive property says that if one number (a) is to be multiplied by the sum of two others $(b + c)$, you may add first $(b + c)$ and then multiply, or you may multiply first, obtaining $(a \times b)$ and $(a \times c)$ and then add $(a \times b) + (a \times c)$. The final answer will be the same in each case.

$$(a) \times (b + c) = (a \times b) + (a \times c)$$

$$3 \times (4 + 2) \nearrow \quad 3 \times 6 = \square$$
$$\searrow (3 \times 4) + (3 \times 2) = \square$$

$$5 \times (3 + 4) \nearrow \quad 5 \times 7 = \square$$
$$\searrow (5 \times 3) + (5 \times 4) = \square$$

$$6 \times (2 + 3) \nearrow \quad 6 \times 5 = \square$$
$$\searrow (6 \times 2) + (6 \times 3) = \square$$

You will recall that this is the same procedure that you used to multiply and factor polynomials in elementary algebra. Remember this: $x (2x + 5) = 2x^2 + 5x$? One good way to help students see the two procedures possible with the distributive property is to solve problems such as those above, working each problem two ways. When students understand the distributive property, it can be used to solve multiplication problems and to explain the multiplication algorithm.

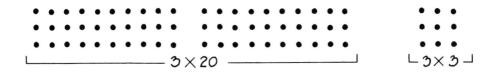

$$\begin{array}{r} 23 \\ 23 \\ +23 \\ \hline \end{array} \longrightarrow \begin{array}{r} 20 + 3 \\ 20 + 3 \\ 20 + 3 \\ \hline 60 + 9 \end{array}$$

If we are presented with a multiplication problem, such as 3 × 23, we may solve it as shown here.

$$3 \times 23 = 3 \times (20 + 3)$$
$$= (3 \times 20) + (3 \times 3)$$
$$= (60) + (9)$$
$$= 69$$

In the first step we write 23 as 20 + 3. To do this, we must understand the meaning of a two-digit number. The next step is to use the distributive property, multiplying the 3 times both the 20 and the 3. To proceed, the student must know that 3 × 20 = 60. Students will work out a few such problems, using arrays such as the one shown for 3 × 23. To succeed in long multiplication, however, children must learn to do these by observing and using the idea that if 3 × 2 = 6, then 3 × 20 = 60. This follows from the associative property of multiplication. For example:

$$3 \times 20 =$$
$$3 \times (2 \times 10) =$$
$$(3 \times 2) \times 10 =$$
$$6 \times 10 = 60$$

We shall digress for a moment to reflect on strings of equations as just presented. The purpose of such strings of equations is to change the form in which the number is represented without changing the number itself; the expression has the same value, though the way it is written changes. For the demonstration to be meaningful to children, they must understand that this is its purpose.

Further, they must be convinced that each step is a "legal" step, a change that merely rewrites but does not change the number. The way in which such expressions are written may also obscure what is going on. The steps proceed from *(A)* to *(B)* and then from *(B)* to *(C)*, etc.

(A) $3 \times 23 = 3 \times (20 + 3)$ (B)
$= (3 \times 20) + (3 \times 3)$ (C)
$= (60) + (9)$ (D)
$= 69$ (E)

Now, let us look in detail at the reasons why each step follows from the previous step, as shown below.

In such demonstrations you may imagine someone saying, at each step, "How do you know you can do that?" We must convince the person that we can. The answer is believable only if the steps in the chain are convincing. Such demonstrations are frequently found in textbooks. Their purpose is to convince. The instructional objective is for the students to "talk their way through it," explaining each step as they write it. There is little point in practicing the demonstration for speed. Reasoning, not speed, is the paramount purpose of these demonstrations.

The procedure used above is quickly converted to the more traditional form of the algorithm.

$$
\begin{array}{rr}
20 + 3 & 2\ 3 \\
\underline{\times \quad 3} & \underline{\times\ 3} \\
60 + 9 = 69 & 9 \\
& 6\ 0 \\
& \overline{6\ 9}
\end{array}
$$

$3 \times 23 = 3 \times (20 + 3)$	In our system of numeration 23 means 2 tens and 3 ones, 20 + 3.
$3 \times (20 + 3) = (3 \times 20) + (3 \times 3)$	Use of the distributive law.
$(3 \times 20) + (3 \times 3) = (60) + (9)$	Known multiplication facts. Derived from multiplication facts.
$(60) + (9) = 69$	Again, a basic meaning in our system of numeration.

From this point, further refinements involve learning to write the algorithm in a more efficient form and learning to use the same reasoning processes on larger numbers.

The place value grid, so effective in teaching addition and subtraction, is just as important in multiplication. Students will work a good many problems using the form shown here.

TH	H	T	O		TH	H	T	O
	3	4	5			3	4	5
×			7		×			7
		3	5		2	4	1	5
	2	8	0					
2	1	0	0					
2	4	1	5					

           A   B

In this problem it is important for students to think the algorithm through as they work it. For example, a student would think (or a teacher would explain) 7 × 4 tens = 280 or 7 × 40 = 280, *not* 7 × 4 = 28. Even though a student will ultimately think, as we all do, 7 × 4 = 28, he or she should begin working this problem by thinking the actual place values rather than the shorter form.

Final abbreviation of this form, as in B, above, is done by holding in mind the number to be grouped in the next place, thus eliminating the need for partial products. So much of this algorithm is done internally that the written steps do not demonstrate the thinking process at all. While 7 × 4 in B should be related to 7 × 40 in A, the thought process for most efficient operation is 7 × 4 = 28, 28 + 3 = 31, and so forth, which is the thought process of adults. This shows the necessity of immediate recall of multiplication and addition facts for efficient performance of the algorithm.

It is frequently observed that children in fifth grade and above are doing multiplications as shown. These students are

$$\begin{array}{r} 37 \\ \times 24 \end{array}$$
‖‖‖‖‖ ‖‖
‖‖‖‖‖ ‖‖ ‖‖‖‖‖ ‖‖
‖‖‖‖‖ ‖‖ ‖‖‖‖‖ ‖‖
‖‖‖‖‖ ‖‖

using an "array" method for finding basic facts. They will get a few problems correct if they are persistent enough, but they will never get sufficient practice for efficient multiplication. They are just too slow. The chapter "Teaching for Computational Skills" contains suggestions for solving this problem.

37	37	37
× 2 4	× 2 4	× 2 4
2 8 →	2 8	→ 1 4 8
1 2 0 →	1 2	7 4
1 4 0 →	1 4	
6 0 0 →	6	

           A   B   C

In the example above, calculation A shows each of the partial products with the zeros included. Thus, there is no question about the placement of the partial products on the grid. Calculation B shows the zeros deleted, and finally C shows the partial products combined to form the traditional algorithm. No matter how careful a teacher may be, an error in the placement of the second partial product is possible.

37	37
× 24	× 24
148	148
74	740

(INCORRECT!)

Working many examples in addition, in which the numbers are aligned at the right, makes this slip a comon one. Replacing the zero in the partial product — because $20 \times 7 = 140$ — can help students to overcome this error.

Discussion Questions

1. Sometimes, in elementary school textbooks, multiplication is presented as the number of choices a child has in order to combine two sets of objects; for example, choosing one of 4 pairs of socks and one of 3 pairs of shoes. Which of the models for multiplication presented in this chapter does this embodiment of multiplication illustrate?

2. What are the two ways children can use models of multiplication? Illustrate.

3. Cite a number of arguments for having children memorize multiplication facts. Agree or disagree with each argument cited.

4. Can a Cartesian product model of multiplication be used to show multiplication by 0 and also by 1?

5. Why is it imperative that children have developed a reasonable understanding of place value and skill in addition in order for them to understand the multiplication algorithm?

6. Show how you could use base ten blocks to show each of the forms of the multiplication algorithm shown in this section.

7. What would you do with a child who is working exercises such as 84×47 correctly but is constantly resorting to making tally marks or finger counting to compute each step in the algorithm and is therefore working very slowly?

5. DIVISION

Models of Division

Several concrete and abstract models of division are frequently used.

Concrete Models
(a) Sets and subsets
(b) The number line
(c) Rectangular arrays

Abstract Models
(a) Repeated subtraction
(b) Inverse of multiplication

Each of these models can be used to represent problems, with or without remainder. Notice in what follows that the use of sets and number line suggest repeated subtraction, while the use of rectangular arrays suggests that division is the inverse of multiplication. Any of these models can be embedded in a story problem to illustrate division.

In using sets of objects to model the division concept, there are two somewhat different procedures to be developed. The first is to begin with a set of objects and arrange them in groups that each have the same specified number. In Figure A, below, we have taken 15 dots and made groups of 5. We are asking, "How many groups of 5 are in a set of 15 dots?" The mathematical problem is $15 \div 5 = \square$. Because we find 3 groups, we know $15 \div 5 = 3$.

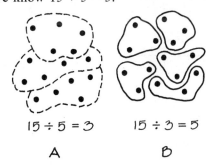

$15 \div 5 = 3$ $15 \div 3 = 5$

A   B

The second procedure for modeling division is shown in Figure B. We begin with 15 elements and create from these a specified number (5) of equivalent sets. Problem: $15 \div 5 = \Box$. We discover there are 3 elements in each of the 5 sets and conclude that $15 \div 5 = 3$.

These models are alike in that each begins with a set of elements and ends with those elements organized in equivalent subsets. In one model we specify how many elements are to be in each subset. "How many sets of 5 can you make out of a set of 15?" In the other model we specify how many subsets are to be made. "If you divide 15 elements into 5 equivalent sets, how many will be in each set?" Problems having a remainder can also be illustrated in each of these ways when there are dots or elements left over—not included in the sets the children construct.

The problem $15 \div 5 = \Box$ can also be modeled on number line A, below. Start at 15 and move left in jumps of 5. Three jumps take us back to 0 and we conclude that $15 \div 5 = 3$. On number line B we illustrate $17 \div 5 = \Box$. Starting at 17, we move left in jumps of 5. Three jumps are possible, but in this case 2 spaces remain "unjumped." We conclude that $17 \div 5 = 3$ R2.

These models, the set model and the number-line model, both suggest the relation between subtraction and division.

This is analogous to the relation between addition and multiplication. Multiplication can be thought of as repeated addition, division as repeated subtraction. This relation will be very important in the development of the division algorithm and is also one of two abstract meanings of division. If we ask, "How many 5's in 15?" we may find the answer by subtraction: Successively subtract 5 and count. We are able to subtract 5 three times, so we say there are three 5's in 15, or $15 \div 5 = 3$.

$$
\begin{array}{cc}
1\,5 & 1\,7 \\
\underline{-\,5}\;(1) & \underline{-\,5}\;(1) \\
1\,0 & 1\,2 \\
\underline{-\,5}\;(2) & \underline{-\,5}\;(2) \\
5 & 7 \\
\underline{-\,5}\;(3) & \underline{-\,5}\;(3) \\
0 & 2
\end{array}
$$

If we ask, "How many 5's in 17?" we may find the answer in the same way, subtracting 5 successively, but at the end we have 2 left. We conclude that $17 \div 5 = 3$ R2.

Rectangular arrays are frequently used to model division problems. We may ask, "If we have 15 objects and place them in rows of 5, how many rows do we get?" This question is also represented mathematically as $15 \div 5 = \Box$. We get 3 rows, and so $15 \div 5 = 3$. Similarly, if we have 17 objects and place them in

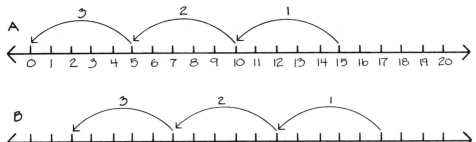

rows of 5, we get 3 rows and 2 objects left.

☐ ☐ ☐ ☐ ☐
☐ ☐ ☐ ☐ ☐   3
☐ ☐ ☐ ☐ ☐   5)‾1‾5‾

The rectangular array model is used extensively in introducing multiplication. The inverse relationship between multiplication and division can be seen in a rectangular array. Using the 3 by 5 array, above, we may write

$$5 \times 3 = 15 \qquad 15 \div 3 = 5$$
$$3 \times 5 = 15 \qquad 15 \div 5 = 3$$

In each case, division is the opposite, or inverse, operation, the operation that "undoes" what multiplication does. This relation is very useful in recalling division facts. $54 \div 6 = \square$ may be recalled by remembering that $9 \times 6 = 54$, and so $54 \div 6 = 9$.

Division may be introduced by a story problem, such as, "John has 15 trading cards. He puts them in rows, 5 in each row. How many rows are there?" or "There are 15 cookies to be shared equally among 5 children. How many does each child get?" Acting out these problems, using concrete materials, can be an effective introduction to division.

The Division Algorithm

Concrete models are not frequently used to explain the division algorithm because they are somewhat cumbersome. However, there are two which are worth doing. The first is based on using place value materials or a whimsical story about dividing jelly beans; the second uses successive subtraction. The students' ability to understand (not simply perform by imitation) the development of the division algorithm is a good check point in elementary arithmetic. Understanding this algorithm requires the student to understand place value, subtraction, and multiplication, and to have a good intuitive feel for the sizes of numbers. If your fourth and fifth graders understand and perform division, you may be confident of their progress. We present the place value model as a manipulation of the model and a parallel step in the algorithm, accompanied by explanatory notes. (See page 248.)

The vocabulary of division is as follows: If 437 is to be divided by 3, then 437 is the *dividend* and 3 is the *divisor*. The answer, 145, is the *quotient* and 2 is the *remainder*. You will note that in the two forms in which division is presented, the example form and the sentence form, the divisor and the dividend are in opposite order as one reads from left to right. This causes considerable confusion and needs careful presentation.

Example form:

QUOTIENT, REMAINDER
DIVISOR)‾D‾I‾V‾I‾D‾E‾N‾D‾

Sentence form:

DIVIDEND ÷ DIVISOR
     = QUOTIENT, REMAINDER

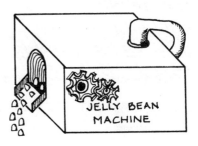

JELLY BEAN MACHINE

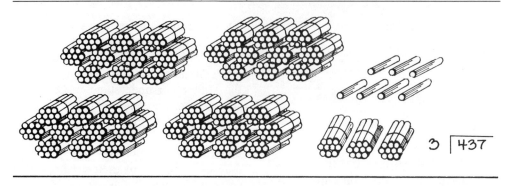

$$3 \,\overline{)437}$$

I WISH TO DIVIDE 437 INTO 3 EQUAL PILES   ONE HUNDRED IN EACH PILE

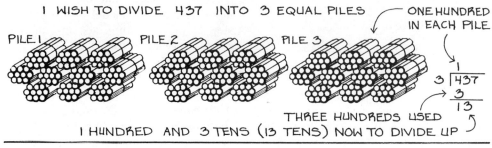

PILE 1   PILE 2   PILE 3

$$\begin{array}{r} 1 \\ 3 \,\overline{)437} \\ 3 \\ \hline 13 \end{array}$$

THREE HUNDREDS USED

1 HUNDRED AND 3 TENS (13 TENS) NOW TO DIVIDE UP

4 TENS ADDED TO EACH PILE

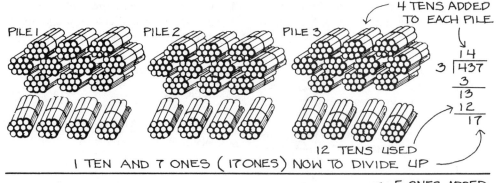

PILE 1   PILE 2   PILE 3

$$\begin{array}{r} 14 \\ 3 \,\overline{)437} \\ 3 \\ \hline 13 \\ 12 \\ \hline 17 \end{array}$$

12 TENS USED

1 TEN AND 7 ONES (17 ONES) NOW TO DIVIDE UP

5 ONES ADDED TO EACH PILE

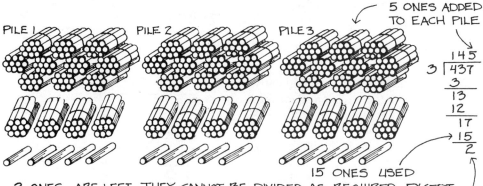

PILE 1   PILE 2   PILE 3

$$\begin{array}{r} 145 \\ 3 \,\overline{)437} \\ 3 \\ \hline 13 \\ 12 \\ \hline 17 \\ 15 \\ \hline 2 \end{array}$$

15 ONES USED

2 ONES ARE LEFT. THEY CANNOT BE DIVIDED AS REQUIRED EXCEPT BY USING FRACTIONS.

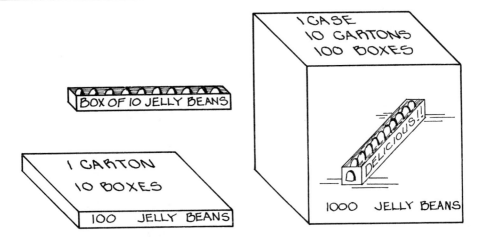

In the jelly bean factory mountains of jelly beans are made each day. As they come out of the jelly bean machine, they are packed in *boxes,* 10 beans to a box, then in *cartons,* 10 boxes (100 beans) to a carton, and then in *cases,* 10 cartons (100 boxes, 1000 beans) to a case.

Now, we may imagine that we have a large number of jelly beans, say 4,685, which we are going to divide evenly among 3 people. So our jelly beans are packed in 4 cases, 6 cartons, and 8 boxes, and there are 5 loose beans. We will write the problem as shown below (a), and we understand that this form of writing a problem can mean dividing 4,685 into 3 equal piles. First, how many full cases can we give each person? Only one (b), which uses up 3 cases (c), so we have 1 full case left (d). If we now think of cartons, the case, when opened, produces 10 cartons to add to the 6 we had at the start. So we now have 16 cartons to divide among three people (e). Each person gets 5 cartons (f), which uses up 15 cartons (g), and there is 1 carton left (h). When this carton is opened, we have 10 boxes to go with the 8 boxes we had

at the start, making 18 boxes (j). Each person gets 6 boxes (i), distributing all 18 boxes (k), and leaving 0 boxes (l). Last, we distribute the single jelly beans. There are 5 of them, and so each person gets 1 (m), using up 3 (n), and 2 remain undistributed (o).

$$3 \overline{)4{,}685} \quad \text{(a)}$$

$$\begin{array}{r} 1, \quad \text{(b)} \\ 3 \overline{)4{,}685} \\ \underline{3} \quad \text{(c)} \\ 1 \quad \text{(d)} \end{array}$$

$$\begin{array}{r} 1, \\ 3 \overline{)4{,}685} \\ \underline{3} \\ 1\,6 \quad \text{(e)} \end{array}$$

$$\begin{array}{r} 1,5 \quad \text{(f)} \\ 3 \overline{)4{,}685} \\ \underline{3} \\ 1\,6 \\ \underline{1\,5} \quad \text{(g)} \\ 1 \quad \text{(h)} \end{array}$$

```
      1,56   (i)
  3) 4,685
      3
      1 6
      1 5
       18    (j)
       18    (k)
        0    (l)


      1,561  (m)
  3) 4,685
      3
      1 6
      1 5
       18
       18
       05
         3   (n)
         2   (o)
```

We hope you like jelly beans—but even if you don't, this story about division makes sense. Please observe that we never said "3 goes into 4" or worse, "3 goes into 46." We have treated each step as division of units (cases, cartons, boxes) into piles. You need only convert these units to thousands, hundreds, tens, and ones to have a meaningful, place-value-based explanation of the division process. We proceed to give this sort of explanation for a larger division problem, 27,941 ÷ 36.

We will divide 27,941 things into 36 equal piles. There are only 2 ten thousands and only 27 thousands, not enough of either to put one in each of 36 piles. There are, however, 279 hundreds in 27,941. How many hundreds go in each pile? To find out, we estimate how many and check by multiplying. As children get better in rounding, estimating, and multiplying, they become more efficient in doing this algorithm.

```
  36) 27,941
```

$36 \times 5 = 180$ — too small
$36 \times 7 = 252$ — ?
$36 \times 8 = 288$ — too large
So 7 is correct.

```
           7
  36) 27,941
      25 2
       2 7
```

```
           7
  36) 27,941
      25 2
       2 74
```

$36 \times 6 = 216$
$36 \times 7 = 252$
$36 \times 8 = 288$

```
         776
  36) 27,941
      25 2
       2 74
       2 52
         221
         216
           5
```

We may interpret the progress of the algorithm thus far: We have divided 279 hundreds into 36 piles, 7 hundreds in each pile and 27 hundreds left. Note that 7 is placed in hundreds' place in the quotient because it *is* 7 hundreds. To proceed, think of the 27 hundreds as 270 tens. We also have 4 tens in the dividend, so we have 274 tens to divide into 36 piles. We find that 7 tens can be put in each of 36 piles, using 252 tens and leaving 22 tens. Finish in the same way—22 tens is 220 ones, and 1 one from the dividend makes 221 ones. We can place 6 ones in each pile and have 5 ones left over.

In this development of the algorithm we deal with larger units first, asking questions such as, "How many hundreds can we put in each pile?" not "How many times does 36 go into 279?" As with other algorithms, children will later work this problem the same way adults do. During the learning process it is important for students to think through the steps, thinking in terms of the place values in the numbers.

The second way in which the division algorithm is developed is to base it on successive subtraction. It has now become the most common way for division to be presented in elementary school textbooks. This algorithm has the advantage that it can be developed and refined gradually. Any student who understands the relation between division and subtraction and who has reasonable facility in subtraction can perform division by using this algorithm. Students who can multiply and who have skill in estimation can use the more efficient refinements of the procedure.

To introduce this algorithm, we ask, "How many times can 37 be subtracted from 189?" We can perform the subtractions one at a time and count the number of times, 5, we have subtracted. The remainder is 4.

```
        5 R 4
37) 189
     37     1
    152
     37     1
    115
     37     1
     78
     37     1
     41
     37     1
      4     5
```

We now look at another problem: $19,652 \div 37$. We *could* find the answer by subtracting 37 time after time but that is clearly impractical. Instead we ask, "Can I subtract one 37, 10 37's, 100 37's, 1,000 37's, and so on?" We can subtract 100 37's (3,700) but not 1,000 37's (37,000). This algorithm is long but it has few prerequisites. Only subtraction and the ability to multiply by powers of ten are required. It is explained in terms of subtracting 37's in bunches — first 100 37's at a time, then 10 37's at a time, and finally one 37 at a time.

```
           531 R 5
37) 19,652
     3,700    100
    15,952
     3,700    100
    12,252
     3,700    100
     8,552
     3,700    100
     4,852
     3,700    100
     1,152
       370     10
       782
       370     10
       412
       370     10
        42
        37      1
         5    531
```

Now, this algorithm may be refined in two ways. One is to subtract more efficiently, using fewer steps; the other is to place quotient digits in the traditional place over the dividend. As in the previous example, we can subtract 37's in bunches of 100. We wish to figure out how many hundreds of 37's there are and subtract them all at once. We see that 500 37's may be subtracted. The 5 is placed in hundreds' place in the quotient. (Note that this example is one of those in which rounding the divisor would have produced an error by underestimating the quotient digit.) The same reasoning shows that 30 more 37's can be subtracted and the 3 located in tens' place. Finally, one more 37 can be subtracted. The quotient figure is complete and the remainder is 5.

$$
\begin{array}{r}
5 \\
37 \overline{)19,652} \\
18,500 \qquad 500 \\
\hline
1,152
\end{array}
$$

$$
\begin{aligned}
100 \times 37 &= 3,700 \\
200 \times 37 &= 7,400 \\
300 \times 37 &= 11,100 \\
400 \times 37 &= 14,800 \\
500 \times 37 &= 18,500 \\
600 \times 37 &= 22,200 \quad (\text{TOO BIG})
\end{aligned}
$$

$$
\begin{array}{r}
53 \\
37 \overline{)19,652} \\
18,500 \qquad 500 \\
\hline
1,152 \\
1,110 \qquad 30 \\
\hline
42
\end{array}
$$

$$
\begin{aligned}
10 \times 37 &= 370 \\
20 \times 37 &= 740 \\
30 \times 37 &= 1,110 \\
40 \times 37 &= 1,480 \quad (\text{TOO BIG})
\end{aligned}
$$

$$
\begin{array}{r}
531 \\
37 \overline{)19,652} \\
18,500 \qquad 500 \\
\hline
1,152 \\
1,110 \qquad 30 \\
\hline
42 \\
37 \qquad 1 \\
\hline
5 \qquad \overline{531}
\end{array}
$$

It is plain that an efficient use of the division procedure is based on some estimation and multiplication skill. The algorithm is quite "forgiving," however — if students overestimate or underestimate, it is not necessary for them to start all over. If they underestimate, they can simply proceed to subtract some more; if they overestimate, they can cross off that step and try again. As the students improve in estimation and multiplication, their procedures will become more efficient.

Discussion Questions

1. Can base ten blocks be used in conjunction with at least one concrete and one abstract model of division? If so, illustrate.

2. In introducing division to children would you use all five of the models presented in this section? Why?

3. Can each concrete model of division be related to each abstract model?

4. If you can, make up a story problem for each of the five models of division.

5. Show how you could use base ten blocks to illustrate both the "jelly bean" approach and the successive subtraction approach to the division algorithm.

6. a. Do both of the approaches to the division algorithm taken in this chapter place heavy emphasis on place value relationship? Compare this with the emphasis on place value in the "goes into" approach started here:

$$
\begin{array}{r}
5 \\
3 \overline{)175} \\
15
\end{array}
$$

Three does not go into 1 but it goes into 17 five times....

b. Under what circumstances would you consider using this "goes into" approach?

7. How much and what kind of practice would you assign to children using the place value or successive subtraction algorithms for division?

8. At what point would you:

a. consider having children shift from a place value or successive subtraction approach to division to using the most efficient paper-and-pencil, "adult" form of the algorithm?

b. permit children to perform division problems involving large divisors and dividends by using a hand calculator?

9. Does the inclusion of decimals as dividends or divisors pose problems for children using the division algorithms presented in this section?

10 · Teaching Fractions

INTRODUCTION

If a popularity contest were held among mathematical topics in elementary school, with both teachers and students being eligible to vote, we think it unlikely that fractions would garner many votes. Perhaps you also feel that fractions are unpopular. Well, take heart; we will try to convince you that fractions can be an enjoyable topic. The suggestions in this chapter have been used successfully by scores of teachers and interns at all grade levels. That's right; they work!

1. SOME BACKGROUND FOR TEACHERS

In elementary school, fractions appear in at least four contexts. We will take a look at each of them in this section. They are related to many physical situations and account for various applications of fractions. The contexts give us models to illustrate fractions and to display the addition, subtraction, multiplication, and division of fractions. We will use them throughout this chapter.

Fractions as Regions of Geometric Figures

This is probably the best known context for fractions. Regions of circles (pies!) and rectangles are popular models for fractions. Drawings of circles, rectangles, and other shapes are partitioned and used in elementary school mathematics textbooks, beginning in the primary grades. Children in the primary grades can understand the concept of a fraction. Among other things, such drawings can be used to represent pizzas, cakes, flags, designs, and maps. Line segments can also be used to depict fractions.

In geometric contexts fractions frequently are referred to as "parts of a whole." It is almost always understood that the whole represents the region of a geometric figure and the parts are regions formed by subdividing the original geometric figure. Usually the figures forming the parts are the same size and shape (congruent). Rarely is one part of a circle or rectangle taken as the unit, although this is possible. Similarly, it is uncommon for the regions of two or more circles or rectangles to be taken as the unit. Thus, one fourth is rarely shown in one of the ways below. In elementary school textbooks, fractions are not usually ascribed to regions where the parts are not congruent. Instead, children are usually given single shapes with uniform divisions or asked to divide given shapes into a specified number of "equal-sized" parts. Given paper strips, or circular or rectangular paper shapes, children can divide them by folding and create fairly accurate, uniform parts.

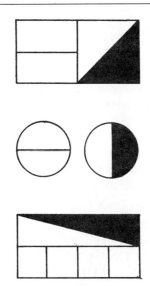

Fractions as Parts of Sets

Suppose a bouquet of flowers was made from 2 daisies, 3 tulips, and 4 roses. The unit in this case can be the entire bouquet. Each flower, although different in size and shape from most of the others, is one ninth of the whole. Sometimes the separate parts are all alike — suppose the bouquet was all roses. The main differences between this context and the preceding one are that the parts are distinct entities in their own right *and*

they do not have to be physically connected or congruent.

The children in your class, a family, or a team are all examples of such sets. The members of these sets are equal in ways other than size and shape. In some cases the members of a set may all look alike — for example, pennies, eggs, or checkers — or they may be connected, such as the charms on a bracelet. But it is not their physical likeness or connection that is important when a fraction is assigned to a portion of the set.

The following are examples of this kind of situation, which could appear in a textbook.

Suppose you had some cupcakes: 1 chocolate, 2 with coconut, and 1 with cherries. What fraction tells the part of the cupcakes having coconut? Write your answer in words and by using a fraction symbol.

In the exercise below, write a fraction that tells what part of each set is shaded. Then write a fraction telling what part of each set is not shaded.

Fractions in Measurement

In making a measurement, an appropriate unit is selected — centimeter, inch,

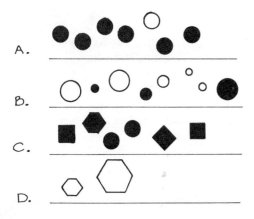

	SHADED	NOT SHADED
A.	$\frac{6}{7}$	$\frac{1}{7}$
B.	——	——
C.	——	——
D.	——	——

liter, degree—and the number of times it is used is counted. Think of the different units we use to measure the following:

a grocery bill	medicine
a gasoline tank	temperature
time	grain
a table top	height
weight	land

In a great many physical situations fractions are needed to record the number of units in the measurement. If you were using centimeters, the width of your thumb, or the length of a pencil to measure the width of this page, it is likely you would find the page measures a certain number of units and a fractional part of a unit.

Sometimes the fractional parts of a unit are given names. In the case of centimeters we have millimeters. Feet and inches are fractional parts of a yard. Milliliters are fractional parts of liters. Frequently, such subunits as millimeters, inches, and milliliters are themselves taken as units of measure. Fractions are still needed, however, because no matter

how small a unit is chosen, those units will not measure each physical situation a whole number of times.

When fractional parts of a unit are used in measuring, the fractional parts are always the same size—the units are always divided into uniform parts. Your students can do this in constructing their own rulers, gauges, and scales and in making measurements by using instruments such as those listed below.

RULER
PROTRACTOR
STOPWATCH
LITER CONTAINER
TRUNDLE WHEEL

SPRING SCALE
BALANCE SCALE
BATHROOM SCALE
EGG TIMER
MEASURING CUP

The procedures for using fractional numbers when you are measuring are as follows:

a. An appropriate unit is chosen.
b. The unit is subdivided into a specified number of equal parts.
c. The number of equal parts in the unit becomes the denominator of the fraction. The name, such as fourths, halves, or eighths, shows the number of equal parts.
d. The number of times the unit is contained in the object being measured is counted.
e. The subdivisions of the unit that are needed are counted. This number becomes the numerator of the fraction.
f. The measurement can be expressed by telling how many whole units are used and how many fractional parts are used.

EXAMPLE
Unit: a foot ruler
Inches

Each inch is $\frac{1}{12}$ of a foot. Counting subdivisions is counting twelfths.

A table measures 3 feet—

and 5 inches. 5 inches is $\frac{5}{12}$ of a foot.

The table is 3 feet and 5 inches long or 3 and 5 twelfths feet long. This is written $3\frac{5}{12}$.

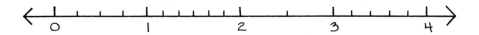

Fractions on the Number Line

The number line is used to illustrate fractions in a way that is similar to the way measurements are used. A unit is chosen and subdivided into a chosen number of equal lengths. The number of equal lengths is the numerator of the fraction, and the number of equal lengths in the unit is the denominator. On the number line, units are almost always the equal lengths between one whole number and the next. On the number line above, the units going from left to right are subdivided into fourths, sixths, halves, and fifths, respectively. The number line is also a popular model for illustrating mixed numbers, e.g., $3\frac{1}{5}$, $1\frac{5}{6}$, $2\frac{1}{2}$, and equivalent fractions, e.g., $\frac{1}{2}$ and $\frac{2}{4}$ and $\frac{3}{6}$, or $\frac{2}{3}$ and $\frac{4}{6}$ and $\frac{8}{12}$.

Discussion Questions

1. Make three or four number lines. How could you have children fold number lines to find halves, fourths, and eighths? Could you fold such number lines to show thirds or fifths?

2. Explain the meaning of this statement.

Fractional numbers can increase the precision of our measurements but they do not make our measurements exact.

3. Equal subdivisions of a unit of measure may be given a name. We often find that they become a unit in their own right. Here is a table of common measuring units and subunits. Complete the table below, and then try to think of a few additional units you could use in your classroom.

4. One of the arguments supporting our use of the metric system is its reduced reliance on fractions. Explain and illustrate what is included in this argument.

5. Name the units and the fractional parts of units used in reading the instruments listed in the section *Fractions in Measurement,* above. Which of those instruments can be read as a ruler bent out of shape?

6. Name some instruments that measure quantities other than length but record their measurements on gauges that are linear or circular in nature. A water meter is one example; a thermometer is another.

Units	Number of Equal Subdivisions	Name and Symbol for One Fractional Part	Common Name for Subunit
Gallon	4	fourth ($\frac{1}{4}$)	quart
Liter	1000		
Day	24		
Hour		$\frac{1}{60}$	
Yard	3		
Foot			
Ton			
Pound			
Meter			centimeter

7. Consider the room you are in. Can you find: geometric shapes, sets or collections where the parts are identical, sets or collections where the parts are different sizes, and measurement contexts that could be used to depict fractions?

2. TEACHING BASIC IDEAS OF FRACTIONS—FOUR OBJECTIVES

Children in primary grades should be taught the basic ideas of fractions. We will condense these ideas into four objectives. The objectives form a basis for developing an understanding of all work with fractions in elementary school mathematics. Consider each one carefully and critically in your teaching. Do not rush through them in one or two lessons as do many mathematics textbooks. Be sure to use all of the contexts of the preceding section in helping children reach these objectives.

A Beginning—The First Two Objectives

At first, avoid the standard symbols used for fractions. They come into play after some fundamental notions have been acquired. What are those notions? Consider the following two objectives:

1. Children should be able to identify and recognize whole objects and complete collections of objects.

2. Children should be able to recognize and count the parts of a whole object and the members of a collection, or set, of objects, and in each case be able to tell in what ways the parts are all the same.

These two objectives deal with a whole, or unit, and the parts that make up the unit. You can work on them at the same time. In physical applications of fractions the user must first see the unit *and* the parts of that unit. Later, in working with symbolic statements like $\frac{2}{3} + \frac{3}{4}$, children should be able (on request) to interpret their work by using diagrams or physical objects. This will require the selection of a model. The model will be composed of wholes and parts of wholes. Without a unit we cannot interpret what we are doing!

Teaching Suggestions for Objectives 1 and 2

Begin by giving and comparing examples and nonexamples of wholes (units) and parts of wholes. Children have had scores of experiences with entire objects or collections and the parts that make up those objects or collections. Use wholes that are continuous or connected, such as the following:

> an orange
> a candy bar
> a cake
> a quart or a liter
>   of liquid
> an hour, a day, a week,
>   or a year
> a circle or a circular object, like a pie
> a rectangle or a rectangular object, like
>   a piece of cloth or a sheet of paper
> a stick, a ruler, or a rod
> a wall or a floor of a room
> a window

Take each whole and divide it into equal parts. Where feasible, try to make the parts all the same size and shape. Break some into 2 parts and then into 4 and 8 parts. Divide others into 3, 4, 5, or 6 parts.

Also take units that are sets, or collections, such as the following:

a dozen eggs
pages of a booklet
a tray of ice cubes
a deck of cards
a box of envelopes
a set of steak knives
a bag of candy having the
    pieces all alike
a bag of candy in which some
    pieces are different
a collection of pictures
sets of hats, dresses, shirts,
    or shoes
a school of fish
parts of a car or bicycle
a bouquet of flowers in which the
    flowers are all alike
a bouquet of three or four
    different kinds of flowers
houses on a street
children in your room
letters of the alphabet
fingers on a hand
islands in a chain
carving knives
windows in a house
a collection of dolls or coins
members of a team
a set of teeth
parts of the body

To reach Objectives 1 and 2, use examples from the two lists above. Place children in situations in which a whole, or unit, is being shown and in which part of the unit is missing. Give them a part or parts and ask them to construct the whole. Circles and rectangles that are intact can be compared with circles and rectangles that have sections missing or broken off. The same types of comparisons can be made with teams, decks of cards, rectangular candy bars, or a sheet of paper. A ruler, a day, and a liter of liquid are other possible units that can be presented as wholes and then subdivided. Like circles and candy bars, parts of rulers and liters can be removed so that they are no longer complete units. This may help children distinguish complete from incomplete units. Taking a bite of an apple is also a good way to exemplify a whole and something that is no longer a whole! Have children describe, identify, or draw wholes and parts of wholes. Ask them to defend their choices and to specify what is needed to complete a unit. Point out the fact that in some cases the parts that make up a whole are the same in some physical way, such as in size and shape (congruent), while in other cases the parts are equal in some other way. For example, how are the children in the class equal? Ask children to count parts of various units and tell how the parts are the same. After one or two lessons begin using the standard verbal names, such as thirds, fourths, and fifths. Encourage children to use these terms as they answer and ask questions.

On to Fractions—Objectives 3 and 4

Objectives 1 and 2, above, are a foundation for all work with fractions in elementary school mathematics. After these objectives have been reached, you should guide children in abstracting certain properties of the parts that make up units and in representing these abstractions with symbols. Specifically, you should strive toward these next two objectives:

3. Children should be able to reflect upon a situation depicting parts of a unit and use *a pair* of numbers to identify the

portion of the unit that is given.
(Note: Children will be making statements such as "three of the five pieces
are red" in reaching this objective.)

4. Children should be able to use fraction names such as "three fourths" and
"two sevenths" and symbols such as $\frac{3}{4}$
and $\frac{2}{7}$ interchangeably with the number
pairs generated in reaching Objective 3. ⸱

Children should have a reasonable
mastery of Objective 3 before working
on Objective 4. When you require a
number pair for an answer, do not ask
"How many?" but ask *"What part?"*
The more familiar fractions, such as
halves, thirds, and fourths, do not get
preferential treatment. Number pairs in
statements, e.g., "three of the eight
parts," "five of the six parts," do not
need to begin with or emphasize halves
or any other fraction. The same can be
said for fractions such as $\frac{1}{2}$, $\frac{1}{3}$, or $\frac{1}{7}$ —
those with a numerator of 1 (unit frac-
tions). Children do not need to learn
about one half, one third, and one fourth
before experiencing other types of fractions. The sequence of Objectives 1–4
is directed at teaching all fractions naming a nonnegative number less than or
equal to one. (Some fractions signify situations where more than one of a unit is
being used, for example, $\frac{9}{5}$ or $\frac{5}{4}$. These
fractions are called improper fractions;
we will discuss them later.)

Objectives 1–3 are about fractions in
general. Objective 4 emphasizes placing
verbal and symbolic labels on the
thoughts expressed in answering questions requiring a pair of numbers
(Objective 3). How early can children
achieve Objective 3? We have seen and
worked with many kindergarten and
first-grade children who have mastered
Objective 3. Of course, these children

had had an ample amount of exploratory
experiences with wholes and parts of
wholes before using number pairs — they
were not rushed through Objectives 1
and 2.

**Teaching Suggestions
for Objectives 3 and 4**

In helping children use a pair of whole
numbers to describe a physical situation,
you should refer to all of the objects or
collections used for Objectives 1 and 2.
Mark or indicate the parts of each whole.

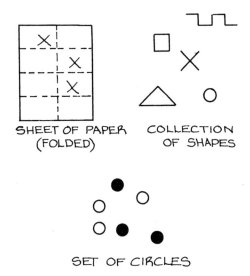

SHEET OF PAPER   COLLECTION
(FOLDED)   OF SHAPES

SET OF CIRCLES

For situations such as those in the diagram, do not just ask "How many parts
of the paper have I marked with an *x*?"
"How many of the shapes are closed?"
or "How many circles are shaded?" Ask
questions that force the children to respond with two numbers. A question
such as, *"What part* of the shapes are
closed figures?" calls for a response such
as, "Three of the five shapes are closed."
Similarly, questions such as, "What two
numbers tell us *how much* of the sheet of

paper is marked with an *x?*" and "*What part* of the set of circles is shaded circles?" require children to give a pair of numbers for their answer. The *pair* of numbers is exactly what we want! In your discussions emphasize that the first number tells how many parts are indicated; the second number tells how many parts comprise the unit.

One way to dramatize the importance of knowing both parts of a number pair is to create situations where children *need* to know *both* numbers to make a decision. The situations may be real or imaginary. For example, it is not enough to know that you are going to get 2 pieces of a cake or 2 pieces of candy, or that you have traveled 2 kilometers. If the cake is cut into 8 or 10 equal pieces, 2 pieces is a considerable amount. If the same cake is cut into 50 or 100 equal pieces, however, 2 pieces does not represent very much cake! The same problem occurs with a "fair share" of candy, the amount of a trip you have completed, or how well one has performed on some test. In these situations we need to know the total number of pieces of candy in the collection, the length of the whole trip, and the maximum number of points on the entire test. There are dozens of situations, involving points in a game, time, weight, and money, in which you can ask questions that will require a *pair* of numbers in order to tell the whole story. In selecting situations to describe with a pair of numbers, be sure to include entire objects, collections, quantities, distances, and lengths.

Children will also be using the notion that one unit can be represented by such names as "seven sevenths," "three thirds," and $\frac{2}{2}$. Children will also use zero. No parts of a unit can be indicated by names like "zero fourths" and $\frac{0}{6}$.

Realization of Objective 4 involves labeling. Some new terms will have to be used. Fortunately, other than *numerator* and *denominator*, the terms make sense to children. Thirds, fourths, fifths, and so on are forms of words children are using in meeting Objective 3. It is not an awkward transition to shift from the expression "three of the four parts" to "three fourths." After writing out expressions such as "two thirds," "four sevenths," and "one fifth," children will likely welcome the shorthand symbols $\frac{2}{3}$, $\frac{4}{7}$, and $\frac{1}{5}$. Over a series of lessons, gradually shift from focusing on Objective 3 to Objective 4. Shift from having children saying *and* writing, "Three of the five parts are shaded," to saying *and* writing, "Three fifths are shaded," and finally to writing, "$\frac{3}{5}$ are shaded." As you guide children in this transition, be careful to say and write what you want them to say and write. In working on Objective 4, look back and use all of the models and situations used in meeting Objectives 1–3.

Discussion Questions

1. Examine at least two primary-level mathematics textbooks. How do they present fractions in a way that is consistent with Objectives 1–4 in this section? In what ways is their presentation at variance with the suggestions given in this section?

2. Illustrate the use of each of the four contexts for modeling fractions (Section 1) in learning activities for Objective 3 and for Objective 4.

3. Make a list of the teaching suggestions, or advice, given in this section on reaching Objectives 1–4. React critically to each suggestion.

4. For each teaching suggestion you rated positively in Question 3, above, briefly describe a way to embody it.

3. MIXED NUMBERS AND IMPROPER FRACTIONS

In a great many physical situations a unit is counted a number of times before a fraction is needed. Each of the displays below shows three and one fourth ($3\frac{1}{4}$) units.

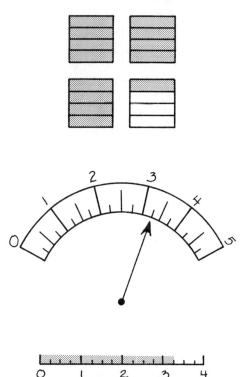

The symbol $3\frac{1}{4}$ is read as "three and one fourth" and is called a mixed numeral or mixed number. If, in each of the situations shown above, we count quarter units—the fourths—we find we have thirteen fourths ($\frac{13}{4}$). The symbol $\frac{13}{4}$

is called an improper fraction—improper because the numerator is larger than the denominator. The symbols $3\frac{1}{4}$ and $\frac{13}{4}$ represent the same quantity and the same point on the number line. We can write the equality $3\frac{1}{4} = \frac{13}{4}$.

If children have been introduced to proper fractions and understand them, they will probably find it easy to assign mixed numbers or improper fractions to situations like those above and to draw geometric, set, measurement, or number-line models for numbers such as $5\frac{1}{3}$ and $\frac{16}{3}$, or $1\frac{2}{5}$ and $\frac{7}{5}$. Improper fractions are just like the number pairs children need for Objective 3. A mixed number can be thought of as a whole number and a number pair. Here are overviews of activities that can help children be involved and alert in working with improper fractions and mixed numbers.

1. Take your pencil as a unit of length and mark its length into four equal parts. Use a piece of string and another pencil to help you do that. Now find out how tall you are to the nearest one fourth of a unit. Record your answer as an improper fraction and also as a mixed number. Also find out how wide and how long your table is in pencil units—give your answer as an improper fraction and as a mixed number. Now see if you can find a way to use your string to measure the circumference of the globe—give your answer in the same two ways. How can two of you find completely different answers for the distance around the globe and still both be right?

2. Take the straw which is marked "$\frac{1}{2}$ a unit" and find one thing in the envelope that is $4\frac{1}{2}$ units long. Now find something else in the envelope that is $\frac{9}{4}$ units long. What are the two things you found? Which is longer? Why?

The activities above can be extended and modified to include other embodiments of improper fractions and mixed numbers. Cut-out squares of grid paper can be used as units or subunits of area; large paper clips and cut-off lengths of these clips can serve as units and subunits of weight; and various sized cups or containers can be used for volume.

In illustrating mixed numbers and improper fractions use all of the geometric, set, measurement, and number-line models used to teach proper fractions. All that is needed to display improper fractions and mixed numbers is to display more than one unit, or whole. Also review the fact that units are composed of $\frac{4}{4}, \frac{5}{5}, \frac{6}{6}$, and so on. Here are some typical questions you can pose to bring out fraction names for whole numbers.

1. Divide a pie into sixths.
   How many sixths in 1?_____
2. Divide a rectangle into fourths.
   How many fourths in 1?_____
3. Divide each unit on a number line into fifths.
   One unit = _____fifths.
4. On a ruler, one inch has been divided into 16 equal parts. Each part is called_____.
   One inch = _____eighths.
5. Each orange in a group of oranges has been divided in half. There are 6 half-oranges. If the oranges were put together to make whole oranges, there would be_____whole oranges.

$$\frac{6}{2} = \square$$

Probably the most difficult aspect of improper fractions and mixed numbers is changing from one to the other. To give a plausible argument for either procedure, we rely on being able to write ones, or units, as $\frac{2}{2}, \frac{3}{3}, \frac{4}{4}, \frac{5}{5}$, or whatever the given situation demands. We present a step-by-step procedure for changing an improper fraction to a mixed number. In this case we are using $\frac{17}{5}$ as our example.

FIRST,
to determine how many of the equal parts make up a whole, use the denominator of the improper fraction.
   For $\frac{17}{5}$ we will use the fact that $\frac{5}{5} = 1$.

THEN,
figure the largest number of units, or "wholes," that can be made from the improper fraction.
   Since $\frac{5}{5} = 1$, then $\frac{10}{5} = 2$ and $\frac{15}{5} = 3$ and $\frac{20}{5} = 4$. There are *3 wholes* in $\frac{17}{5}$.

NEXT,
construct all the units you can from the parts of the improper fraction and count the number of equal parts that are left.
   Of the $\frac{17}{5}$, we use $\frac{15}{5}$ to make 3 wholes. $\frac{2}{5}$ are left. We write this: $\frac{17}{5} = \frac{15}{5} + \frac{2}{5} = 3 + \frac{2}{5}$

FINALLY,
express the result as a mixed number.
   $3 + \frac{2}{5} = 3\frac{2}{5}$

Now, consider the mixed number $3\frac{2}{5}$. To change $3\frac{2}{5}$ to an improper fraction, we first must think of it as $3 + \frac{2}{5}$. Since $1 = \frac{5}{5}$, $3 = \frac{15}{5}$. So $3 + \frac{2}{5} = \frac{15}{5} + \frac{2}{5} = \frac{17}{5}$. We are, in effect, undoing the work we did above.

Discussion Questions

1. How could the model below be used to depict $2\frac{1}{2}$ or $\frac{5}{2}$? Could it also be used to illustrate $2\frac{2}{4}$ or $\frac{10}{4}$?

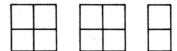

2. How could a set of colored rods of graduated lengths, e.g., Cuisenaire Rods, be used to model improper fractions and mixed numerals? What kind of model are such rods—geometric shapes, sets, measurement, or number line? Could a set of such rods be used to model proper fractions? Explain.

3. Why are representations of 1, such as $\frac{2}{2}$, $\frac{3}{3}$, $\frac{4}{4}$, and so on, necessary to change improper fractions to mixed numbers?

4. Use a geoboard, or draw sketches, to illustrate: $\frac{9}{5} = 1\frac{4}{5}$; $\frac{12}{8} = 1\frac{1}{2}$; and $\frac{7}{2} = 3\frac{1}{2}$.

5. Make 11 small squares. Make them one centimeter on a side. Call each square $\frac{1}{3}$ of a unit. Arrange them to show $\frac{11}{3} = 3\frac{2}{3}$. Notice in this application of fractions how vital it is to establish a whole, or a unit.

6. Does $6\frac{1}{3} = 6 + \frac{1}{3}$?

7. In converting improper fractions to mixed numbers, at which point are we doing some preliminary work in adding and subtracting fractions?

4. EQUIVALENT FRACTIONS

Just as there are many fractions to represent 1, 2, or any other counting number, we can write various fractions for any other fraction. There are an infinite number of fractions indicating the same amount or quantity or naming the same point on the number line. Here are seven fractions equivalent to $\frac{2}{5}$: $\frac{2}{5} = \frac{4}{10} = \frac{6}{15} = \frac{8}{20} = \frac{10}{25} = \frac{12}{30} = \frac{14}{35} = \frac{16}{40}$. Being able to generate equivalent fractions is needed in adding and subtracting fractions with unlike denominators.

Models for Equivalent Fractions

Geometric regions and the number line can be used to illustrate equivalent fractions. A sheet of paper can be taken as a unit and folded into halves with one of the halves shaded. This same paper can then be folded into fourths, eighths, and even sixteenths. Opening the paper after each fold can reveal the same shaded area being assigned a new name; one half becomes two fourths, four eighths, and so on.

The drawing below shows the fraction $\frac{1}{3}$ established by vertical folds and shading and then the results of folding the paper in half horizontally twice to illustrate $\frac{1}{3} = \frac{2}{6} = \frac{4}{12}$.

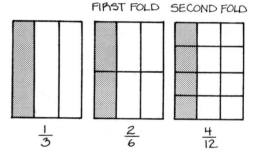

FIRST FOLD   SECOND FOLD

$$\frac{1}{3} \qquad \frac{2}{6} \qquad \frac{4}{12}$$

A unit length can also be subdivided by folding to indicate some equivalent fractions. Any unit segments, marked by subdivisions, can be used to mark or make a number line showing equivalent improper fractions. Sometimes thirds and fourths, or fourths, fifths, and sixths are placed on the same number line to illustrate order relations.

Objects of graduated lengths, such as Cuisenaire Rods, can also be used to

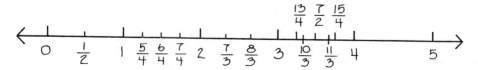

EACH WHITE ROD IS $\frac{1}{8}$ OF A UNIT

WHITE	WHITE	WHITE	WHITE	WHITE	WHITE	WHITE	WHITE
$\frac{1}{4}$ UNIT - RED		$\frac{1}{4}$ UNIT - RED		$\frac{1}{4}$ UNIT - RED		$\frac{1}{4}$ UNIT - RED	
$\frac{1}{2}$ UNIT - PURPLE				$\frac{1}{2}$ UNIT - PURPLE			
1 UNIT - BROWN							

model equivalent fractions. The diagram above depicts an arrangement of colored rods placed on top of an arbitrarily chosen unit rod. Order relationships among fractions are illustrated as well as equivalent fractions.

One very useful device for helping children use Cuisenaire Rods to model equivalent fractions, and for adding and subtracting fractions, is a *fraction board*. Fraction boards are relatively easy and inexpensive to construct from cardstock; children can take a few minutes and construct their own using pre-cut materials. On page 266 you see a 12-step fraction board with all but its bottom slot—a working space—filled. Each slot in the fraction board is constructed to be 12 equal parts in length. The length of a slot is *one*. Since 12 is a multiple of 1, 2, 3, 4, and 6, we can illustrate twelfths, sixths, fourths, thirds, and halves. The colors of the rods highlight the relationships. Again, order relationships and equivalent fractions are shown.

Generating Equivalent Fractions

You may have noticed two things about equivalent fractions. The first is that for any two equivalent fractions, such as $\frac{3}{5}$ and $\frac{9}{15}$, the "cross products"

are the same. In this case, we have $3 \times 15 = 5 \times 9$. It is always true that the product of the numerator of one of two equivalent fractions and the denominator of the other will equal the product of their counterparts; and if this is the case for two fractions, then these fractions are equivalent.

The second point is that one can generate fractions equivalent to any given fraction by multiplying the numerator and the denominator by the same number. Multiplying *both* the numerator and the denominator of $\frac{2}{7}$ by 3 yields $\frac{6}{21}$. Multiplying *both* the numerator and the denominator of $\frac{3}{5}$ by 4 gives $\frac{12}{20}$. The fractions $\frac{2}{7}$ and $\frac{6}{21}$ are equivalent. The fractions $\frac{3}{5}$ and $\frac{12}{20}$ are equivalent. Apply the cross-product test as a check. Students often must generate equivalent fractions to add or subtract fractions; for example, in the case of $\frac{3}{16} + \frac{5}{18}$.

Reducing Fractions

A fraction can be "reduced" by dividing both the numerator and the denominator by the same number. The numerator and the denominator of $\frac{6}{30}$ can *each* be divided by 6, giving $\frac{1}{5}$. This same reduction can also be done in two steps: first by dividing by 3 and then dividing

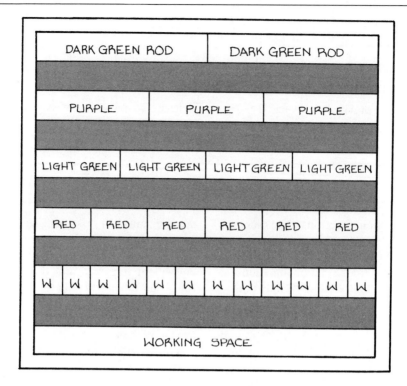

by 2 (or vice versa). Students often reduce fractions in a series of steps and frequently do not make all the reductions possible. This is not a serious error. Unfortunately, some standardized tests and some teachers seem to make a major issue out of always reducing fractions as far as possible—to "lowest terms."

Discussion Questions

1. In generating equivalent fractions by multiplying the numerator and the denominator by the same number, we are in essence multiplying the original fraction by what counting number? When reducing fractions, are we really dividing by this same counting number?

2. What equivalent fractions are shown on the fraction board illustrated above?

3. Use a 12-step fraction board and give the fractions shown in each slot if the length of the slot is *one*. If everyone agrees to let the length of the slot be *two,* then what fractions are shown?

4. Draw a 20-step fraction board and indicate how the various slots could illustrate halves, fourths, fifths, and tenths. What additional fractions can be shown? What fractions cannot be shown? What fractions can be shown on an 18-step board? On a 16-step board?

5. Does $\frac{128}{152} = \frac{32}{38}$? Why?

6. Fold a unit segment and a sheet of paper to illustrate $\frac{2}{5} = \frac{4}{10}$. Can you show this equality on a geoboard? How?

7. Why does one often need to use equivalent fractions in adding or subtracting fractions?

8. Use a set of objects of the same size and shape and a set of objects of different sizes and shapes to model pairs of equivalent fractions.

5. ADDING AND SUBTRACTING FRACTIONS

Like fractions are fractions with the same denominators. For example, $\frac{3}{4}$ and $\frac{2}{4}$ are like fractions, as are $\frac{1}{8}$, $\frac{5}{8}$, $\frac{11}{8}$, and $\frac{16}{8}$. *Unlike fractions,* such as $\frac{2}{3}$, $\frac{3}{4}$, and $\frac{9}{5}$, have different counting numbers as denominators. It is relatively easy to add or subtract two like fractions. It is harder to perform these operations on unlike fractions.

Adding and Subtracting Like Fractions

Like fractions are added according to the rule $\frac{a}{b} + \frac{c}{b} = \frac{a+c}{b}$; for example, $\frac{4}{5} + \frac{3}{5} = \frac{7}{5}$. All the contexts for representing fractions—geometric regions, sets, measurement, and the number line—can be used to model adding and subtracting like fractions. As with whole numbers, we can join or remove parts of sets or regions, and we can count on or count back. Three of eight pieces of a pie added to two more pieces result in five of the eight, or $\frac{5}{8}$, of the pie. The same is true for ounces in a cup. One can also move forward or backward on the number line or add to or remove elements of a set to depict addition and subtraction.

Adding mixed numbers whose fractional parts have like denominators introduces an element of special note. This occurs in such situations as $3\frac{3}{4} + \frac{2}{4}$. The addition problem results in a sum of $3\frac{5}{4}$. While the answer is correct, it is custom-

ary to change a mixed number containing an improper fraction to a mixed number with a proper fraction. In this case, $3\frac{5}{4}$ can be thought of as $4 + \frac{1}{4}$, or $4\frac{1}{4}$. Children can use a number line, ruler, or geometric model to guide or check their work.

Sometimes subtracting mixed numbers whose fractional parts contain like denominators poses a borrowing problem. Consider the subtraction exercise: $2\frac{5}{8} - \frac{7}{8}$. In the diagram, removing $\frac{7}{8}$ of a

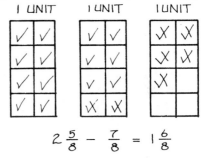

$$2\frac{5}{8} - \frac{7}{8} = 1\frac{6}{8}$$

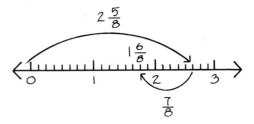

TWO MODELS OF SUBTRACTING $\frac{7}{8}$ OF A UNIT FROM $2\frac{5}{8}$ UNITS

unit (seven pieces) from $2\frac{5}{8}$ units, where the units have been subdivided into eighths, will give $1\frac{6}{8}$ units. Counting backwards on a number line from $2\frac{5}{8}$ likewise yields $1\frac{6}{8}$. Such a subtraction may be harder for some children to visualize when only symbols are employed since one of the units has been thought of as $\frac{8}{8}$ and then part of it removed.

One tactic to use in teaching operations is first to have children work exercises by using models and have them explain what they are doing as they draw or manipulate objects. Next, encourage children to give up their manipulative aids or drawings when finding the answer and use aids only to check answers. When children reach reasonable proficiency using models to check work, most of the use of models can be dropped.

Adding and Subtracting Unlike Fractions

Unlike fractions, such as $\frac{2}{3}$ and $\frac{3}{4}$ have unlike denominators. Children cannot add unlike fractions in one step, as they add like fractions. First, the fractions have to be transformed into like fractions. This means finding an equivalent fraction for at least one of the addends. After the unlike fractions have been changed to like fractions, the children add these like fractions and, perhaps, reduce the answer to lowest terms.

If students are able to generate equivalent fractions and add like fractions, they may initially find the addition of unlike fractions to be a challenging problem. With some guidance and perhaps resorting to certain models such as a fraction board, many children can feel a sense of accomplishment by finding a way to add unlike fractions. You may wish to start with exercises such as $\frac{3}{5} + \frac{2}{10}$ and $\frac{1}{4} + \frac{5}{8}$, where only one of the addends has to be replaced by an equivalent fraction. In the two additions above we can replace $\frac{3}{5}$ and $\frac{1}{4}$ by their equivalents $\frac{6}{10}$ and $\frac{2}{8}$. The additions then become $\frac{6}{10} + \frac{2}{10}$ and $\frac{2}{8} + \frac{5}{8}$—exercises children already know how to complete.

Additions such as $\frac{3}{4} + \frac{2}{3}$ require finding equivalent-fraction replacements for

both addends. This is more difficult and children often make careless errors or get confused in the process. Textbooks usually present these additions in both horizontal and vertical arrangements. In a horizontal format work proceeds this way:

$$\frac{3}{4} + \frac{2}{3} = \frac{9}{12} + \frac{8}{12} = \frac{17}{12}$$

In a vertical arrangement the work looks like this:

$$\frac{3}{4} = \frac{9}{12}$$
$$+\frac{2}{3} = \frac{8}{12}$$
$$\overline{\frac{17}{12}}$$

One of the keys to adding or subtracting unlike fractions is being able to find the "new" denominator for one or both of the addends. Since the new denominator results in both of the addends having the same denominator, it is called a "common denominator."

Finding common denominators. We recommend teaching either of two methods for finding common denominators. The first depends on children being able to multiply whole numbers. The second requires ability to divide as well as multiply whole numbers.

Consider the addition of $\frac{3}{4}$ and $\frac{2}{3}$, above. The common denominator is 12—the product of the two original denominators. To add or subtract $\frac{3}{7}$ and $\frac{2}{5}$, we also multiply the denominators 7 and 5 and get 35—a common denominator. Working vertically, we have enough information to write:

$$\frac{3}{7} = \frac{\Box}{35}$$
$$+\frac{2}{5} = \frac{\Box}{35}$$

At this point, it is clear why children studying addition and subtraction of fractions need to have reasonable mastery of being able ... equivalent fractions. To res ... and $\frac{2}{5} = \frac{\square}{35}$, children should r...ze that the numerator and denominator of $\frac{3}{7}$ *both* need to be multiplied by 5. Also, the numerator and denominator of $\frac{2}{5}$ must *both* be multiplied by 7. It is no accident that each multiplier is the denominator of the other addend. It should be noted that we are really multiplying the fractions by $\frac{5}{5}$ and $\frac{7}{7}$, respectively. But $\frac{5}{5}$ and $\frac{7}{7}$ are each equal to 1. And multiplying by 1 does not change the value of any number.

Another way to find a common denominator of two fractions — besides multiplying their denominators — is to generate a sequence of multiples of one of the denominators, stopping when the other denominator exactly divides a member of this sequence. For the denominators of fractions $\frac{3}{7}$ and $\frac{2}{5}$ we could start with 7 — the denominator of $\frac{3}{7}$: 7, 14, 21, 28, 35, . . ., checking each member to see if it is divisible by 5 — the denominator of $\frac{2}{5}$. We stopped at 35 because 35 is divisible by 5. If we start with 5 — the denominator of $\frac{2}{5}$ — we generate the sequence: 5, 10, 15, 20, 25, 30, 35, ... Again, we check each member of the sequence to see if it is divisible by the other denominator. Thirty-five is the first member of either sequence to pass this divisibility test.

If you use the method of generating sequences to find a common denominator, you will always find the smallest whole number that is a common denominator. This is called the "least common denominator." The least common denominator has the advantage of having children work with the smallest numbers possible for the given computation. However, children in Grades 4 and 5 rarely need to add fractions with denom-

inators exceeding 16. Such fractions are rarely encountered by adults. In fact, keeping denominators restricted to the first dozen counting numbers will serve to reinforce previously learned multiplication and division facts.

The second method of finding a common denominator works very well when one denominator is a multiple of the other. The method of multiplying denominators together works efficiently in other cases. Both methods work all of the time. There is still another method that uses prime factors and works nicely when the denominators are relatively large numbers, but this method is not needed in the intermediate grades.

Models for teaching addition and subtraction. You may have noted we discussed the addition and subtraction of unlike fractions without relying on diagrams or manipulative aids. We assumed a reasonable understanding of the following: addition, what fractions are, multiplication and division of whole numbers, and equivalent fractions. Based on these assumptions, we proceeded at a symbolic, or abstract, level. We relied on reasoning and plausible arguments. You will have some children in Grades 4 and 5 who are capable of taking such an approach to some mathematical topics. Do not deny them the opportunity to think in this fashion. For those children following such an approach, it is always appropriate that they look back and interpret their abstract work with physical apparatus. This interpretation can broaden their understanding and help them understand applications of mathematics. For these children story problems can be presented along with the models.

For other children you will want to

start with models similar to those described below. Many children in Grades 4 and 5 will need to construct diagrams and manipulate objects when they are working with symbolic statements, such as $\frac{3}{5} - \frac{1}{10}$. As noted earlier, encourage these children to use models only if they get stuck or to check their work.

1. Fraction Boards

Fraction boards can be used to model the addition of fractions if the total length of the slots in each board can be divided by the denominators of the fractions. For a fraction board of length 12 we can model the addition of twelfths, sixths, fourths, thirds, and halves.

Consider the fraction board displayed in Section 4. Since a red rod is $\frac{1}{6}$ and a purple rod is $\frac{1}{3}$, we could place one red and two purples in the bottom working slot to model $\frac{1}{6} + \frac{2}{3}$. The answer can be obtained by "trading in" any or all of the working rods so that the working slot contains rods of all the same color. In our example, $\frac{1}{6} + \frac{2}{3}$, the two thirds can be traded for four sixths; that is, the two purple rods can be replaced by four red rods, since they are the same length. The diagram below shows the working slot before and after this trade.

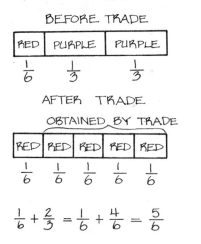

$$\frac{1}{6} + \frac{2}{3} = \frac{1}{6} + \frac{4}{6} = \frac{5}{6}$$

Figures
...t rectangles or unit circles can be ...d to model addition and subtraction of fractions. We will use unit rectangles. This model is similar to the fraction board in that we replace sections with new sections having the same area.

Consider the subtraction $\frac{3}{4} - \frac{2}{3}$. First, we can create a unit rectangle and mark $\frac{3}{4}$ of it — using vertical divisions.

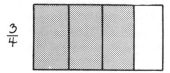

Next, we make another unit rectangle (congruent to the first rectangle) and mark $\frac{2}{3}$ of it — using horizontal divisions.

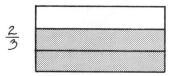

Then we have to find some way to remove the amount of *shaded area* in the second unit *from the shaded area* in the first unit. One way to do this is to take the first region — divided into vertical divisions — and divide it horizontally, just like the second region. Then divide the second region vertically, just like the

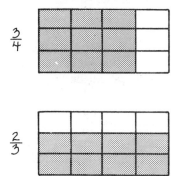

first region. We now have 12 smaller rectangles in each unit. The 8 smaller rectangles comprising the $\frac{2}{3}$ unit tell us to remove 8 rectangles from the $\frac{3}{4}$ region. This leaves us with 1 shaded rectangle. This rectangle is $\frac{1}{12}$ of a unit. Thus, $\frac{3}{4} - \frac{2}{3}$ becomes $\frac{9}{12} - \frac{8}{12} = \frac{1}{12}$.

Discussion Questions

1. Try to create a number line and a set model for adding or subtracting two unlike fractions, such as $\frac{2}{5}$ and $\frac{1}{3}$. Which model do you prefer for adding and subtracting fractions: geometric figures, fraction board (a measurement model), number line, or set?

2. In the fraction-board model we trade pieces; in the geometric-figure model we subdivide each region twice. Mathematically, what are we doing in these steps?

3. In adding two unlike fractions, when will only one of the two fractions have to be changed to an equivalent fraction?

4. The rule for adding two fractions with like denominators is $\dfrac{a}{b} + \dfrac{c}{b} = \dfrac{a+c}{b}$.
Devise a similar rule for adding two unlike fractions: $\dfrac{a}{b} + \dfrac{c}{d}$.

5. Make sketches to show how unit rectangles can illustrate $\frac{1}{3} + \frac{1}{2}$.

6. Can you make a sketch of an 18-unit fraction board showing $\frac{5}{9} - \frac{1}{3}$? Sketch a 12-unit fraction board showing $\frac{1}{6} + \frac{3}{4}$.

7. Consider the two methods presented for finding a common denominator.
a. Find some instances in which multiplying the denominators gives a common denominator that is not a least common denominator. In general, when is this the case?

b. In finding a common denominator by generating sequences of multiples of either denominator, one can choose to generate sequences starting with the larger or the smaller denominator. Which do you recommend? Why?

6. MULTIPLICATION AND DIVISION OF FRACTIONS

Models for Multiplication

There are a variety of models for multiplication of fractions, which can be used to introduce and explain the meaning of the operation. Joining regions and using the number line lead to repeated addition and can be used to show multiplication of a fraction by a whole number. Parts of sets, geometric figures, and use of a unit geometric region do not lead conveniently to repeated addition but can be used to depict multiplication of a fraction by a fraction. There are many models related to the multiplication of fractions; the operation has many applications.

Joining regions. Selecting a circle as a unit region, we may join fractional parts, for example, three one-quarter pieces or five one-quarter pieces. The drawings below show $3 \times \frac{1}{4}$ and $5 \times \frac{1}{4}$. They are simple and effective *only* when one factor is a whole number.
To show $3 \times \frac{1}{4}$, we can draw and write:

$$\frac{1}{4} + \frac{1}{4} + \frac{1}{4} = \frac{3}{4}$$

$$3 \times \frac{1}{4} = \frac{3}{4}$$

To show $5 \times \frac{1}{4}$, we can draw and write:

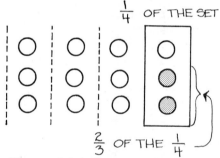

$$\frac{1}{4} + \frac{1}{4} + \frac{1}{4} + \frac{1}{4} + \frac{1}{4} = \frac{5}{4}$$

$$5 \times \frac{1}{4} \qquad\qquad = \frac{5}{4}$$

The number line. The number line also can be used as a model when one factor is a whole number. The multiplication of $5 \times \frac{1}{4}$ is shown below.

$$5 \times \frac{1}{4} = \frac{1}{4} + \frac{1}{4} + \frac{1}{4} + \frac{1}{4} + \frac{1}{4} = \frac{5}{4} = 1\frac{1}{4}$$

Both the regions model and the number-line model show multiplication as repeated addition.

These illustrations can lead to an algorithm for multiplying a whole number and a fraction. The algorithm is shown by the rule $a \times \dfrac{b}{c} = \dfrac{a \times b}{c}$. For example, $3 \times \dfrac{1}{4} = \dfrac{3 \times 1}{4} = \dfrac{3}{4}$. This may be done first in Grade 4 or 5 and is usually repeated each time multiplication of fractions is encountered. Students can be challenged to seek a "short cut" for the process of drawing regions or number lines and may discover the algorithm for themselves.

In multiplying a fraction by a whole number, equalities of the form $3 \times \frac{1}{4} = \frac{3}{4}$ are established. These equalities will be of use later.

In multiplying two fractions such as $\frac{2}{3} \times \frac{1}{4}$, the repeated-addition meaning is not much help. While adding 3 addends has meaning ($3 \times \frac{1}{4} = \frac{1}{4} + \frac{1}{4} + \frac{1}{4}$), it is not clear what it would mean to add $\frac{2}{3}$ of an addend. For problems such as $\frac{2}{3} \times \frac{1}{4}$ we must turn to other models.

Parts of parts. A set or region may be divided into parts, and "parts of the parts" may be used as a model for multiplication of fractions. We take $\frac{2}{3} \times \frac{1}{4}$ as an example. The set of 12 dots in the diagram below is the unit in this example.

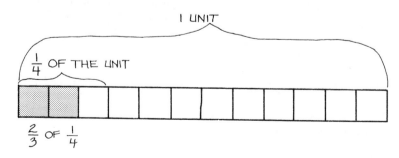

The model is interpreted as follows: Take $\frac{2}{3}$ of $\frac{1}{4}$ of the dots—which we show by taking $\frac{1}{4}$ of the dots and then taking $\frac{2}{3}$ of this $\frac{1}{4}$. What part, or fraction, *of the whole* is the resulting set? The answer is $\frac{2}{12}$, or $\frac{1}{6}$, of the whole set, so $\frac{2}{3}$ of $\frac{1}{4}$ is $\frac{2}{12}$. So $\frac{2}{3} \times \frac{1}{4} = \frac{2}{12}$.

Exactly the same reasoning is applied in solving the problem by using geometric regions. The figure above shows that $\frac{2}{3}$ of $\frac{1}{4}$ is $\frac{2}{12}$ of a rectangular unit region. Again, we conclude that $\frac{2}{3} \times \frac{1}{4} = \frac{2}{12}$.

From these examples and others like them children may discover or you can demonstrate an algorithm for multiplying two fractions. If you give the children some problems to work by using regions, they may see the algorithm as a short cut, for it is easier than tedious drawing of figures.

Examples in which no reducing is possible are perhaps the clearest for showing the algorithm for multiplying two proper fractions. The drawing below shows how we may find the answer to $\frac{2}{5} \times \frac{3}{7}$. The diagram shows that $\frac{2}{5}$ of $\frac{3}{7}$ is $\frac{6}{35}$. The conclusion is clear! The algorithm is: multiply the numerators and multiply the denominators,

$$\frac{2}{5} \times \frac{3}{7} = \frac{2 \times 3}{5 \times 7} = \frac{6}{35}.$$

$\frac{3}{7}$ OF THE UNIT

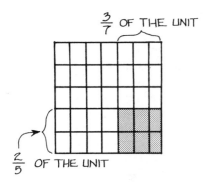

$\frac{2}{5}$ OF THE UNIT

The algorithm for multiplying two fractions is carried over to problems that are more difficult to illustrate, such as multiplying a fraction and a mixed number or two mixed numbers. Here are two such calculations:

$$\frac{2}{3} \times 1\frac{3}{5} = \frac{2}{3} \times \frac{8}{5} = \frac{2 \times 8}{3 \times 5} = \frac{16}{15} = 1\frac{1}{15}$$

$$1\frac{2}{3} \times 1\frac{3}{4} = \frac{5}{3} \times \frac{7}{4} = \frac{5 \times 7}{3 \times 4} = \frac{35}{12} = 2\frac{11}{12}$$

It is customary to change back to mixed numbers at the end of the calculation, although it is not actually necessary. In fact, the improper form of a fraction is usually easier to use in further calculations.

The Multiplication Algorithm:

$$\frac{a}{b} \times \frac{c}{d} = \frac{a \times c}{b \times d}$$

If the development of the models has been well done, the students should be convinced that the algorithm that can be derived from the models is correct and widely applicable. We may also derive the multiplication algorithm by a logical argument, provided we accept two conclusions from our work with models. First, when we multiplied a whole number times a fraction, we noted

$$3 \times \frac{1}{4} = \frac{3 \times 1}{4} = \frac{3}{4},$$ or in general that

$$a \times \frac{1}{b} = \frac{a \times 1}{b} = \frac{a}{b}.$$ In this case, a and b

stand for any whole numbers, except that b cannot be zero. Second, we need

to assume that $\frac{1}{a} \times \frac{1}{b} = \frac{1 \times 1}{a \times b} = \frac{1}{a \times b}$, a

conclusion that must also rest on our work with regions or parts of parts of sets. We will use these ideas several times. Our argument goes as follows:

$$\frac{3}{5} \times \frac{2}{3} = \left(3 \times \frac{1}{5}\right) \times \left(2 \times \frac{1}{3}\right)$$

because $a \times \frac{1}{b} = \frac{a}{b}$

$$= \left(3 \times 2\right) \times \left(\frac{1}{5} \times \frac{1}{3}\right)$$

application of the commutative and associative properties of multiplication

$$= 6 \times \frac{1}{15}$$

because $\dfrac{1}{a} \times \dfrac{1}{b} = \dfrac{1}{a \times b}$

$$= \frac{6}{15}$$

because $a \times \dfrac{1}{b} = \dfrac{a}{b}$

This answer $\left(\dfrac{6}{15}\right)$ is the same as we would have obtained using the algorithm $\dfrac{a}{b} \times \dfrac{b}{c} = \dfrac{a \times b}{b \times c}$.

This argument could have been made longer. We did not use the commutative and associative laws separately. We did not attempt logically to establish $a \times \dfrac{1}{b} = \dfrac{a}{b}$ or $\dfrac{1}{a} \times \dfrac{1}{b} = \dfrac{1}{a \times b}$; rather, we accepted these conclusions from our work with models.

Models for Division

The models we will use for division of fractions are sets, regions, and repeated subtraction. These are effective only in explaining very simple problems and in giving the student an intuitive grasp of division of fractions. For more complex problems, however, interpretation of the model becomes more difficult than grasping a mathematical explanation of the algorithm. Our procedure here will be first to illustrate the use of the models with appropriate problems and then to present ways to establish four different algorithms.

Sets. Division of whole numbers can be introduced using sets in problems such as "How many sets of 5 can you make from a set of 32?" In division of fractions a similar problem can be presented: "I have 2 dozen eggs and use $\frac{1}{2}$ dozen each morning. How many mornings will the eggs last?" Essentially, this question asks, "How many times can $\frac{1}{2}$ be subtracted from 2?" or "How many $\frac{1}{2}$'s are in 2?" We can draw a figure and simply count the half dozens. We conclude that $2 \div \frac{1}{2} = 4$. If the answer had not been a

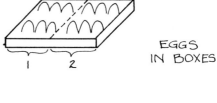

EGGS IN BOXES

1   2

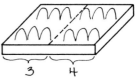

3   4

whole number, we would have had a remainder as in the problem $2\frac{3}{4} \div \frac{1}{2}$. In the division of fractions it is very difficult to interpret remainders. The best procedure in introducing division of fractions is to stick to examples in which the answer is a whole number.

Regions. The same consideration applies here; if the answer is not a whole number, the interpretation is too complex to be of much use. Simple problems will carry the message. "Elizabeth made one pan of fudge. She will keep $\frac{1}{2}$ of the fudge for her family and will sell $\frac{1}{2}$ of the fudge at the bake sale. She will sell it in packages which hold $\frac{1}{8}$ pan. How many packages can she sell?" How many $\frac{1}{8}$'s are in

$\frac{1}{2}$? This problem is easily solved with a drawing.

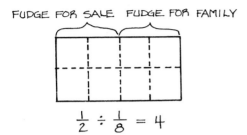

FUDGE FOR SALE   FUDGE FOR FAMILY

$$\frac{1}{2} \div \frac{1}{8} = 4$$

Note that in division children may be expecting a relatively small answer. In division of whole numbers the quotient is smaller than the dividend. Problems like $\frac{1}{2} \div \frac{1}{8}$ show graphically why the answer can be large when the divisor is a fraction. Story problems can play an important role in developing understanding. They can clarify the meaning of the operation.

Repeated subtraction. Each of the models above suggests repeated subtraction as a model for division. We may ask, "How many times can $\frac{1}{2}$ be subtracted from 2?" We do the subtractions and, as in whole-number division, count the number of times we are able to subtract.

2	$1\frac{1}{2}$	1	$\frac{1}{2}$
$-\frac{1}{2}$	$-\frac{1}{2}$	$-\frac{1}{2}$	$-\frac{1}{2}$
$1\frac{1}{2}$	1	$\frac{1}{2}$	0

Again, we conclude $2 \div \frac{1}{2} = 4$, or $\frac{4}{2} \div \frac{1}{2} = 4$.

Establishing Division Algorithms

There are several different ways to explain a procedure for division of fractional numbers. They are used in various textbook series, and we will include most of them here. An evaluative comment is included following each explanation. Each method is presented by using the problem $\frac{7}{12} \div \frac{3}{4}$ as an example.

1. "Invert the Divisor and Multiply"

Algorithm: $\dfrac{a}{b} \div \dfrac{c}{d} = \dfrac{a}{b} \times \dfrac{d}{c}$

$$\frac{7}{12} \div \frac{3}{4} = \frac{7}{12} \times \frac{4}{3} = \frac{28}{36} = \frac{7}{9}$$

In this case, the teacher simply tells the students, "To divide fractions, you invert the divisor and multiply." Of course, this explains nothing. Why one should invert and change from division to multiplication is a mystery. The only justification that can accompany an "authoritative" assertion is to show that the rule does give the same answers we get by using sets, regions, or repeated subtraction on problems in which the answer is a whole number. This latter means of justification has considerable merit — it is pragmatic.

2. The "Common Denominator" Algorithm

$$\frac{7}{12} \div \frac{3}{4} = \frac{7}{12} \div \frac{9}{12}$$

As in addition, find a common denominator and use it in writing equivalent fractions.

$$\frac{7}{12} \div \frac{9}{12} = \frac{7 \div 9}{12 \div 12}$$

This is a difficult step to justify. A plausible explanation goes as follows: "When we multiply fractions, we multiply numerators and denominators, so when we divide fractions, we should divide numerators and denominators." This is a weak justification.

$$\frac{7 \div 9}{12 \div 12} = \frac{7 \div 9}{1}$$

A fact of whole-number arithmetic is that $12 \div 12 = 1$.

$$\frac{7 \div 9}{1} = 7 \div 9$$

If any number is divided by 1, the number itself is the quotient; that is, $a \div 1 = a$.

$$7 \div 9 = \frac{7}{9}$$

This change makes use of the interpretation of a fraction as an "indicated division."

This method of doing division of fractional numbers has two shortcomings. There is no place in the explanation where the student can observe—"discover"—the "invert and multiply" rule as a short cut and one must find a common denominator. Finding common denominators is often as difficult as the division problem itself!

3. The "Complex Fraction" Algorithm.

$$(1) \ \tfrac{7}{12} \div \tfrac{3}{4} = \frac{\frac{7}{12}}{\frac{3}{4}}$$

This algorithm is usually first presented in about Grade 7 since we have a fraction whose numerator and denominator are fractions! The explanation is, "Since a fraction is an indicated division, for example $\frac{2}{3}$ means $2 \div 3$, we can use the fraction form to indicate the division problem $\frac{7}{12} \div \frac{3}{4}$." *From here on one must assume that the knowledge we have learned about ordinary fractions applies to complex fractions!*

$$(2) \ \frac{\frac{7}{12}}{\frac{3}{4}} = \frac{\frac{7}{12} \times \frac{4}{3}}{\frac{3}{4} \times \frac{4}{3}}$$

The reason justifying what has been done is that multiplying the numerator and the denominator of a fraction by the same number—in this case $\frac{4}{3}$—does not change the "value" of the fraction. But why use $\frac{4}{3}$? Looking ahead, we can see that having 1 in the denominator of this complicated fraction will simplify it a great deal. What number can we multiply

$\frac{3}{4}$ by to obtain 1? The answer is $\frac{4}{3}$. This step is easier if children have previously learned to find the reciprocal of a fractional number.

$$(3) \ \frac{\frac{7}{12} \times \frac{4}{3}}{\frac{3}{4} \times \frac{4}{3}} = \frac{\frac{7}{12} \times \frac{4}{3}}{1}$$

Because $\frac{3}{4} \times \frac{4}{3} = 1$. Note that here or in the following step a child can observe the "invert and multiply" short cut.

$$(4) \ \frac{\frac{7}{12} \times \frac{4}{3}}{1} = \tfrac{7}{12} \times \tfrac{4}{3}$$

Because $\dfrac{a}{1} = a$, or, put another way, $a \div 1 = a$.

A child who works problems this way may find a short cut from step (1) to step (4). This means the child will have *invented* the "invert and multiply" rule. One advantage of this method (as well as the method which follows) is that while working on it a student can see why "invert and multiply" works. However, the approach will not make sense to a child who has not considered fractions as indicated divisions. We have not taken this approach in this chapter. We have considered fractions as a pair of numbers indicating an amount or number on the number line. Considering fractions as indicated divisions is discussed in the chapter on teaching decimals.

4. The "Equation Method" Algorithm.
As was the case with the preceding method, explaining the "equation" algorithm requires some knowledge of mathematics usually taught at Grade 6 and above.

$$(1) \ \tfrac{7}{12} \div \tfrac{3}{4} = \square$$

The $\square$ is the answer to the division problem.

Consider the relationship between multiplication and division:

$12 \div 3 = 4$ because $4 \times 3 = 12$,
$36 \div 4 = 9$ because $9 \times 4 = 36$,
$12 \div \frac{1}{4} = 48$ because $48 \times \frac{1}{4} = 12$.

Now, assuming that this relationship holds for all fractional numbers and that $\frac{7}{12} \div \frac{3}{4} = \square$, we have

$$(2) \; \square \times \tfrac{3}{4} = \tfrac{7}{12}$$

If $a \div b = c$, then $c \times b = a$.

$$(3) \; (\square \times \tfrac{3}{4}) \times \tfrac{4}{3} = \tfrac{7}{12} \times \tfrac{4}{3}$$

If we have an equation, we can multiply both sides by the same number. In this case we multiplied both sides by $\frac{4}{3}$. The reason why we did this can be seen by looking ahead. We would like to get $\square$ on one side by itself—in step (2) it is multiplied by $\frac{3}{4}$. We use a number which when multiplied by $\frac{3}{4}$ will give 1 as a product. The result can be seen in the following steps:

$$(4) \; \square \times (\tfrac{3}{4} \times \tfrac{4}{3}) = \tfrac{7}{12} \times \tfrac{4}{3}$$

Use of the associative property of multiplication

$$(5) \; \square \times 1 = \tfrac{7}{12} \times \tfrac{4}{3}$$

Because $\frac{3}{4} \times \frac{4}{3} = 1$

$$(6) \; \square = \tfrac{7}{12} \times \tfrac{4}{3}$$

Any number when multiplied by 1 gives itself as a product; that is, $a \times 1 = a$.

Note that in steps (4) to (6) the student can observe the "invert and multiply" short cut by comparing the problem in step (1) and the result in step (6).

Discussion Questions

1. Create two different models to show each of the following:

(a) $4 \times \frac{1}{3} = \frac{4}{3}$ (b) $\frac{1}{3} \times \frac{1}{2} = \frac{1}{6}$ (c) $\frac{3}{4} \times \frac{2}{5} = \frac{6}{20}$
(d) $5 \div \frac{1}{3} = 15$ (e) $\frac{5}{2} \div \frac{1}{4} = 10$

2. Consider the procedure for multiplying two fractions summarized by the rule $\frac{a}{b} \times \frac{c}{d} = \frac{a \times c}{b \times d}$. Paraphrase this rule. Then give the advantages and disadvantages of each of the following strategies for teaching children to multiply two fractions:

Strategy A

(1) Write the rule down.

(2) Show the children two or three instances of the rule, $\frac{a}{b} \times \frac{c}{d} = \frac{a \times c}{b \times d}$.

(3) Have the children work a few exercises using the rule.

(4) Have the children paraphrase the procedure.

(5) Present a series of models of the multiplication of two fractions and show that the models give the same answer as following the rule.

(6) Have the children create drawings modeling the multiplication of fractions.

(7) Have the children practice multiplying fractions. Ask them to draw a picture for every 10th exercise.

Strategy B

(1) Present children with some problems in multiplying fractions—help them create different models for the problems.

(2) After the children can solve these problems using objects or drawings, ask them to work a seemingly long assignment. Tell them they don't have to draw pictures if they can figure out a short cut.

(3) Ask leading questions of those children that do not see a short cut. If necessary, to avoid frustration, privately tell them how the short cut works.

(4) Same as step (7) in Strategy A.

3. Repeat Discussion Question 2, substituting the division of fractions for the multiplication of fractions and the rule $\frac{a}{b} \div \frac{c}{d} = \frac{a}{b} \times \frac{d}{c}$.

11 · Teaching Decimal Fractions

INTRODUCTION

Up to now, decimal fractions have been introduced late in the elementary grades. Students in third and fourth grades have used decimal notation only for money. In these early presentations, however, $4.37 is taken by children to mean 4 dollars and 37 cents, actually two whole numbers and not a decimal fraction. The introduction of decimal fractions has been in fifth grade. At that time the symbol .1 is presented as one tenth, associated with fractional parts of regions and with common fractions. The values of places to the right of the decimal point—tenths, hundredths, and so forth—are introduced. We will examine these ideas in detail in this chapter.

There are present trends in our society which will probably—almost certainly—result in the earlier introduction of decimals as fractions and in some deemphasis of common fractions. Almost all textbooks will present the metric system as the primary, if not the only, system of measurement. The use of the metric system, based on subdivisions and multiples of 10 and expressed conveniently in decimals, will increase the need for an early presentation of decimal fractions. The increased use of calculators, in which both input and output are in decimal form, is a major influence in our society. Teachers are wondering what to do with calculators brought to school and how to respond to calculator-done homework. The fact that this instrument does not handle common fractions will have an influence on our curriculum. Because of these influences, it seems likely that we will have, in the near future, a full presentation of decimal fractions in Grade 3. This presentation will be based on money and the metric system. It may involve calculators and will be supported by a strong semiconcrete development. The presentation may not be associated with common fractions at all.

We now present a development of decimal fractions which, with minor modifications, could be used in Grades 3 through 6.

1. MODELS FOR DECIMAL FRACTIONS

In representing whole numbers, a *small* object or region was chosen as the unit, the "one," and a number of these were grouped into tens of units, hundreds of units, and so on. In representing decimal fractions, a *large* unit is chosen for "one," and the fractions are represented by dividing that unit into 10 parts, 100 parts, and so on. The concrete and semiconcrete aids that were used in teaching whole numbers can be used in a similar way to build understandings of decimal fractions.

Base ten blocks and place value cards can be used in this way. The large block is designated as "one" and the flat then becomes one tenth, .1, because it takes

10 of them to make a block. Similarly, a long block becomes .01, one hundredth, and a small cube becomes .001, one thousandth.

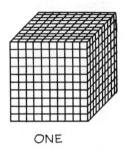

ONE

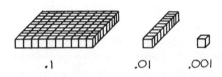

.1   .01   .001

Place value cards can be used the same way. The large square becomes the unit, "one," the strip becomes .1, and the small square becomes .01.

Pictures of subdivided regions are often used to represent decimals, just as they are used to represent common fractions. A region is divided into 10 parts and 4 are shaded. This is familiar to the children as $\frac{4}{10}$. The decimal representation, .4, is associated with the picture and with the common fraction. Similarly, a square is divided into 100 small squares and 60 are shaded, in columns of 10. This represents $\frac{6}{10}$, .6, $\frac{60}{100}$, or .60 and introduces the equality .6 = .60.

Other devices that were used to represent whole numbers can be altered to represent decimal fractions. Pockets on a place value chart and wires on a bead abacus can stand for decimal fractions as well as for whole numbers.

The number line is a valuable device for helping children understand numbers represented by decimal fractions.

We may begin by representing tenths and proceed to represent hundredths, thousandths, and so on by using "magnified" pictures of the number line. As an example, let us locate pi (π), 3.1416 approximately, on a sequence of number lines that have increasing magnification. In each number line below, the smallest subdivision in the preceding number line is magnified and divided into 10 subdivisions. Thus, we go from a line on which tenths are the smallest division to a line that shows hundredths, and so on. In each case, π is marked on the line.

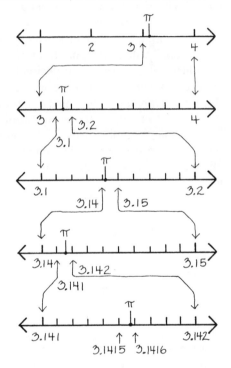

Plotting points on the number line magnified to show tenths or hundredths helps children see the richness of points on the line and the order of points on the line. The number line is used to illustrate simple problems involving decimal fractions. We must emphasize again that as long as a student continues to study mathematics the number line and extensions of the number-line idea will be used. It is extremely advantageous for students to encounter and use the number line at every oppotunity.

In the metric system the basic unit of length is a meter. The meter is subdivided into 10 decimeters, 100 centimeters, and 1,000 millimeters. As children learn to measure using the metric system, it will be natural for them to record a measurement as 7.3 meters, interpreting this as 7 meters and 3 decimeters. Thus, the tenths, hundredths, and thousandths places will have special meanings in measurement situations. As the conversion to the metric system proceeds, "ruler fractions" will be decimal fractions.

Children also learn to use decimals to represent dollars and cents. The tenths' place can represent dimes and the hundredths' place can represent cents. These social or applied uses of the decimal system are essential in giving significance to the study of decimal fractions.

The use of a grid is very effective in explaining concepts of decimal fractions and operations done on them. The grid below shows a variety of ways to represent place values. At first the names of the places are written out and the values associated with common fractions, (A) and (B). The decimals are shown in line (C). The exponential forms, (D) and (E), may be introduced in Grade 6 and the expression using negative exponents, (F), in later grades.

There are many patterns in this place value display. Students should come to recognize them because the patterns contribute to their understanding of fractions, decimals, and exponents, as well as helping them to read decimal fractions. The value of each place is 10 times the value of the place to the right and $\frac{1}{10}$ the value of the place to the left. In row (D) the values of the places are expressed as products of tens. Beginning with 1 in ones' place, places to the left are 10, $10 \times 10 = 100$, $10 \times 10 \times 10 =$

	HUNDREDS	TENS	ONES	TENTHS	HUNDREDTHS	THOUSANDTHS	
NAMES OF PLACES							(A)
VALUES OF PLACES	100	10	1	$\frac{1}{10}$	$\frac{1}{100}$	$\frac{1}{1,000}$	(B)
	100	10	1	.1	.01	.001	(C)
	10×10	10	1	$\frac{1}{10}$	$\frac{1}{10 \times 10}$	$\frac{1}{10 \times 10 \times 10}$	(D)
	10^2	10^1	10^0	$\frac{1}{10^1}$	$\frac{1}{10^2}$	$\frac{1}{10^3}$	(E)
	10^2	10^1	10^0	10^{-1}	10^{-2}	10^{-3}	(F)

1,000, and so on. Beginning with 1 in ones' place, places to the right are $\frac{1}{10}$, $\frac{1}{10 \times 10} = \frac{1}{100}$, $\frac{1}{10 \times 10 \times 10} = \frac{1}{1000}$, and so on.

$$10,000 = 10 \times 10 \times 10 \times 10 = 10^4$$
$$1,000 = 10 \times 10 \times 10 \qquad = 10^3$$
$$100 = 10 \times 10 \qquad\qquad = 10^2$$
$$10 = 10 \qquad\qquad\qquad = 10^1$$
$$1 = 1 \qquad\qquad\qquad\quad = 10^0$$
$$.1 = \frac{1}{10} = \frac{1}{10^1} \qquad\qquad = 10^{-1}$$
$$.01 = \frac{1}{100} = \frac{1}{10^2} \qquad\quad = 10^{-2}$$
$$.001 = \frac{1}{1,000} = \frac{1}{10^3} \qquad = 10^{-3}$$

When the values are expressed in terms of exponents, a question arises regarding the exponents for 10, 1, $\frac{1}{10}$, and so on. They do not fit the early definition of an exponent as the number of times a number is used as a factor. For example, 2^3 means 2 used as a factor 3 times; $2^3 = 2 \times 2 \times 2$. Then 10^1 should mean 10 used as a factor 1 time. To do multiplication, however, you must have two factors (at least) and so the definition cannot apply—you cannot have only one factor in multiplication. The problem is resolved by defining $10^1 = 10$, $10^0 = 1$, $\frac{1}{10^1} = 10^{-1}$, $\frac{1}{10^2} = 10^{-2}$, and so on. The pattern in the table is consistent. As you read down the table, each number is $\frac{1}{10}$ of the number that preceded it and each exponent is one less than the one that preceded it. For 10^4, 10^3, and 10^2 this pattern comes from simply counting the number of times 10 is used as a factor. The definitions for 10^1, 10^0 and negative exponents continue the pattern. Also, some very useful properties of multiplication and division of powers can be preserved only be defining the zero exponent and negative exponents in that way.

Discussion Questions — Exercises

1. A national study committee has recommended that beginning in Grade 8 all children have access to calculators for all mathematical activities, including tests. What reasons can you give *for* and *against* this policy? You may wish to make up teams and debate the issue.

2. Illustrate 3.47 using an abacus, a place value pocket chart, and a picture of place value cards.

3. Using a succession of increasingly magnified number lines, show the location of 2.4163.

4. Draw an illustration that shows that $.4 = .40$. Draw an illustration that shows that $\frac{1}{4} = .25$.

5. Fill in this table, following the patterns you observe. What can you conclude about 2^0? about 2^{-2}? Do not try to write a product where the table is crossed out; use the pattern.

$$2^6 = 2 \times 2 \times 2 \times 2 \times 2 \times 2 = 64$$
$$2^5 = 2 \times 2 \times 2 \times 2 \times 2 \qquad = 32$$
$$2^4 = 2 \times 2 \times 2 \times 2 \qquad\quad = 16$$
$$2^3 = \underline{\qquad\qquad} \qquad\qquad = \underline{\quad}$$
$$\underline{\quad} = \underline{\qquad\qquad} \qquad\qquad = \underline{\quad}$$
$$\underline{\quad} = /\!/\!/\!/\!/\!/\!/\!/\!/\!/\!/\!/\!/ \qquad = \underline{\quad}$$
$$\underline{\quad} = /\!/\!/\!/\!/\!/\!/\!/\!/\!/\!/\!/\!/ \qquad = \underline{\quad}$$
$$\underline{\quad} = /\!/\!/\!/\!/\!/\!/\!/\!/\!/\!/\!/\!/ \qquad = \underline{\quad}$$
$$\underline{\quad} = /\!/\!/\!/\!/\!/\!/\!/\!/\!/\!/\!/\!/ \qquad = \underline{\quad}$$

2. COMPUTATION WITH DECIMAL FRACTIONS

Developing computational skill with decimal fractions is considerably easier than with common fractions. This is another reason to look forward to increased importance of decimal fractions in the curriculum. The computational procedures for decimal fractions parallel the procedures for whole numbers. The models and explanations which are used to teach these algorithms are extensions of the models and explanations used to teach whole-number operations. It is likely, and much to be desired, that a curriculum in which metric measures and decimal fractions predominate will be meaningful to a larger proportion of children than is the present curriculum.

Addition and Subtraction

Decimal fractions can be represented as parts of things and parts of pictures, just as common fractions can be. Decimal place values can also be represented on an abacus, a place value pocket chart, a place value grid, or by using expanded notation. Each of these representations can be used to model the addition and subtraction algorithms. Measurements in the metric system and decimal representation of money can also be used to explain computation with decimals. Because of the likely trend toward earlier introduction of decimals, we will illustrate *more* concrete aids to decimal computation than are typically used at the present time.

Earlier we illustrated place value cards. They can be used to do the addition problem $1.6 + 1.55$. Base ten blocks can be used in a similar manner. There are a number of comments to be made about this problem. Regrouping is involved — 11 tenths are grouped as 10 tenths (one) and 1 tenth. With place value cards, this is done by the exchange of 10 strips for a large square. Alternative methods of doing the problems include expanded notation or a place value grid, as shown below.

$$\begin{array}{rrrr} & 1 \text{ one} & + \ 6 \text{ tenths} & + \ 0 \text{ hundredths} \\ + & 1 \text{ one} & + \ 5 \text{ tenths} & + \ 5 \text{ hundredths} \\ \hline & 2 \text{ ones} & + 11 \text{ tenths} & + \ 5 \text{ hundredths} \end{array}$$

or 3 ones + 1 tenth + 5 hundredths

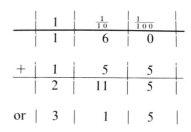

	1	$\frac{1}{10}$	$\frac{1}{100}$
	1	6	0
+	1	5	5
	2	11	5

or | 3 | 1 | 5 |

The problem involves the addition of "ragged decimals," so called because when the decimal points are aligned, the right-hand digits are not all in one column. The column presents a ragged appearance. Addition and subtraction of ragged decimals have some special features, which we discuss later. At this point, we will simply fill the empty places with zeros, using the argument that $1.6 = 1.60$, that is, $1\frac{6}{10} = 1\frac{60}{100}$, which most students will readily accept.

The algorithms for addition and subtraction of decimal fractions differ from the corresponding algorithms for whole numbers in that the decimal points are aligned but the right-hand column may not be in line. Children frequently ask why the decimal points must be aligned if we are to add columns. The answer is that we are then adding digits that have the same place value. If I misalign the columns, I may add tenths to hundredths. What would the answer mean? Not a number of tenths and not a number of hundredths. This would be like adding 3 cents and 4 dimes and getting 7 for an answer. 7 what?

The abacus and the place value pocket chart may be labeled to represent decimal fractions. These may then be used for addition and subtraction, just as they were for whole numbers. As a reminder, the decimal point can be placed on the abacus or the chart to emphasize the position of the whole numbers and the decimal fractions.

The addition and subtraction of amounts of money and metric measures can be done in the primary grades. In some countries in which the metric system is well established, these two socially useful topics (money and measurement) are used to begin work with decimals in Grade 3. Problems can be used to introduce the operations. For example, what is the distance around a rectangular garden that is 3.4 meters long and 2.7 meters wide? The problem can be solved using decimal fractions of a meter or using meters and decimeters. These two forms of the algorithm should both be used.

3.4 m	3 m 4 dm
2.7 m	2 m 7 dm
3.4 m	3 m 4 dm
2.7 m	2 m 7 dm
12.2 m	10 m 22 dm
	or 12 m 2 dm

The use of decimeters will help the students understand the decimal fraction form. Note that in working with both meters (m) and decimeters (dm) only whole numbers are used. The student adds decimeters as whole numbers and

then changes 20 decimeters to 2 meters. The process of changing decimeters to meters can be used to explain regrouping in decimal fractions. All this, of course, is dependent on familiarity with the metric system.

Problems with money can be used to give concrete meaning to addition, subtraction, and to regrouping.

$$\begin{array}{r} \$3.42 \\ -1.27 \\ \end{array} \qquad \begin{array}{r} {}^{3\ 12} \\ 3.\cancel{4}\cancel{2} \\ -1.27 \\ \hline 2.15 \end{array}$$

The regrouping can be explained as changing 1 dime to 10 cents in order to have enough cents to subtract 7 cents. This explanation will support the more abstract presentations of place value which students will get in later grades.

Regrouping. When regrouping is necessary, the procedures used are explained in the same way that regrouping of whole numbers is explained. When we regroup, we may change 1 to 10 tenths, 1 tenth to 10 hundredths, and so on. We may illustrate the transformations by using place value cards or an abacus, or we may use expanded notation. The display below shows how the steps in the regrouping process are presented in expanded notation.

$$\begin{array}{r} 3.42 \\ -\ 1.57 \end{array} \qquad \begin{array}{l} \text{3 ones, 4 tenths, 2 hundredths} \\ -\text{ 1 one, 5 tenths, 7 hundredths} \end{array}$$

$$\begin{array}{r} {}^{3\ 12} \\ 3.\cancel{4}\cancel{2} \\ -\ 1.57 \\ \hline 5 \end{array} \qquad \begin{array}{l} \text{3 ones, 3 tenths, 12 hundredths} \\ -\text{ 1 one, 5 tenths, 7 hundredths} \\ \hline \text{5 hundredths} \end{array}$$

$$\begin{array}{r} {}^{13} \\ {}^{2\ \cancel{3}\ 12} \\ \cancel{3}.\cancel{4}\cancel{2} \\ -\ 1.57 \\ \hline 1.85 \end{array} \qquad \begin{array}{l} \text{2 ones, 13 tenths, 12 hundredths} \\ -\text{ 1 one, 5 tenths, 7 hundredths} \\ \hline \text{1 one, 8 tenths, 5 hundredths} \end{array}$$

It is frequently easier to use a place value grid to illustrate regrouping. The use of a place value grid can accomplish the same objective—understanding how the values of the places are used in regrouping—and is less tedious to use. The diagram below shows the same problem solved on a place value grid.

<pre>
ONES TENTHS HUNDREDTHS
	3	12
3	A̶	2̶
− 1	5	7
		5

	13	
2	3̶	12
3̶	A̶	2̶
− 1	5	7
1	8	5
</pre>

In some cases, for example in the problem 7.3 − 1.126, there are no digits in the minuend in places from which we are to subtract. In such cases we fill the empty places with zeros.

$$
\begin{array}{r} 7.3 \\ -\,1.126 \end{array}
\qquad
\begin{array}{r} 7.300 \\ -\,1.126 \end{array}
$$

If this is an applied problem, however, one in which the numbers represent measures, a special matter in computation with ragged decimals must be considered. Problems involving ragged decimals appear in both addition and subtraction. We will discuss them in the next paragraph.

Ragged decimals. In teaching decimal fractions we emphasize that .3 and .30 are symbols for the same number, that they are equal. Our experience with regions and with common fractions leads us to this conclusion. *However, if these numbers are related to measurements of real objects, they mean different things!* Let us take two measurements: one of .3 meters and one of .30 meters. A measure of .3 meters means, "I have measured the object to the nearest .1 meter—the length is closer to .3 meters than to .2 meters or .4 meters." Put another way, the length is *between* .25 and .35 meters. On the other hand, a measure of .30 meters means, "I have measured the object to the nearest .01 meter—the length is closer to .30 meters than to .29 meters or .31 meters." The length is *between* .295 and .305 meters. The measure .30 meters is more *precise* than .3 meters. It uses a smaller unit of measure

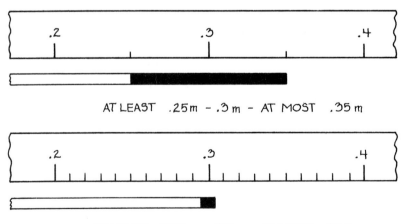

AT LEAST .25m − .3 m − AT MOST .35 m

AT LEAST .295 m − .30m − AT MOST .305m

and has a smaller "margin of error."

Let us look carefully at a problem in addition in which the addends are measures. If we add 2.4 meters and 3.74 meters, the usual procedure would be to annex a zero to 2.4 meters.

$$\begin{array}{r} 2.40 \text{ m} \\ + \underline{3.74} \text{ m} \\ 6.14 \text{ m} \end{array}$$

The answer *looks like* a measure to the nearest hundredth of a meter. However, the addend 2.4 meters is precise only to the nearest tenth of a meter. The measures have different "margins of error." We can see that, in the extreme cases in which both addends are as small or as large as they can be, the answers may not agree even in tenths' place.

		Smallest Value		Largest Value
2.4	meters $\longrightarrow$	2.35	$\longleftrightarrow$	2.45
+ 3.74	meters $\longrightarrow$	3.735	$\longleftrightarrow$	3.745
6.14	meters $\longrightarrow$	6.085	$\longleftrightarrow$	6.195

$$6.1$$

Recognizing that extreme error is somewhat unlikely, we may state the answer as 6.1 meters. In general, the answer may be as precise as the *least* precise addend. In this case, the least precise addend was a measure to the nearest one tenth meter, so the answer can be expressed only to tenths of a meter.

Because of these problems, which are more complex than we can present fully here, many authorities recommend that ragged decimals be rounded to conform to the least precise addend. If this is done, students do not need to annex zeros to decimals for purposes of addition.

$$\begin{array}{r} 2.4 \\ + \underline{3.74} \end{array} \qquad \begin{array}{r} 2.4 \\ \underline{3.7} \\ 6.1 \end{array}$$

Both procedures are typically used. There is a tendency to emphasize the annexing of zeros in elementary school. Because of the complexity of the problem of precision of a measure, this topic is frequently not presented until the junior high school.

Discussion Questions — Exercises

1. Work the problem $3.47 + 5.89 = \square$, using a place value grid and using expanded notation.

2. Make and label a place value pocket chart to use in teaching decimal fractions.

3. Illustrate the regrouping that occurs in the problem $2.39 + 1.47$, using a place value pocket chart and an abacus.

4. How will the increased use of the metric system make the teacher's job easier? more difficult?

5. Here is an example of subtraction of decimal fractions: $3.42 - 1.73 = \square$. The whole-number parts represent meters. What measures do the other places represent? Explain the regrouping which is necessary, using fractions of a meter and again using the smaller units. Which explanation is easier to understand?

6. How are 1.3 and 1.300 alike? How are they different?

Multiplication

If a student is skillful in multiplication of whole numbers, it is deceptively easy to teach multiplication of decimal fractions. "Just tell the rule for handling the decimal point and the student's got it!" By teaching that way, one misses a most important objective: Introducing the multiplication of decimal fractions *with care* provides many opportunities to review and build understanding of the place value system and the operation of multiplication itself.

As with common fractions and whole numbers, multiplication of decimal fractions has many practical applications and many models, which may be used to explain the operation. If one factor is a whole number, repeated addition can be used to obtain the answer:

$$3 \times 6.2 = 6.2 + 6.2 + 6.2 = 18.6$$

The area of a rectangle can be used to show how the multiplication of "tenths times tenths" gives hundredths as the answer. If the rectangle is 1.4 m by 1.2 m, we can see the problem and the answer in the diagram. The diagram shows 1 square meter, 6 strips each one tenth of a square meter, and 8 small squares each one hundredth of a square meter.

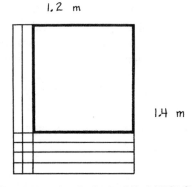

1.2 × 1.4 = 1.68 SQUARE METERS

At an early stage, looking at any problem in decimal fractions, we may explain why the format and algorithm utilized for multiplication of whole numbers also works for the multiplication of decimals. Use the problem 3.28 × 4.6 as an example. Below, we successively change this

problem from decimal form to mixed numbers to improper fractions. We see that to perform the multiplication we multiply in whole numbers 328 × 46.

$$3.28 \times 4.6$$

$$3\frac{28}{100} \times 4\frac{6}{10}$$

$$\frac{328}{100} \times \frac{46}{10}$$

$$\frac{328 \times 46}{100 \times 10} = \frac{15,088}{1,000}$$

Look at the answer. By changing the answer to a mixed number, the placement of the decimal point is clear: It follows the whole-number part.

$$\frac{15,088}{1,000} = \frac{15 \times 1,000}{1,000} + \frac{88}{1,000}$$
$$= 15 + \frac{88}{1,000} = 15\frac{88}{1,000}$$
$$= 15 + .088$$
$$= 15.088$$

A second way to place the decimal point is to select the place which will give the farthest right place the proper place value.

$\dfrac{15,088}{1,000}$ The decimal fraction must be in thousandths.

15.088   Therefore, place the decimal point so there are three places to the right—tenths, hundredths, thousandths.

Any problem in multiplication of decimal fractions may be done by multiplying whole numbers and placing the decimal point appropriately. It is important to notice that if we prematurely give the *rule* for placing the decimal point, we will cut off discussion of how this may be done. There is little motivation to think carefully about a problem if one knows an easy rule for solving that problem.

The algorithm. Students quickly change from the common-fraction and mixed-number approach to the "finished form" of the algorithm. Again, this amounts to practice in multiplying two whole numbers and placing the decimal point.

$$
\begin{array}{r}
3.\,2\,8 \\
\times \quad 4.6 \\
\hline
1\,9\,6\,8 \\
1\,3\,1\,2 \\
\hline
1\,5\,0\,8\,8
\end{array}
$$

In the calculation shown here, where will the decimal point be placed and, more important, what reasoning do we follow to place it in a meaningful way? One method is to look at the values of the places in the factors. You will note that in one factor the decimal fraction is in hundredths and in the other factor the decimal fraction is in tenths. Consequently, the first product is a number of *thousandths* (48 in this case).

$$
\frac{6}{10} \times \frac{8}{100} = \frac{48}{1000}
$$

That determines the "grid" for the partial products and the final product.

When we know that in the answer the right-hand place must be thousandths' place, we can move left and locate the decimal point between the ones' place and tenths' place. Actually, this process is easier done than said: Showing students how to do it is far simpler than writing an explanation of the process!

This explanation of the location of the decimal point began by determining the place value of the smallest place. The next explanation is based on determining the magnitude of the whole-number part of the answer.

Estimating the answer. Consider again the problem 3.28×4.6 with the partial products and the product but lacking the decimal point.

$$
\begin{array}{r}
3.\,2\,8 \\
\times \quad 4.6 \\
\hline
1\,9\,6\,8 \\
1\,3\,1\,2 \\
\hline
1\,5\,0\,8\,8
\end{array}
$$

We may estimate the size, or magnitude, of the product by rounding off the factors to convenient whole numbers. In this case 3.28 is a little more than 3 and 4.6 is a little less than 5, so the product will be close to 15. Our choices for placing the decimal will give us 1.5088, 15.088, 150.88. The obvious choice to obtain an answer close to 15 is 15.088.

Problems having larger factors present more difficult problems in estimation.

$$
\begin{array}{r}
3\,4\,9.2\,5 \\
\times \quad 3\,2.3 \\
\hline
1\,0\,4\,7\,7\,5 \\
6\,9\,8\,5\,0 \\
1\,0\,4\,7\,7\,5 \\
\hline
1\,1\,2\,8\,0\,7\,7\,5
\end{array}
$$

In the problem shown here, we may round off 32.3 to 30, the nearest ten. The factor 349.25 is 300, rounding to the nearest hundred. So we expect the product to be close to 9,000.

$$1,128.0775$$
$$11,280.775$$
$$112,807.75$$

Of our choices, some of which are listed above, only 11,280.775 is "close" to 9,000. The other choices all differ by a factor of 10, as we would expect.

It is well worth the time spent to work hard on placing the decimal point by estimation before introducing the rule. The rule, by the way, is to count off as many places from the right in the answer as there are places to the right of the decimal point in both factors together. The work on estimation helps students develop a feeling for the magnitude of a product and the relation between an estimate and an exact answer.

Adding zeros. One complication that causes some students difficulty is the need, in some problems, to annex zeros to the left of the answer in order to locate the decimal point properly.

$$
\begin{array}{r}
.0\ 2\ 7 \\
\times\quad .1\ 2 \\
\hline
5\ 4 \\
2\ 7\quad \\
\hline
.\underline{\ \ }\underline{\ \ }3\ 2\ 4
\end{array}
$$

- Hun. th.
- Ten th.
- Thousandths
- Hundredths
- Tenths

In the problem shown here, the right-hand place must be hundred thousandths' place because it is thousandths times hundredths. Naming places as we move to the left, we find that tenths' and hundredths' places must be represented

but have no digits in them. They will be filled with zeros to preserve the standard form of the numeral.

The rule. The rule for placing the decimal point in the product is, "Count the number of places to the right of the decimal points in both factors; place the decimal point that many places from the right in the product." In the example below there are 3 decimal places in one factor and 2 in the other. We locate the decimal point in the product so there will be 5 places to the right of the decimal point, adding zeros as necessary.

$$
\begin{array}{r}
.0\ 2\ 7 \longleftarrow 3 \text{ places}\\
\times\quad .1\ 2 \longleftarrow 2 \text{ places}\\
\hline
5\ 4\\
2\ 7\quad\\
\hline
.0\ 0\ 3\ 2\ 4 \longleftarrow 5 \text{ places}
\end{array}
$$

How can this rule be presented so that it is more than a mechanical trick? Change each factor to a common fraction. Express the denominators — tenths, hundredths, thousandths, and so forth — as products of tens.

$$.0\ 2\ 7\qquad \times\ .1\ 2 =$$

$$\frac{27}{10\times 10\times 10}\times\frac{12}{10\times 10}=$$

$$.00324$$

When these common fractions are multiplied, the number of tens in the denominator will be the sum of the numbers of tens in the denominators of the factors. Thus, the rule is derived from known procedures, using common fractions.

$$\frac{27}{10^3}\times\frac{12}{10^2}=\frac{324}{10^5}$$

If the students are familiar with exponential notation, you may call attention to the fact that the exponent in the product is the sum of the exponents in the factors. While these rules for exponents will not be formalized until sometime later, it is helpful to call attention to this relationship when the opportunity arises.

Discussion Questions — Exercises

1. Draw an area picture showing that 1.3 × 2.2 = 2.86.

2. Using common fractions in your argument, show why you can use the same algorithm for multiplication of decimals that is used for multiplication of whole numbers.

3. Discuss two ways to place the decimal point correctly in the product in this example of multiplication of decimal fractions.

$$
\begin{array}{r}
3\,5.2\,6 \\
\times\quad 8.4 \\
\hline
1\,4\,1\,0\,4 \\
2\,8\,2\,0\,8 \\
\hline
2\,9\,6\,1\,8\,4
\end{array}
$$

Division

As with multiplication of decimal fractions, the introduction of division of decimal fractions is a good review of the process of division and an opportunity to extend students' understanding of the decimal system. In working exercises in division of decimals, we frequently change the problem into an easier problem that has the same answer. Students should be aware of what is being done: They should know that we are changing from one problem to another, why it is convenient to do that, what reasoning process is employed, and certainly that the two problems have the same answer.

An applied problem involving metric measures or money can be used to give meaning to division of decimals. We will shortly explain the development of the algorithm needed to solve these problems. Note here that the application gives the problems significance, and the situation suggests a way to begin the solution. For example, the shelf problem suggests repeated subtraction as the carpenter cuts off one shelf at a time.

A carpenter cuts shelves each 1.2 meters long from a board 7.8 meters long. How many shelves can he get? How much wood is left over?

$$1.2\overline{)7.8}$$

A carpenter cuts a board 2.61 meters long into 3 equal pieces. How long is each piece?

$$3\overline{)2.61}$$

We can use successive subtraction to divide decimals. Consider 41.82 ÷ 3.4. In this case we are asking, "How many 3.4's are in 41.82?" It is important to estimate the answer before starting. Because this problem is close to 40 ÷ 3, we could expect the answer to be near 13. This procedure is used extensively in the early presentation of division of whole numbers.

$$3.4 \overline{)\ 4\ 1.8\ 2}$$

$$\begin{array}{r} 3\ 4 \\ \hline 7.8\ 2 \\ 3.4 \\ \hline 4.4\ 2 \\ 3.4 \\ \hline \end{array}$$

(A) → 1.0 2

(B) $\left\{ \begin{array}{r} .3\ 4 \\ \hline .6\ 8 \\ .3\ 4 \\ \hline .3\ 4 \\ .3\ 4 \\ \hline 0 \end{array} \right.$

10. × 3.4

1. × 3.4

1. × 3.4

.1 × 3.4

.1 × 3.4

.1 × 3.4
_____
12.3

Let us examine in detail how this problem is solved beginning at [A], at which point we have subtracted 3.4 12 times. We cannot subtract 3.4 another time, but we can subtract one tenth of 3.4. In fact, we can do that 3 times [B], so in a manner of speaking, we have subtracted twelve-and-three-tenths 3.4's. The remainder is 0. This algorithm is normally not used for decimals but may be used to emphasize that division is related to subtraction.

We *could* do a problem like 36.84 ÷ 2.4 without any change in the position of the decimal point in the divisor or dividend. Using the rule for changing the position of the decimal point is not absolutely necessary. A student may ask, "Why do we have to change the position of the decimal point?" The answer should be, "We don't, really, but it is certainly easier to work the problem if we do." If we are dividing by a whole number, the position of the decimal point in the quotient will be the same as the position of the decimal point in the dividend. Because of this fact, our manipulations are designed to produce a problem in which the divisor is a whole number. The procedure for moving decimal

points is justified and explained by the familiar operations on fractions.

$$2.4 \overline{)\ 36.84} \rightarrow \frac{38.84}{2.4} \rightarrow$$

(A)   (B)

$$\frac{36.84 \times 10}{2.4\ \times 10} = \frac{368.4}{24} \rightarrow 24 \overline{)\ 368.4}$$

(C)   (D)   (E)

The problem is presented in example form [A]. The example form is changed to a fractional form [B]. One of the meanings of a fraction is indicated division; for example, ¾ means 3 ÷ 4. To obtain a whole-number divisor (the denominator of the fraction), we multiple by 10, 100, or whatever is necessary. We must also multiply the numerator by the same number [C]. It is this step, multiplying by the same power of ten in numerator and denominator, which "moves the decimal point the same number of places in divisor and dividend." The denominator is now a whole number [D], and we convert back to example form [E]. The crucial thing to recognize, and to communicate to students, is that in all these manipulations we have changed the *problem* but not the *answer*. The quotient of 368.4 ÷ 24 is the same as the quotient of 36.84 ÷ 2.4. It is this characteristic—that these steps change the problem but not the answer—which enables us to solve [E] when we want the answer to [A].

We will now show by example that the decimal point in the quotient will fall directly above the decimal point in the dividend. The quotient can be estimated to be between 10 and 20. Thus, the first digit in the quotient will be in tens' place. Placing the decimal point in the quotient just above the decimal point in the dividend and proceeding to divide, will result in the proper placement of the digits in the quotient.

$$\begin{array}{r} 15. \\ 24)\overline{368.4} \\ \underline{24} \\ 128 \\ \underline{120} \end{array}$$

In some division problems the quotient is a "terminating" decimal, that is, the division "comes out even" and all further quotient figures will be zero. In the problem $7.8 \div 1.2$ we may annex a zero, changing 7.8 to 7.80, and continue to divide. The quotient is a terminating decimal: All places to the right of the 5 are 0.

$$\begin{array}{r} 6.5 \\ 1.2)\overline{7.8\ 0} \\ \underline{7\ 2} \\ 6\ 0 \\ \underline{6\ 0} \\ 0 \end{array}$$

Examine the problem $7.8 \div .7$. We annex zeros again and again, and the quotient does not terminate; in fact, this problem will never "come out even."

$$\begin{array}{r} 1\ 1.1\ 4\ 2 \\ .7)\overline{7.8\ 0\ 0\ 0}\ldots \\ \underline{7} \\ 8 \\ \underline{7} \\ 1\ 0 \\ \underline{7} \\ 3\ 0 \\ \underline{2\ 8} \\ 2\ 0 \\ \underline{1\ 4} \\ 6\ 0 \end{array}$$

There are two considerations to this procedure. In the case of a "theoretical" problem, we may annex as many zeros as we desire and continue to divide as long as we wish. This will result in many interesting patterns of digits in the quotient and a deeper understanding of the relation between common fractions and decimals and what makes a problem "come out even."

If the problem is a "practical" one, annexing zeros has the effect of making the dividend and the quotient look more precise than in fact they are. In the problem $7.8 \div .7$ it appears that our answer is precise to the nearest thousandth. In a measurement sense, however, 7.8 is a measure to the nearest tenth and thus is between 7.75 and 7.85. Therefore, in the quotient we are sure only of the two digits in tens' and ones' places. One should consider, before starting the problem, which interpretation, the theoretical or the applied, is being taken and treat the problem accordingly.

Discussion Questions – Exercises

1. Draw a picture showing 3.5 divided into 7 equal parts. How much is in each part?

2. Write a story problem in which the required operation is $\$35.80 \div \$6.10$.

3. Do the problem $89.46 \div 7.1$ by successive subtraction.

4. What is the relative importance of attaining computational skill and being able to explain the process being done? How does the increased availability of small calculators affect the answer to this question?

5. To do the division problem $3.42)\overline{1.923}$, we change to $342)\overline{192.3}$ and divide. Show the steps in the process of changing the positions of the decimal points and explain why we can work the second problem to obtain the answer to the first.

12 · Geometry and Measurement

INTRODUCTION

The geometry taught in elementary school mathematics should be taken from and related to the visual world. Children should use their eyes and hands to see, touch, create, and measure models of geometric concepts. In the current mathematics curriculum (as reflected in commercial textbooks) there is a great deal of geometry.

In the following pages we will present lists of many of the principal geometric objectives children should attain. Following each list, we describe some activities teachers may use in reaching many of the stated objectives. The lists of objectives outline what we believe to be a mathematically significant curriculum. The activities convey and depict our belief that geometry can and should be taught in an intuitive way.

A condensed scope-and-sequence chart is presented below to help show the nature and general placement of geometric topics in elementary school mathematics. The grade placement of topics is approximate. You should adjust placement to the maturity of your children.

Kindergarten
1. To order shapes according to size
2. To compare lengths, distinguishing between longer and shorter
3. To recognize inside and outside
4. To recognize some simple geometric shapes

Grade 1
1. To measure to the nearest inch
2. To measure to the nearest centimeter
3. To recognize and draw or sketch geometric shapes: circle, triangle, square, rectangle
4. To draw the other half of a figure
5. To locate a line of symmetry
6. To work with inside, outside, and on

Grade 2
1. To recognize and draw line segments
2. To identify symmetrical shapes, congruent shapes, and right angles
3. To identify points inside, outside, and on a shape

Grade 3
1. To see the difference between a line, a line segment, and a ray
2. To recognize closed curves and simple closed curves, polygons, angles, right angles, triangles, quadrilaterals, rectangles, squares
3. To recognize symmetry and congruence
4. To find the perimeter of a triangle and a quadrilateral
5. To find distances on a map
6. To recognize properties of a circle, a cube, a sphere
7. To find the area of a region by counting unit squares

Grade 4

1. *To identify intersecting, perpendicular, and parallel lines in a plane*
2. *To identify congruent, acute, and obtuse angles*
3. *To make two shapes fit by sliding, flipping, or turning, and by turning and flipping (transformations)*
4. *To measure to the nearest millimeter*
5. *To identify a rectangular prism*
6. *To compare kilometers, meters, decimeters, centimeters, millimeters, liters, deciliters, centiliters, and milliliters*

Grade 5

1. *To identify scalene, isosceles, and equilateral triangles; cones, cylinders, and pyramids*
2. *To use standard units to find areas by multiplying*
3. *To name points inside, outside, and on intersecting curves*
4. *To measure and draw angles with a protractor*
5. *To find the area of a right triangular region*
6. *To construct circles and draw the parts of a circle*
7. *To give the measure of an arc*
8. *To construct congruent segments*
9. *To bisect a segment by using a compass*

Grade 6

1. *To bisect angles*
2. *To construct perpendicular lines*
3. *To construct isosceles, equilateral, and congruent triangles*
4. *To use some nonstandard units of measure: cubit, palm, digit*
5. *To use formulas to find perimeter and area*
6. *To identify parallel planes*
7. *To find the circumference of a circle*
8. *To find surface area and volume*

Grade 7

1. *To use betweenness to determine segments*
2. *To use separation to determine half-planes, half-lines, and rays*
3. *To identify the interior and exterior of an angle*
4. *To identify adjacent and vertical angles; complementary and supplementary angles*
5. *To identify angles formed by the intersection of two lines and a transversal*
6. *To find the unknown measure of an angle of a triangle*
7. *To add and subtract with measurements having the same or different precisions*
8. *To find the area of a parallelogram and a circle*
9. *To find the surface area of a triangular prism and a cylinder*
10. *To find the volume of a triangular prism and a cylinder*
11. *To work with rigid motions: translations, reflections, and rotations*

Grade 8

1. *To use betweenness for points to identify midpoints and bisectors of line segments*
2. *To relate angle measures with arcs of circles*
3. *To identify and use the congruence property*
4. *To work with similar triangles*
5. *To use the Pythagorean Rule*
6. *To find the area of a trapezoidal region*
7. *To find the surface area of a cone and a sphere*
8. *To find the volume of a pyramid, a cone, and a sphere*
9. *To find the distance between two points in the coordinate plane*

In the following sections objectives for various geometric topics and activities for achieving the objectives will be presented.

1. OBJECTIVES AND ACTIVITIES FOR BASIC GEOMETRIC CONCEPTS

This section is concerned with concepts often encountered in the child's first school experiences with geometry.

Key Objectives

Students should be able to do the following:

1. Draw and label pictures of points, planes, segments, lines, rays, angles, circles, squares, rectangles, and triangles.

2. Recognize and identify points, segments, lines, rays, circles, squares, rectangles, and triangles in given diagrams and from descriptions in mathematical statements.

3. Name instances in the environment that approximate points, segments, lines, rays, angles, circles, squares, rectangles, and triangles.

4. Draw or identify examples of: curves, closed curves, simple closed curves.

5. Identify a given point as being inside, outside, or on a closed curve, circle, square, rectangle, or triangle.

6. Describe how the following are the same and how they are different:
    a. line, ray, segment, angle, curve
    b. curve, closed curve, simple closed curve
    c. square, rectangle

Activities

In using the following activities you will probably need to adapt them to your own teaching situation.

Activity 1. The picture below is a scene looking out a classroom window. Consider the room in which you are teaching. In the picture and in your classroom there are examples of many of the concepts given above in the objectives. A good activity is to have students find as many examples of planes, angles, segments, squares, or triangles as they can in the room. It is important for the students to realize that geometric concepts exist outside their mathematics textbooks. An alternative is to tell the children you can see something that represents a triangle or some other shape and then ask them to identify your example. Of course, they may identify others in addition to the one you are thinking about. That should be encouraged. By the way, can you find any examples of triangles and circles in the picture opposite?

Activity 2. A related activity is to have a "brainstorming" session with the students on identifying or describing examples of a geometric figure. Their example may be an object in the classroom or something they have seen—perhaps on television. For example, you might ask students to identify as many examples of rays as they possible can. Their list might include: beam from flashlight, light from the sun, sound from a megaphone, laser beam, bullet shot from a "powerful" gun, or a light beam from the headlight of a car.

Activity 3. An activity similar to Activity 2 is to identify an object and ask the stu-

dents what that object exemplifies. For example, a teacher might identify a pencil and ask the students to state the concept it exemplifies. Further, students could suggest objects and have their classmates name the geometric figures they depict.

Activity 4. To teach the concepts *interior, exterior,* and *on* (with reference to a curve), figures could be arranged as shown. The figures could be made from hula-hoops or yarn. Yarn or similar material could be formed into circles, triangles, squares, or rectangles. Children could be asked to step inside the red figure but outside the blue figure. Other conditions could be identified. For example, a teacher might ask if it is possible to be inside the triangle but outside the square. This acitivity could be used in a "Simon-says" format, with commands such as:

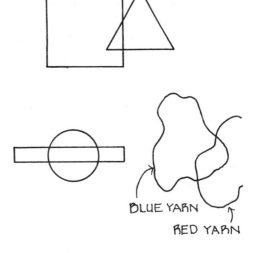

BLUE YARN

RED YARN

Simon says — "Step on the triangle."
         — "Step inside the square."
Simon says — "Step on both the triangle and the square."
         — "Now step inside both the triangle and the square."

Note that the first two commands contain only one condition. The third and fourth commands require children to meet two conditions. Primary-age children cannot always keep two conditions in mind. Encourage them to explore and experiment but try to prevent them from becoming frustrated.

Activity 5. To compare and contrast figures, students could play a "Who am I?" game. For example, a child could give the following clues.

I am like a segment because I have an endpoint.
I am different from a segment because I have no definite length.
Who am I?

Or the following clues could be given.

I am a closed curve.
I have no corners.
Every part of me is the same distance from my center.

Students could make up the clues and play, or the teacher could provide the clues. The activity could be done in a game format or as a group activity.

Activity 6. Primary-age children will enjoy identifying objects as examples of segments, triangles, rectangles, squares, points, and circles when they have to make their decision using only their sense of touch. To do this, children can be blindfolded or reach into a large paper bag. Models of points should be very small objects like grains of rice. Agreements can be made that objects with "arrowheads" on the end can be called rays or lines, since the arrowhead signals that the figure "keeps on going" in the indicated direction. An appealing name for an activity designed along these lines is "betchacantguessme!"

2. OBJECTIVES AND ACTIVITIES FOR STUDYING ANGLES

Key Objectives

Students should be able to do the following:

1. Name, identify, and distinguish among acute, right, and obtuse angles.

2. Give numerical examples of complementary and supplementary angles and, given a drawing of an acute angle, find its complement and supplement.

3. Construct, using a compass and straightedge, right angles and congruent angles.

4. Copy or bisect angles and segments, using a compass and straightedge.

5. Measure and draw angles, using a protractor.

Activities

Activity 1. Angles, like the fundamental geometric figures in the preceding section, can be seen in the classroom and in virtually every aspect of the environment. Have children find them in pictures and in the classroom. Acute, right, and obtuse angles can be seen in animals (bend in your elbow — wings of a bird in flight), in plants (veins of leaves — branches and stems), in buildings (corners of rooms — a door in various positions), and in every other physical situation one can imagine. Airplanes depict angles when they are taking off and landing. Frequently, an angle and its complement or supplement can be seen in a physical situation, as is shown with angles 1 and 2 in this diagram of an airplane making a landing.

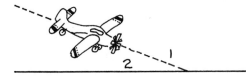

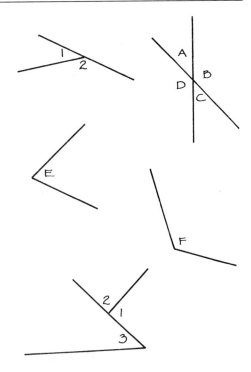

Activity 2. Angles and segments can be made by folding paper, as well as by drawings. The creases made by folding paper can depict each type of angle. These angles can be formed and measured. An angle formed by paper folding can be bisected by another fold of the paper. Just fold so that the sides of the angle are superimposed. The resulting crease bisects the original angle. Try it. Also experiment and discover how to bisect a segment by folding. A right angle can result if a segment is bisected through paper folding. If you use waxed paper, the lines formed by folding show up nicely and you can fold one line on top of another easily because you can see through the paper.

Activity 3. Present children with a page of angles or have them use a straightedge to fill a page with angles. Name each angle with a symbol, placed in the interior, close to the vertex. Children can then practice measuring these angles with their protractor. When they have a grasp of angle measurement, it is a good idea to ask them to predict the measure of each angle first. They can mark their predictions and encircle them and then indicate their measurements and see how accurate their predictions were. If the number of angles on a given page is not too great, children can predict which angles will be congruent and which may be complementary or supplementary. Besides measuring with a protractor, they can check their guesses by cutting out the angles and placing them side by side or on top of each other.

Activity 4. Challenging verbal problems can be constructed, using the concepts of complementary or supplementary angles. Consider the following for upper elementary students:

I am twice as big as my complement — find me.
My supplement is 40° bigger than I am — find me.
If I was twice as big as I am now, I would be the same size as my supplement — find me.

3. OBJECTIVES AND ACTIVITIES FOR STUDYING PARALLEL AND PERPENDICULAR LINES AND PLANES

Key Objectives

Students should be able to do the following:

1. Identify examples of parallel and perpendicular lines and planes.

2. Identify properties of parallel and perpendicular lines and planes.

3. Construct perpendicular lines, using a ruler and a protractor.

Often, students will be required to learn properties of three-dimensional figures from two-dimensional drawings, such as the following. Some attention

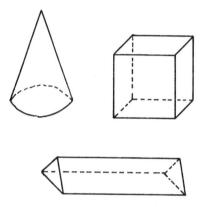

should be given to the sketching of the figures, such as the significance of the dotted lines, and to recognizing properties of three-dimensional figures from two-dimensional drawings.

Activities

Activity 1. Capital letters in the printed alphabet are an excellent source of examples of perpendicular and parallel lines. Of course, the segments forming the letters are only portions of lines. Some capitals, such as F, contain both perpendicular and parallel segments. Others, such as T, exemplify only perpendicular lines. Note also that some numerals model parallel and perpendicular lines. Which ones?

Activity 2. Ask the children to find examples of parallel and perpendicular lines and planes around them at school and in magazine pictures at home. Walls, table tops, book covers, floors, doors, shelves, seats and backs of some chairs, benches, pages, and chalkboards all model planes. Pencils, edges of things like books and shelves, intersections of walls and floors, seams in blocks and tiles, and designs on clothing can all exemplify lines. Perpendicularity and parallelism will jump out all over the place!

Some objects, such as ladders, chairs, tables, and books, depict both perpendicular and parallel situations. Children should be asked to find objects showing certain properties—find something that shows parallel lines or find something that shows perpendicular planes and parallel lines—and also to identify the parallel and perpendicular aspects of given objects or situations.

Activity 3. Using just their fingers and hands, children can approximate perpendicular lines, parallel lines, parallel planes, perpendicular planes, a line perpendicular to a plane, and a line parallel to a plane. Two examples are shown below.

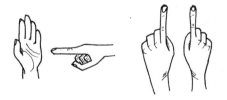

After the children learn to make "hand signals" for each of the above situations, you can again use the "Simon says"

game to provide practice in modeling these concepts. The commands might sound like this:

Simon says — Perpendicular lines
           — Parallel lines
Simon says — Line perpendicular to a plane

4. OBJECTIVES AND ACTIVITIES FOR STUDYING TRIANGLES, QUADRILATERALS, AND OTHER POLYGONS

Key Objectives

Students should be able to do the following:

1. Recognize and draw these polygons: triangle, quadrilateral, pentagon, hexagon, octagon. Be able to give models of these polygons from the environment.

2. Be able to identify and distinguish among triangles according to
a. measure of sides: equilateral, isosceles, scalene
b. measure of angles: acute, right, obtuse

3. Given a quadrilateral, be able to classify it as a parallelogram, rectangle, rhombus, or square.

4. Recognize properties of these quadrilaterals: quadrilateral, parallelogram, rectangle, rhombus, and square.

5. Draw all of the diagonals from one vertex of a polygon.

6. Find the measure of the third angle of a triangle, given the measures of the other two angles.

7. Find the third side of a right triangle, given the other two sides, using the Pythagorean Theorem.

Activities

Activity 1. Matching drawings of various polygons with their names is an unspectacular yet useful activity. The matchings can be relatively straightforward, as illustrated below, or they can be more difficult, as shown in the next exercise, where the children have to consider more than one characteristic.

Match the models in Column *A* with their names in Column *B*.

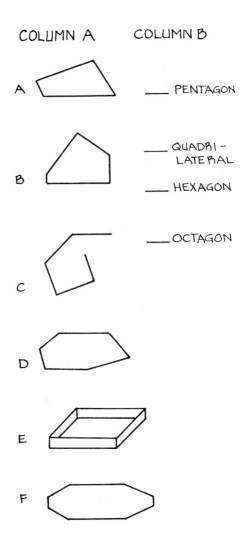

COLUMN A   COLUMN B

A ___ PENTAGON

B ___ QUADRI-LATERAL
  ___ HEXAGON

C ___ OCTAGON

D

E

F

Match the pictures with the descriptions below. Be careful—some figures match up with more than one set of words.

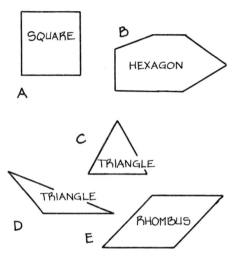

a. I have all my sides the same length.
_____

b. I have an obtuse angle. _____
c. All my sides have different lengths.
_____

d. Two of my sides are the same length.
_____

e. I am called scalene by my friends.
_____

f. My angles are all acute. _____

Activity 2. Children can be helped to discover properties concerning the lengths of sides and sums of angles by making measurements on given figures. Be sure to draw accurately any figures you use for this purpose. Tell students to measure lengths to the nearest unit. Use units such as a centimeter or half inch. When using a protractor, draw your figures so that the angles come out to a multiple of 5 degrees and tell your children to measure to the nearest degree. Use these activities to introduce the notion of approximation in measurement.

SAMPLE WORKSHEET: GEOMETRY

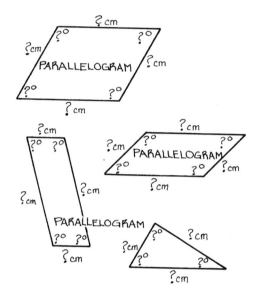

When presenting figures for students to use, a variety of sizes and shapes should be used. Presenting a variety of different-looking figures helps children learn what properties are essential for a parallelogram, for example.

Activity 3. Children like to find missing measurements by thinking rather than by measuring directly. Here are some figures whose missing measurements can be obtained by using the generalizations concerning the sum of the measures of the angles of a triangle being 180° and the sum of the squares of the sides of a right triangle equaling the square of the length of the hypotenuse (Pythagorean Theorem). Children also need to use the properties of special quadrilaterals, such as rectangles, squares, rhombi, and parallelograms. Hints often help in problems like these—try them yourself.

SAMPLE WORKSHEET: GEOMETRY

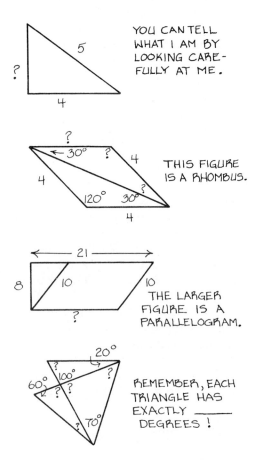

YOU CAN TELL WHAT I AM BY LOOKING CARE- FULLY AT ME.

THIS FIGURE IS A RHOMBUS.

THE LARGER FIGURE IS A PARALLELOGRAM.

REMEMBER, EACH TRIANGLE HAS EXACTLY _____ DEGREES !

Activity 4. Here is an example of a laboratory activity that guides children toward discovering the Pythagorean Theorem. The activity terminates after step 3. If you are having children work this exercise, you may want to add one or two more steps, in which the children are encouraged to write down their observation and perhaps build a few more squares to check their conjecture. Or you might want the children to come to you after step 3 to talk about their work and to verbalize their discovery.

SAMPLE WORKSHEET: GEOMETRY

The following is a sample worksheet for use with students. Of course, you may wish to revise it depending on the nature of your students. Before you start: You will need 200 small, cut-out squares all the same size and a ruler. You can work with a partner.

Follow these steps:

1. Use a corner of your large paper to draw a right triangle with sides as long as 3 squares and 4 squares. (See diagram).

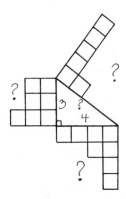

A. Use the small, cut-out squares to build a 3-by-3 square on one side of the triangle and a 4-by-4 square on the other side of the triangle.

B. Now build a square on the hypotenuse (marked "?").

C. How many small, cut-out squares are in the 3-unit square?_____ the 4-unit square?_____

D. How many small squares are in the square you built on the hypotenuse? _____

E. How many are on *one side* of the hypotenuse square?

2. On another corner of your worksheet, draw a right triangle with legs 5 and 12 units long.

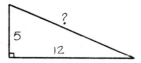

A. Use your small squares to build a large square on the 5-unit side. How many squares did you use?_____

B. Use the small squares to build a large square on the 12-unit side. How many squares did you use?_____

C. To build the large square on the hypotenuse, start by using the 144 small squares from the 12-unit side. Do you have any left over?_____ If you need more squares, use the ones from the square on the 5-unit side. Do you have any left over?_____ Do you need more squares?_____ How many pieces are in the square on the hypotenuse?_____ How many along each side of the square on the hypotenuse?_____

3. On the reverse side of your large paper, draw a right triangle so that the legs have the measures of 6 and 8 units.

A. Build a large square on the 6-unit leg. How many unit squares are in this square?_____

B. Build a square on the 8-unit side. How many unit squares did you use?
_____

C. How many have you used altogether to build squares on the 6-unit side and the 8-unit side?_____

D. Use these 100 squares to start building a square on the hypotenuse. Do you need more?_____ Do you have any left?_____ How many are in one side of the square on the hypotenuse? _____. What is the length of the hypotenuse?_____.

When giving students problems to work involving the Pythagorean Theo-

rem, be careful to choose lengths of sides so that the answer is a whole number. For example, if the legs of a right triangle are assigned measures of 2 and 3, as indicated below, then the square to be built

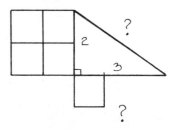

on the hypotenuse must contain 13 small squares. You cannot construct a large square on the hypotenuse using 13 small squares! One way to avoid answers that are not whole numbers is to select measures of sides of the right triangle that are multiples of 3, 4, and 5; or 5, 12, and 13; or 8, 15, and 17. Below are multiples of these combinations. Remember, the longest side is the hypotenuse.

3 – 4 – 5
6 – 8 – 10
9 – 12 – 15
12 – 16 – 20
Can you add others?

5 – 12 – 13
10 – 24 – 26
15 – 36 – 39
20 – 48 – 52
Can you add others?

8 – 15 – 17
16 – 30 – 34
Can you add others?

Activity 5. To review the properties of the various quadrilaterals with your students, you could play "Who am I?" with them. To prepare for this game, write clues (such as those below) on cards.

Students pick a card, read the clues, and try to name the quadrilateral described, thus earning a predetermined number of points for their team.

1. I am a parallelogram. My diagonals have the same measure, but my sides do not all have the same measure. Who am I? _____

2. I am a quadrilateral. All my sides have the same measure. My diagonals are not equal in measure. Who am I?

_____

3. I am a quadrilateral. My diagonals meet to form right angles. My sides also meet to form right angles. Who am I?

_____

4. I am a quadrilateral. Each pair of opposite sides has the same measure.

My diagonals bisect each other, but are not equal in length. Who am I?_____

5. I am a quadrilateral. All my sides have the same measure. My diagonals are equal in length. Who am I?_____

6. I am a quadrilateral. None of my sides has the same measure as any other. Who am I?_____

7. I am a special type of parallelogram. My diagonals are perpendicular, but not equal in measure. Who am I?

Activity 6. Here is another activity reviewing properties of certain polygons. Place a check in the column of the figure possessing the indicated property. If you are not sure, get some of the models and measure them or carefully draw each figure and make your measurements.

SAMPLE WORKSHEET: GEOMETRY

	Parallelogram	Rectangle	Rhombus	Square	General Quadrilateral
Sample: All sides are equal.			✔	✔	
1. Opposite sides are equal length.					
2. Diagonals bisect each other.					
3. Diagonals are equal length.					
4. Diagonals are perpendicular (form right angles).					
5. The sum of the measures of the angles is 360°					
6. Opposite angles have equal measure.					

5. OBJECTIVES AND ACTIVITIES FOR STUDYING THREE-DIMENSIONAL FIGURES

Key Objectives

Students should be able to do the following:

1. Associate the terms *cube, rectangular prism, triangular prism, pyramid, sphere, cylinder,* and *cone* with objects in the environment or pictures or drawings of these objects.

2. Identify vertices, edges, and faces (where appropriate) of the figures listed in Objective 1.

3. Identify properties of those same figures.

Activities

Activity 1. Here is another example of finding geometry all around us. Consider leading a discussion along these lines: Look around you. Chances are you are sitting inside a rectangular prism. Were you ever inside a cube? a pyramid? a cylinder? a sphere? Can models be found in the classroom of each of the three-dimensional figures given in Objective 1 in this section?

Activity 2. With upper elementary-age children, a teacher could take styrofoam or clay models of three-dimensional objects and ask the students to guess what new figure will result when a certain object is cut all the way through. The cut could then be made and the guess accepted or rejected. On the figures below, cuts are indicated with dotted lines. See if you can predict the figures resulting from the cuts.

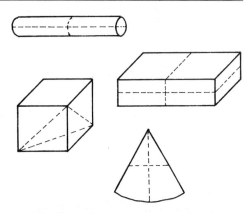

Activity 3. An interesting game for one or more children is to put one of the three-dimensional figures listed in Objective 1 in a shoe box and then have students guess the object inside. The shoe box should be securely fastened so the students can pick the box up, roll it from side to side, and up and down. The students' ability to predict what is inside will depend in part on their knowledge of the properties of the objects. For example, an object that rolls cannot be a cube. The objects you select might include a can of soup (cylinder), a book (rectangular prism), or other objects representing the figures. In some cases, the objects could be made (by the students!) from cardstock.

6. OBJECTIVES AND ACTIVITIES FOR STUDYING PERIMETER, CIRCUMFERENCE, AREA, AND VOLUME OF GEOMETRIC FIGURES

Key Objectives

Students should be able to do the following:

1. Compute the perimeter of a polygon, given the lengths of its sides; be able to find the length of a side, given the perimeter and the lengths of the remaining sides.

2. Find the circumference of a circle, using the formula C = πd.

3. Given the lengths of sides and altitudes, determine the area of these polygons: rectangle, square, parallelogram, triangle.

4. Find the area of a circle, given its diameter or radius.

5. Calculate the volume of a rectangular prism, given the base, width, and height.

Activities

Activity 1. The following activity focuses on the circumference of a circle. The materials needed include: string, scissors, and the following worksheet. You may wish to have students work in pairs or in small groups.

SAMPLE WORKSHEET: GEOMETRY

The following is a sample worksheet for use with students. Some revisions may be necessary, depending on the nature of your students.

1. Find a circular object that is approximately 4 inches in diameter.

2. Have students determine its circumference by wrapping string around a circular edge. Cut the string so that its length represents the circumference.

3. Determine the diameter of the object by using string stretched across the center of the circular object. Cut the string so that its length represents the length of the diameter.

4. Now consider the following questions.
    a. How many diameter-string-lengths

does it take to make one circumference-string-length?

b. Does it take more than 3?

c. More than 3½ diameter-string-lengths?

d. What is your best estimate of how many diameter-string-lengths it takes to make one circumference-string-length?

5. Repeat Exercises 1–4 using circular objects of various sizes.

6. Approximately how many string-lengths equal to the radius of the various objects does it take to equal the length of the corresponding circumference?

On each circle, you found that the measure of the circumference is "a little more than three times the measure of the diameter." Mathematicians using computers have calculated this "little more than three," carrying it out to hundreds of decimal places. However, for computation purposes, we use an *approximation* of the number, such as 3.14 or 3.1416 or $3\frac{1}{7}$ or $\frac{22}{7}$.

In order to talk more easily about this number that is a "little more than three," mathematicians have assigned a name to it: "pi." Pi is a letter from the Greek alphabet and is written "π". So pi, or π, is approximately 3.14, 3.1416, $3\frac{1}{7}$, or $\frac{22}{7}$.

The circumference of a circle, then, is found by multiplying pi by the diameter. This can be written:

$$C = \pi \times d$$

Using this relationship, find the circumference of a circle with a diameter of 8". Let π = 3.14. Circumference: _____

Suppose you knew the radius of a circle. How could you use "$C = \pi \times d$" to find its circumference? _____

If a circle has a radius of 3 feet, what is its circumference? (Use 3.14 for π.) _____

Find the circumference:

a. diameter $= 14''$; use $\pi = \frac{22}{7}$.

_____inches

b. diameter $= 10''$; use $\pi = 3.14$.

_____inches

c. radius $\quad= 50''$; use $\pi = 3.14$.

_____inches

d. radius $\quad= 14''$; use $\pi = 3\frac{1}{7}$.

_____inches

List some everyday circular objects that you and your students could use to demonstrate that the distance around a circle is a little more than 3 times the diameter of the circle.

Activity 2. This activity is designed to promote a basic concept of area. The materials needed to determine the area are squares of paper, perhaps 1 inch by 1 inch or 1 cm by 1 cm, and larger rectangular or square figures. It is suggested that the larger figures be exact multiples of the unit square being used. Children can work individually or in groups, using the steps below.

1. Provide the students with drawings of squares and rectangles of various sizes. Let us assume that one square inch is being used as the unit of measure for area. Then the dimensions of the figures might be 4 in. by 4 in., 9 in. by 9 in., 4 in. by 6 in., 10 in. by 6 in., etc.

2. Have the students determine the area of each of the figures by placing the unit squares inside the drawn figures and counting the number of squares.

3. If the students have the concept of multiplication, then formulas for the area of squares and rectangles can be discovered, perhaps using a chart similar to the one below.

Figures *A, B, C, D,* and *E* represent different sized rectangles and squares.

Figure	No. of squares covering the figure (area)	Width	Length
A			
B			
C			
D			
E			

Areas of other figures can be found by placing the unit squares over the given figures and counting and estimating the number of unit squares required to cover the figure. One such example is given below, where units are divided into $\frac{1}{2}$ units to approximate fractional units of area.

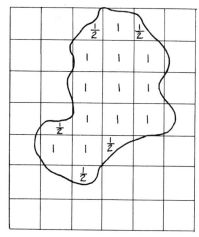

APPROXIMATE AREA : $14\frac{1}{2}$ UNITS

Activity 3. This activity can be used to teach the area of a triangle. Again, changes can be made to make it appropriate for your classroom needs. Students will need the worksheet, grid paper, scissors, colored pencils, and ruler.

SAMPLE WORKSHEET: GEOMETRY

The following sample worksheet can be used with your students, perhaps with some revisions.

1. On your grid paper draw a rectangle that is 6 units by 8 units. What is the area of this rectangle? _____.

2. In the rectangle draw a triangle like △ABC, below.

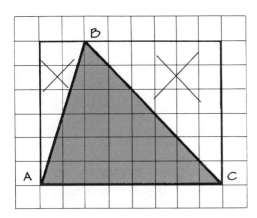

A. Shade the interior of △ABC.
B. Cut out the rectangle.
C. Put an "X" on each part of the interior of the rectangle that is not in the interior of triangle ABC.
D. Cut along $\overline{AB}$ and $\overline{BC}$ and save the triangles marked with X's.
E. Place your two triangles with X's on the original (shaded) triangle so all of △ABC is covered, and there is no overlapping of the smaller triangles.
F. Do all three triangles together have the same area as the rectangle? _____ What is the total area of the three triangles?

_____

G. Do the two smallest triangles (the triangles that have X on them) have the same total area as triangle ABC? _____
H. Would the total area of triangle ABC be the same as ½ the area of the rectangle? _____
I. What is the area of triangle ABC? _____ square units.

3. On your grid paper draw three more rectangles that are 6 units by 8 units. Draw triangles in the rectangles similar to those below and shade the triangles as before.

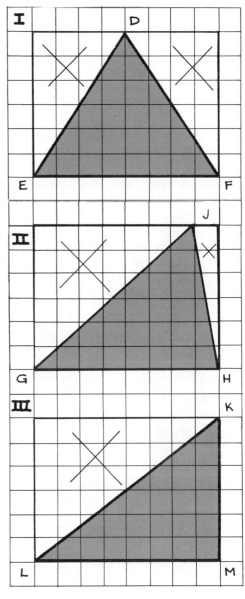

A. What is the total area of rectangle I?
_____ square units. rectangle II?
_____ square units. rectangle III?
_____ square units. Cut out the three
rectangles.

B. Cut out △DEF by cutting along $\overline{DE}$ and
$\overline{DF}$. Test to see if the total area of the two
smaller triangles is the same as the area
of triangle *DEF* by placing the smaller
triangles on triangle *DEF*. Is the area of
△*DEF* one half the area of rectangle I?
_____. What is the area of rectangle
I? _____. What is the area of △*DEF*?
_____.

C. Repeat the activity in *B* for △*GHJ*. Is
the area of △*GHJ* one half the area of
rectangle II? _____ What is the area
of △*GHJ*? _____

D. Repeat the activity in *B* for △*KLM*,
noting that there is only one triangle to
place over △*KLM*. What is the area of
△*KLM*?_____

4. What did you notice about the area of
each of the triangles that were in the 6 × 8
rectangles?_____

5. In each case below, the dimensions of
the sides of the rectangles are given. Your
job is to find the area of the shaded triangle drawn in the rectangle. You can count
unit squares, cut out the triangles, or use
any other method you think will work. Fill
in the table at the top of page 309.

6. In each case, how is the area of the triangle related to the area of the rectangle?

7. Often, the formula below is used for
finding the area of a triangle:

$$\text{Area of } \triangle = \tfrac{1}{2} \times b \times h$$

where *b* represents "base" and *h* represents "height." The base is simply the
length of one side of the triangle. The
height is the distance coming down to the
base.

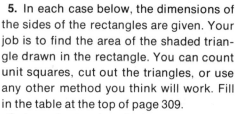

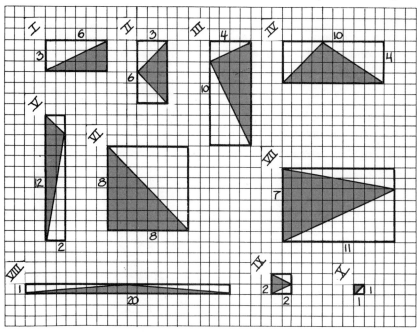

Dimensions of rectangle	Area of rectangle	Area of triangle
I. 3 by 6	_____sq. units	_____sq. units
II. 6 by 3	_____sq. units	_____sq. units
III. 10 by 4	_____sq. units	_____sq. units
IV. 4 by 10	_____sq. units	_____sq. units
V. 2 by 12	_____sq. units	_____sq. units
VI. 8 by 8	_____sq. units	_____sq. units
VII. 7 by 11	_____sq. units	_____sq. units
VIII. 1 by 20	_____sq. units	_____sq. units
IX. 2 by 2	_____sq. units	_____sq. units
X. 1 by 1	_____sq. units	_____sq. units

A. On triangle *QRS*, the base, *RS*, is 6 units, and the height, *QP*, is 4 units. The area is $\frac{1}{2} \times 6 \times 4$, or 12 square units.

B. Is the area of $\triangle QRS$ $\frac{1}{2}$ the area of the rectangle? _____

Notice that the base of the triangle is always one of the sides of the triangle, while the height of the triangle is the same length as one side of the *rectangle* and not necessarily one of the two remaining sides of the triangle. (See figures at right.)

8. Now go back to the diagrams for Exercise 5. Your job, now, is to compute the area of eight of these triangles using the formula: Area of $\triangle = \frac{1}{2} \times b \times h$. Notice that the *height* of each triangle is the same length as one of the sides of the rectangle. The height "comes to" the side you choose as a base. Fill in the table below.

9. Compare these areas with your answers for Exercise 5. Do they agree?

10. State in words the procedure for finding the area of a triangle. _____

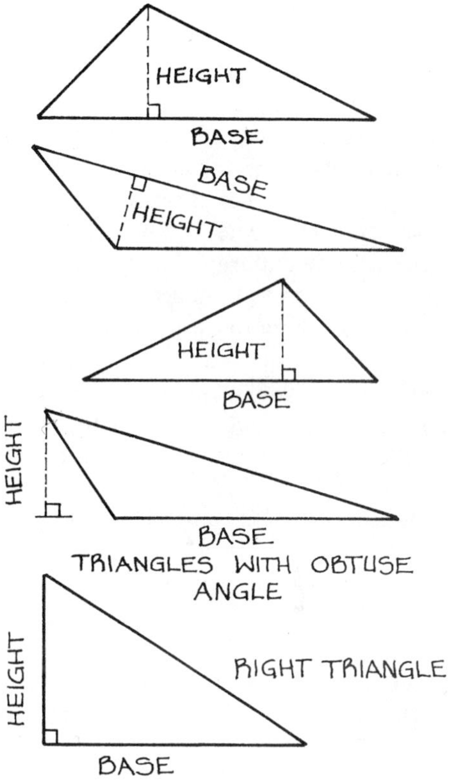

HEIGHT
BASE

BASE
HEIGHT

HEIGHT
BASE

HEIGHT
BASE
TRIANGLES WITH OBTUSE ANGLE

HEIGHT
RIGHT TRIANGLE
BASE

Triangle	A of $\triangle = \frac{1}{2} = b = h = ?$	
Samples: I	A of I = $\frac{1}{2} \times 6 \times 3 = 9$ sq. units	
II	A of II = $\frac{1}{2} \times 3 \times 6 = 9$ sq. units	
III	_____	_____sq. units
IV	_____	_____sq. units
V	_____	_____sq. units
VI	_____	_____sq. units
VII	_____	_____sq. units
VIII	_____	_____sq. units
IX	_____	_____sq. units
X	_____	_____sq. units

Activity 4. In the chapter "Teaching Aids and Laboratory Activities," Section 4, the laboratory problem "Let's Go on a Scavenger Hunt!" was outlined. A scavenger hunt can be a stimulating way to provide practice in measuring length, area, perimeter, volume, and weight. The hunt can be restricted to items on one or two tables (or shelves), or it can apply to the entire room. Children can make up lists and check one another's work. If the entire room is used, there can be many correct answers. It is suggested that measurements be made to the nearest half inch, centimeter, pound, or 5 grams. Smaller divisions than this may serve to create conflict or frustration for some children. A scavenger hunt forces children to look around them and encourages them to estimate. Estimating is an important and valuable skill in arithmetic as well as geometry. Estimating is a way of checking to insure an answer makes sense. Remember, estimates are supposed to be close—not exact.

7. OBJECTIVES AND ACTIVITIES FOR STUDYING SYMMETRY, REFLECTIONS, AND ROTATIONS

Key Objectives

The students should be able to do the following:

1. Draw the reflection of a figure, given the line of symmetry.

2. Recognize two figures that are reflections of each other and draw the line of reflection.

3. Recognize a figure that is symmetric; draw the line of symmetry of a symmetric figure.

4. Determine if two figures can be made to coincide by rotating one of the figures about a given point.

Activities

Activity 1. The purpose of this activity is to learn how to draw the reflection of a given figure. The steps below can be illustrated for students. The students will need tracing paper for this activity.

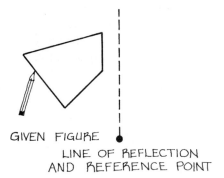

GIVEN FIGURE
LINE OF REFLECTION
AND REFERENCE POINT

1. Place the tracing paper over the figure and the line of reflection and trace both the figure and the line of reflection, being careful to mark the reference point.

2. Flip the tracing paper over, making sure the line of reflection and the reference point on the tracing paper coincide with the original line and point.

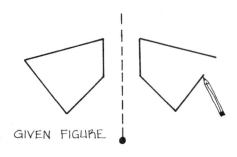

GIVEN FIGURE

3. Trace over the figure on the tracing paper to get an impression on the original paper.

4. After getting an impression, remove the tracing paper and darken the impression. The resulting figure will be the reflection of the given figure with respect to the line of reflection.

A variety of figures can then be given for the students to use.

Activity 2. The purpose of this activity is the same as that of Activity 1. But the method of drawing the image is different. To use this procedure, follow the steps below.

1. Fold the paper along the line of reflection.

2. On the folded-over part of the paper trace the original figure. Make sure the traced figure is dark.

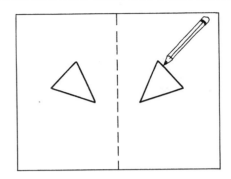

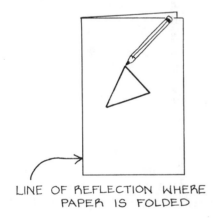

LINE OF REFLECTION WHERE PAPER IS FOLDED

3. Then unfold the paper and flatten it out.

4. Darken the impression made on the underneath side of the paper.

Some students may prefer the method discussed in Activity 1, others may prefer the method in Activity 2. In the latter method the paper must be thin enough so

that you can see the drawing through it.

On page 312, column 1, are a few examples of figures that might be reflected. This activity is especially appropriate for the primary grades.

Activity 3. Below is another sample worksheet that could be used by your students. Other similar worksheets could also be constructed.

SAMPLE WORKSHEET: GEOMETRY

Looking in a mirror
For this exercise use the drawings on page 312, column 2.

Activity 4. In order for students to do this activity, they must remember that symmetric figures must have at least one line of reflection, or line of symmetry, which passes through the figure. To help students recognize symmetric figures, you might point out various symmetric or approximately symmetric objects in our environment. Objects that are not symmetric can also be identified. Examples of symmetric or approximately symmetric figures are the face of a brick or cinder block, the letter O (among others), a picture of the human face (approximately symmetric), leaves, some floor tiles, electric light outlets, or a chalkboard.

A

B

C

D

E

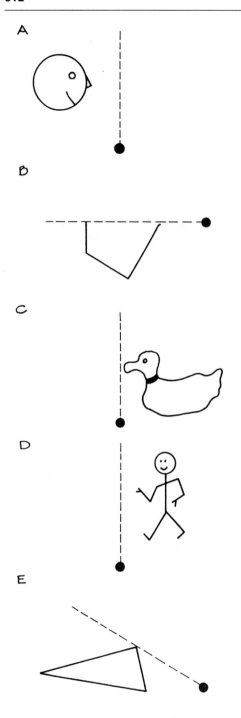

THIS FISH IS LOOKING IN A
MIRROR. WHICH DRAWING
SHOWS WHAT IT WILL SEE?

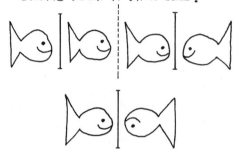

DRAW WHAT THE FISH WILL SEE.
DRAW IT HERE.

DRAW THE REST OF THE
BEADS IN THE MIRROR.

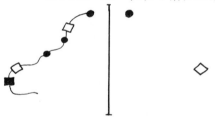

The following are figures that students could point out that are not symmetric figures: one side of a door, the front of most books, the letter J (among others), a knife, or a footprint.

Besides identifying figures in the environment that have or do not have symmetry, figures can be drawn—by the teacher or the students—and classified as symmetric or not symmetric. Letters of the alphabet can also be presented. Below are samples of figures and letters that might be considered. Students should be encouraged to draw more than one line of symmetry where possible.

tions of each other and to draw the reflection of a figure, given the line of reflection. In addition to the worksheet, tracing paper will be needed.

SAMPLE WORKSHEET: GEOMETRY

Draw the line or lines of symmetry through the figures that are symmetric.

SAMPLE WORKSHEET: GEOMETRY

1. Use a sheet of tracing paper to help you draw each image with respect to the given line of reflection and the given reference point.

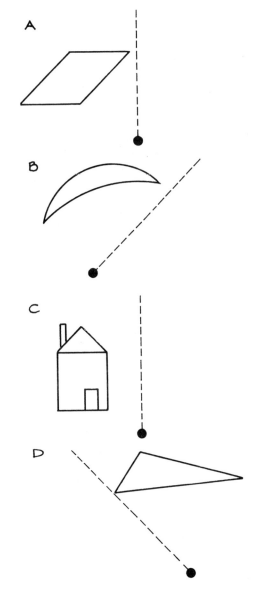

Activity 5. The purposes of this activity are to recognize figures that are reflec-

2. In each exercise below, use tracing paper to determine if Figure *B* is a reflection of Figure *A* with respect to the given line of reflection.

3. In each exercise on page 315, column 1, complete the second figure so that it is a reflection of the complete figure. Use tracing paper to help you.

4. Draw the line of reflection for each set of figures in Exercise 3.

Activity 6. This activity involves rotations. The purposes of the activity are to recognize and draw the image of a figure under a given rotation and to identify figures that have turn symmetry. In addi-

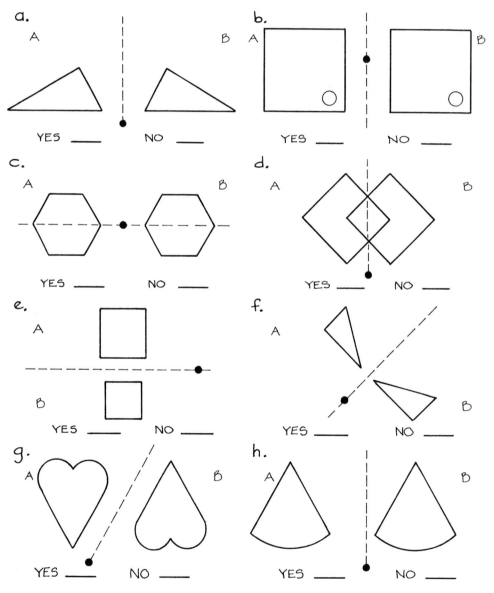

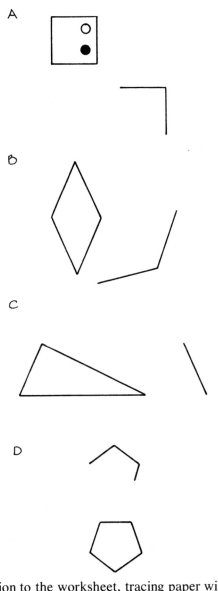

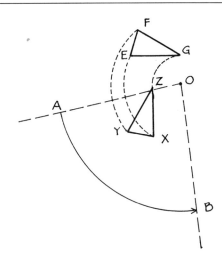

tion to the worksheet, tracing paper will be needed.

SAMPLE WORKSHEET: GEOMETRY

In this lesson you will use tracing paper to help you draw the image of a figure under a given rotation. Below is an example of how to do your drawings.

1. A. Trace the original drawing. In this case, it is triangle *EFG*.
   B. Be sure to mark the pivot point *O* on your tracing paper. The pivot point and its image should always coincide. Also mark point *A* on your tracing paper.
   C. The arrow indicates which way to turn your tracing paper. The length of the arc *AB* indicates how far to turn your tracing paper.
   D. Turn the tracing paper on pivot point *O* in the direction indicated and for the distance indicated. Point A will move along arc *AB* until it reaches *B*. Triangle *EFG* should be congruent to triangle *XYZ*.
   E. Go over your tracing to get an impression on the original paper. Remove the tracing paper and darken the impression lines you made.
   F. The angle *AOB* is called the "angle of rotation." In *this* example, the angle of rotation is 90°. (Notice that, *if drawn*, angles *EOX*, *FOY*, and *GOZ* would also measure 90°)

2. Use tracing paper to help you draw the image under the indicated rotation:

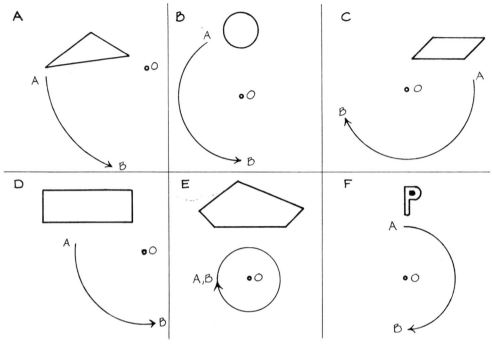

3. For each exercise below, decide whether the figure drawn with a dashed line is the image of the other figure under the rotation indicated by the arrow. Check the appropriate response. Use tracing paper to help you decide.

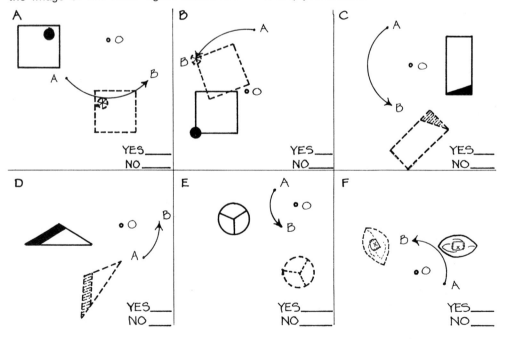

4. Some figures have what is called "turn symmetry." This means that there is a pivot point and a rotation of more than 0 degrees and less than 360 degrees which leaves the resulting image on top of and matching the original figure.

Consider the examples below:

A

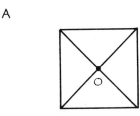

A square has turn symmetry. If a square is rotated through 90°, 180°, or 270°, using point *O* as the pivot point, its image will be on top of and will match the original figure.

B

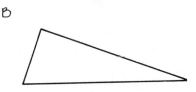

This triangle does not have turn symmetry. There is no rotation (except through an angle of 360°) such that the image will be on top of and match the original figure.

C

The letter "H" has turn symmetry. If the letter is rotated around the indicated pivot point through an angle of 180°, then the image will be on top of and match the original letter.

D

The letter "A" does not have turn symmetry.

Determine whether the figures at the top of page 318 have turn symmetry. Check the appropriate response. If the figure does have turn symmetry, indicate the pivot point with a large dot.

8. OBJECTIVES AND ACTIVITIES FOR STUDYING CONGRUENCE, SIMILARITY, AND COORDINATES

Key Objectives

The students should be able to do the following:

1. Pick out congruent figures from given figures.

2. Name pairs of congruent angles and segments, given two congruent figures.

3. Pick out similar figures from given figures.

4. Given the ratio of the sides of two similar polygons and the length of one side of one of the polygons, find the length of the corresponding side of the other polygon.

5. Determine the size of an object from a scale drawing.

6. Determine the distance between points on a map.

Activities

Activity 1. One way to illustrate similar figures is to use a slide projector. Consider the lower drawing on page 318.

Students will enjoy putting their hands in front of the projector and observing the various shadow figures on the screen. After these initial experiences,

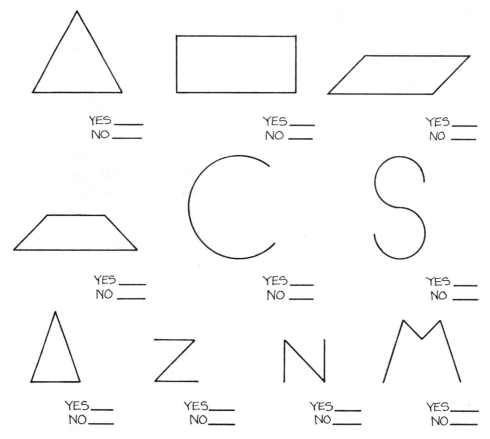

YES ___
NO ___

YES ___
NO ___

YES ___
NO ___

YES ___
NO ___

YES ___
NO ___

YES ___
NO ___

YES ___
NO ___

YES ___
NO ___

YES ___
NO ___

YES ___
NO ___

shapes such as squares, rectangles, or triangles can be used to make shadow figures. Then questions can be posed concerning the relative sizes of the shadow figures in comparison to the shapes being projected. The shadow figure and the original figure will be similar.

The students might be interested in placing the object so that it is half way between the light source in the projector and the screen. For example, place the object so that distance a (see diagram) is equal to distance b or, to say it another way, the distance from the light source

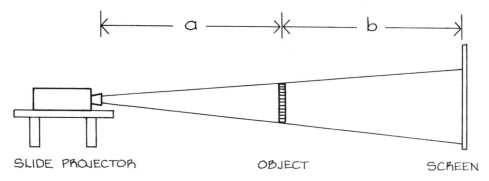

SLIDE PROJECTOR   OBJECT   SCREEN

to the screen is twice the distance from the light to the object. The students can then measure the figures and observe that the length of any side of the shadow figure is twice the length of the corresponding side of the object.

Activity 2. Here is a procedure for "enlarging" any two-dimensional shape. This technique was developed by the late Kenneth Kidd of the University of Florida. If all the parts of a shape are increased by the same factor, the original figure and the enlarged figure are similar. Since this technique can be used on any shape, enlargements of cartoon characters and other appealing figures can serve to exemplify similarity.

To begin, tie a string of 3 or 4 rubber bands together end to end, as illustrated below. Secure one end of the string of rubber bands to a drawing surface, perhaps with a thumbtack. Stretch the bands moderately tight, using a pencil hooked on the other end of the string of bands. Place the figure to be enlarged so that any part of its border is directly under any one of the knots in the string of rubber bands. Then begin moving your pencil at the end of the string, being careful to keep the chosen knot always over a portion of the border (or feature) of the original figure. Keep your eye on

the knot! Keep the knot moving along the border of the shape you are enlarging. Your pencil will trace out a similar figure. The degree of enlargement will be the ratio of the distance between the pencil and the thumbtack to the distance between the knot and the thumbtack.

This technique works as well for regular geometric shapes as it does for cartoon characters.

Activity 3. This activity emphasizes coordinates. The sample worksheet below could be altered for use with your students. The game "Tic Tac Toe, Four in a Row" can be played on an overhead projector with the entire class or between individuals.

SAMPLE WORKSHEET: GEOMETRY

A. On your grid paper, draw a coordinate system in which both axes extend from −5 to +5. Plot the points below on your system, labeling each point with its letter.

A (−1,5)   D (−1,3)   G (1,−5)
B (1,5)   E (−5,−3)   H (3,−3)
C (−1,4)   F (−3,−5)   I (−1,−3)
                        J (−1,2)

B. Now use a straightedge to draw the segments listed below:
$\overline{AB}$ $\overline{BC}$ $\overline{DE}$ $\overline{FG}$ $\overline{EH}$ $\overline{AI}$ $\overline{JH}$ $\overline{EF}$ $\overline{GH}$

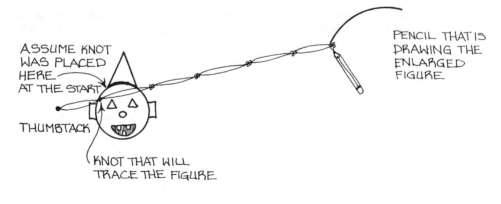

ASSUME KNOT WAS PLACED HERE AT THE START

THUMBTACK

KNOT THAT WILL TRACE THE FIGURE

PENCIL THAT IS DRAWING THE ENLARGED FIGURE

C. What figure did you draw? _____
Note: While the artistic quality of this "drawing" is questionable, we do suggest this type of activity (perhaps with objects that are more familiar to your students) for classroom use.

D. Did segment $\overline{AI}$ go through any named point(s)?_____. Which one(s)?_____. Name the coordinates of these points: A_____ C_____ D_____ I_____ J_____ What did you notice about the first coordinate of each of those points?

_____

E. Did $\overline{EH}$ go through any named point(s)? _____ Which? _____ What did you notice about the coordinates of each of those points? _____

Suppose the coordinates of a point B are (3,1), and the coordinates of point C are (1,1), and the coordinates of point N are (0,1). What are the coordinates of another point that line $\overleftrightarrow{BN}$ will go through? _____ (You can work this out on your graph paper.)

A. On your graph paper, draw a coordinate system extending from −5 to +5 horizontally and −5 to +5 vertically. Plot these points: A (−5,−3) B (−2,−1) C (1,1) D (4,3)

B. Suppose E was the next point in this series. Can you predict its coordinates? _____ Name them. _____

To play the game "Tic Tac Toe, Four in a Row," the class is divided into two teams, one marking with X's, the other using O's. The teacher (or students) elicits a pair of coordinates from the members of each team (taking turns) and marks them on a large 10 × 10 grid on the chalkboard or overhead projector. To win, a team must have claimed four points in a row—vertically, horizontally, or diagonally. These points must be consecutive.

Example: Mark these on the graph:

1. Team *X* starts with (2,3)

2. Team *O* claims (3,3)

3. Team *X* claims (2,2)

4. Team *O* claims (2,1)

5. Team *X* claims (2,4)

6. Team *O* claims (5,2) [wanted (2,5) but *named* it wrong]

7. So team *X* wins, choosing (2,5).

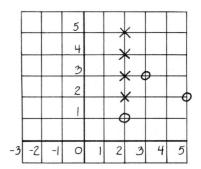

Activity 4. This activity involves the use of a road map. If possible, each student should have a copy of a map, preferably of the area in which the students live. Besides skills in map reading, there are a variety of other mathematical skills that can be prompted. Before actually having the students read the map, the questions below might be posed.

a. How many miles does 1 inch represent?

b. Forty miles is represented by how many inches?

Questions can be raised about where camping grounds, state parks, or recreation areas are located. If a state map is used, questions about counties and county seats can be posed.

Once the students have some familiarity with the map, they can be asked to identify two cities or towns — perhaps the one that the students live in or near and one other city or town. Alternate routes for getting from one place to the other can be identified. The mileage of the different routes can then be determined. In addition, you can specify routes from one town to another and then ask the students to determine the mileage of each route. To provide computational practice, the students can be given a route and an odometer reading, say 20,562, and asked to find out what the odometer reading will be at the conclusion of the trip.

Students can also be asked to estimate the time of a trip. Discussions can be held on the expected miles per hour one might drive. Then, by determining the number of miles to be driven, an estimate of the time can be made. Travel times can be estimated for trips from Atlanta to Tampa, from Chicago to St. Louis, or from Phoenix to Los Angeles. Perhaps the students have grandparents or friends living in another city. They can estimate the time it would take to drive there. Questions can also be asked such as, "If you left Detroit at 9:00 AM, when would you arrive in Cleveland?"

Expenses of traveling can also be determined. Have the students find the distance between two cities. They can then ask their parents how many miles per gallon of gasoline their family car goes. They can also check the prices of gasoline at several service stations. With this information they can determine the cost of gasoline used in driving from one city to another and then returning.

9. OBJECTIVES AND ACTIVITIES FOR STUDYING MEASUREMENT USING NONSTANDARD UNITS

The main purpose of the activities in this section is to suggest students' activities with units of their choosing to estimate length, area, and volume. The emphasis should be placed on the reiteration of a unit, an estimation of the measure of the object being measured, and comparison of objects according to their measures.

The following questions relate to understandings that help children profit from the study of measure. If a child cannot answer them correctly, you will want to approach measure gradually and in an exploratory, informal manner. All students can profit from the activities but less achievement, naturally, is expected from less mature students.

1. If line segment AB is 1 unit, then how long is line segment AC?

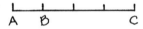

2. Take two pencils of the same length and ask the child which is longer or if they are the same length. Have the pencils placed side by side as shown.

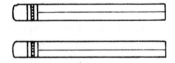

Now rearrange the same two pencils as illustrated at the top of the next page. Does the child still maintain that the two pencils are the same length, or does he or she now maintain that one of the pencils is longer than the other? In order to profit from measurement activities, the student should assert that the two pencils

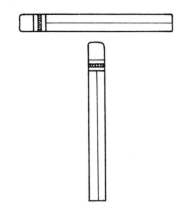

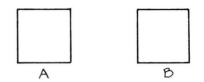

a. *A* and *B* are sheets of paper or any other objects which contain the same area. Do *A* and *B* contain the same amount of space? (Use whatever phrase communicates the idea of area to the child.)

b. Now tear *B* into several parts and rearrange as follows:

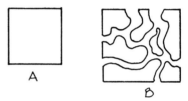

Now do *A* and *B* contain the same space or does one have more than the other?

If the child can correctly answer the second question, assuming that the answer to *a* is correct, then there is evidence that the student conserves the idea of area.

are the same length regardless of their position.

3. The same sort of question can be posed using two pieces of string. The two pieces can be positioned side by side, so the student can determine that they are of the same length.

Then string A can be twisted, so that it "appears shorter."

STRING A

STRING B

The student should be able to conserve the idea of length in the sense of realizing that the length of the strings has not changed.

4. For activities involving area, students must be able to conserve the idea of area in the sense that the number of square units of a given region remains constant regardless of how that region is positioned. To determine if students can "conserve" area, the following two questions can be posed.

5. Conservation of the idea of volume can be determined in a similar way by taking two bunches of an equal amount of clay and tearing one lump into smaller lumps. The "conserver" should then realize that the second bunch still consists of as much clay as the "single bunch."

Of course, each of these questions could become the basis for developing an activity in itself. You may wish to do this and create your own materials for the students to use in considering the questions. Assuming that the students have the above prerequisite knowledge, we state the objectives for the activities that follow.

Key Objectives

The students should be able to do the following:

1. Estimate and then measure the length of an object, using some nonstandard unit of length.

2. Estimate and then determine the area of various objects, using some nonstandard square unit of area.

3. Estimate and then determine the volume of various objects, using some nonstandard cubic unit of volume.

Activities

Activity 1. Have the students identify some unit that they would like to use to measure length. Any object that is easy to handle and is not "too long" or "too short" is acceptable. For example, a paper clip would be fine. Other units could be the width of the student's mid-dle finger or the width of the hand. Perhaps the students would like to create their own unit on a sheet of paper and cut it out, so the "unit paper" could be easily held, like this:

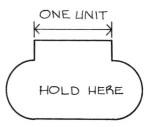

Names might be assigned the units — for example, clip unit, pencil unit, Hank's unit, or Karen's unit. Using whatever unit the student devises, various objects can be measured. Some are suggested below. In each case the student should guess how many of his or her units the object measures *before* the object is actually measured. Then the approximate number of units can be determined. The chart below might facilitate the activity.

To illustrate, suppose the length of a pencil is being measured by Jim's unit, which is the width of Jim's middle finger.

Name of your unit_____			
	Estimate	*At least*	*No more than*
1. Width of desk			
2. Width of math book			
3. Length of homework paper			
4. Length of various used pencils			
5. Height of a classmate (more appropriate for "longer units")			
6. Length of a baseball bat			

The length is estimated to be 10 units. Upon actually measuring the pencil, the number of units is found to be at least 11 units but not quite (no more than) 12 units.

It should be pointed out to students that whatever unit is selected, the unit must not be changed when one is measuring. That is, one should not select a paper clip as a unit but then use paper clips of different length when measuring. Further, students should realize that if one pencil has a measure of 3 Janet units and another pencil measures 7 Bill units, nothing can be determined about the relative lengths of the two pencils. That is because a common unit is not used. On the other hand, if one pencil is 5 Frank units long and another is 7 Frank units long, the longer pencil can be determined. The chart above can be used to emphasize these ideas. For example, the actual widths of the desks are probably the same. Yet this will not be apparent because each will have been measured with a different unit of measure. But if the same unit is used to measure various pencils, then the longest and the shortest pencil can be determined without comparing them.

Activity 2. This activity parallels Activity 1 in that nonstandard units are used to determine the areas of different regions.

In this activity it might be best to provide the students with various units. The units could be represented on grid paper. Several examples are illustrated below.

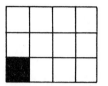

EACH SQUARE IS ONE UNIT OF AREA

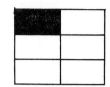

EACH RECTANGLE IS ONE UNIT OF AREA

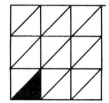

EACH TRIANGLE IS ONE UNIT OF AREA

Various objects can be selected for measuring. Examples are provided in the chart below. The comments made in Activity 1 about drawing conclusions when different units are used also pertain to this activity. The activity should also emphasize estimating the area before actually determining the area of a region.

The areas of various irregular shapes can also be found. The areas of parts of the human body can be found by tracing

	Estimate	*At least*	*No more than*
1. Top of desk			
2. Top of math book			
3. Sheet of paper			
4. Chalkboard (larger unit of area should be used)			
5. The top of a glass			

the part—or even the entire body by tracing the outline of someone lying on the ground—and then using the grid paper.

Activity 3. This activity relates to finding perimeters and areas of various figures on a geoboard. The perimeter and the area should be determined by direct count. The figures should be constructed so that the length of a side is either a unit or several whole units—to avoid fractional units of length and area. Below are possible figures for students to investigate.

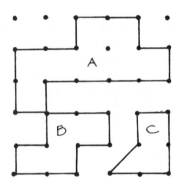

A figure like *C* should not be used to find perimeters because of the "slant" line segment, which is $\sqrt{2}$ units long.

Activity 4. This is an introductory activity for the concept of volume. Take several containers, such as cereal boxes, and ask students to guess which box holds the most. Following these informal discussions, the containers can be filled with cubes of some sort—preferably small cubes, such as cubic centimeters (the smallest Cuisenaire rod). It should be pointed out that the container that "holds the most" is the one that contains the largest number of cubes. Remember that the number of cubes contained in a box represents the measure of the volume of the box. Such an exercise will help the student have a firm, concrete foundation for studying volume.

Activity 5. This activity deals with volume. Various units of volume can be devised. Here are several suggestions: a cup of rice, a cup of kidney beans, or a cup of water. Of course, little cubes can be constructed, or cubes of sugar can be used. Probably a variety of units should be used to emphasize the nature of volume.

The following objects can be used for investigations of volume: boxes of cereal (a Quaker Oats box is good), shoe boxes, empty soup cans, and glasses (plastic cups are better). Estimation should be emphasized. If various objects are measured with the same unit, then students can compare the different objects by the number of cubic units the objects contain.

Activity 6. This activity consists of measuring the volumes of various three-dimensional objects and comparing results. For example, find a cone—or make one—and a cylinder, like a soup can, that has the same base as the cone and the same height. Fill the cone with sand. Then empty the sand into the cylinder. If the students repeat this two more times, they will find that 3 fillings of the cone will exactly fill the cylinder. This illustrates the fact that the volume of a cone is one third the volume of a cylinder, if the cone and the cylinder have the same base and the same height.

The activity also can be done by defining the cubic unit as a certain amount of sand. Preferably, the cubic unit should be small. The ratio of the number of cubic units of sand for the cylinder to the number of cubic units for the cone should be approximately three to one. The actual ratio is exactly 3:1, of course.

Activity 7. This same type of activity can be used with a pyramid and a rectangular prism. The bases of the two figures must be equal in area — probably congruent — and their heights must also be the same. The ratio of the amount of sand used to fill the prism compared to the amount used to fill the pyramid is three to one.

10. OBJECTIVES AND ACTIVITIES FOR STUDYING MEASUREMENT USING STANDARD UNITS

Once students have had experience in measuring with nonstandard units, the advantages of standard units can be discussed. Students should realize that standard units allow comparisons that are not possible when various nonstandard units are used. The following activities use measurements in the metric system. Of course, the same activities could be used with English-system measures.

Generally, having students memorize conversion factors for changing from the English system to the metric system and vice versa is a poor use of time. Hence, the activities below make use of measurements solely within the metric system.

Key Objectives

The students should be able to do the following:

1. Convert from one metric measure to another, for example, from decimeters to centimeters.

2. Determine which metric measure is most appropriate for measuring in a given situation.

3. Estimate and then measure the length of an object, using an appropriate metric measure.

4. Estimate and then measure the area of an object, using an appropriate metric measure.

5. Estimate and then determine the volume of various objects, using an appropriate metric measure.

Activities

Activity 1. Select various objects for the students to measure using a cenitmeter ruler. Have them measure the objects in centimeters and in decimeters. Have the students compare the measures to reinforce the fact that 10 cm = 1 dm. The same sort of activity can be done with square units. A square meter can be determined and then the number of square centimeters or square decimeters inside the square meter can be found. This should help the students realize that 1 square meter = 100 square decimeters or 10,000 square centimeters. Similarly, measurements can also reinforce the fact that a liter contains 1,000 cubic centimeters.

Activity 2. The purpose of this activity is to help the students realize the approximate sizes of the various metric measures. To begin, have the students construct a ruler to represent a centimeter, decimeter, millimeter, and meter, and to suggest a kilometer. Then ask which measure would be best to measure the following objects: a pencil, the width or length of the room, the thickness of the mathematics book, the width or length of the mathematics book, the distance from Chicago to Detroit, or the thickness of different wooden or paper objects.

The emphasis of the activity should be on the identification of the appropriate unit and not on the actual measurement of the object. A second way to reinforce this understanding is to have students react to sentences such as the following or create their own sentences for someone else to consider.

Mark the following as true or false.

a. Yesterday, Frank ran 125 cm.
b. When Ann checked the oil in her car, it was low. So she added 7 ml of oil.
c. In track, Bill runs the 100-meter race.
d. When Grace measured her bedroom, she found that the room was approximately 4 meters by 5 meters.
e. Most men are approximately 2 dm tall.
f. A glass of water generally contains about 300 cc of liquid.
g. Mr. Rug wanted to carpet his living room. He thought he would need about 25 square meters of carpet.

Activity 3. This activity emphasizes linear measures. Students are divided into small groups. Each group should provide an estimate of the lengths of the given objects. After each group has estimated the length of an object, then the object can be measured by several individuals. Once the object's measure has been found, then the group with the best estimate can be determined. You may decide to reward that group with praise or perhaps something more tangible. Possible measurements include: the length or the width of a desk or a mathematics book, the height of a person—perhaps a student or yourself, the length of tiles or cement blocks in the room, or any object that is easy for students to reach and is convenient to measure.

A slightly different version of this activity is to select some measure, such as 17 cm, 6 dm, or 2 meters, and then have each group identify some object which best approximates the given length. The objects can then be measured and the best estimate determined.

Activity 4. This activity also consists of linear measures but is listed as a separate activity because it primarily deals with the human body. Possible features to be measured are listed below.

Distance between eyes	_____cm
Width of hand	_____cm
Waist (circumference)	_____cm
Head (hat size)	_____cm
Length of shoe	_____cm
Length of middle finger	_____cm
Wrist (circumference)	_____cm
Elbow to end of hand	_____cm

Activity 5. This activity focuses on measuring the areas of different figures. In many respects it resembles Activity 3 in this section and Activity 2 in the section on measuring with nonstandard units. Various objects can be selected, such as the tops of students' desks, the tiles in the floor, writing paper, or whatever. Then grid paper can be used to ascertain the areas of the selected regions. The grid paper must be transparent, of course, and probably should contain square centimeters. These activities should be a forerunner to the development of the area formulas.

Estimates should also be made. If you desire, you can make a game out of the activity by seeing which estimate comes closest to the measured area. Students should make estimates of the fractional units of area as best they can—perhaps counting the area as 0 if it is less than $\frac{1}{2}$ of a square unit or 1 if more than $\frac{1}{2}$ of the unit is covered.

Activity 6. An activity on volume could use either a cubic centimeter or a liter as the unit of volume. If cubes can be purchased or made that represent a cubic centimeter, then the volume of an object can be determined by filling the object— cereal box or pan—with the cubes and counting them. If the cubes are not available, graduated cylinders can usually be obtained which are calibrated by the number of cubic centimeters. Again, such activities should be a forerunner to

developing formulas for volume, such as $V = lwh$.

Containers for measuring in liters can also be obtained. Using either water or sand, the volume of various objects can be found by repeatedly filling the objects with liters of sand or water. The measurements will not all come out to be whole liters. The fractional part of a liter can be estimated, or the fractional part can be better determined by using cubic centimeters.

One of the important outcomes of activities involving liters is to develop some sense of approximation of what a liter contains. For example, could the student look at a pan of water and reasonably estimate how many liters it contains? If given a gallon jug, could students make a reasonable guess as to how many liters it might contain? These are the kinds of outcomes that should be deemed important in doing activities on volume.

13 · Statistics and Probability

INTRODUCTION

Statistics and probability do not occupy many pages in most elementary textbook series. Even so, these topics are most important as applications of mathematics in the elementary curriculum. Every citizen needs to understand some of the numerical information that describes the world of economics, business, government, and science. Virtually all this information is presented in statistical form. *Probability concepts are useful in many fields and are a part of our daily life.*

At the elementary school level statistical concepts are fun to teach and easy to learn. No new arithmetic operations are introduced in statistics; the familiar operations are used for the necessary calculations. The material presented should make sense and its purpose should be readily understandable. In Section 1 of this chapter we will present statistical concepts. We also suggest some laboratory activities that will help children not only to learn statistics but to appreciate how these concepts are used for understanding complex numerical data. Section 2 of the chapter will examine probability concepts.

1. STATISTICAL CONCEPTS

Data — Information

Statistical concepts begin with a collection of data, or information, which we would like to understand, visualize, or use. The question, "How tall is George?" can be answered by a measurement. The question, "How tall are boys in the fifth grade?" must be answered by statistics. Here are the heights of 20 fifth-grade boys. The heights are in centimeters and the students are listed in alphabetical order. This table would be fine for some purposes. If you are interested in finding quickly the height of a particular child, an alphabetical list is best. George is number 7 on the list, so we can quickly find his height: 150 cm—taller than some, shorter than others.

TABLE 1 • Heights of Fifth-grade Boys	
1. Al	140 cm
2. Bill	146 cm
3. Bob	130 cm
4. Ed	125 cm
5. Elvis	162 cm
6. Fred	156 cm
7. George	150 cm
8. Jack	146 cm
9. John	145 cm
10. Marco	157 cm
11. Morris	136 cm
12. Ned	132 cm
13. Owen	145 cm
14. Paul	128 cm
15. Peter	142 cm
16. Ralph	158 cm
17. Sam	153 cm
18. Tom	137 cm
19. Virgil	145 cm
20. William	147 cm

If we want to obtain some information about the heights of fifth-grade boys in general, Table 1 is not very informative or, at least, the information is not easily seen. The first change we can make in the table is to arrange the numbers from smallest to largest. The data are then said to be arranged in *rank order*. We can now draw some conclusions simply by inspecting Table 2: The shortest boy is 125 cm tall, the tallest is 162 cm tall, and there is a "cluster" in the middle, in the 140's. George is taller than 14 boys and shorter than 5 boys.

TABLE 2 • Heights of Fifth-grade Boys in Rank Order	
Elvis	162 cm
Ralph	158 cm
Marco	157 cm
Fred	156 cm
Sam	153 cm
George	150 cm
William	147 cm
Bill	146 cm
Jack	146 cm
John	145 cm
Owen	145 cm
Virgil	145 cm
Peter	142 cm
Al	140 cm
Tom	137 cm
Morris	136 cm
Ned	132 cm
Bob	130 cm
Paul	128 cm
Ed	125 cm

A second way to simplify the task of drawing conclusions from a set of data is to group the data into intervals that seem to go together. Most of the time the interval selected is simply the choice of whoever is organizing the data. The interval that produces the clearest organization is chosen. Table 3 is called a *fre-quency table*. It is now clear that there is a cluster in the 140's and that there are few students at the extreme ends, the 120's and the 160's. Further, the tally marks suggest a visual presentation of the data, a graph.

TABLE 3 • Frequency Table Heights of Fifth-grade Boys		
Interval (cm)	Tally	Frequency
160 – 169	I	1
150 – 159	NHI	5
140 – 149	NHI III	8
130 – 139	IIII	4
120 – 129	II	2

Graphic Presentation

We now illustrate a variety of graphs which may be used to present the data in the frequency table above.

Having studied the tables and the graphs made from the data, we now have a reasonable answer to the original question, "How tall are boys in the fifth grade?" They are mostly around 140 to 150 centimeters tall, but a few are as short as 125 centimeters and a few are as tall as 160 centimeters. Not a bad answer when you consider that *we have not performed even one arithmetical operation*. We have only arranged and illustrated the data in sensible ways.

Are there numbers that summarize the data and give us a numerical overview of the data, somewhat as the graphs do? Yes! There are numbers called statistics that describe a collection of data. We will examine four of them. The first three give us an estimate of the middle of the data, or a number typical of the entire set of data. The fourth tells how spread out

HEIGHT IN
CENTIMETERS

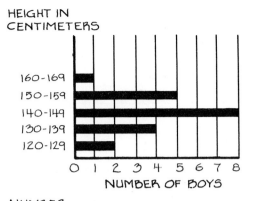

NUMBER OF BOYS

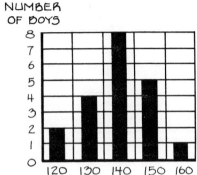

BAR GRAPHS

ALSO CALLED

FREQUENCY HISTOGRAMS

NUMBER
OF BOYS

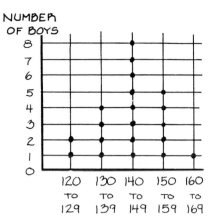

HEIGHT IN CENTIMETERS

FREQUENCY DOT DIAGRAM

NUMBER
OF BOYS

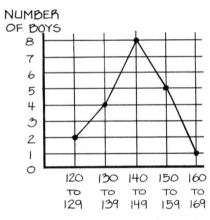

HEIGHT IN CENTIMETERS

LINE GRAPH

HEIGHT IN
CENTIMETERS

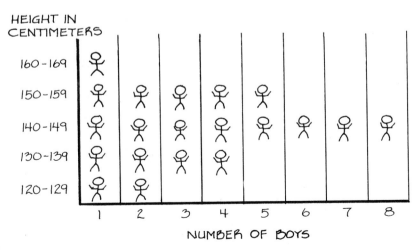

NUMBER OF BOYS

PICTOGRAPH

the data are. The numerical information, then, indicates the middle of the data, the most frequent score, and the dispersion of the data.

Measures of Central Tendency

In order to give a more precise meaning to our observation that fifth-grade boys are "mostly around 140 to 150 centimeters tall," we will look for a number that is in some sense typical of this distribution. There are three common ways to find such a typical number.

The mean. The mean is obtained by adding all the numbers in the distribution and dividing by the number of addends.

$$\frac{\text{Sum of the 20 heights}}{20} = \frac{2880}{20} = 144$$

Performing this calculation, we may now say that the mean height is 144 centimeters. In this case, the mean fits quite nicely into the center of the distribution, even though it happens that no boy is exactly that tall. George, who is 150 centimeters tall, is taller than the average by 6 centimeters.

The mean can be strongly influenced by extreme scores, either high or low. Examine the list of test scores in Table 4. If you compute the mean, you will find that it is 64. This score is not typical of the set of scores. Most students scored in the 50's, while four had 100. In cases like this, where the scores do not "bunch up in the middle," a mean may not be a typical score.

TABLE 4 • Test Scores

1	100
2	100
3	100
4	100
5	65
6	64
7	62
8	60
9	57
10	57
11	57
12	56
13	55
14	55
15	52
16	49
17	49
18	48
19	47
20	47
	Sum: 1280

$$\text{Mean: } \frac{1280}{20} = 64$$

The median. In the case shown in Table 4, the median is a better typical score. The median is a number that has as many scores above it as below it. It is the "halfway point" in the distribution. If there is an odd number of scores in the distribution, the median is simply the middle one when they are rank ordered. In a list of 37 scores in rank order the median is the 19th score.

When there is an even number of scores, take the two in the middle and find their mean (the point halfway between them); that is the median. Look at the 8 scores in Table 5. The two scores in the middle are 24 and 20. Find the mean of those two scores:

$$\frac{24 + 20}{2} = \frac{44}{2} = 22$$

So 22 is the median of that distribution.

TABLE 5

1.	35	
2.	30	
3.	26	
4.	24	22 is the
5.	20	median
6.	19	
7.	16	
8.	11	

The median of the distribution of heights of fifth-grade boys is the mean of the tenth and eleventh numbers in Table 2. We calculate the median as follows:

$$\frac{145 + 145}{2} = 145$$

Calculate the median test score of the scores in Table 4.

The mode. The mode is the most frequently occurring score, no matter where it may be in the distribution. When a distribution contains a large number of scores and the scores are nicely bunched in the middle, the mode is likely to be near the mean and the median. The distribution of heights of fifth-grade boys is of that type. The mode is 145; that height occurs 3 times, more often than any other score. It is in the middle, near the mean and the median.

Now find the mode for the test scores in Table 4. What conclusion can you draw? Does the mode represent a typical score?

The Range

The range of a set of data is the difference between the highest and the lowest numbers in the set. The range is one measure of the "dispersion" of a set of data; it tells how spread out the numbers are. The range answers the question, "Is there a large difference between the largest and the smallest numbers in a distribution?"

TABLE 6 • Heights of Fifth-grade Boys in Rank Order	
Elvis	162 cm
Ralph	158 cm
Marco	157 cm
Fred	156 cm
Sam	153 cm
George	150 cm
William	147 cm
Bill	146 cm
Jack	146 cm
John	145 cm
Owen	145 cm
Virgil	145 cm
Peter	142 cm
Al	140 cm
Tom	137 cm
Morris	136 cm
Ned	132 cm
Bob	130 cm
Paul	128 cm
Ed	125 cm

The data in Table 6 are the heights of 20 fifth-grade boys, exactly the same data as displayed in Table 2. The mean, median, and mode are 144, 145, and 145, respectively. The range of this distribution is obtained by subtracting the smallest score from the largest:

$$162 - 125 = 37$$

We now have a fairly complete picture of the heights of fifth-grade boys.

Discussion Questions

1. Table 7 shows germination time in days of seeds from a particular plant. Analyze

the data and draw what conclusions you think are reasonable. Rank order the data, make several different kinds of graphs, and calculate the mean, median, mode, and range. Do these statistics agree with your general description of the data?

TABLE 7 • Germination Time (Days)					
27	27	30	28	35	25
35	32	30	27	39	35
30	25	32	32	22	30
32	25	28	35	27	28
28	30	27	37	32	30

2. Later, some seeds from the same plant were treated with a certain chemical before they were planted. The results are shown in Table 8. Do the same things to these data that you did to the numbers in the previous table. Do you think that the chemical treatment had any effects? What do you think the effects were? Can you think of any reason why these might be desirable effects? undesirable?

TABLE 8 • Germination Time (Days)					
31	35	33	35	33	34
33	34	32	31	33	34
33	31	33	33	34	35
32	32	32	32	33	32
34	33	34	32	34	33

3. Decide whether the mean, mode, or median is the best statistic to describe each of the following distributions.

a. Mr. Hatesmoke interviewed 20 men and women about smoking. He found that 15 did not smoke, 1 person smoked 1 pack a day, 3 people smoked 2 packs a day, and the last person was a chain smoker who smoked no less than 4 packs a day.

b. The average incomes for 5 people were: $250,000; $22,000; $17,500; $16,000; $12,800.

c. In five years Henry Homer had 42, 36, 39, 28, and 41 home runs.

4. If the average income of each of 10 people is $10,000 and if one person gets a raise of $10,000, is the median, the mean, or the mode changed and, if so, how much?

5. Identify some data for which the best description is the mean; the mode; the median.

6. What is the mean of the following numbers: 17, 15, 13, 20, 32?

7. Calculate the mean, median, mode, and range of the scores on the last test you took in the class in which you are using this textbook.

Activities and Laboratory Projects

We turn next to laboratory activities, which can be used with children to teach these statistical concepts and to apply them to problems. Many of these are "project" or laboratory activities involving data collection and analysis while seeking the answer to some question.

1. Some children will enjoy collecting examples of graphs and uses of statistics that are found in newspapers and magazines. If data are presented, the children can make graphs of the data and calculate the mean, median, mode, and range. These can be used to enrich the study of statistics, to make a bulletin board display, and for discussion. This is one of the best opportunities a teacher has to coordinate mathematics with other subjects. Statistics are used frequently in social science, world affairs, and other areas. When a social science project is begun, look for ways to use statistics in the study.

2. How tall are the students in our class? The set of data we used on the heights of fifth-grade boys is an example of what might be done to answer the question.

3. Are girls or boys taller in our class? Students can arrange the data on boys and girls separately and compare them, graph them, and calculate the mean, median, mode, and range for each. They can construct a display, including data, graphs, statistics, and conclusions. You may correlate this project with a health class. At about seventh grade, the average height of girls exceeds the average height of boys, but by tenth grade, boys are taller, on the average.

4. How much will I grow during the next year? Of course, this is a complex question. Collecting and analyzing data from one class and from a class in the next grade will give some indication about likely growth.

5. The weather and weather reports provide rich sources of data. How does the daily high temperature in October compare to the daily high in January? in May? What about low temperatures? How does the daily temperature *range* change over the school year? All this information can be recorded (or weather reports clipped and saved) and data graphed and analyzed.

6. The daily "average temperature" is reported as the mean of the daily high and the daily low. Does the mean represent a "typical" temperature during the 24-hour period? Have a weather man come to class and explain! The "average daily temperature" is not such a simple concept; taking the mean of highest and lowest temperatures gives only a very rough approximation.

7. Graphs are useful in summarizing the results of polls on various issues. Students can gather and report the opinions of other students on issues such as candidates for public office, pets, sports, and so forth.

8. Young children can collect, graph, and interpret information. They are particularly interested in information about themselves. If each child writes his or her name on a square of paper and pastes it on a chart above the birth month, the result will be a bar graph. The graph can be used to answer simple questions, such as: In what month do we have the most birthdays? In what month the fewest birthdays? Which months have the same number? and many others.

2. PROBABILITY

People use probability concepts more frequently than they realize. A decision based on probability is involved when one decides to go on a picnic (Proba-

6									SAM			
5									SAM			
4			ALICE			JERRY		NED				
3			TED	JIM		ED	TOM	JULIE				
2			CAROL	LARRY		ANNIE	KAY	JIM	BILL		BETH	
1	BERT		PETE	BOB	LES	JOE	MIKE	BEA	KATHY	JOAN	ANGIE	DOUG
	JAN	FEB	MAR	APR	MAY	JUNE	JULY	AUG	SEPT	OCT	NOV	DEC

bility of rain is 40 percent today.), cross a busy street (Come on, we can make it!), or bet on a game. The uses of probability in technical work are extensive and continue to increase. In work or play, probability is used; furthermore, the activities through which probability can be taught are interesting and fun to do.

We have included in this topic a series of activities you may use in teaching probability. You may also wish to work through these activities yourself first to gain familiarity. If you work through the activities ahead of time, you will be more comfortable teaching the topic. Probability experiments do not work out exactly the same each time but will tend to be "close" to the same outcomes.

Probability is the measure or estimate of the likelihood of an event. A fraction is frequently used to state the probability of an event. If we say, "The probability of getting heads on the flip of a coin is $\frac{1}{2}$," we mean that on 1 out of 2 flips we would expect the result to be heads. Of course, we might flip 10 times and get 8 or 9 or (very rarely) 10 heads. But over a very large number of flips the fraction

$$\frac{\text{Number of heads}}{\text{Number of flips}}$$

would get closer and closer to $\frac{1}{2}$.

The coin flip is a simple probability to calculate. There are two outcomes and the outcomes are equally likely. In simple cases, particularly those that can be broken down into equally likely outcomes, it is usually easy to figure out the probability of an event. In other situations, especially those influenced by many factors, the probabilities are difficult or impossible to calculate. What is the probability that it will be a mild winter? What is the probability that the

Dolphins will win the Super Bowl? For these and other complex situations there is no simple way to calculate probabilities.

The first concepts we wish to discuss are the related ideas of outcomes and equally likely outcomes. In elementary school mathematics probability experiments are usually simple and the outcomes can usually be listed with a little reflection.

Outcomes

For many probability problems the first step is to think about the experiment and to list all the possible outcomes of that experiment. Examples of this could be a coin flip (heads, tails), drawing one card from a deck (list of all cards in the deck), rolling one die (1, 2, 3, 4, 5, 6), spinning an arrow spinner (list of places where the spinner may point), or choosing the winner of a football game (Team A, Team B, tie). Notice that in some cases we ignore outcomes which are theoretically possible but extremely unlikely; we don't list "landing on edge" as an outcome of the coin flip. Notice also that in these examples all except the last two have equally likely outcomes. That is, heads is as likely as tails to come up on a fair coin, and no number is more likely than any other number on one roll of a die. On a spinner the probability is determined by the sizes of the zones around the spinner. The outcome of a football game is influenced by so many factors that the probability of one team winning is difficult to estimate. Complete Table 9—list all the outcomes for each experiment and tell whether you believe the outcomes you have listed are equally likely.

TABLE 9

Event	Outcomes	Equally Likely?
Coin toss	Heads, tails	Yes
Spin spinner *A*		
Spin spinner *B*		
Spin spinner C		
Tomorrow's weather		

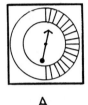

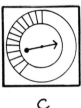

A   B   C

Calculating the Probability

When we have listed all the outcomes, and especially if we have equally likely outcomes, we are ready to calculate the probability of any particular outcome. To show how this is done, we will describe an experiment: The numbers from 1 to 10 are written on slips of paper, placed in a paper bag, and mixed. The experimenter is to draw, without looking, one slip of paper from the bag. We may assume that, because all slips of paper are the same size and the papers are thoroughly mixed, the experimenter is just as likely to draw one slip as another; these outcomes are *equally likely*.

Suppose we want to draw an even number. There are five even numbers in the bag, 2, 4, 6, 8, and 10, so the probability is $\frac{5}{10}$, 5 chances out of 10, of drawing an even number. In general, if we have listed equally likely outcomes, the probability of the specified event is a fraction:

P (specified event) =

$$\frac{\text{Number of specified outcomes}}{\text{Number of all possible outcomes}}$$

In the case of drawing an even number, the specified outcomes are 2, 4, 6, 8, or 10. All possible outcomes are the 10 numbers in the bag. The probability of drawing an even number is $\frac{5}{10}$.

$$P\,(2, 4, 6, 8, 10) = \tfrac{5}{10}$$

A probability of 1 would represent certainty, an event sure to occur. For example, suppose we calculate the probability of drawing a number less than 20 from the bag. All 10 numbers are less than 20, so

$$P\,(n < 20)^1 = \frac{\text{successful}}{\text{possible}} = \tfrac{10}{10} = 1$$

The probability of drawing a number greater than 20 is

$$P\,(n > 20) = \frac{\text{successful}}{\text{possible}} = \tfrac{0}{10} = 0$$

A probability of 0 means that an event is impossible, that it will never occur.

Suppose several events are described and these events, first, include all possible outcomes of an experiment and, second, include each outcome only once.

---

¹Read $P\,(n < 20)$ as "The probability that the number drawn is less than 20."

The sum of the probabilities of these events will be 1. That seems reasonable because a probability of 1 represents certainty; if all possible outcomes are included, one of them is certain to occur.

Consider a coin flip and the events heads and tails. These two events include all possible outcomes and include each outcome only once.

$$P \text{ (heads)} = \tfrac{1}{2} \qquad P \text{ (tails)} = \tfrac{1}{2}$$

$$\tfrac{1}{2} + \tfrac{1}{2} = \tfrac{2}{2} = 1$$

As a second example consider again the bag with 10 numbers on slips of paper. Calculate the probability of drawing a prime number, 2, 3, 5, 7, the probability of drawing a composite number, 4, 6, 8, 9, 10, and the probability of drawing a 1 from the bag. The probability of drawing a prime number is $\tfrac{4}{10}$; the probability of drawing a composite number is $\tfrac{5}{10}$; the probability of drawing a 1 is $\tfrac{1}{10}$.

$$\tfrac{4}{10} + \tfrac{5}{10} + \tfrac{1}{10} = \tfrac{10}{10} = 1$$

Problem. List all the outcomes of rolling one die. Calculate the probability of each event described in the table below.

Expected Outcomes

If the probability of an event is $\tfrac{4}{10}$, then, over a number of trials, we would expect that on approximately $\tfrac{4}{10}$ of the trials the event would occur. If, for example, we conduct 200 trials of this event, then $\tfrac{4}{10} \times 200 = 80$ is the number of times we would expect the event to occur. To find the expected number, multiply the number of trials by the probability of the event. This *almost never* works out exactly in experiments but is *almost always* close.

Experiments. After we have calculated the probability of an event, we frequently do an experiment to see how closely the experimental results correspond to our calculation. Indeed, the understanding of probability and more than half the

TABLE 10

EXPERIMENT: ROLLING ONE DIE OUTCOMES: 1, 2, 3, 4, 5, 6		
Event	Specified outcomes	Probability of the event
An odd number	1, 3, 5	$\tfrac{3}{6} = \tfrac{1}{2}$
An even number	2, 4, 6	
A number less than 10		
A prime number		
A composite number		
A 3 or a 4		
$n < 3$		
$n > 6$		

fun of studying probability lies in analyzing and performing experiments. There are two things to note about experiments: If, over a large number of trials, the results are *much* different from the probability you calculated, you should check your calculation and the way you conducted the experiment; the experimental results arc usually close to the calculated probability. On the other hand, experimental results are almost never in *exact* agreement with calculations. To illustrate this relationship between calculated probability and experimental results, we show the results of an experiment here.

A bag contains 10 cards, numbered 1 through 10. Draw 10 cards, replacing each card after it has been drawn and mixing the cards each time. Go through this procedure 10 times to obtain 100 trials. A "successful" draw will be a 7, 8, 9, or 10. The probability of a successful draw is calculated to be $\frac{4}{10}$. The actual and the expected results are shown in Table 11.

As you examine the table, notice that individual sets of 10 trials vary quite widely from expectations. As few as 2

and as many as 6 "successful" outcomes occurred when 4 were "expected." However, the cumulative result is very close to the expected fraction, $\frac{4}{10}$.

The best way for you *or* your students to learn this, to really get a feel for what happens, is to perform several experiments. You might wish to get a die and perform an experiment of 60 rolls or more. The event might be rolling a 5 or a 6. Make a table such as the one below and analyze the results. Do your experimental results agree closely with the expected results?

Several more experiments are described below in the Laboratory Activities section.

Independent experiments. When two experiments are independent, that is, when the outcome of one has no influence on the outcome of the other, we may calculate the probability of a specified event in each of the experiments. Suppose the two experiments are (1) flipping a coin and (2) rolling one die. The coin flip has no influence on the roll and vice versa. First, list the outcomes of each experiment. We will use, for

Draws	Cumulative Draws	Successful	Cumulative Successful	Expected	Cumulative Expected	Successful Trials	Expected Fraction, Expressed as a Decimal
10		3		4		$\frac{3}{10} = .30$	.40
10	20	3	6	4	8	$\frac{6}{20} = .30$	.40
10	30	2	8	4	12	$\frac{8}{30} =$	.40
10	40	4	12	4	16	$\frac{12}{40} =$	.40
10	50	5	17	4	20	$\frac{17}{50} =$	.40
10	60	6	23	4	24	$\frac{23}{60} =$	.40
10	70	3	26	4	28	$\frac{26}{70} =$	.40
10	80	5	31	4	32	$\frac{31}{80} =$	.40
10	90	4	35	4	36	$\frac{35}{90} =$	.40
10	100	4	39	4	40	$\frac{39}{100} = .39$	.40

simplicity, only experiments for which equally likely outcomes can be listed. Second, make a chart of all combinations of outcomes of the two experiments.

Coin	Die
Heads (H)	1, 2, 3,
Tails (T)	4, 5, 6

Combinations Die-Coin	
1, H	1, T
2, H	2, T
3, H	3, T
4, H	4, T
5, H	5, T
6, H	6, T

Notice that there are $6 \times 2 = 12$ different outcomes in the chart. Each of these 12 outcomes is equally likely because each of the outcomes of the coin and the die were equally likely. Thus, the probability of any one of the outcomes listed in the chart is $\frac{1}{12}$.

Experimentally Determined Probability

In some situations the analysis of an experiment into equally likely outcomes is virtually impossible; the situation is just too complex. Think about the problem of attempting to calculate the probability that a new light bulb will be defective. Many factors could contribute to the production of a defective bulb: quality of component parts, quality of raw materials, operation of automated machines, etc. The probability that a new bulb is defective can be determined, however, by testing a large number of bulbs and calculating

P (defective bulb) =
$$\frac{\text{Number of defective bulbs}}{\text{Total number of bulbs}}$$

Suppose that, of 100,000 light bulbs manufactured in one week, 1,000 are found to be defective. What is the probability that a bulb manufactured in that plant will be defective?

P (defective bulb) =
$$\frac{1,000}{100,000} = \frac{1}{100} = 1\%$$

If the factory went for some time with a fairly steady rate of 1 percent defective bulbs, that might be considered "normal" for the parts, raw materials, and manufacturing process used. If the rate of production of defective bulbs increased suddenly to, say, 3 percent or if the rate began to show a steady increase, that might indicate something wrong in the process. Thus, knowledge of the normal rate of production of defective bulbs and checking samples of the production can provide information about the manufacturing process.

Discussion Questions and Activities

We now present some discussion activities and some laboratory activities which can be used to develop the concept of probability and help children learn to estimate and calculate probabilities. To gain increased understanding of probability, it is recommended that you answer the questions and perform the experiments as part of your study of this chapter.

Activities for young children
In each of these activities the idea is to think about the situation and to list all the outcomes or try to. Then, with the list of

outcomes before the class, engage the children in discussion of which outcome might happen most often in a large number of trials. In some of these activities it is easy to go on to the next step, to try the event many times and to keep a record of the number of times each outcome occurs.

1. "What do you think the weather *might* be tomorrow?" The list of possible conditions is quite extensive. Ask, "What do you think the weather probably *will* be tomorrow?" and "What kind of weather is the most likely?"

2. Here is a spinner for a game. If we spin it, what could the arrow point to? What shading do you think it will point to most often? What shading will it point to least often? Why?

3. Questions that ask children to list all possible combinations of several things are more difficult. Allow more time for discussion; help and encourage the children but don't expect complete analysis of the problem.

Angela, Mary, Ted, and Bob are all on school patrol. Two are to be picked for outside stations. All the names are written on slips of paper and two names are drawn, without looking. Who might be picked?

Angela and Mary	Mary and Ted
Angela and Ted	Mary and Bob
Angela and Bob	Ted and Bob

4. A number cube is a die with numbers instead of spots. If I roll the cube, what number might come up on the top? Do you think all the numbers will come up about the same number of times? Children may roll the cube a large number of times and keep track of how many times each number does come up.

5. If you have a small block which is a rectangular solid but *not* a cube, you may write numbers on the faces and repeat Activity 4, using the rectangular solid. Depending on the shape of the block, it will come to rest on the small end much less often than on the larger faces. Will the children be able to guess this from the shape of the block?

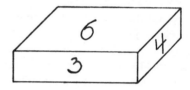

6. Activities 4 and 5 contrast *equally likely* and *not equally likely* outcomes in similar situations. Another such contrast is flipping a coin and flipping a thumbtack. In the coin flip the two outcomes, heads and tails, are equally likely. In flipping a tack the two outcomes, point up and point down, usually are not equally likely. Discussion of outcomes and guesses as to which outcomes are most likely can be followed by "trying it out" a large number of times to see what happens.

UP   DOWN

Laboratory activities for older children
The following activities are laboratory lessons in which the main function of the

teacher is to guide rather than to tell students what to do. The emphasis is on independent thinking and experimentation. To help guide students through these activities, questions are suggested to highlight the next step that might be taken. As long as students are working toward a solution, there is no need to use the suggested questions. When they are stumped, and after reasonable effort can't figure out what to do next, use a question or even more direct suggestion to get them started again. Let us look at activities you might use in the upper elementary grades or junior high school.

1. The problem we wish to consider is, "If we throw one die, what is the probability that a 6 will come up on top?"

a. Make a list of the possible outcomes of this event. Certainly, that is easy: 1, 2, 3, 4, 5, 6.

b. Ask, "Is it reasonable to assume that all these outcomes are equally likely?" Because the die is uniform, symmetrical, and not loaded, this assumption is reasonable.

c. Therefore, what is the probability that a 6 will come up? $\frac{1}{6}$

d. Conduct an experiment to see whether the experimental probability and the theoretical probability are close. Each student can record the results of 48 rolls. We pick 48 because *if* our calculation of the probability is correct, this will give us an expectation of $\frac{1}{6} \times 48 =$

8 sixes in 48 rolls. Ask, "How do we tell whether or not the experiment has confirmed our probability calculation?" Record the results in a table such as Table 12.

Examine the table to see whether or not *each student's* 48 rolls conformed to the $\frac{1}{6}$ hypothesis. Probably not; there will be some who rolled more than the 8 sixes expected and some who rolled fewer. Then look at the cumulative results. While individual results vary quite a bit, the cumulative results will tend to be close to the expected results. That is, *if* the probability has been estimated correctly in the first place! To see the relationship, you may make a table which compares the cumulative results with the "expected cumulative" results. If the students are familiar with decimal fractions, the decimal columns in the table will show more clearly the tendency of cumulative results to get closer and closer to the expected frequency.

2. The problem of flipping two coins is an interesting one. The flips of the two coins are independent experiments like the coin flip and die roll described earlier. There are two ways students usually think out the theoretical probability, and these lead to different results. Performing an experiment will confirm one and reject the other. Look for these two different hypotheses as students discuss the problem, and make

TABLE 12

Name	Number of 6's	6's/Rolls	As a Decimal	Expected 6's/Rolls	As a Decimal
Sam	11	11/48	.229	8/48	.167
Bob	8	19/96	.198	16/96	.167
Carol	3	22/144	.153	24/144	.167
John	5	27/192	.141	32/192	.167
Ted	12	39/240	.162	40/240	.167
Alice	8	47/288	.163	48/288	.167

sure students understand both hypotheses and the significance of the experiment in choosing between them. The question to be investigated is, "If I flip two coins, what is the probability that they will both come up heads?"

a. What are all the possible outcomes of tossing two coins? You will see the beginnings of the two different hypotheses here:

2 heads	head-head
1 head, 1 tail	head-tail
2 tails	tail-head
	tail-tail

b. Are these outcomes equally likely? The supporters of each hypothesis will probably state that the outcomes in their list are equally likely. The question probably cannot be settled to the students' satisfaction until the experiment is performed.

c. What is the probability of each outcome? On the basis of assuming equally likely outcomes, we assign probabilities:

2 heads	$\frac{1}{3}$
1 head, 1 tail	$\frac{1}{3}$
2 tails	$\frac{1}{3}$

head-head	$\frac{1}{4}$
head-tail	$\frac{1}{4}$
tail-head	$\frac{1}{4}$
tail-tail	$\frac{1}{4}$

Of course, the difference is not large: One scheme has a probability of $\frac{1}{3}$ for the 2-heads outcome, the other has a probability of $\frac{1}{4}$. Consequently, the experiment needed to investigate the question must have a large number of trials.

d. You might suggest that the students plan an experiment and that they state in advance how many "2-heads" events are predicted under each of the

schemes above. If your experiment has 1,200 trials, you will almost certainly see the results as convincing evidence for one of the hypotheses. If the probability of 2 heads is $\frac{1}{3}$, then you would expect 2 heads to come up 400 times; if the probability is $\frac{1}{4}$, you would expect 2 heads 300 times. As before, keep records of each student's contribution and of the cumulative count.

A similar experiment is the rolling of two dice. This is more complicated to analyze and requires more detailed record keeping.

3. "Extra sensory perception" (ESP) is an ability to know something you could not have learned through your normal senses. Some scientists believe it exists but others do not. Here is one of the now-classic experiments performed to determine whether or not a person has ESP.

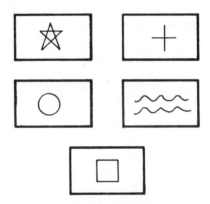

Make a set of cards with the symbols shown here—star, plus, circle, waves, square. Use 3 in. × 5 in. cards and make 5 of each kind of symbol. The experiment consists of having a person shuffle the deck *without* looking at the cards and having another person guess the order of the symbols from the top of the deck down. Before we start this experiment, we want to know something about the outcomes.

a. *Outcomes.* In guessing one card, what are the possible guesses? List them.

b. *Probability.* How many of these possible guesses are correct? Only one each time. What is the probability that a person will guess correctly? Assuming that the five outcomes are equally likely, the probability is $\frac{1}{5}$.

c. *Expectation.* Since the probability of guessing correctly on a single card is $\frac{1}{5}$ and we have 25 tries, we would expect to get $\frac{1}{5} \times 25 = 5$ correct guesses. However, we know that we may guess correctly more or less than 5 times.

d. *Experiment.* Have one student shuffle the cards without looking at them. All other students number their papers from 1 to 25, guess which symbol will be on each card, starting at the top of the deck, and write their choices. Then the student who shuffled the cards turns each one up, reads the symbol, and shows it to the class. Students keep records of their scores as this experiment is done a number of times, say 20 times in two weeks. A student who scores *consistently* better than 5 correct for each test may have ESP!

Make a spinner. Turn a stiff paper plate upside down. Attach a cardboard arrow in the center with a pin. Now you can predetermine the probability by using different regions around the plate. You may assume that a region which runs one quarter of the way around the circle has a probability of $\frac{1}{4}$, and so on. Conduct an experiment like those described above to see whether the probability of the spinner stopping in a particular place is about what you thought it would be.

Check the weather. For a long-term project, children interested in weather can keep track of forecasters' predictions and successes. Normally, forecasts are given in terms of "percent probability of rain." We may make a table to keep track of predictions and outcomes. The forecasts quote 0 percent, 10 percent, 20 percent, . . . 90 percent, 100 percent probability of rain. Each day mark a tally by the percent-of-rain forecast and a tally if rain actually occurred. When the experiment is over (and it might run for months), calculate the number of rains expected. If, for example, the forecast was for "40 percent probability of rain" on 20 days, then rain would be expected on 8 of those days (40% × 20 = 8). When you have completed the study, compare the number of times rain occurred with the number of times rain was expected. Do this by adding the numbers in the "Rain Occurred" column and the "Rain Expected" column and comparing the totals.

TABLE 13

Percent Probability of Rain		Number of Days on Which Rain Occurred (Tally)	Number of Days on Which Rain Was Expected (Percent Probability × Number of Days)
Forecast %	(Tally of days)		
0			
10			
20			
30			
40			
50			
60			
70			
80			
90			
100			
		Sum:	Sum:

14 · Teaching Relations and Functions

INTRODUCTION

Functions and relations are extremely important topics in mathematics and have wide application. An understanding of functions and relations is essential in virtually every mathematics course a student may take. Functions and relations are found everywhere in daily life; recognizing and using these concepts are as important as recognizing and using concepts in arithmetic and geometry. We will begin the development of the topic with ideas introduced in kindergarten and Grade 1 and trace it through the seventh-grade level. At that level students learn formal mathematical definitions of function *and* relation.

1. RELATIONS AND RELATIONSHIPS

The ideas most people have about relationships are quite close to the proper technical definition of the term. Two people can be related by the relationship "is the brother of," and we may identify two people and state that the relation exists between them: Bill *is the brother of* Glenna. A relation of "is less than" can exist between two numbers: 7 *is less than* 10. Thus, we can rely to some extent on the nontechnical meaning of the word *relation* to understand the mathematical meaning of that term.

Sets

In kindergarten and the primary grades children work extensively with sets of objects or pictures. They are expected to recognize certain relations that may exist between two sets. These relations can be seen when an attempt is made to pair off two sets in one-to-one correspondence. In Figure *A*, below, it is not possible to place the sets in one-to-one correspondence. There is one circle not paired with a square. We can state the relation in two ways: (1) there are *more* circles than squares, and (2) there

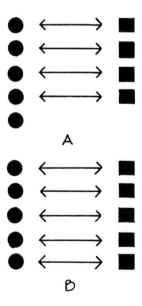

A

B

are *fewer* squares than circles. In Figure B, the pairing is possible; the two sets are in one-to-one correspondence. In this case, we say there are *the same number* of squares as circles. Working with these relationships between sets provides the experience needed to understand the relations "greater than," "less than," and "equal" between numbers.

There is a vocabulary problem in the discussion of sets such as those in Figure B. Children and teachers frequently say these sets are *equal,* meaning that each has the same number of elements. When mathematicians discuss two sets having the same number of elements, they call them *equivalent* sets; they reserve the term *equal* sets to refer to sets that contain exactly the same elements. Teachers should be aware of this distinction and use the vocabulary correctly but not let overemphasis on word usage interfere with a free flow of sensible dialogue in the classroom.

Whole Numbers

Growing out of comparisons of sets are relations between numbers. Figure *A* shows that a set of 5 is more than a set of 4. Because this *always* is the case when we compare sets of 5 and 4 elements, we conclude that 5 is a larger number than 4; 5 *is greater than* 4, or $5 > 4$. Similarly, 4 *is less than* 5, or $4 < 5$. Other than by sets, there are at least two ways a child may investigate the relation between 4 and 5. One way is counting: 1, 2, 3, 4, 5, 6, 7, ... In counting order the smaller number comes first and the larger number after. The other way is to visualize the numbers on the number line.

On the number line, shown below, the numbers increase to the right — 5 is larger than 4 because it is farther right. (Of course, the direction of increase, to the right, is purely a convention — it could be done some other way but it is not.) When children have been introduced to the number line, it may be used extensively to compare numbers because it is an effective model for comparing fractions, decimals, and integers as well as whole numbers. The comparison of whole numbers is an important foundation for later work.

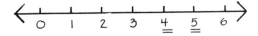

Comparing larger numbers depends on an understanding of the place value system of numeration. It is not always made clear to children that 1,012 is greater than 989. Children know that 8 and 9 are large digits and 0, 1, and 2 are small, and so they frequently pick 989 as the larger number. Counting order places 989 before 1,012, and so $989 < 1,012$. A whole number with more digits is greater than one with fewer digits. If two numbers have the same number of digits, the largest decimal place in which they differ will determine which is greater. A good knowledge of counting order is necessary if students are to avoid difficulty in comparing large numbers.

We have not touched on the *equals* relation for whole numbers. Children have problems with this relation. It will help to understand these problems if we first discuss fractions, decimals, and integers and then return to the *equals* relation for whole numbers.

Fractional and Decimal Numbers

Counting order cannot be used to determine which of two fractional numbers is greater. One way to compare fractions is to mark the fractions on the number line. This also contributes to students' understanding of fraction concepts as well as the order. On the number line below, we have marked $\frac{3}{2}$ (★) and $\frac{5}{3}$ (■). Because $\frac{5}{3}$ is farther to the right, it is greater than $\frac{3}{2}$. We write $\frac{5}{3} > \frac{3}{2}$.

We can compare $\frac{3}{2}$ and $\frac{5}{3}$ by changing the fractions to equivalent fractions having a common denominator. When the denominators are the same, we compare numerators just as we compare whole numbers.

$$\frac{3}{2} = \frac{9}{6} \text{ and } \frac{5}{3} = \frac{10}{6}$$
$$\frac{9}{6} < \frac{10}{6}$$
$$\text{So}$$
$$\frac{3}{2} < \frac{5}{3}$$

In some comparisons of fractional numbers, we find that the fractional numbers are equal. This means that the two fractions are two different ways of writing the same number. The same comparison procedure, finding a common denominator and comparing numerators, will identify equal fractional numbers. Compare $\frac{10}{15}$ and $\frac{6}{9}$. We see that each is equal to $\frac{30}{45}$, so they are equal.

$$\frac{10}{15} = \frac{30}{45} \qquad \frac{6}{9} = \frac{30}{45}$$
$$\frac{30}{45} = \frac{30}{45}$$
$$\text{So}$$
$$\frac{10}{15} = \frac{6}{9}$$

Another means of comparing two fractional numbers is to convert each to a decimal and compare the decimals. We will compare $\frac{3}{2}$ and $\frac{5}{3}$, as in a previous example. By dividing, write

$$\frac{3}{2} = 1.5000 \ldots$$
$$\frac{5}{3} = 1.6666 \ldots$$

Since $1.5 < 1.666 \ldots$, we know $\frac{3}{2} < \frac{5}{3}$. Comparing decimal fractions is done in the same way as the comparison of whole numbers. If the numbers differ in any decimal place, then they are not equal, and the number having the larger digit in the first decimal place in which they differ (reading from left to right) is the larger. This rule is far easier to understand than to state. Compare 2.3619 and 2.3497. The digits in the ones' places and tenths' places are the same. The two numbers differ first in hundredths' place, and 6 hundredths is greater than 4 hundredths, so $2.3\underline{\underline{6}}19 >$ $2.3\underline{\underline{4}}97$. This will hold no matter what digits the other places may contain. Plotting such numbers on magnified number lines (see the chapter on decimal fractions) can make this comparison more meaningful to children. Several examples will help them understand this rule.

Examples: $56.32\underline{\underline{1}}7 > 56.32\underline{\underline{0}}9$
$53.\underline{\underline{4}} > 53.3\underline{\underline{2}}617$
$.71\underline{\underline{3}}2 > .70\underline{\underline{}}$
$.6\underline{\underline{7}} > .6\underline{\underline{6}}66 \ldots$

When a decimal is nonterminating and all the repeating digits are 9's (for example, .2999. . .; .999. . .; .00999. . .), the above rule does not always hold. Students should not be unduly pushed on this point, but the nonterminating decimal with repeating 9's is *equal* to a terminating decimal formed by increasing the last non-9 digit by 1 and dropping the nines (for example, .2999 . . .= .3; .999. . .= 1; .00999. . .= .01).

Do you agree that $\frac{1}{3} + \frac{1}{3} + \frac{1}{3} = 1$? Certainly! Now $\frac{1}{3} = .333$. . . and .333. . .+

.333. . . + .333. . . is .999. . . . But
.333. . . + .333. . . + .333. . . $= \frac{1}{3} + \frac{1}{3} + \frac{1}{3} = 1$. So .999. . . $= 1$.

One is tempted to describe the process of writing .2999. . . $= .3$ as "rounding." Strictly speaking, it is not. The two numbers are equal and a thorough discussion would require the concept of limit.

Equality of Whole Numbers

In a discussion of fractional numbers we can ask if two different fractions may be equal. There are many fractional numerals that stand for the same number. This is also the case with whole numbers. In those instances where we are studying another system of numeration, children may be asked, "Do 134_5 and 44_{10} stand for the same number?"

There are many cases in which we want to emphasize equality of different-looking whole numbers and in order to do this we must build proper background. The set picture—Figure B, above—should be used as a springboard for statements like "Five squares is the same number as five circles, so five equals five," and we write $5 = 5$. When working on addition facts, we usually start with 3 and 2 and put them together, writing $3 + 2 = 5$. We can also start with 5 and separate five objects into sets of 3 and 2 and write $5 = 3 + 2$. Because we have not provided such experiences, children tend to reject as "wrong" both $5 = 5$ and $5 = 3 + 2$. Their concept of the *equals* relation is not what teachers have tried to teach them.

We use equality of whole numbers in some very crucial ways in expanded notation and in regrouping. These equations are the kind frequently used to pre-

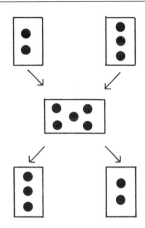

sent the regrouping procedure for subtraction.

$325 = 3$ hundreds $+ 2$ tens $+ 5$ ones;
 or $325 = 300 + 20 + 5$
$325 = 3$ hundreds $+ 1$ ten $+ 15$ ones;
 or $325 = 300 + 10 + 15$

If children do not grasp the relationship that "$=$" signifies two different ways of writing the same quantity, these procedures for regrouping can hardly make sense to them.

As mentioned earlier, we will return to the topic of relations later and introduce a mathematical definition for the term. The *greater than, less than,* and *equals* relations will be explored further, showing how they can be represented as part of our mathematical definition.

2. FUNCTIONS

Tables of Values

A function is a special kind of relation. The fact that it is special in certain ways makes it easy to introduce and explore with children. One of the first exposures children have to functions is the function machine. Many programs use this notion at early grade levels. Some programs delay the use of the word *function* until later grades. The function machine accepts numbers as input and "does something" to these numbers, giving the result as output. The "+ 4 machine" pictured here adds 4 to whatever is put into the top and feeds the results out the side. If 3 goes in, 7 comes out. This concept of function leads us to two of the ways to express or represent a function: a table of values and a rule.

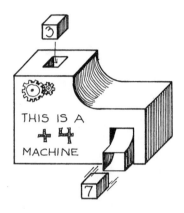

The table of values shown here is the table produced by using the "+ 4 Machine." An unlimited number of other pairs could also be generated and listed in the table.

Table of Values

Input	Output
3	7
0	4
5	9
6	10
9	13
2	6
15	19
.	.
.	.
.	.

When we have a table of values, we can present the information in a diagram in several different ways. Below are two different diagrams of this function. In each of the diagrams the arrows connect an input number to its associated output number. Another important and useful way to illustrate a function is by a graph.

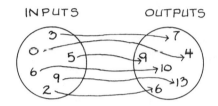

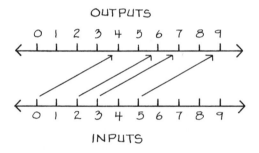

Graphs of Functions

Although some readers already know it, we must review the basic terminology of graphing, referring to the figure below. The graph begins with two *coordinate axes,* one horizontal, the other vertical. These are perpendicular number lines that intersect at their zero points. The axes permit us to identify locations in much the same way that intersecting streets identify locations in a city. Each point in the plane has an "address" that consists of two numbers. We may wish to find the "address," the *coordinates,* of a point such as point *A* in the graph shown here. To do this, we draw a line from point *A* straight down to the horizontal axis. The number associated with that point on the horizontal axis is the first coordinate. Then draw a line from point *A* straight across to the vertical axis. The number associated with that point is the second coordinate. Thus, the coordinates of point *A* are (4,2).

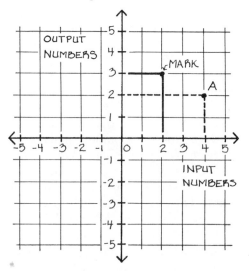

Now we describe the reverse procedure, marking a point whose coordinates are given. In the example, the point to be marked has coordinates (2,3). The input number, 2, is located on the horizontal (input) axis. The output number, 3, is located on the vertical (output) axis. Move *up* from the 2 on the horizontal axis to a point opposite the 3 on the vertical axis and mark that point. This process is called *plotting* a point. The point is named by the two numbers; the point plotted in the graph is the point (2,3). You will note that the coordinates (3,2) represent a different point. *Order counts* in naming points.

When you have a table of values for a function, each pair of values from the table is entered on the graph in the same manner. Locate the first coordinate

number on the horizontal axis. From that point move straight up or straight down until you are opposite the second coordinate number. The graph below shows some of the points from the table of values given above. We can complete the graph of the function within the limits of the size of our paper by plotting all the pairs. That is, to graph a function, one plots all the points for which the function is true. Since we are working at this time only with whole numbers, we have not plotted any points having negative or fractional coordinates.

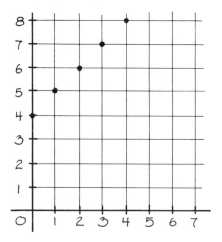

Rules for Functions

The "rule" for a function can be stated in a variety of ways. In the early grades the rule would be simply a statement of what the function machine does: To any number you put in, add 4 and that is the number that comes out. Later, more concise symbolic statements can be made, and finally in the upper grades an equation using x and y will be the statement of the rule: $y = x + 4$. This equation says that x is the input and y, the output, is $x + 4$.

Over a period of years children should learn to express and illustrate functions in each of these ways and to change from one form of expression to another.

(1) Given the rule, make a table of values, diagrams, and a graph.

(2) Given a diagram or graph, make a table of values and state the rule.

(3) Given a table of values, state the rule and make a graph.

It is fairly easy to start with a rule and produce a table of values and from that a graph. It is more difficult to start with a table or a graph and figure out the rule. This requires more than simply following a procedure; the student must examine the table, make a guess about the rule, and test each guess. In simple problems in elementary school it is safe to assume that a rule that works for all given pairs is correct. Different rules may be possible. Hunting for a rule that fits a table of values can be a time-consuming process. Many rules may be suggested and tested before a correct rule is found. Hunting for a rule, however, is well worth the time it takes; it encourages higher-level thought and provides the excitement of having to hunt down a correct answer rather than merely calculating it.

In Table *A* we are presented with a table for which we do not know the rule. Looking at the first pair, (1,2), we might hope that the rule is "add 1" or "multiply by 2," but neither of these rules fits the second pair. One thing that will frequently help is to put the data in an organized form. Table *B* shows the data arranged so that values of *x* appear in increasing order. You can observe that the output numbers increase much faster than the input numbers (the *x*'s). How much faster? If *x* goes up 1, how much does the output increase? If *x* goes up 2, as from 4 to 6, how much does the output increase? Another approach is to ask, as in Table *C,* for some output numbers not given in the original table. What would the output be if 5 is the input? What would be the output if 10 or 30 is the input? Then ask, "What could I do to 5 to get that number as the output?"

If students are stuck, it is a good idea to let them have a day or so to think about it. Don't be too quick to give the answer. You may also give a variety of different easier rules for them to discover, leading up to the rule on which they are stuck. Did you get it? The rule is multiply *x* by 4 then subtract 2, or $y = 4x - 2$.

A

x	?
1	2
4	14
3	10
8	30
2	6
7	26
6	22

B

x	?
1	2
2	6
3	10
4	14
6	22
7	26
8	30

C

x	?
1	2
2	6
3	10
4	14
5	
6	22
7	26
8	30
9	
10	
11	
12	
18	
30	

Exercises

1. Identify the larger and the smaller number in each pair, or state that they are equal.

A. $\frac{3}{14}$, $\frac{12}{55}$ B. $\frac{3}{14}$, .2142794

C. $\frac{3}{11}$, .272727 . . .   D. $\frac{12}{52}$, $\frac{15}{65}$

2. For this function machine generate a table of values and state the rule. Diagram the function by drawing arrows from inputs to outputs on these number lines.

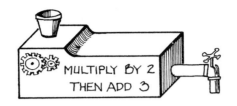

OUTPUTS

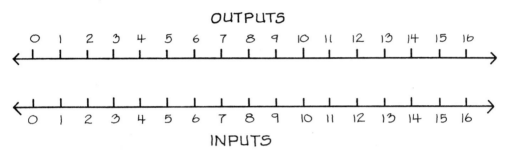

INPUTS

3. What is the rule for the function shown
in this diagram?

OUTPUTS

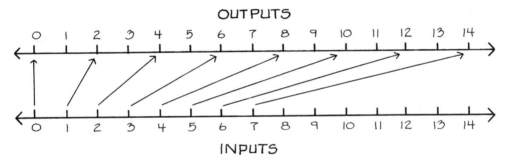

INPUTS

4. Describe how a child who cannot yet
count may find out who has more cookies.

5. Describe how a child may use the number line, counting order, and place value to
compare 23 and 35.

6. Make a table of values and a graph for
each of these functions. Use coordinate
axes like the ones here for each of your
graphs.

a. $y = x - 2$
b. $y = 2x - 4$
c. $y = \frac{1}{2}x + 3$

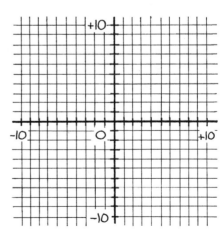

7. State the rule for each of the following tables.

A

x	y
3	5
12	23
1	1
6	11
2	3
7	13
4	7

B

x	y
8	5
2	2
6	4
18	10
14	8
4	3
10	6

C

x	3	1	6	4	2	10	8	20	5
y	10	2	37	17	5	101	65	401	26

First Number	Second Number
0	4
0	3
0	2
0	1
1	4
1	3
1	2
2	4
2	3
3	4

{(0,4), (0,3), (0,2), (0,1), (1,4), (1,3), (1,2), (2,4), (2,3), (3,4)}

Finally, take the pairs of numbers out of the table and group them as a set of the pairs. For the original set, {0, 1, 2, 3, 4}, this set of ordered pairs tells all about the *less than* relation, even though it is in a rather abstract form. *A relation is a set of ordered pairs.* This is sometimes taken as the formal mathematical definition of a relation. As we have seen in the cases of functions, we can list the pairs in a table, diagram them in several ways, make a graph of them, or simply list them as ordered pairs, as shown earlier. Each of these ways of describing a relation has certain advantages. Sets of pairs, tables, and graphs are most frequently used.

3. WORKING WITH RELATIONS

Sets of Ordered Pairs

We now return to the topic of relations and examine a more formal mathematical definition. Let us begin the development of the definition with a small set of numbers; the set {0, 1, 2, 3, 4} is convenient. Suppose we wish to explain what is meant by *less than* in this set. One could describe it, define it, discuss it, *or* simply list all of the *less than* statements that could be made about elements in the set. Because the set is small, making

$$0 < 4, 1 < 4, 2 < 4, 3 < 4$$
$$0 < 3, 1 < 3, 2 < 3$$
$$0 < 2, 1 < 2$$
$$0 < 1$$

such a list is easy. The fact that each item in the list contains two numbers suggests a table such as we constructed for a function. We can observe that order counts in this list. Because it is a *less than* list, (0,4) is in it, while (4,0) is not.

Graphs of Relations

We will continue to use the relation *less than* on the set {0, 1, 2, 3, 4} as an illustration. We have already made a table and a set of ordered pairs from it. Now make a graph. We plot each pair in the table as a point on the graph. In this case, the set we started with is finite and we have listed all of the pairs in the relation, so we have a complete graph.

SECOND
NUMBER

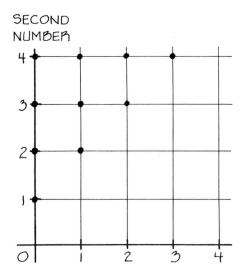

FIRST NUMBER

Let us examine some other relations and their graphs. We will see that the set of numbers used in the relation makes a difference in the appearance of the graph. The convention, in mathematics, is to call the first member of the pair x, the second member y. Below is the graph of the relation $x > y$, graphed using the set of all integers (positive, negative, zero) as members. Because the set is infinite, the graph is incomplete; the pairs that fall outside the limits of the graph are not shown.

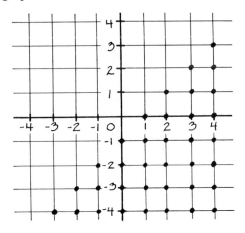

Suppose now, instead of the integers, we use the rational numbers as coordinates. The spaces between the integers will be "filled in" as we plot more and more points with rational numbers as coordinates.[1]

The result will look like the graph below, in which the region where $x > y$ is shaded. The line of points for which $x = y$ is *not* a part of the graph. This is indicated by a dashed line. If the relation had been $x \geq y$, this line would have been included in the set, and we would have drawn a solid line as the boundary of the shaded region.

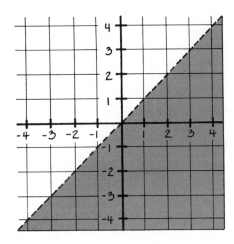

4. WORKING WITH FUNCTIONS

Remember that a relation is a set of ordered pairs. A function is a special kind of relation. That is, *a function is a relation in which there is only one pair having a given first member.* Examine the tables below. Table *A* has two pairs having the same first element, (2,3) and

---

[1]There are points that do not have fractional coordinates, for example, $(\sqrt{3}, \sqrt{2})$, $(\pi, \frac{\pi}{2}$.

(2,4); thus, while it is a relation it is not a function. Table *B* has no two pairs having the same first element, so it is a function.

A			B	
x	*y*		*x*	*y*
1	1		1	1
2	3		3	2
2	4		4	3
3	4		5	1
4	5		6	3

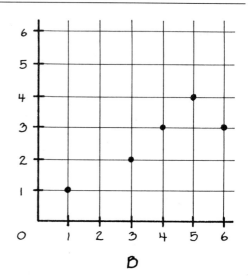

B

Another way to determine whether a relation is a function is to examine the graph. If there are two or more pairs having the same first element, these pairs will show up on the graph as points directly above each other. In graph *A* the two points (2,3) and (2,4) are on the same vertical line; graph *A* does *not* represent a function. In graph *B* no two or more points are on the same vertical line; graph *B* *does* represent a function.

The graph of the relation *less than* shows many points that have the same first coordinate. The graph below shows the relation $x < y$, plotted on the graph with "·'s." There are many, in fact infinitely many, pairs having the same first coordinate. The function $x = y$ is plotted on the graph with "*'s." In this case, there is never more than one point having a given first coordinate.

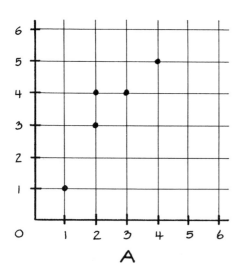

A

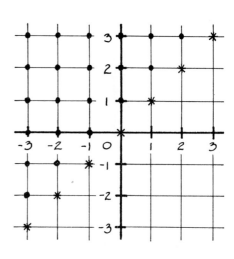

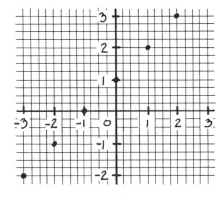

A

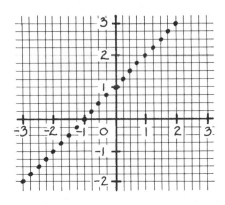

B

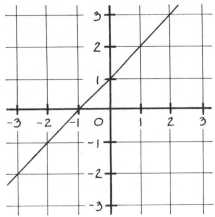

When functions are expressed as ordered pairs of rational numbers, the pairs "fill in" the graph between the integer points, giving the appearance of a complete line.[1] Here are three graphs of $y = x + 1$. In A only integer points are plotted, in B points having as coordinates integers and halves ($1\frac{1}{2}$, $2\frac{1}{2}$, $-1\frac{1}{2}$, etc.) are plotted, and in C the quarters ($1\frac{1}{4}$, $2\frac{3}{4}$, etc.) are added. You can imagine that as more and more fractions are used, the graph will take on the appearance of a solid line. The figure below shows this graph. Since any points from $y = x + 1$ will lie on a straight line when graphed, we say that $y = x + 1$ is a *linear function*.

Exercises

1. Here is a partial list of ordered pairs of whole numbers. Can you figure out what the relation is?

(1,1)
(1,2), (2,2)
(1,3), (3,3)
(1,4), (2,4), (4,4)
(1,5), (5,5)

---

[1]You should be aware that some points cannot be expressed with rational-number coordinates. Thus the line is densely packed with points but not "completely filled."

C

(1,6), (2,6), (3,6), (6,6)
(—,8), (—,8), (—,8), (—,8)
(1,7), (7,7)
(1,9), (3,9), (9,9)
(1,10), (2,10), (5,10), (10,10)
(1,11), (11,11)
(—,12), (—,12), (—,12)

2. Plot the ordered pairs in the relation in Exercise 1 on a graph like this one. Use graph paper if you have it or use lined notebook paper for your graph

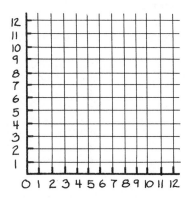

3. Make partial tables and plot the graphs of these relations. Use coordinate axes like the ones below.
a. $y = x$ (integers)
b. $y = x - 3$ (integers)
c. $y < x$ (rational numbers)

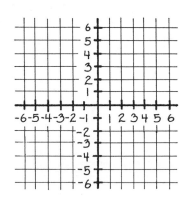

4. Which of these tables represent functions?

A		B		C	
x	y	x	y	x	y
1	2	1	2	3	5
3	5	2	3	1	4
4	5	4	3	6	2
2	6	1	4	4	4

5. Which of these sets of ordered pairs represent functions?
a. (3,5), (4,2), (5,1), (1,3), (4,3), (7,2)
b. (4,5), (3,4), (5,3), (1,2), (6,2), (2,2)

6. Which of these graphs represent functions?

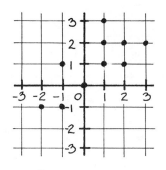

A

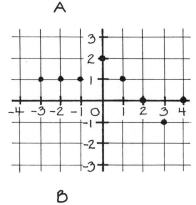

B

7. Graph these functions using integer values of x and y and again using rational-number values for x and y.

a. $y = x - 1$

b. $y = 3$ (That's different, isn't it?)

c. $y = \frac{1}{2}x + 1$

8. Give an example of a relation in mathematics that is not a function.

9. Give an example of a relation in a nonmathematical context that is not a function.

ACTIVITIES

The exercises in this chapter are not unlike textbook problems for functions and relations. There is a substantial strand in the elementary curriculum devoted to functions and relations. To augment this material, we provide here a small number of laboratory activities that make use of these concepts.

1. *Variation in Temperature.* Make a large graph showing how temperature changes during the day. Record the outside temperature every 30 minutes. Draw lines between the points. Using different colors, repeat this for several days. Place the graph of these data on the bulletin board. Discuss the variation of temperature during the day. Is the temperature during one day a function or a relation?

2. *Cost of Travel.* Get a schedule of bus or air fares and a map. By checking the cost of trips of various distances, make a graph showing how cost of travel is related to distance.

3. *Cost of Power.* Investigate the rates charged by local utilities for electric power. Make a graph showing how much the cost will be for different amounts of electric power. From the graph you may be able to see the effect of a minimum billing or a change of rate for large users.

4. *Taxi Ride.* Many functions have very interesting graphs. Graph the cost of a taxi ride if the taxi charges 50 cents for the first $\frac{1}{5}$ mile and 25 cents for each $\frac{1}{5}$ mile after that.

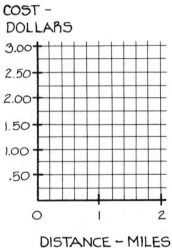

COST – DOLLARS

DISTANCE – MILES

5. *Functions Everywhere.* Make a list and a bulletin-board display of areas in daily life in which functions are important. Cut out and post examples of graphs that show functions and those that show relations.

Bibliography

The readings listed here by chapter provide mainly two kinds of information: readings which amplify the ideas developed in the chapters and readings which provide suggested activities for use in teaching. In particular, many articles in *The Arithmetic Teacher* contain suggestions for teaching activities.

PART ONE – METHODS

Chapter 1. An Overview

Begle, E. G., and Wilson, J. W. "Evaluation of Mathematics Programs." Chapter 10 in E. G. Begle (ed.), *Mathematics Education,* 69th Yearbook of the National Society for the Study of Education, Part I. Chicago: University of Chicago Press, 1970.

Hollis, L. Y., and Houston, W. R. *Acquiring Competencies to Teach Mathematics in Elementary Schools.* Lincoln, Neb.: Professional Educators Publications, Inc., 1973.

Mager, R. F. *Preparing Instructional Objectives.* Palo Alto, Calif.: Fearon Publishers, 1962.

McKillip, W. D., et al. "Developing a Competency-Based Teacher Education Program: a Report on a Project." *The Arithmetic Teacher,* 1974, 21:220–223.

Popham, W. J., and Baker, E. L. *Establishing Instructional Goals.* Englewood Cliffs, N.J.: Prentice-Hall, Inc., 1970.

Popham, W. J., and Baker, E. L. *Evaluating Instruction.* Englewood Cliffs, N.J.: Prentice-Hall, Inc., 1973.

Shulman, L. S. "Psychology and Mathematics Education." Chapter 2 in E. G. Begle (ed.), *Mathematics Education,* 69th Yearbook of the National Society for the Study of Education, Part 1. Chicago: University of Chicago Press, 1970.

Weaver, J. F. "Evaluation and the Classroom Teacher." Chapter 9 in E. G. Begle (ed.), *Mathematics Education,* 69th Yearbook of the National Society for the Study of Education, Part 1. Chicago: University of Chicago Press, 1970.

Weigand, J. E. (ed.). *Developing Teacher Competencies.* Englewood Cliffs, N.J.: Prentice-Hall, Inc., 1971.

Wilson, J. W. "Evaluation in Secondary School Mathematics." Chapter 19 in B. S. Bloom, T. Hastings, and G. M. Madaus, *Handbook of Formative and Summative Evaluation of Classroom Learning.* New York: McGraw-Hill Book Co., 1971.

Chapter 2. Teaching for Understanding

Ashlock, R. B. "Teaching the Basic Facts: Three Classes of Activities." *The Arithmetic Teacher,* 1971, 18:359–364.

Beecher, W. J., and Faxon, G. B. (eds.) *Methods, Aids, and Devices for Teachers.* Dansville, N.Y.: F. A. Owen Publishing Co., 1918.

Brownell, W. A. "Psychological Considerations in the Learning and Teaching of Arithmetic." In *The Teaching of Arithmetic,* 10th Yearbook of National Council of Teachers of Mathematics. Reston, Va.: NCTM, 1935.

Bruner, J. S. *Toward a Theory of Instruction.* Cambridge, Mass.: Harvard University Press, Belknap Press, 1966.

Dienes, Z. P. "A Theory of Mathematics Learning." Chapter 2 in *Building Up Mathematics,* 3rd ed. London: Hutchinson Publishing Group, Ltd., 1967.

Ginsburg, H. *Children's Arithmetic: the Learning Process.* New York: D. Van Nostrand, 1977.

Margenau, J., and Sentlowitz, M. *How to Study Mathematics.* Reston, Va.: National Council of Teachers of Mathematics, 1977.

National Council of Teachers of Mathematics. *Experiences in Mathematical Ideas.* Vols. 1 and 2. Reston, Va.: NCTM, 1970.

Payne, J. N. (ed.). *Mathematics Learning in Early Childhood.* 37th Yearbook of National Council of Teachers of Mathematics. Reston, Va.: NCTM, 1975.

Menchinskaya, N. A., and Moro, M. I. "Questions in the Methods and Psychology of Teaching Arithmetic in the Elementary Grades." In Kilpatrick, J., et al., (eds.), *Soviet Studies in the Psychology of Learning and Teaching Mathematics,* Vol. 14. Stanford, Calif.: SMSG, 1975. (Distributed by NCTM, Reston, Va.)

Nibbelink, W. H. *Math from Rock Bottom: from Ideas to Computations.* Columbus, Ohio: Charles E. Merrill Publishing Co., 1972.

Platts, M. E. *Plus.* Stevensville, Mich.: Educational Service, Inc., 1975.

Suydam, M. N., and Dessart, D. J. *Classroom Ideas from Research on Computational Skills.* Reston, Va.: National Council of Teachers of Mathematics, 1976.

Wirtz, R. *Drill and Practice at the Problem Solving Level.* Palo Alto, Calif.: Creative Publications.

Chapter 3. Teaching for Computational Skills

Davis, E. J. "Some Comments and Suggestions on Teaching the Basic Facts of Arithmetic." In *Computation and Practice,* 1978 Yearbook of National Council of Teachers of Mathematics. Reston, Va.: NCTM, 1978.

Ginsburg, H. *Children's Arithmetic: the Learning Process.* New York: D. Van Nostrand, 1977.

Hamrick, K. B., and McKillip, W. D. "How Computational Skills Contribute to Meaningful Learning of Arithmetic." In *Computation and Practice,* 1978 Yearbook of National Council of Teachers of Mathematics. Reston, Va.: NCTM, 1978.

Chapter 4. Teaching for Problem-Solving Skill

Biggs, E. E., and Maclean, J. R. *Freedom to Learn.* Don Mill, Ontario: Addison-Wesley (Canada) Ltd., 1969.

Brown, I. M. "Headlines." *The Arithmetic Teacher,* 1977, 24:272.

Butts, T. *Problem Solving in Mathematics.* Glenview, Ill.: Scott, Foresman & Company, 1973.

Greenes, C., Gregory, J., and Seymour, D. *Successful Problem Solving Techniques.* Palo Alto, Calif.: Creative Publications.

Henney, M. "Improving Mathematics Verbal Problem Solving through Reading Instruction." *The Arithmetic Teacher,* 1971, 18:223–229.

Menchinskaya, N. A., and Moro, M. I. "Questions in the Methods and Psychology of Teaching Arithmetic in the Elementary Grades." In Kilpatrick, J., et al., (eds.), *Soviet Studies in the Psychology of Learning and Teaching Mathematics,* Vol. 14. Stanford, Calif.: SMSG, 1975. (Distributed by NCTM, Reston, Va.)

Nelson, D., and Kirkpatrick, J. "Problem Solving." In J. N. Payne (ed.), *Mathematics Learning in Early Childhood,* 37th Yearbook of National Council of Teachers of Mathematics. Reston, Va.: NCTM, 1975.

Orans, S. "Go Shopping! Problem-Solving Activities for the Primary Grades with Provisions for Individualization." *The Arithmetic Teacher,* 1970, 17:621 – 623.

Payne, J. N. (ed.). *Mathematics Learning in Early Childhood.* 37th Yearbook of National Council of Teachers of Mathematics. Reston, Va.: NCTM, 1975. (Chapters 9, 10.)

Polya, G. *How to Solve It.* 2nd ed. Princeton, N.J.: Princeton University Press, 1973.

Reidesel, C. A., and Burns, P. C. *Handbook for Exploratory and Systematic Teaching of Elementary School Mathematics.* New York: Harper & Row, Publishers, 1977. (Chapter 6.)

Richardson, L. L. "Role of Strategies for Teaching Pupils to Solve Verbal Problems." *The Arithmetic Teacher,* 1975, 22: 414 – 421.

Thompson, M. *Experiences in Problem Solving.* Reading, Mass.: Addison-Wesley Publishing Company, 1976.

Thompson, M. *Number Theory.* Reading, Mass.: Addison-Wesley Publishing Company, 1976. (Section II, Problems and Problem Solving.)

Wilson, J. W. "The Role of Structure in Verbal Problem Solving." *The Arithmetic Teacher,* 1967, 14:486 – 497.

Wirtz, R. *Banking on Problem Solving.* Palo Alto, Calif.: Creative Publications.

Chapter 5. Diagnosis and Remediation

Ashlock, R. B. *Error Patterns in Computation.* Columbus, Ohio: Charles E. Merrill Publishing Co., 1972; or 2nd ed., 1975.

Copeland, R. W. *Diagnostic and Learning Activities in Mathematics for Children.* New York: Macmillan Publishing Co., Inc., 1974.

Ginsburg, H. *Children's Arithmetic: the Learning Process.* New York: D. Van Nostrand, 1977.

Menchinskaya, N. A., and Moro, M. I. "Questions in the Methods and Psychology of Teaching Arithmetic in the Elementary Grades." In Kilpatrick, J., et al., (eds.), *Soviet Studies in the Psychology of Learning and Teaching Mathematics,* Vol. 14. Stanford, Calif.: SMSG, 1975. (Distributed by NCTM, Reston, Va.)

Reisman, F. K. *A Guide to the Diagnostic Teaching of Arithmetic.* Columbus, Ohio: Charles E. Merrill Publishing Co., 1972; or 2nd ed., 1977.

Reisman, F. K. *Diagnostic Teaching of Elementary School Mathematics.* Chicago: Rand McNally Publishing Co., 1977.

Chapter 6. Individualization of Instruction

Clark, H. C. "Individualized Instruction — It Can't Be Done with a Screw Driver." *The Arithmetic Teacher,* 1976, 23:50 – 53.

Crosswhite, F. J. (ed.). *Organizing for Mathematics Instruction.* 1977 Yearbook of National Council of Teachers of Mathematics. Reston, Va.: NCTM, 1977.

Hlavaty, J. H. (ed.). *Enrichment Mathematics for the Grades.* 27th Yearbook of National Council of Teachers of Mathematics. Reston, Va.: NCTM, 1963.

Lipson, J. I. "Hidden Strengths of Conventional Instruction." *The Arithmetic Teacher,* 1976, 23:11 – 15.

Lowry, W. C. (ed.). *The Slow Learner in Mathematics.* 35th Yearbook of National Council of Teachers of Mathematics. Reston, Va.: NCTM, 1972.

National Council of Teachers of Mathematics. *The Arithmetic Teacher,* 1972, 19: No. 1. (Issue devoted to individualization of instruction.)

O'Daffer, P. G. "Individualized Instruction—a Search for a Humanized Approach." *The Arithmetic Teacher,* 1976, 23:23 – 28.

Schoen, H. L. "Self-Paced Mathematics Instruction: How Effective Has It Been?" *The Arithmetic Teacher,* 1976, 23:90 – 96.

Chapter 7. Teaching Aids and Laboratory Activities

Berger, E. J. (ed.). *Instructional Aids in Mathematics.* 34th Yearbook of National Council of Teachers of Mathematics. Reston, Va.: NCTM, 1973. (Chapter 9.)

Buckeye, D. A., Eubanks, W. A., and Ginther, J. L. *Cheap Math Lab Equipment.* Troy, Mich.: Midwest Publications Co., Inc., 1972.

Cathcart, W. G. (ed.). *The Mathematics Laboratory.* Readings from *The Arithmetic Teacher.* Reston, Va.: NCTM, 1977.

Collier, M. J., Forte, I., and Mackenzie. J. *Kids' Stuff: Kindergarten and Nursery School.* Nashville, Tenn.: Incentive Publications, 1969.

Curatalo, C. *Teacher Made Materials for Math.* Belmont, Calif.: Fearon Publications, Inc., 1975.

Fitzgerald, W. M., et al. *Laboratory Manual for Elementary Mathematics.* Boston: Prindle, Weber & Schmidt, Inc., 1973.

Forte, I., and Mackenzie, J. *Creative Math Experiences for the Young Child.* Nashville, Tenn.: Incentive Publications, 1973.

Higgins, J. L., and Sachs, L. *Mathematics Laboratories and Games for Elementary Schools.* Columbus, Ohio: ERIC Information Analysis Center for Science, Mathematics, and Environmental Education, 1974. (Distributed by NCTM, Reston, Va.)

Hlavaty, J. H. (ed.). *Enrichment Mathematics for the Grades.* 27th Yearbook of National Council of Teachers of Mathematics. Reston, Va.: NCTM, 1963.

Kidd, K. P., Myers, S. S., and Cilley, D. M. *The Laboratory Approach to Mathematics.* Chicago, Ill.: Science Research Associates, 1970.

Mahaffey, M. L., and Perrodin, A. F. *Teaching Elementary School Mathematics.* Itasca, Ill.: F. E. Peacock Publishers, Inc., 1973. (Part III, Teaching-Learning Aids.)

Marshall, K. *Opening Your Class with Learning Stations.* Palo Alto, Calif.: Learning Handbooks, 1975.

National Council of Teachers of Mathematics. *The Arithmetic Teacher.* 1971, 18: No. 8. (Entire issue on mathematics laboratories.)

National Council of Teachers of Mathematics. *The Arithmetic Teacher.* 1976, 23: No. 7. (Entire issue on hand calculators.)

Nuffield Foundation. *I Do and I Understand.* New York: John Wiley & Sons, Inc., 1967.

Pearson, C., and Marfuggi, J. *Creating and Using Learning Games.* Palo Alto, Calif.: Learning Handbooks, 1975.

Post, T. R. "A Model for the Construction and Sequencing of Laboratory Activities." *The Arithmetic Teacher,* 1974, 21:616–622.

Reys, R. E., and Post, T. R. *The Mathematics Laboratory, Theory to Practice.* Boston: Prindle, Weber & Schmidt, Inc., 1973.

Smith, S. E., Jr., and Backman, C. (eds.). *Teacher Made Aids for Elementary School Mathematics.* Reston, Va.: National Council of Teachers of Mathematics, 1974.

Chapter 8. Teaching Reading Skills and Using Textbooks

Barney, L. "Problems Associated with the Reading of Arithmetic." *The Arithmetic Teacher,* 1972, 19:131–133.

Feeman, G. F. "Reading and Mathematics." *The Arithmetic Teacher,* 1973, 20:523–529.

Hater, M. A., Kane, R. B., and Byrne, M. A. "Building Reading Skills in the Mathematics Class." *The Arithmetic Teacher,* 1974, 21:662–668.

Henney, M. "Improving Mathematics Verbal Problem Solving through Reading Instruction." *The Arithmetic Teacher,* 1971, 18:223–229.

Kane, R. B., Byrne, M. A., and Hater, M. A. *Helping Children Read Mathematics.* New York: American Book Co., 1974.

Mahaffey, M. L., and Perrodin, A. F. *Teaching Elementary School Mathematics.* Itasca, Ill.: F. E. Peacock Publishers, Inc., 1973. (Chapter 7, "Using a Textbook.")

Reidesel, C. A., and Burns, P. C. *Handbook for Exploratory and Systematic Teaching of Elementary School Mathematics.* New York: Harper & Row, Publishers, 1977. (Chapter 6.)

PART TWO—CONTENT

Chapter 9. Teaching Whole Numbers

Bruni, J. V., and Silverman, H. J. "Let's Do It—the Multiplication Facts: Once More, with Understanding." *The Arithmetic Teacher,* 1976, 23:402–409.

Cleminson, R. A. "Developing the Subtraction Algorithm." *The Arithmetic Teacher,* 1973, 20:634–638.

Heddens, J. W. *Today's Mathematics.* Chicago: Science Research Associates, Inc., 1974. (Units 2 through 5, 7, 8, and 11.)

King, I. "Giving meaning to the Addition Algorithm." *The Arithmetic Teacher,* 1972, 19:345–348.

LeBlanc, J. F. *Addition and Subtraction.* Reading, Mass.: Addison-Wesley Publishing Co., 1976.

LeBlanc, J. F. *Multiplication and Division.* Reading, Mass.: Addison-Wesley Publishing Co., 1976.

LeBlanc, J. F. *Numeration.* Reading, Mass.: Addison-Wesley Publishing Co., 1976.

National Council of Teachers of Mathematics. *Experiences in Mathematical Ideas.* Vols. 1 and 2. Reston, Va.: NCTM, 1970.

Payne, J. N. (ed.). *Mathematics Learning in Early Childhood.* 37th Yearbook of National Council of Teachers of Mathematics. Reston, Va.: NCTM, 1975. (Chapters 9, 10.)

Reidesel, C. A., and Burns, P. C. *Handbook for Exploratory and Systematic Teaching of Elementary School Mathematics.* New York: Harper & Row, Publishers, 1977. (Chapters 9–11.)

Reidesel, C. A., and Callahan, L. G. *Elementary School Mathematics for Teachers.* New York: Harper & Row, Publishers, 1977. (Chapters 1–11.)

Thompson, M. *Number Theory.* Reading, Mass.: Addison-Wesley Publishing Co., 1976. (Units 2 through 5, 7, 8, and 11.)

Tucker, B. F. "The Division Algorithm." *The Arithmetic Teacher,* 1973, 20:639–646.

Wahl, J., and Wahl, S. *I Can Count the Petals of a Flower.* Reston, Va.: National Council of Teachers of Mathematics, 1976.

Chapter 10. Teaching Fractions

Armstrong, C. "'Fradecent'—A Game Using Equivalent Fractions, Decimals, and Percents." *The Arithmetic Teacher,* 1972, 19:222–223.

Bruni, J., and Silverman, H. J. "Using Rectangles and Squares to Develop Fraction Concepts." *The Arithmetic Teacher,* 1977, 24:96–102.

Green, G. F., Jr. "A Model for Teaching Multiplication of Fractional Numbers." *The Arithmetic Teacher,* 1973, 20:5–9.

Heddens, J. W. *Today's Mathematics.* Chicago: Science Research Associates, Inc., 1974. (Units 12, 13, 14.)

LeBlanc, J. F. *Rational Numbers with Integers and Reals.* Reading, Mass.: Addison-Wesley Publishing Co., 1976.

National Council of Teachers of Mathematics. *Experiences in Mathematical Ideas.* Vols. 1 and 2. Reston, Va.: NCTM, 1970. (Chapter 5.)

Payne, J. N. (ed.). *Mathematics Learning in Early Childhood.* 37th Yearbook of National Council of Teachers of Mathematics. Reston, Va.: NCTM, 1975. (Chapter 8.)

Reidesel, C. A., and Burns, P. C. *Handbook for Exploratory and Systematic Teaching of Elementary School Mathematics.* New York: Harper & Row, Publishers, 1977. (Chapter 13.)

Reidesel, C. A., and Callahan, L. G. *Elementary School Mathematics for Teachers.* New York: Harper & Row, Publishers, 1977. (Chapters 19, 20, 21.)

Swenson, E. J. *Teaching Mathematics to Children.* New York: The Macmillan Company, 1973. (Chapters 9, 10, 12.)

Chapter 11. Teaching Decimal Fractions

Heddens, J. W. *Today's Mathematics.* Chicago: Science Research Associates, Inc., 1974. (Units 15 and 16.)

Mayor, J. R. "Science and Mathematics: 1970's—a Decade of Change." *The Arithmetic Teacher,* 1970, 17:293–297.

National Council of Teachers of Mathematics. *Experiences in Mathematical Ideas.* Vols. 1 and 2. Reston, Va.: NCTM, 1970. (Chapter 6.)

Reidesel, C. A., and Burns, P. C. *Handbook for Exploratory and Systematic Teaching of Elementary School Mathematics.* New York: Harper & Row, Publishers, 1977. (Chapter 14.)

Reidesel, C. A., and Callahan, L. G. *Elementary School Mathematics for Teachers.* New York: Harper & Row, Publishers, 1977. (Chapter 22.)

Swenson, E. J. *Teaching Mathematics to Children.* New York: The Macmillan Company, 1973. (Chapters 11, 12.)

Winzenread, M. "Repeating Decimals." *The Arithmetic Teacher,* 1973, 20: 678–682.

Chapter 12. Geometry and Measurement

Arithmetic Teacher. 1973, 20: No. 3. (Entire issue on metric system.)

Arithmetic Teacher. 1973, 20: No. 10. (Entire issue on geometry.)

Arithmetic Teacher. 1977, 24: No. 3. (Geometry theme.)

Bitter, G. G., Mikesell, J. L., and Maurdaff, K. *Activities Handbook for Teaching the Metric System.* Boston: Allyn & Bacon, Inc., 1976.

Bruni, J. V., and Silverman, H. "Let's Do It—Developing the Concept of Linear Measurement." *The Arithmetic Teacher,* 1974, 21:570–577.

Bruni, J. V., and Silverman, H. "Let's Do It—an Introduction to Weight Measurement." *The Arithmetic Teacher,* 1976, 23: 4–10.

Bruni, J. V., and Silverman, H. "Let's Do It—Developing Intuitive Ideas about Time." *The Arithmetic Teacher,* 1976, 23: 582–591.

Bruni, J. V., and Silverman, H. "Let's Do It—from Shadows to Mathematics." *The Arithmetic Teacher,* 1976, 23:232–239.

Bruni, J. V., and Silverman, H. "Let's Do It—Organizing a Metric Center in Your Classroom." *The Arithmetic Teacher,* 1976, 23:80–87.

Bruni, J. V., and Silverman, H. "Let's Do It—Using Geostrips and 'Angle Fixers' to Develop Ideas about Shapes and Angles." *The Arithmetic Teacher,* 1976, 23:256–268.

Bruni, J. V., and Silverman, H. "Let's Do It." *The Arithmetic Teacher,* 1977, 24: 172–180. (Many premeasurement and comparison activities for Kindergarten and Grade 1.)

Brydegaard, M., and Inskeep, J. E., Jr. (eds.). *Readings in Geometry from The Arithmetic Teacher.* Reston, Va.: National Council of Teachers of Mathematics, 1970.

Del Grande, J. J. *Geoboards and Motion Geometry.* Glenview, Ill.: Scott, Foresman & Company, 1972.

Epstein, S. L. "Weighing Ideas." *The Arithmetic Teacher,* 1977, 24: 293–297. (Introducing metric weights.)

Glenn, W. H., and Johnson, D. A. *The Pythagorean Theorem.* Atlanta: Webster Publishing Company, 1960.

Heddens, J. W. *Today's Mathematics.* Chicago: Science Research Associates, Inc., 1974. (Units 17 through 20.)

Johnson, D., Hansen, V., Peterson, W., Rudnick, J., Cleveland, R., and Bolster, C. *Activities in Mathematics—Geometry.* Glenview, Ill.: Scott, Foresman & Company, 1971.

Kerr, D. R. *Analysis of Shapes.* Reading, Mass.: Addison-Wesley Publishing Co., 1976.

Kerr, D. R. *Awareness Geometry.* Reading, Mass.: Addison-Wesley Publishing Co., 1976.

Kerr, D. R. *Measurement.* Reading, Mass.: Addison-Wesley Publishing Co., 1976.

Kerr, D. R., Jr. *Transformational Geometry.* Reading, Mass.: Addison-Wesley Publishing Co., 1976.

Konkle, G. S. *Shapes and Perceptions: an*

Intuitive Approach to Geometry. Boston: Prindle, Weber & Schmidt, Inc., 1974.

Leffin, W. W. *Going Metric.* Reston, Va.: The National Council of Teachers of Mathematics, 1975.

Morris, J. P. "Investigating Symmetry in the Primary Grades." *The Arithmetic Teacher,* 1977, 24:181–186.

National Council of Teachers of Mathematics. *A Metric Handbook for Teachers.* Reston, Va.: NCTM, 1974.

National Council of Teachers of Mathematics. *Experiences in Mathematical Ideas.* Reston, Va.: NCTM, 1970. (Chapter 4.)

National Council of Teachers of Mathematics. *Measurement in School Mathematics.* 1976 Yearbook of National Council of Teachers of Mathematics. Reston, Va.: NCTM, 1976.

Nuffield Foundation. *Environmental Geometry.* New York: John Wiley & Sons, Inc., 1969.

Nuffield Foundation, *Shape and Size.* New York: John Wiley & Sons, Inc., 1967, 1968.

O'Daffer, P., and Clemens, S. R. *Geometry: an Investigative Approach.* Reading, Mass.: Addison-Wesley Publishing Company, 1976.

O'Daffer, P., and Clemens, S. R. *Metric Measurement for Teachers.* Reading, Mass.: Addison-Wesley Publishing Company, 1976.

Payne, J. N. (ed.). *Mathematics Learning in Early Childhood.* 37th Yearbook of National Council of Teachers of Mathematics. Reston, Va.: NCTM, 1975. (Chapters 9 and 10.)

Reidesel, C. A., and Burns, P. C. *Handbook for Exploratory and Systematic Teaching of Elementary School Mathematics.* New York: Harper & Row, Publishers, 1977. (Chapters 15 and 16.)

Reidesel, C. A., and Callahan, L. G. *Elementary School Mathematics for Teachers.* New York: Harper & Row, Publishers, 1977. (Chapters 14–18, 23–25.)

Steffe, L. P. "Thinking about Measurement." *The Arithmetic Teacher,* 1971, 18:332–338.

Trueblood, C. R. *Metric Measurement—Activities and Bulletin Boards.* Dansville, N.Y.: The Instructor Publications, Inc., 1973.

Walter, M. I. *Boxes, Squares, and Other Things.* Reston, Va.: National Council of Teachers of Mathematics, 1970.

Chapter 13. Statistics and Probability

Burns, M. "Ideas." *The Arithmetic Teacher,* 1974, 21:686–696.

Burt, B. C. "Drawing Conclusions from Samples (an Activity for the Low Achiever)." *The Arithmetic Teacher,* 1969, 16:539–541.

Coltharp, F. L. "Mathematical Aspects of the Attribute Games." *The Arithmetic Teacher,* 1974, 21:246–251.

Flory, D. W. "What Are the Chances?" *The Arithmetic Teacher,* 1969, 16:581–582.

Girard, R. A. "Development of Critical Interpretation of Statistics and Graphs." *The Arithmetic Teacher,* 1967, 14:272–277.

Grass, B. A. "Statistics Made Simple." *The Arithmetic Teacher,* 1965, 12:196–198.

Green, G. F., Jr. *Elementary School Mathematics Activities and Materials.* Lexington, Mass.: D. C. Heath & Company, 1974. (Chapter 10.)

Heddens, J. W. *Today's Mathematics.* Chicago: Science Research Associates, Inc., 1974. (Unit 22.)

Higgins, J. E. "Probability with Marbles and a Juice Container." *The Arithmetic Teacher,* 1973, 20:165–166.

Hildebrand, F. H., and Johnson, N. "An Ordered Pair Approach to Addition of Rational Numbers in Second Grade." *The Arithmetic Teacher,* 1965, 12: 106–108.

Immerzeel, G., and Wiederanders, D. "Ideas." *The Arithmetic Teacher,* 1971, 18: 239–242.

Johnson, D., Hansen, V., Peterson, W., Rudnick, J., Cleveland, R., and Bolster, C. *Activities in Mathematics—Probability.* Glenview, Ill.: Scott, Foresman & Company, 1971.

Niman, J., and Postman, R. D. "Probability on the Geoboard." *The Arithmetic Teacher,* 1973, 20:167–170.

Page, D., and Beattie, I. D. *Probability: A Programmed Supplement.* Prindle, Weber & Schmidt, 1969.

Schaefer, A. W., and Mauthe, A. H. "Problem Solving with Enthusiasm—the Mathematics Laboratory." *The Arithmetic Teacher,* 1970, 17:7–14.

Schell, L. M. "Horizontal Enrichment with Graphs." *The Arithmetic Teacher,* 1967, 14:654–656.

School Mathematics Study Group (SMSG). *Probability for Primary Grades and Probability for Intermediate Grades.* Stanford, Calif.: SMSG, 1965, 1966.

Sherrill, J. M. "Egg Cartons Again?" *The Arithmetic Teacher,* 1973, 20:13–16.

Swenson, E. J. *Teaching Mathematics to Children.* New York: The Macmillan Company, 1973. (Chapter 15.)

Thompson, M. *Graphs: the Picturing of Information.* Reading, Mass.: Addison-Wesley Publishing Co., 1976.

Thompson, M. *Probability and Statistics.* Reading, Mass.: Addison-Wesley Publishing Co., 1976.

Wilkinson, J. D., and Nelson, O. "Probability and Statistics—Trial Teaching in Sixth Grade." *The Arithmetic Teacher,* 1966, 13: 100–106.

Wonka, W. G., *What Are the Chances I Will Graduate?* Stanford Honorary Institute of Technology, Occasional Paper 37, June, 1967.

Chapter 14. Teaching Relations and Functions

Bruni, J. V. and Silverman, H. J. "Let's Do It—Graphing as a Communication Skill." *The Arithmetic Teacher,* 1975, 22:354–366.

Heddens, J. W. *Today's Mathematics.* Chicago: Science Research Associates, Inc., 1974. (Unit 21)

Johnson, D., Hansen, V., Peterson, W., Rudnick, J., Cleveland, R., and Bolster, C. *Activities in Mathematics—Graphs.* Glenview, Ill.: Scott, Foresman & Company, 1971.

Nuffield Foundation. *Pictorial Representation.* New York: John Wiley & Sons, Inc., 1967.

Payne, J. N. (ed.). *Mathematics Learning in Early Childhood.* 37th Yearbook of National Council of Teachers of Mathematics. Reston, Va.: NCTM, 1975. (Chapters 9 and 10.)

Pereira-Mendoza, L. "Graphing and Prediction in the Elementary School." *The Arithmetic Teacher,* 1977, 24:112–113.

Reidesel, C. A., and Callahan, L. G. *Elementary School Mathematics for Teachers.* New York: Harper & Row, Publishers, 1977. (Chapter 3.)

Fun and Frolic

These references identify materials which, though mathematical in nature, contain activities that are mainly for fun and motivation.

Brandes, L. G. *Math Can Be Fun.* Portland, Maine: Weston Walch, Publisher, 1976.

Buechner, K. *File Folder Math.* Palo Alto, Calif.: Creative Publications, 1976.

Burns, M. *The I Hate Mathematics Book.* Boston: Little, Brown & Company, 1975.

Corle, C. *Building Arithmetic Skills with Games.* Dansville, N.Y.: The Instructor Publications, Inc., 1973.

Frank, M. *Kids' Stuff Math.* Nashville, Tenn.: Incentive Publications, 1974.

Hlavaty, J. H. (ed.). *Enrichment Mathematics for the Grades.* 27th Yearbook of National Council of Teachers of Mathematics. Reston, Va.: NCTM, 1963.

Juster, N. *The Dot and the Line: A Romance in Lower Mathematics.* New York: Random House, 1963.

Kennedy, L., and Michon, R. *Games for Individualizing Mathematics Learning.* Columbus, Ohio: Charles E. Merrill Publishing Company, 1973.

Platts, M. E. *Plus.* Stevensville, Mich.: Educational Service, Inc., 1975.

Seymour, D., et al. *Aftermath.* Palo Alto, Calif.: Creative Publications, 1975.

Smith, D. E. *Number Stories of Long Ago.* Classics in Mathematics Education Series. Reston, Va.: National Council of Teachers of Mathematics, 1969.

Smith, S. E., Jr., and Backman, C. A. (eds.). *Games and Puzzles for Elementary School Mathematics.* Reston, Va.: National Council of Teachers of Mathematics, 1975.

Thomason, M. E. *Modern Math Games, Activities and Puzzles.* Belmont, Calif.: Lear Siegler, Inc./Fearon Publishers, 1970.

Wagner, G., and Hosier, M., and Gilloley, L. *Arithmetic Games and Activities.* New York: Macmillan Publishing Co., Inc., 1964.

Wahl, J., and Wahl, S. *I Can Count the Petals of a Flower.* Reston, Va.: National Council of Teachers of Mathematics, 1976.

For Enrichment and Enjoyment

Burns, M. *Good Time Math Event Book.* Palo Alto, Calif.: Creative Publications.

Chilicote, E., and Blaine, J. *Happy Math.* Ft. Collins, Colo.: Scott Resources, Inc., 1975.

Chilicote, E., Blaine, J, and Blaine, B. *Mathways.* Ft. Collins, Colo.: Scott Resources, Inc., 1975.

Hestwood, D., and Huseby, E. *Crossnumber Puzzles, Books I and II.* Palo Alto, Calif.: Creative Publications.

Judd, W. *Math Mat Activities.* Palo Alto, Calif.: Creative Publications.

National Council of Teachers of Mathematics. *Teacher-Made Aids for Elementary School Mathematics.* Reston, Va.: NCTM, 1974.

Suydam, M. N., and Dessart, D. J. *Classroom Ideas from Research on Computational Skills.* Reston, Va.: National Council of Teachers of Mathematics, 1976.

Index

3 4 5 6 7 8 9 10–RRD–83 82 81